Ruud Gullit

THE CHELSEA DIARY

Ruud GULLIT

THE CHELSEA DIARY

Harry Harris

ORION

First published in Great Britain in 1997 by
Orion
An imprint of Orion Books Ltd
Orion House, 5 Upper St Martin's Lane,
London WC2H 9EA

A CIP catalogue record for this book is available from the British Library

ISBN 0 75281 189 4

Typeset by Selwood Systems, Midsomer Norton

Printed in Great Britain by
Butler & Tanner Ltd, Frome and London

ACKNOWLEDGEMENTS

Thanks to Ruud Gullit for being one of the most open, honest and frank managers you'd ever come across in world football.

Thanks, too, for the co-operation from Chelsea FC, notably chairman Ken Bates, managing director Colin Hutchinson, Gwyn Williams and Graham Rix. Ken's secretary Jayne McGuinness was always ready and willing to help out with details. FIFA licensed football agents Jon and Phil Smith, Ruud's UK representatives, are old and dear friends who have been more than helpful. So I should mention their company First Artist Corporation.

My appreciation goes to Cathal Morrow of the New Nation Newspaper for permission to use extracts from a wonderfully revealing interview by Garth Crooks on Ruud covering a wide range of personal and private issues.

Use of exceptional photographs from The Mirror Syndication Department – where Phil Le Blanc provided expert photo selection – Sky Sports, PR company Fleishman Hillard UK for providing information and pictures on Ruud's M&M's advert.

None other than 'Spy' himself, Neil Barnett, editor of the club programme, *Onside and Clubcall*, supplied his top secret behind-the-scenes snap shots taken with his own candid camera.

Special thanks to Giancarlo Galavotti of *Gazzetta dello Sport* for his insights into the Italian players.

Grateful thanks to Gerard Farrell for the use of his copyrighted photographs and to Kevin Batt at Hammersmith and Fulham Council for his assistance.

Dedicated to Linda, Jean and Ken
– a true Blue family

CONTENTS

INTRODUCTION

History was made at a muggy Wembley on May 17, 1997. And the game might never be quite the same again in England as a consequence.

The first foreign coach to reach the FA Cup Final masterminded victory to claim the most traditional of English trophies on the day sixteen foreigners paraded their talents in the showpiece game. Mark Hughes became the first player this century to claim four winners' medals, and the fastest Wembley Cup Final goal, by Roberto Di Matteo, came after just 42.4 seconds.

Chelsea's first major trophy for more than a quarter of a century was achieved by a man in only his first season in management.

When Ruud Gullit was informed that he had already made English soccer history after the FA Cup semifinal demolition of Wimbledon at Highbury it was a moment to savour, a special achievement even in his distinguished career. 'I have just been told that I am the first foreign coach to take a team to Wembley in an FA Cup Final and am very proud of that. But it is important we win it as first place is the only thing that matters in any competition.'

English football has been a graveyard for foreign coaches. Their track record is a litany of disaster. In recent years Dr Joe Venglos at Aston Villa and Ossie Ardiles at Newcastle and then Tottenham have flopped. Gullit broke the mould, and Chelsea's success would surely encourage other clubs to do the continental.

He is the first black coach, the first foreign coach, the youngest manager in the Premiership and he brought with him a host of Italian and overseas superstars. Ironically, Chelsea Football Club was once synonymous with racism, infested by the National Front, the home of bigotry. The Shed was its symbol, its breeding ground and recruitment centre. The Shed was not alone, of course. There were several other terraces in English football plagued with violent, unsavoury and unwanted fans, who threw bananas onto the pitch and imitated monkey noises. Chelsea's few black players were hardly welcome and it was hell for black opponents. Fans used to shave their heads out of homage to unpalatable and dangerous right-wing groups – now they shave their heads out of hero-worship of Vialli.

Chairman Ken Bates presided over years of racial tension. 'Paul Cannoville was our first black player and our own fans would throw bananas at him when he warmed up at the side of the pitch. Now we have the first black manager in the Premiership. But don't forget that we were also the first club to have closed-circuit TV. Now that has become mandatory in football, and paid for by the Football Trust. We introduced it at our own expense.' Bates battled to improve racist problems, but Gullit has completely changed the atmosphere.

Bates would, however, rather confine Gullit's impact purely to football. 'Hoddle bought Gullit, but Hoddle couldn't have bought the players Gullit has done! Four years ago we would have been on par with the likes of QPR and Crystal Palace. Hoddle produced that quantum leap by transforming the club. Gullit has made it a European club, and has made people realise that England doesn't stop at the White Cliffs of Dover, that there is a Channel Tunnel.'

Asked how it felt, before he embarked on his first season as coach and the highest-profile black manager in the English game, there wasn't a flicker of emotion as Gullit responded: 'Although you are black or white, what is important is the talent. My father, who studied economics at night school, told me that I would have to work harder than others for what I would achieve with my talent. For me, that was the stimulation. I took it positively. If you feel attacked by the way you are then you have a problem. I felt proud of what I was – of the colour, everything. Of course I am aware I'm black and that I stand out. I use it to my advantage. If you feel attacked by your difference then *you* have the problem. You have to view it positively. It's the same with a very intelligent child. No one wants to be with him because he knows everything already. So he has to prove himself in a different way.'

Gullit's first season in charge was a whirlwind of activity at the Bridge – a kaleidoscope of goals, famous victories and disappointing defeats. Things went from the sublime to the ridiculous at times, winning at Old Trafford and beating mighty Liverpool twice at the Bridge in a matter of weeks – including that epic 4–2 FA Cup win after being two goals down. The nation mourned along with Chelsea the tragic death of their vice-chairman, Matthew Harding. Ruud Gullit and his team felt the most fitting tribute to his memory would be to win a trophy in his honour. They did it.

Managing director Colin Hutchinson explained how the club had come to the decision to appoint Ruud and how he operates within a new continental system. 'English football is entering the era of the coach. It is the continental way and Chelsea are pioneering this with Ruud working in a classic continental set-up. He identifies the players he wants and I try to get them. Chelsea were fortunate that Ruud had a Premiership year, getting to know the English game and Blues players before he took over as player-manager. It would have been too much to have asked him when he first arrived in London from Sampdoria to play, coach and manage!

'Had Ruud turned down the player-manager role in May, Chelsea might still have gone continental as there were few available options in England. Arsène Wenger was on a list of possibles, although indications at the time suggested he might not be available until mid-November and this would have been a major stumbling block. Sven Eriksson, who has had European success with Malmö, Benfica and Sampdoria, was another. Premiership squads will continue to be multi-national and the next big invasion could be continental coaches – another step on the road to helping raise standards and technical quality. If that makes English clubs a stronger force in European competitions then it will be to the good. Until England's club representatives start winning European cups we won't be seriously considered as the number one league in the world.'

Ruud's innovations were a breath of fresh air for the traditional English game. And Mr Super-Cool did it without any grey flecks in football's most famous dreadlocks. While Kevin Keegan and other high-profile bosses were struck down by burn-out, it was a stress-free zone for a manager who sat on the bench in the summer in an Armani suit and no socks and in the winter with a bobble hat to cover the dreadlocks. 'I think the very best time is the relief of scoring a goal or watching the celebrations of the players after scoring.'

Voted Britain's Best-Dressed Man, Ruud was signed up for his own designer label 'Ruud Wear'. The BBC negotiated a two-year contract after his roaring success with Des Lynam and Alan Hansen during Euro '96, and he signed a lucrative TV commercial deal and a money-spinning computer contract.

In his first six months in charge he bought and sold twelve players for a transfer turnover of more than £18m. He imported Gianluca Vialli, Gianfranco Zola, Roberto Di Matteo and Frank Leboeuf at a cost of £12m, and sold off old favourites like John Spencer, Terry Phelan and Gavin Peacock. Ruthless Ruud also sold off Paul Furlong and youngsters like Anthony Barness and Muzzy Izzett, with Mark Stein and David Rocastle loaned out. The reconstruction on the field went apace with the hotel, flats and new stands off it.

More arrivals and departures are planned for next season as the Chelsea quest for silverware doesn't end with the FA Cup, but with the Champions League. Gullit's long term goal – the cup 'with the big ears', as he put it – was his ultimate prize.

MAY

Exit Hoddle – Ruud Gullit is the new boss of the Bridge

WEDNESDAY, MAY 1

It had been widely mooted that the FA would move for Glenn Hoddle as their successor to Terry Venables. Immediately, Ruud Gullit was favourite to take over at the Bridge.

Gullit and the Chelsea players were stunned by the cloak-and-dagger events that led to Hoddle's elevation to Lancaster Gate. The atmosphere reached fever pitch toward the end of April when the FA's international selection committee met the day after England's goalless draw with Croatia to decide on Venables's successor. The five-man committee unanimously voted for Hoddle. Others on the original short list had ruled themselves out.

Speculation also mounted that the FA planned to team up Hoddle with Gullit. This provoked an outburst from Ken Bates, insisting Gullit was under contract for one more year as a player and wouldn't be going anywhere. Hoddle was still suggesting he would sign a new four-year Chelsea contract before the end of the season – if the directors gave him the assurances he wanted. But once FA headhunter Jimmy Armfield made the first formal approach in a phone call to Hoddle's Ascot home on April 29 there was little or no chance he would stay with Chelsea. On Tuesday, April 30 at 9.00am, FA officials contacted Bates for official permission to talk to Hoddle. Bates reluctantly agreed. Half an hour later, Hoddle called Matthew Harding to tell him of the FA's offer, but promised not to make a decision before further discussions with Chelsea's board. At noon on that eventful day, Hoddle informed Ruud and his players of the FA offer at the club training ground. He said he'd give his answer within a couple of days.

Hoddle's appointment was confirmed on Wednesday, May 1, a significant day in Chelsea's history:

7.30am: Harding admitted newspaper stories were true, but insisted he still hoped to persuade Hoddle to stay. Few gave him much hope.

9.30am: Hoddle left home in his N-reg BMW for further discussions with Harding.

9.45am: Bates blasted the FA and revealed that Chelsea first offered a new contract to Hoddle last September.

10.10am: Harding and Hoddle met at an outer London hotel. Harding underlined his offer of major finance for further team strengthening in the summer. Chelsea repeated their £7,000-a-week contract offer to Hoddle, worth £1.4m over four years, countering the FA's deal worth £1.2m.

2.15pm: Harding admitted he still didn't know what Hoddle would do. Hoddle asked for twenty-four hours to make up his mind but it was certain he would accept. The lure of England proved too much for Hoddle, who won fifty-three caps.

Was Gullit wanted by the FA? Bates flattened any notion of losing Gullit: 'If Ruud has any spare time he can coach Chelsea.' Blunt. Typical Bates.

Gullit dismissed the idea. 'I have not been approached but I want to play football. You are retired a long time.' Another erroneous suggestion was that Harding would consider pulling out his money once Hoddle left.

Bates criticised the FA over their approach to his manager and had an early-morning meeting with Hoddle's agent. Bates said: 'I'm very disappointed with the FA. If they had Glenn on their short list, they should have approached him a month or so ago so the matter could have been resolved. It's very bad behaviour on their part to leave it so late.' High on Hoddle's CV was his foresight in bringing Gullit to English football. Gullit was lured to Chelsea by Hoddle's reputation. 'When you are asked to come to play in England you consider many things. But when Glenn Hoddle asks, you are flattered – and you come.'

George Graham was reportedly the favoured choice of Bates to succeed Hoddle, a suggestion that infuriated Bates himself. Graham, seeking employment, put himself in the frame, although the tip within the game was that he would go to Leeds. Graham said at the time: 'I'd be interested in any job that presents a challenge – and Chelsea would be that. I'm banned until July 1 but that doesn't mean I can't talk to a club.' Graham's one-year FA ban expired in a month, but Graham's football philosophy is diametrically opposed to Hoddle's. He clearly did not meet Chelsea's criteria.

Bates insisted: 'I seem to read quite a lot that I want George Graham as manager – that's simply not true. I haven't expressed any opinion at all on who our new manager should be. There is a different name mentioned every day. But I can assure all Chelsea supporters we don't intend to make a rash decision. We're conscious of the fact that we're at a crossroads where we can go back or forward – and we intend to go forward.'

THURSDAY, MAY 2

Named International Sportsman of the Year by the Variety Club of Great Britain, Ruud was presented with his handsomely mounted trophy by the Duke of Edinburgh at the London Hilton Hotel. A spokesman for the children's charity said: 'These awards go to sports personalities who by word or work have inspired or helped disadvantaged children.'

Bates again hammered speculation that Chelsea's player of the season would join Hoddle, saying 'Let me reassure Chelsea supporters on one matter: there is no way Ruud will be leaving Chelsea. He is under exclusive contract to Chelsea to June 1997 and under no circumstances would we release him from it.' Gullit reiterated that the FA had not approached him and 'that it would not be a question of "if Glenn goes I go". I am Chelsea through and through and I have another year of my contract to run.'

Gullit advised Hoddle to take the England job. 'It's a great honour for Glenn and he thoroughly deserves it. It would mean things changing at Chelsea but you cannot think only of yourself. That would be selfish.'

FRIDAY, MAY 3

Hoddle met the Chelsea players for the first time since making his decision. He tried to raise their spirits for his final Premiership game against Blackburn. Hoddle's departure left his Stamford Bridge coaching staff uncertain of their positions and goalkeeping coach Eddie Niedzwiecki believed it was vital that Bates moved quickly to appoint a replacement. 'We need a clear vision of what lies ahead for the club. We have come so far under Glenn in the last three years and it would be nice to think that can be taken on by the next man. In Glenn's time here we have played the same system throughout the club, from youth level to first team, so it is natural we want to continue the work.'

Gullit reacted to being favourite to succeed Hoddle: 'Chelsea want to continue playing the way we played this year and I want to play as long as I enjoy it. That is my priority. Glenn has had a great opportunity which does not come very often. For me, it's important that he is an independent person. He doesn't depend on what others might say. He can do what he likes.'

Harding said: 'As far as I'm concerned, we have the lovely advantage of having three years of Glenn's work at Chelsea to build upon. There aren't many clubs who would be in such an advantageous position having just lost their manager. We have to carry on in Glenn's image. I would hope we would want to keep playing in the Hoddle style, not tear up the blueprint, throw it away and play an entirely different sort of football.'

Bates revealed the contents of his conversation with Hoddle on the morning he lost his manager to the FA. 'Glenn rang to tell me he was taking the England job and I simply told him "I thought you were going to take it. I appreciate what you have done for this club over the last three years and I wish you well with England." '

Nigel Spackman, a senior Chelsea player at the time, urged the club's directors to look for a replacement who would use the same tactics as Hoddle. 'It's important for Chelsea to find someone who can carry on the same style that Glenn has got us playing, just as it was vital for England to find someone who could take over from Terry Venables. We've got used to playing the way Glenn wanted and it was proving very successful, so it would be a great shame if the new manager went back to a 4–4–2 formation.'

Colin Hutchinson was 'delighted for Glenn', but described his departure as a sad day for Chelsea. 'It is a very emotional time,' he said. 'He has been an absolute joy to work with and we're all a bit down.' Hutchinson reassured fans that the playing style at Stamford Bridge would be continued whoever was eventually chosen as Hoddle's successor. 'The structure in the club is good. Everyone can see the continental style that we have here, but what is good for us is that this system prevails throughout the club. Every team from the under-12s through to the first team play the same way. The situation we have reached so far under Glenn is something we will consider carefully when we come to appoint a new manager.'

SATURDAY, MAY 4

Gullit was the supporters' choice. Ruud said: 'I am very honoured by the reaction of the fans and the players, and if the job is offered to me I would have to consider it. I need to know what the task will be. I want to carry on playing but it is not easy to concentrate on your football if you are a manager as well. The feeling among the players is that we want to continue the style we are playing. We hope that whatever the decision about a new manager will be, we can carry on like that. We don't want to play kick and rush football, so it would be wise for the board to consider someone who has the same ideas that Glenn has.'

Gullit was beginning to come to terms with the likelihood that he would take an earlier-than-expected leap into management. 'I haven't heard anything officially, but because of all the rumours you are thinking about how you would do it. I would need to talk to them about how things would be run, what would you like to change. There are so many things to think about, but the job hasn't been offered yet. It is wise to consider it now because everyone is talking about it. I can say with one hundred per cent certainty that I will stay with Chelsea next season. People appreciate what I am doing and I want to give something back.'

SUNDAY, MAY 5

Prior to Hoddle's farewell game in charge, the board discussed his successor. In the small board room beside the Trophy Room behind the directors' box, the big decision was taken. They considered experienced men like Dave Bassett and Sven Goran Eriksson. Harding flirted with the notion of hiring Venables. The name of Graham was raised and dismissed.

In that room, as you enter, there is a table laid out for a pre-match lunch – strictly directors only. On the left are trophies, on the right the drinks cabinet where the directors toasted the unanimous choice for their next manager – Gullit.

Gullit was growing more excited by the minute at the prospect of taking over. 'I would want the same preconditions as Glenn set down regarding the structure and finances of the club. That is the first thing the board must do – it's important and for me it will have to be sorted out soon. It's good news that Matthew Harding has said he will keep his money in the club as we need to spend that on new players.'

Hoddle was in the Bates camp regarding Gullit. 'Obviously Ruud is a strong option and he would be exceptionally good for continuity of the style and tactics here. But I've been a player-manager for the last four years and it's very hard. I think Ruud might find it difficult as his first job in management. He still wants to be a player and the fans might find his form on the pitch would suffer as a result.' Hoddle had Gullit on an extensive list of 'possibles' to join the England coaching staff, but felt that it was more likely he would be appointed as his successor at the Bridge. Hoddle said: 'I need to have people around me that I feel right with. I must look at Ruudi in the same circumstances as Ray Wilkins – but I have not had the time to make any decision yet. I must sit down, look at the pluses and the minuses and wait and see whether Ruud gets the job here first. If that happens it will dictate a few things, which is only fair to the club. To be honest I haven't really made any decision who my number two will be or who the backroom staff will be. I have to form a list of names, look at the people who are already with the FA and go from there.' He chose John Gorman, Ray Clemence and Peter Taylor – the Tottenham connection.

'The King is dead. Long live the King.' So declared Bates somewhat melodramatically as Hoddle signed off with a 3–2 defeat by Blackburn. The fans voted with their voice, with chants in support of Gullit and suggestions to Bates that they would rather have one candidate, George Graham, inserted in a delicate part of his anatomy.

In one sense, a scrappy performance suggested Hoddle had left Chelsea much as he found them three years ago: halfway down the Premier League, with an inconsistent side well short of genuine challengers for honours and their off-field situation still unclear. But, as Hoddle pointed out, the club was in a healthier state because of the work at junior levels. Blackburn were chasing a place in Europe determined to end their year as champions on a high note. As the then-manager Ray Harford said: 'I thought we had qualified for Europe when the final whistle went because we'd heard that Arsenal were losing.' They missed out, finishing seventh – four places above Chelsea.

Gullit played to the gallery. One fifty-yard pass midway through the first half was straight out of the Hoddle lexicon, landing perfectly on Hughes's chest only for the Welsh striker to volley over. Another inspired back-heel from Gullit caught Minto on the hop. Wise opened the scoring, but Blackburn equalised two minutes later when a fifty-yard run by Gullit was halted and the ball was quickly transferred to the other end, with Tim Sherwood heading in Graham Fenton's cross from close range. Blackburn took the lead shortly after half-time when poor marking allowed Billy McKinlay to head in. The result was beyond doubt in the fifty-ninth minute, following Fenton's goal.

It had been one of the most emotional days of Hoddle's career. 'I'm sure there will be greater days to come at the club. The foundations are in place and Chelsea can go on to win things.' The sole source of satisfaction for the home fans was the performance of Gullit, their unanimous choice to be Hoddle's successor – not least the sight of the Dutchman still making eager runs upfield in the second minute of injury time. There were many at the start who questioned Gullit's durability, but this was his fortieth match of the campaign and his touch and vision were as irresistible as ever.

Hoddle blew kisses to the crowd at the end; they applauded him off. 'Personally, it's been a lovely way to leave the club. It's been an emotional week.'

'Thank you Glenn, bring on Ruud Gullit,' read one banner.

'There could be a big surprise,' Bates, the chairman, wrote in his programme notes. Mischievous as ever. The only surprise would have been if Gullit had not been appointed.

TUESDAY, MAY 7

The club opened talks with Gullit. One of his conditions was to sign three players. Chelsea opened negotiations for Gianluca Vialli. Hutchinson, who joined the club in 1987, is a tall, no-nonsense figure with experience at Carlisle and Wimbledon, now in charge of recruitment. He travelled to Turin to meet the Juventus striker, who had expressed an interest in teaming up with Gullit. Vialli's former Sampdoria team-mate, David Platt, wanted him at Highbury, but Rioch showed little interest, and likewise there was no reaction from Chelsea's north London rivals, Spurs. Only Glasgow Rangers were ready to meet Vialli's massive wage demands, and a deal had been set up by chairman David Murray when the pair met a month earlier. Vialli was offered a three-year deal worth almost £2m a season to sign for the Ibrox club. Juventus were also keen to keep him, but Vialli had not been impressed by the way they went about it and he opted to play Premiership football in London. He had been attracted by good reports from his friend Gullit. He would have been happy to work under Hoddle, but he was equally content with Gullit in charge.

Klinsmann and Ian Wright were on the transfer hit list, but Vialli topped either of those names, even at thirty-one. He had helped Juventus to the final of the Champions Cup against Ajax and that was to be his farewell performance. Vialli was out of contract after the final.

*

At Planet Hollywood, pop star and Chelsea nut Damon Albarn left his soccer hero Gullit looking embarrassed when he introduced him as 'the next Chelsea manager' at a sports awards ceremony. Security was tight at what has become a venue for many showbiz events, a theme restaurant launched by Bruce Willis, Sly Stallone and Arnie Schwarzenegger, packed with Hollywood memorabilia, and with screens all over the large interior showing clips of hit movies. The Blur pop star was invited to present his hero with the Best International Player award.

Ruud was unfazed, always relaxed, willing to stop and talk to anyone who approached him. When he entered the restaurant every head turned. An instantly recognisable star, those dreadlocks his trademark, he looked smart even though casually attired, a real presence in any company.

I sat with my girlfriend Linda and *Daily Mirror* editor Piers Morgan, sandwiched between Ruud and Damon. Ruud was always smiling, laughing, happy to hear a joke or tell one, and equally willing to talk more seriously about his football. When Ruud left the table, Damon shared with us his secret plan to ensure Gullit became the Chelsea boss. Damon said: 'I couldn't resist it. I hoped Ruud would say something but he's above all that. He is a god after all. I hope he gets the job.'

There was almost a diplomatic incident when Ruud entered Planet Hollywood. Everyone wanted to talk to him, and he was cajoled to sit at Dani Behr's table. Ruudi's agent Phil Smith had to smooth over the problem by persuading Ruud to sit at his allotted place – with Damon threatening to walk out if he couldn't meet the man of his dreams! It's amazing how much Ruud is liked. Linda ended up affectionately nursing Ruudi's glass when he left! It must have been the booze, I assured myself.

I had plenty of time to discuss the Chelsea job with Ruud and it became clear he was keen to accept it. I suggested that, rather than Hoddle's demands for £15m to strengthen the side, he asked for the three players of his choice and left it to the club to work out the wages and transfer fees. It was a suggestion he clearly took on board – unless he'd thought about it already, and didn't want to give too much away.

WEDNESDAY, MAY 8

Gullit and Hoddle turned out for Paul Merson's testimonial at Highbury. His big night attracted a host of top stars, including Paul Gascoigne and Matt Le Tissier. The game raised more than £400,000 for twenty-eight-year-old Merson.

THURSDAY, MAY 9

Ruud was one of my many guests at the annual Footballer of the Year award dinner at the Royal Lancaster Hotel. I introduced him to Spurs chairman Alan Sugar. Among my other guests was Vinnie Jones! But his old adversary was diplomatically seated at the other end of a very large table for fourteen. I need not have worried, the pair were ultra-pleasant to each other. Vinnie's verbal attack on Ruud that earned the Wimbledon hard man a disrepute charge has been forgotten, if not forgiven. Ruud's reception was equal to that of the winner, Eric Cantona. In the end, Ruud finished in second place.

There were many in the room who felt Gullit would be a much better recipient of the old established award. Ruud was wonderful company. Naturally most people in the room wanted an autograph, but he wasn't pestered. Every time he was asked he politely signed. I should note that Gullit and Cantona were the only two guests in the room without a tie!

FRIDAY, MAY 10

Gullit was confirmed as Chelsea player-manager after a final meeting with Colin Hutchinson. His contract was extended to June 1998 to allow him to be one of England's first continental-style coaches. Hutchinson took control of financial matters for signings and contracts, with Gullit concentrating on the playing side. Graham Rix stepped up from reserve-team coach to first-team coach, ousting Hoddle's first-team coach, Peter Shreeves. Gwyn Williams, one of Hoddle's backroom team, took charge of administration.

Ruud was a 'dream' to deal with in re-negotiating his terms, making a verbal commitment to stay long term. Hutchinson said: 'When I talked to him in the afternoon I jokingly said that he would use his management experience at Chelsea to one day become manager of AC Milan. But he surprised me when he said: "I don't think so, I hope to stay here for many years to come."'

Hutchinson continued: 'I had a brief chat with Ruud last Sunday and then another half-hour with him after the tremendous reception he received at the end of our last match. We went through things with him and then I gave him until today to sort it all out. When I knew Glenn was leaving, Ruud was one of the first people we thought of and it was a unanimous decision to offer him the job. His responsibility will be purely for team matters and that's how he likes it.' The official investiture had to wait, since Gullit was in Holland for the weekend. Hutchinson added, 'Ruud's chief concern was to have a more involved role without it affecting his playing career. We've made sure he is as far away from day-to-day administrative matters as possible. We are delighted. He desired the job and we were happy to give it to him. We acted quickly to halt speculation and allow us to build on the foundations laid by Glenn. Everyone has seen Ruud's playing quality and he is obviously a deep thinker about the game. He has worked with some of the best coaches in Europe and probably the world, and he was clearly the fans' choice in a big way last Sunday.'

With Gullit in charge, Chelsea had a distinct advantage when foreign superstars became available. Gullit's policy was to recruit only quality. One of Ruud's favourite analogies, during his first season in English football, was to liken the game to a car. 'You have five gears and the trouble with English teams is that they drive all the time in fourth and fifth.' Ruud wanted players capable of utilising all five gears. He wasted no time. Bates said: 'We finished our negotiations after forty-five minutes with Ruud and ten minutes later he went straight from the boardroom to the terraces – the only place where he can get privacy – with his mobile phone, and was talking to players throughout Europe that he wanted to bring to Chelsea.'

The continental approach was the only one that would suit Gullit. Bates put it succinctly: 'You would not expect Ruud to go to Peterborough on a wet Tuesday night in November to watch a player we fancy.'

The set-up drew little or no criticism from within the dressing room – at least at the outset. There was no hint of possible disillusionment among those who would eventually be ousted in the whirlwind of change. Even John Spencer said: 'A player of Ruud's standing will influence the club's ability to bring in top-class players. We are already being linked with the likes of Gianluca Vialli, and it will be fantastic if we can get him. We may have lost a world-class manager in Glenn Hoddle – but we've got another in his place!' Spencer added: 'I have two years left at Chelsea and

I'm looking forward to pre-season already so that I can work with Ruud. You cannot fail to learn just by training with him.' Minto said: 'Ruud's pulling power is even better than Glenn's – he is one of the greatest names in world football. He has been a great success here and I'm sure other foreign players will look at him and want to give it a go themselves. The reception he got from the fans in our last game of the season was so great that the other ten of us need not have bothered to go on the pitch.'

The entire Chelsea team welcomed Gullit's appointment. Eddie Newton said: 'The players are delighted that Ruud has got the job, and at the same time we're all relieved. He was the only choice, if the good work Glenn had done at Stamford Bridge was to continue. Chelsea have gone through a major transformation under Glenn. If someone else had taken over, it could have spelt disaster.' But Newton warned his new boss that he can no longer be Mister Nice Guy. 'It will be interesting to see how Ruud's relationship with the players changes. He enjoys a good laugh with the lads, and has become something of a practical joker at the club. But he can't afford to have a relationship like that with the players any more.'

Ruud's appointment was well received in the media. Neil Harman, chief soccer correspondent of the *Daily Mail*, was typical. 'If Hoddle was the man who sent the wind of change through the old glamour club and raised its profile to new heights, then his talisman on the field was the dreadlocked Dutchman who was the personification of class and charm. Gullit is everything – on the field and off it – that Chelsea could have wanted. A superb athlete, who at thirty-three has shown a remarkable ability to make the Premiership play at his pace, Gullit has the charisma which comes with learning football at the knee of Holland's greats. When the ever-thirsty media have wanted an opinion on anything to do with football, out has stepped Gullit to speak in whatever language has been required.' Chris Lightbown of the *Sunday Times* wrote: 'Ruud Gullit's appointment as Chelsea's player-coach took a week to settle, but will have an effect on English football for years to come. At one stroke, Gullit has killed the last nagging doubt about prominent foreign players coming to England, namely that they were seeking a soft year or so in the Premier League in order to tag English football on to their CV. Not Gullit.' The esteemed Michael Parkinson wrote in the *Daily Telegraph*: 'The foreign players have provided the catalyst which is why the best news of the week was Ruud Gullit becoming player-manager of Chelsea. Particularly when the rumour factory had George Graham in the job.'

MONDAY, MAY 13

On his first day as the new Chelsea player-manager, Gullit experienced some of the problems which made it easy for his predecessor to depart: Bates tore up the agreement that would have seen Harding eventually take over as chairman. Diplomacy was the key for Ruud in the continuing feud. 'I don't know the details of what has gone on between the chairman and Mr Harding and I don't want to. I don't think it will affect me directly but obviously it would be better if they sorted things out quickly. There is a lot of work to be done and players to be signed. The uncertainty is obviously not the best thing at this stage and it would be better for all concerned if things were settled. At the meeting I had with the club I asked questions and got the answers and assurances I needed. I hope they keep their word. The row between the two of them has been going on a long time. How it is resolved is not vital to me. As long as I get what I want to build the team I am happy. I know Glenn was always concerned about it, and the sooner it's resolved the better for everyone at Chelsea. Bates and Harding are two proud men and neither is prepared to give in. But I don't want to be distracted. I'm very excited about this job.' Gullit was informed that, even without Harding, Chelsea had the financial clout to sign the players he wanted.

Equally he was not concerned how much the club lavished in salaries to land his signings. 'I am not interested in how much the players cost or earn. I just want them. I know I will attract good players to Chelsea. Not necessarily big players, but those who will fit in with my ideas and the team. I wouldn't discount someone even if it means paying them more than me. And I don't care if they're English or European – they could come from Timbuktu for all I care as long as they fit into our style of play.'

Worried fans called on Bates and Harding to end the board room war. The Independent Supporters Association feared there would be a lot more blood-letting before their power struggle was resolved. 'We are very disappointed with this new turn of events just days after the club took the positive step of appointing Ruud Gullit,' said ISA vice-chairman Mark Pulver. Bates issued assurances. 'There is more than one fish in the sea and we've made arrangements elsewhere to ensure that Ruud Gullit is not disadvantaged. His negotiations with two continental players will not be affected by this.'

TUESDAY, MAY 14

Chelsea's hopes of capturing Vialli rose as he steered away from Glasgow Rangers despite the better terms on offer – a £6m three-year contract – because he wouldn't be under enough pressure. He adored the constant attention the Italian media gave him. 'I would have to think long and hard before I leave for a country where nothing happens. It would be strange to move to a country where at the training grounds you only find two reporters – without TV cameras. There is constant pressure in Italy and that's what I'm used to. I would have to consider all aspects very seriously – not just my wallet, but also the charms and beauty of the city and the quality of life. I can say that Rangers have made me a very tempting offer. They want to make me King of Scotland. But in the last fifteen years I have grown accustomed to a particular psychological set-up. The effect is similar to a drug. Meanwhile, I have faith that Juve will keep their word not to take any decision regarding myself until May 22.' Vialli's determination to stay in the spotlight was in marked contrast to Paul Gascoigne, who used the excuse that he was turning his back on the Premiership because he was being hounded by the press.

Vialli was reputedly offered £27,000 a week to sign for Chelsea. The deal would make him the highest-paid player in the Premier League, topping Gullit himself and Arsenal's Dennis Bergkamp. The three-year contract would bring Vialli £4.2m. Hutchinson said: 'Our hat is in the ring, and Ruud will play a significant role in getting him. They are good friends and played together in Italy. There are exciting times ahead for Chelsea with Ruud going even further down the continental road after the start made by Glenn Hoddle.' The Bates–Harding conflict wouldn't affect Gullit's transfer plans.

Season ticket prices rose by 21 per cent with £654 for the best seats – the highest in the Premiership. The money would help pay for Vialli, one of the first big-name beneficiaries of the Bosman ruling, a free transfer enabling him to negotiate a reported £1m signing-on fee and an annual salary of at least that much to match his remuneration in Italy. Such a deal illustrated the current financial quandary of the English game. It has saved money on fees, but is in danger of squandering its new-found wealth gleaned from television money and increasing ticket prices on wages, worries which will be redundant if Chelsea receive some return on the field during Vialli's contract. Vialli was concerned that Chelsea would not be good enough to compete for honours and was seeking reassurance about their buying plans. He would have preferred to sign for Arsenal, as telephone conversations with David Platt indicated. London, though, was his preferred home after Turin, where he would ideally liked to have remained, but he considered Juventus's offer of a one-year deal without a pay rise unworthy.

Juventus superstar Alessandro Del Piero begged Vialli not to quit the club. The Italian superkid admitted: 'It will be a huge loss to Juve and to me when Luca moves to another club. I am still a boy. Everything has happened so quickly for me that I have needed his advice and he has always been willing to give it. I owe him so much.' Juve relied on the golden triangle del Piero formed with Vialli and Ravanelli to end the Dutch reign in the European Cup Final in Rome on May 22. Del Piero added: 'Ajax are outstanding and rightly are the favourites to win once again. But we have a chance if we perform to our best.'

Meanwhile the BBC enlisted the talents of Gullit for Euro '96 as a studio pundit alongside Des Lynam and Gary Lineker, who had been handed the task of fronting the nightly round-up of highlights. ITV signed England's two top managers – Manchester United's Alex Ferguson and Newcastle's Kevin Keegan – to join their TV panel for the championships. Gullit ruled England out of finishing Euro '96 in the last four. He tipped his native Holland – best-priced at 13–2 – for glory ahead of Italy, Germany and Croatia.

Peter Shreeves became the first victim of the new managerial regime. Shreeves, who spent three years as assistant manager to Hoddle, said: 'There are no ill feelings or anything like that. What I want is to get back into football as soon as possible. The club went about things in the correct fashion, there was nothing underhand. I've enjoyed every minute of my time at Chelsea. They are probably the best set of lads that I have worked with.'

THURSDAY, MAY 16
The Ruud Revolution was well underway; specialist goalkeeping and conditioning coaches were hired. Hoddle first introduced strict controls on the players' diet and fitness; now Chelsea's keepers would be coached individually by a specialist and an expert would monitor each player's fitness. Gullit said: 'I'm used to certain ways of working and that means a specialist for keepers, and for the fitness side of things.'

Gullit could not, and would not, try to change attitudes overnight. It was to be a gradual, educational process. He explained: 'It is impossible to make the English player change his thinking completely. Take his diet. They are too accustomed to the sausage. They must have it. What can I do? I have tried to make Chelsea players change. It is no good. I would like to introduce Italian professionalism. I have spoken to the players on how the Italians live. Sadly, they think it boring.' He found one disciple in Hoddle. He encouraged the Chelsea squad to arrive early for training and eat breakfast. Muesli and yoghurt were on the menu, with lunch including pasta and other health dishes to follow. But the players still went for bangers and ketchup. Gullit admitted: 'You cannot break tradition.'

Robert Philip of the *Daily Telegraph* amusingly pointed out: 'He certainly has some innovative ideas. The Dutchman's first move, as I understand it, will be to arrange blood tests for all the Stamford Bridge players to detect any possible food allergies. It would be a crushing blow were the average professional footballer to discover he was allergic to a diet of beer and biryani.'

SUNDAY, MAY 19
The fans were certainly behind Ruud, judging by this letter in the *Sunday Mirror*:

> Thanks, FA, for taking that impressive mediocrity, Glenn Hoddle, to England. It allows Ruud Gullit to mould Chelsea from a team of towering expectations to one that will make any argument between Messrs Ferguson and Keegan next season irrelevant. Ruud will show Hoddle how serious you need to be to win silverware.
>
> C Rossini, Harwich, Essex

WEDNESDAY, MAY 22
The European Cup Final. Vialli planned to announce his decision once the clash with Ajax was concluded. But it was clear that he had already chosen Chelsea. Vialli's business adviser Claudio Pasqualin confirmed: 'It is probable he will sign for Chelsea. He prefers London, even though Rangers are in the Champions League. He believes the standard of English football is rising. And Chelsea are going to get better. He expects that the season after next they will be in the UEFA Cup, and then the Champions League.'

Vialli would only say: 'I am flattered so many clubs want me, especially from Britain. I will announce my decision after the final, probably on Friday. The final is the biggest match of my career. First I must give Juventus one hundred per cent. Then I can sit down with the directors to confront my contract.'

Europe's dream final ended in the nightmare of penalties but also the reawakening of one of football's grandest clubs. Juventus poured their very soul into this hyper-charged exorcism of the ghost of Heysel. The Old Lady, as this stately club is known, had never felt able to celebrate fully her only previous European Cup triumph, which came that black night in Brussels eleven years ago when thirty-nine of her family were stampeded to death by Liverpool fans.

Two shoot-out saves by Angelo Peruzzi dethroned the reigning champions. Vialli captained Juve to victory. Amid the jubilation and festivities, Vialli said: 'It's unfair to ask me about my future in this moment of intense joy and great happiness. On a joyous occasion like this, I think it is right that we only talk about the game and the victory.' Vialli led the lap of honour, with tears of delight and relief streaming down his face – he had missed an open goal and another golden chance to give Juventus victory in normal time. By the time the penalties came, Vialli was suffering from cramp and exhaustion and coach Marcello Lippi admitted: 'Gianluca would not have taken the fifth penalty if we had needed it. He was due to take the twelfth.' Vialli admitted he'd had a nightmare match, adding: 'Yes, there was a nasty smell around me when it came to taking the penalties. But it is a magnificent feeling to win the European Cup. So many great players have never tasted it and I am so lucky.'

Behind the scenes, his friends and advisers were finalising the details of his move to join Gullit at Stamford Bridge. Vialli was replaced by Alen Boksic from Lazio. Vialli gave the game away when he waved emotionally in a farewell gesture to the Juventus fans before leaving the field. Then Vialli's agent, Claudio Pasqualin, dropped a heavy hint that Vialli had chosen Gullit's team. Referring to the Friday press conference when Vialli would reveal his intentions, Pasqualin said: 'If you are an English journalist you should definitely come. The announcement will be very interesting for you.' Asked if Gullit and the Chelsea directors would join Vialli for the announcement on Friday, Pasqualin said: 'No, they will have their own announcements to make in England.' Then Pasqualin hurriedly added: 'That is, of course, if he has decided to join Chelsea.'

Gullit's wisdom in signing Vialli was questioned. On the evidence of his part in the final, would he score the twenty-five goals a season Chelsea needed if they were to win a trophy? The Italians do not let strikers go without a reason. To them, men who can break down the best defences in the world are like gold dust. So why were Juventus allowing Vialli to leave? Was it because he had lost that explosive pace that all men up front need to have? Against Ajax, Vialli worked tirelessly. He was still strong, and led his attack impressively. But Patrick Barclay in the *Sunday Telegraph* wrote: 'How can England be worried about losing its status as the financial centre of Europe? Not while star players – one minute Gianluca Vialli, the next Paulo Futre – keep choosing it as the place to take out massive pension schemes. To the Euro '96 slogan "Football Comes Home" might be added ... To Retire.'

Ajax boss Louis van Gaal – one of the most respected coaches in the world – cast doubt on Vialli's staying power. The Dutchman smirked when asked if Vialli had at least one or two more good years left in him. 'I think that will be very difficult,' said van Gaal. 'You see, he needs so much energy for the aggressive, bustling type of game he plays. So when you are thirty-two it is a question of just looking to the next match and the one after that and trying to get through the forty-odd a season that way.'

FRIDAY, MAY 24

Yes to Chelsea. No to Glasgow Rangers. Hutchinson finalised the deal. Vialli's signature on a contract at 1 am in his private apartment in Turin. Vialli knew just enough English 'to read a contract'.

Rangers chairman David Murray said: 'Vialli has sent me a personal letter to say he will not be signing for Rangers. He says he is very, very sorry but that he will be joining Chelsea instead. He feels he achieved everything there is for him to achieve in football when he lifted the Champions Cup. That win made it easier for him to decide to move to London for lifestyle reasons. I replied to Vialli by sending him a fax today. I said it was very nice of him to write to me and explain his decision.'

Announcing his decision in Turin, Vialli said: 'Ruud asked me what I wanted out of life, both sporting and non-sporting. After discussing it, he said Chelsea was the place for me because London has everything. My desire to go to London was greater than going to Scotland. Gullit is a friend, he speaks Italian and knows Italian soccer. His presence was certainly a factor. Ruud, like me, is a winner. I hope to win the Premiership or the FA Cup and score many goals. But my English is poor and I'll have to take courses in London. I do know the value of the pound, though. There were other top possibilities in Italy, but it was hard to imagine a future in Italy after Sampdoria and Juventus. I gave and received a lot during four years with La Juve. It was a terrific experience and we divorced by mutual consent.'

No European competition for a season at least but that didn't bother him as he had nothing left to win. 'I've won all the European trophies in my career. I can take a season off from the international scene and help Chelsea win a place in Europe next year. There is more fair play in England and less drama than in Italy. And I feel more English than Italian as a player. In Italy we say that leaving is a little like dying, but change is a little like being reborn. I feel like a kid going to a new environment with new challenges. I'm leaving without a grudge and I hope to return to Italy one day, possibly as a manager. Soccer is my whole life. I can't wait to arrive in London. It is the best city in Europe, if not the world. I'll settle down there with my girlfriend, Giovanna. All the contract formalities have been completed and I'll be in London next month. I know some of the players' reputations very well. Dmitri Kharine is one of the best keepers around and I know all about Ruud. Then there's Mark Hughes, John Spencer and Dennis Wise. I will get to know the rest at training. I feel like a kid going off to play in a completely new environment. In England there will not be all the weight on my shoulders. There you are not judged by goals alone but by what you can achieve for the team.'

Juve vice-president Roberto Bettega said: 'We separated as friends. In the future he could return in a managerial role.'

Matthew Harding said: 'Since Vialli is a world-famous player, the very fact he has come here proves that Chelsea really is a club that means business now, and is entitled to be taken seriously. There is no doubt about it. One of the things in Chelsea's favour is that we are situated in the best part of London. For talented and financially successful footballers used to living well in Europe, it makes sense to come here. Ruud Gullit has been tremendously important in attracting these players – as was Glenn Hoddle in attracting *him*. Vialli has captured the imagination. I should think that Chelsea is every Italian restaurateur's favourite club at the moment.'

The Chelsea players were celebrating as well as the fans. But was Spencer psychic? He said: 'He's an unbelievable signing and Ruud is probably going to get other world-class players in. I just hope he wants them for positions other than mine. Ruud was brilliant as a player and we all learned from him, but if I say too many nice things he'll think I'm trying to talk my way into the team! I know I've got it all to prove again. Ruud might have liked me when we played together but that can all change and I need to do better again now he's the boss. I'll not fail for the want of trying. Let's hope he does for us what Jurgen Klinsmann did for Tottenham. He pulled them right up into the top six and to the FA Cup semifinals.'

Vialli was installed at 14–1 with William Hill to top the Premiership goalscoring charts. Chelsea were 40–1 with the firm to win the Premiership title but they suddenly became 25–1.

SUNDAY, MAY 26

Speculation over Hughes's future, inevitably fuelled by the arrival of Vialli. Everton were linked in a £2m deal, but Hughes was far more interested in linking up with Vialli in the Chelsea attack. 'I've admired him for some time. He is a great player because he works very hard, he has skill and scores goals. That's not a bad combination. It's good for Chelsea and for English football that stars like him keep coming. Stamford Bridge is a good place to be now.' 'Sparky' added: 'I don't think he is here to replace me and I haven't been told anything different by the boss. I'm looking forward to him coming and I want to play alongside him.' Hughes was amazed how many changes he witnessed since moving from Manchester United a year before. 'I would never have thought a year ago Ruud Gullit would be manager, Vialli would be coming and Glenn Hoddle would be the England boss. It's nice to be part of the excitement. You have to keep your interest going in your career and this has kept me on my toes.'

The first U-turn. Sweeper David Lee changed his mind and agreed a new Chelsea contract. But Muzzy Izzett stayed at Leicester where he had been on loan and had helped them win promotion to the Premier League. Izzett said: 'I can't stand the thought of going back to Stamford Bridge.'

WEDNESDAY, MAY 29

A run-down looking Bridge was in the embryonic stages of becoming one of the grand stadia and development sites in the country. You walked across the builders' rubble, over the broken tarmac and through the swing doors into the reception area. A couple of girls sat behind the desk, manning the switchboard and greeting callers. Theresa was in control, a highly experienced official at the club who doubled as the press box organiser. The two lifts to the right of the entrance took visitors to the grander levels of the large dining area on the first floor and the directors' landing on the second. Once the West Stand was the pride of the club, but it was nearly twenty years old and in urgent need of upgrading. The stand was responsible for the financial crisis that eventually drove Bates to salvage the situation by purchasing the football enterprise for one pound, while the £1.5m debts went into the holding company that owned the ground.

Appearances can be deceptive. Behind the ramshackle facade, it was boom time in terms of finance and interest. A new long term lease with the Royal Bank of Scotland, taken over by Harding, made the security of the club's tenure at the Bridge safer than for nearly two decades.

Vialli's arrival led to a massive boost in season ticket sales. Chelsea banked £2.6m before the start of the new season, a club record, easily eclipsing the previous season's £1.8m, despite having some of the dearest tickets in the Premiership. That would help pay Vialli's wages! Chelsea received fifteen sacks of season ticket applications. Staff were rushed off their feet dealing with a jammed switchboard and queues at the box office. Sales manager Eddie Barnett said: 'I can easily predict a huge increase over our previous best which stood at 4,673 sales. Early indications are for sales of at least 6,500 and compared with the situation this time last year it's much, much higher.'

JUNE

Euro '96, a TV Star is Born ... in his daytime job
Gullit unveils Vialli

SATURDAY, JUNE 8

Ruud took his place in the TV gantry as a key analyst for the BBC during Euro '96. His performance as a pundit whetted appetites for the moment Gullit would take control for the first time in his new managerial capacity. A question of putting theory into practice. 'New signing Ruud Gullit is the jewel in BBC's crown,' was the verdict of the *Daily Record* as the competition progressed and the BBC were clear winners in the ratings. The *Sunday Express* tempted new readers with 'Ruud Gullit's eight-page guide to Euro '96'.

MONDAY, JUNE 10

Gullit, who played against Gazza in the 1990 World Cup, was critical of the England midfield player's performance against the Swiss in the opening game. He pointed out: 'What was most worrying was the lack of physical fitness in the England side, particularly after the break. The midfield were unable to get up and back and that meant the team suddenly became very exposed.'

In the build-up to the Holland–Scotland clash, Spencer and the rest of his Brave-heart team-mates were incredibly relaxed. Gullit publicly criticised Scotland's stars after watching them fool around at a press conference. Spencer said: 'I'd better be careful what I am saying here – I wouldn't like to be caught smiling on camera. I believe Ruud gave a couple of my team-mates some stick for laughing and joking. He said that the Dutch and the Germans wouldn't behave like that when they talked in the media. He said they would be too busy concentrating and certainly wouldn't be smiling ...' Spencer added: 'The difference between us and the English is that they are surrounded by all the hype every day. The whole country expects them to win the championship and it's put them under tremendous pressure. That must put such a strain on their energies, so I'm not surprised they tired the way they did against Switzerland at Wembley. But we aren't feeling anything like that. The pressure will only start for us when we walk off the team bus and go into the dressing room at Villa Park.'

FRIDAY, JUNE 14

Ruud was one of the early stars of Euro '96 – including those on the pitch! The *Sporting Life*'s verdict of the battle for TV viewers: 'Talking of Hansen, the best match of Euro '96 so far has been his battle with Ruud Gullit for the starring role alongside Des in the BBC studio. Des, Ruud and Jockey Hansen. The absolute dream team, the dog's bollards. A brilliant broadcasting trio whose combination is made all the more watchable by the merest hint of tension between Hansen and Gullit. See, the thing is Hansen's been top boy a good while now and he's in no mood to let some Dutch upstart nick the limelight. For Gullit's part, you've got some minor problem with the acidic jock. It's as if one of his mates has dug out an old *Match of the Day* clip in which Hansen is watching Gullit in action for Chelsea and saying something like "He flicks it too much for my liking."' The *Daily Record*: 'Ruud Gullit continues to impress and he even managed not to say the word "technical" after the last Dutch game ... until well into his second sentence.' The *Evening Standard*'s verdict: 'The dread chin of Hill has been replaced by the dreadlocks of Ruud Gullit. This was a brave move ... Ruud has begun to toss his hair about as if he's actually enjoying the football, a fine contrast with the unforgiving Calvinism of Jocky Hansen. What's more, Ruud has brought a European sense of style to the commentary box.'

The *Daily Record* continued their eulogy: 'The wise words of Dutchman Ruud Gullit on the telly are thought-provoking. He speaks so sensibly he's putting Alan Hansen in the shade – and Jimmy Hill's chin out of joint.' The *Daily Telegraph*: 'Ruud Gullit is the star turn. The man is brilliant. His charm, gentle wit and deep knowledge of the modern game produced the most impressive debut in televised sport since the arrival of Sue Barker ... From the body language on display, Hansen is clearly not amused to have the Dutchman starring on his patch.' The *Independent on Sunday*: 'Ruud Gullit has been an eloquent television star and there would be little doubt about the answer if you asked any Premier player to say from whose lips he would care to hear team talks next season.' The *Sunday Times*: 'The Boy Gullit leans back, jiggles his locks, does everything in his power to keep the beautiful game beautiful, then makes his move with the deliberation of a Kasparov. Jock leans forward, itching to pounce, ego in conflict with respect for an intellectual equal (if not superior).' The *Sunday Mirror* was more direct: 'Gullit is the best soccer mastermind television has given us for years, and though Hansen can see his crown slipping he is hanging on bravely for at least a draw.'

Ruud easily won when it came to the women's vote. Lynne Truss of *The Times*: 'If it hadn't been for ogling Ruud Gullit in the BBC intervals (or whatever they call them), I'd have rigged up my Euro '96 pager to the mains, and killed myself.'

MONDAY, JUNE 17

Drake's Bar, named after Ted Drake, the manager who last brought the championship to Chelsea, was the venue for Vialli's media unveiling. Drake's Bar nestles comfortably in the club's fashionable new £5m stand and was a most unlikely venue for the entrance of Vialli. A pub. Really, nothing grander than a carpeted, chrome and painted wall lounge with a long bar. The only reason to distinguish it from any bar in town was the clientele on this particular occasion: the room was packed with gesticulating Italians in Armani suits, a ponytail here and a single gold earring there.

The star of the show arrived fashionably late, accompanied by Gullit. That might have confused one or two since a helpful factsheet distributed by Chelsea officials listed Glenn Hoddle as manager! Vialli walked into the room with great poise. Instantly, his bald head symbolised the start of the new Chelsea under Gullit.

Vialli's English is 'nod gudd', so Chelsea hired an interpreter, who spoke at a volume undetectable to the human ear, and in heavily accented English of her own. 'I hope between three and four months I can speak English proper and good,' said Gianluca. Pending that, he elected to answer most questions through the interpreter.

Vialli grinned contentedly throughout a long address by Hutchinson, of which he understood very little. Hutchinson invited questions, and a voice at the back of the room asked, frankly mystified: 'So why Chelsea?' He said: 'I wanted to work with my friend, Ruud. I like English football very much. They are the masters of fair play. Also, I think it is very important that they pay me very well.' Hutchinson interceded. 'Not *too* well,' he said, with an over-hearty laugh. Vialli continued: 'Success for me this year will mean enjoying myself and making sure the fans enjoy the game.'

No way back into the Italian team while Sacchi was still around? 'It will be difficult for me to get back into the national team with Sacchi as manager. But I hope to score as many goals as possible for Chelsea to put Sacchi in trouble.'

Gullit answered questions fluently in both English and Italian. He provided the most eloquent statement on why a Serie A star might want to come to England. 'For me,' he said, 'London gave the ability to walk freely on the street. I wanted again to have an ordinary life and that is what I find here.'

Gullit was convinced Vialli would prosper in the Premiership. 'English football is less technical than the Italian game. It is more open and with the passing game I want Chelsea to play, Vialli will be perfect for the team.' Out on the pitch, removing his shirt and jacket to put on a Chelsea top for photographs, Vialli revealed a set of frighteningly well-honed muscles. The tattoo of an eagle on his right shoulder is virtually life-size.

Vialli's first competitive game since captaining Juventus to victory in the European Champions Cup would be at the humble Dell. Vialli had played on all the world's great stages, the Stadium of Light, the Bernabeu and the San Siro. He was about to make his Premier League debut at – the Dell! Worse to come … Ken Monkou promised him a red-raw welcome. Monkou had faced Vialli when Saints had drawn 2–2 with Juventus in a friendly two years earlier. Monkou said: 'He had Roberto Baggio alongside him and we didn't do too badly then.'

Vialli knew little of the Premier League other than what he had seen on television, and he was experienced enough to realise 'it's very different on the pitch'. He envisaged no problems teaming up with Hughes. 'The pitch is very big.' Well, that was a profound enough tactical explanation of the new attacking force. In reality, he didn't have a clue how it would work out, but he's an optimist, who feels good players can play together irrespective of the formation.

Gullit planned to change the face of English football. 'I already have players who are good for English football but I want to change that style. When I went to Milan a lot of people thought Arrigo Sacchi was crazy when he altered their methods. But after we started to gain success everyone copied us. Sacchi changed the mentality of the Italian game and I want to do the same here. We will carry on with the style which Glenn Hoddle introduced at Chelsea but I want players to realise that it's not just about passing the ball. If we got a point for every ten passes we'd win the championship, but it's winning the game which is important and we have to play more for the result. It's not always possible to play beautiful football. I want them to be more efficient.' Gullit was also looking for greater fitness levels, and would work the players harder to achieve it. 'The players here have got to get fitter so I've been asking a number of top athletes for the best physical conditioning coach around.'

It was pointed out to Vialli that John Major supports the club. Given the choice, would Vialli rather it were Tony Blair? Vialli looked blank. 'Who is Tony Blair?' he asked. After an intermission for laughter, a more formal response came back through the interpreter: 'The realities of politics in England are still unknown to me.'

FRIDAY, JUNE 21

Gullit won the race for Leboeuf. He moved in after the Strasbourg defender turned down a £2.5m move to Marseille; his preference was English football. Strasbourg had been in talks with Gullit, Hutchinson and Rix. Gullit was delighted that Leboeuf, with eight caps, had not made an appearance in Euro '96, alerting other English clubs. Leboeuf was told by French national coach Aimé Jacquet not to comment on the deal, but he said: 'It is my ambition to play in England and join my friend David Ginola in the Premiership. I'm definitely leaving Strasbourg and am now waiting to hear what is happening with Chelsea.' The centre-back, regarded as the natural successor in the national side to the highly regarded Laurent Blanc, made his international debut at the start of the season, scoring twice in the 10–0 victory against Azerbaijan. He scored seventeen goals in 106 games for Strasbourg.

Hutchinson completed the deal worth a new club record of £2.5m at the French team hotel with Rix acting as translator. He signed a four-year contract. Leboeuf, twenty-eight, said: 'When I knew Ruud Gullit wanted me at Chelsea, I could not wait to sign. I am very happy because it has been my ambition to play in England for some time. I am very excited that Ruud Gullit wants to sign me, and that I will be playing with Vialli. I am looking forward to meeting my new team-mates and the Chelsea fans.' Hutchinson said: 'Frank has had very enthusiastic reports about English football from his friend Ginola. We've been tracking him since Ruud was appointed and as soon as he knew we were interested he wanted to come here despite very strong interest from his home club, Marseille. We were negotiating for four hours before we convinced Strasbourg to let him go. It's like Southampton losing Matt Le Tissier – that's how important he was to them.'

With Mad Cow Disease the major issue of the day, and Europe shunning British beef, typical of Gullit to bring a Frenchman called Leboeuf!

Gullit had to wait an extra twenty-four hours before beginning his managerial career in the Premiership. The dictates of *Sky Sports* coverage selected Chelsea for first match of the season at Southampton. Back on TV, Jimmy Hill suggested that even his wife, who didn't usually watch him, was making an exception for England's game with Spain, such was Euro '96 mania taking a grip. Ruud had his own theory. 'She's tuning in to watch Des Lynam,' he said, 'the sexiest man on television.'

WEDNESDAY, JUNE 26

The BBC enjoyed a runaway win in the Euro '96 battle of the box, thanks to smooth performers Ruud, Des, Alan and Gary winning the popularity stakes against ITV's big guns. More than twenty-six million viewers tuned into the England–Germany sudden-death semifinal shoot-out. Three-quarters of those were watching the Beeb's coverage, which kicked off ten minutes earlier than ITV's. The BBC boasted: 'We are thrilled by our share of the market.' The figure, though, was down on the twenty-eight million for the England–Germany semifinal of Italia '90. The *Daily Telegraph* verdict: 'Not for the first time in this tournament, ITV were playing the patriotism card. The problem is, at the top level of television punditry, international experience for the home nation guarantees nothing. Consider the BBC's Ruud Gullit, analyst of the tournament by a mile, and he's never represented England at anything.'

Some of Ruud's 'Colemanballs' were the quotes of the tournament. 'It's a clash of the Titanics!' – on England v Germany. 'It's the men without the balls who should decide the play!' – Gullit on the importance of running off the ball.

On a more serious note, Ruud paid tribute to England's brave attempts to reach the final. He said: 'I admire the Germans but I don't know how they do it, because they seem to get into the final every time. They are lucky, too, because England had all the chances to win with a golden goal.'

Chris Lightbown of the *Sunday Times*: 'the excellent impression Ruud Gullit made on BBC makes a difference, too. Try hating all foreigners after hearing his incisive comments. It's impossible.'

THURSDAY, JUNE 27
Next on Gullit's transfer hit list was Italy's Euro '96 midfield star Roberto Di Matteo. Talks were already in progress with Lazio, but there were still delicate negotiations over the fee. Di Matteo, twenty-six, was under contract for another two years. Hutchinson journeyed to Rome to close a £4.9m deal.

FRIDAY, JUNE 28
Gullit recruited former Olympic sprint ace Ade Mafe to train his players. Mafe, the youngest ever Olympic 200 metres finalist, was offered the post of personal fitness trainer. Gullit was startled by the poor fitness of his team and made it clear that he wouldn't tolerate players who abused their bodies. The criticism was general, not aimed at any individuals but at the team's lack of stamina in the final third of a game. In Italy, Gullit had experienced how experts were used in a variety of fields to ensure the players were in peak condition. Gullit would embark on a programme of gentle persuasion and understanding rather than a sergeant major approach. He wanted to provide his new charges with the benefit of his vast experience, something he had started gradually in his first season as a player. But now he had the opportunity to put them into practice in his first season as a manager.

JULY

Gullit splashes out on Leboeuf and Di Matteo

MONDAY, JULY 1

Ruud's BBC persona during Euro '96 brought a rash of bets with William Hill for Chelsea to win the FA Carling Premiership. The offer was down to 20–1 from 33–1. Graham Sharpe, Hill's spokesman, said: 'We took one bet of £1,500 each-way for Chelsea at 33–1 and have seen a steady flow of three figure bets for them throughout Euro '96. We can only put it down to Gullit's impressive display on TV. We're already looking at a potential payout of £200,000 should Chelsea win the title and they are now seventh favourites and our biggest liability.'

TUESDAY, JULY 2

No sooner had Gullit introduced record-buy Leboeuf to the media than he was splashing out more millions on Di Matteo. Lazio spokesman Mario Pennacchio said: 'It is true that a Chelsea director is in Rome. The player has refused to sign again for Lazio and therefore the deal looks inevitable.' Di Matteo's personal terms were more modest than Vialli's: £800,000 a year over the next four years. He ran a gauntlet of hate in Rome as Lazio fans heard of the Chelsea talks. They went berserk at the news of Di Matteo's imminent departure and hundreds rioted outside the club offices. Fans yelled 'traitor' and 'don't come back', stoning the taxi as he left the club after completing the deal with Hutchinson. Di Matteo, close to tears, said: 'Ruud Gullit called me and said he wanted me at all costs for the new Chelsea team he is trying to put together. I am leaving Lazio for personal reasons. I decided in October that I was going to leave. I did not have a good relationship with Zdenek Zeman, the Lazio coach. Our ideas were different. We had different philosophies on life and on football. I am happy to go to Chelsea. It is nothing to do with money. The fans were pretty angry when I left. I had to put up with quite a bit of abuse, some even spat at me. But once things had calmed down, I spoke to them and now there's no problem. They understood my decision as did my team-mates. I knew what I was letting myself in for by joining Chelsea. It wasn't like I was walking into the unknown. I had heard about Hoddle, Wise and Gullit. Then there was Vialli's move as well.'

Di Matteo's relationship with Lazio fans had turned sour the previous season, reaching a peak when supporters set fire to the intercom outside his home. They had already seen Alen Boksic leave for Juventus and Aaron Winter for Inter in two months – and Di Matteo's departure was the last straw.

Despite his success, his relationship with Zeman had become strained. 'Pinocchio', as he was nicknamed at Lazio, was left out of a league game by Zeman. The coach, renowned for his fetish for fitness, was not convinced that Di Matteo was fully recovered after turning out for Italy in two games in one week. At the time Di Matteo said, somewhat perplexed: 'I thought that playing for a national team would be an advantage, not the opposite.' Parma made an offer but Lazio and Zeman insisted he wasn't for sale. However, the damage had been done and by the time Di Matteo arrived in England for Euro '96, Lazio's Zoff openly declared that the player was for sale, at a price. Zoff said: 'The deal is done. Roberto wanted to leave for personal reasons. It is a great loss to us – he is a very good player.'

Di Matteo is a tough character who grew up in Switzerland, suffering racist taunts from school pals over his Italian parents. Lazio signed him from Swiss club Aarau in 1993 for only £550,000. He was invited to join the Swiss squad by boss Roy Hodgson, but declined saying Italy was his first choice. Less than a year after joining Lazio he was called up by Sacchi and, by the start of Euro '96, was a vital part of the side. The only game he missed in Euro '96 was the disastrous defeat by the Czech Republic when Sacchi made shock sweeping changes. A 2–1 defeat condemned a shaken Italy to an early exit, and sealed Sacchi's fate as coach.

Gullit had taken his spending to £7.4m with Di Matteo. Bates was splashing out in unprecedented style knowing the club would receive £9m in Sky TV money, once the new TV deal kicked in next season. The board room war was also over; Bates and Harding made their peace. Harding agreed to plough £5m into the club's holding company, Chelsea Village. Harding became club vice-chairman. This news sent shares in Chelsea Village soaring by 23p to 91p.

Back to the unveiling of Leboeuf. The latest recruit paid tribute to Gullit, a major reason for choosing Chelsea ahead of his local side Marseille. Leboeuf said: 'Ruud was a factor, as were Dan Petrescu, Mark Hughes and Gianluca Vialli. At Strasbourg I was the only international, but that is not the case at Chelsea. It will be a great sensation to play for them. I want to win everything at Chelsea and play at Wembley next year, because I've never won anything in France.'

FRIDAY, JULY 5
Yet another unveiling of a new superstar at the Bridge. Enter Roberto Di Matteo. With Gullit in touch by phone from Holland, where he was relaxing on holiday, Rix introduced the new player to the Bridge. It was yet another stunning signing for English football, coming hours after Vialli's Juve strike partner Fabrizio Ravanelli moved to Middlesbrough for £7m.

Di Matteo said: 'The Italian league is the most important in the world at the moment but within the next two years the Premiership will overtake it. Quite a few foreign players are moving here because they know the Premier League. We watch English football on Italian TV every Saturday. I know from that it is a strong league, both physically and competitively. I didn't talk to Gianluca Vialli, only to Ruud, and I was impressed at the way he handled the move. Chelsea will have a strong squad and that is one of the reasons I came here. We will try our hardest to compete with the likes of Manchester United and Liverpool. I don't think coming here will be a problem for my international career. It is important that I play well and, as long as I do this, I will still be in the national side. I think with Vialli here the team is very strong. I have had many battles with him in the past – and he's won!'

Di Matteo wears the number sixteen shirt that he has always had. 'I know the fans were upset at me leaving. I am sorry for them but I had to make a decision.' Hutchinson said: 'Lazio took a lot of persuading. There were still two years on his contract and they were under no pressure to sell. Ruud identified various players he wanted to sign when he took over. We have now brought in three and they were the ones he particularly wanted. This has been a unique week – not one but two Italian internationals have moved here.'

Harding said: 'Chelsea can become the biggest and most successful club side in Britain and Europe. My dream is that Chelsea will challenge the best in Europe within the next eight years. I have invested first as a fan and then because of my love for football.'

Players' union chief executive Gordon Taylor voiced his fears that soccer's new-found wealth, from Sky TV cash, was rapidly disappearing into the pockets of a handful of mercenary Euro stars. The PFA boss said: 'I've been banging my head against a brick wall for the past few years trying to convince clubs that our players are as good as anyone in the world. I thought the success of England at Euro '96 would have proved that. But all of a sudden we are seeing an awful lot of money going out of our game and now clubs need to be reminded of their responsibilities. Terry Venables's team raised the flag for Britain and proved we have nothing to fear from anyone. Teams such as Manchester United and Liverpool have already enjoyed success by developing home-grown talent. But it seems clubs are still looking abroad for a quick fix and it's money which is being lost to our game. All fans want a successful team. But while they like to see big-name foreign players coming here on massive salaries, they are also far-sighted enough to realise that the best long term approach is to encourage home-grown talent.'

Rix retorted: 'There is no way players like Ruud Gullit, Gianluca Vialli and Roberto Di Matteo are going to block the development of any young players at Chelsea. Those lads will watch and learn from the very best. And in five to six years we will all reap the benefit.'

MONDAY, JULY 8

The backroom system was already working smoothly. Gullit had left the poolside at his holiday hotel in Mauritius and returned to the reception area. He'd collected a fax which conveyed a simple and concise message: 'It is good news' – signed 'Colin'. The 'good news' was that Chelsea had signed Vialli. This was a perfect example of how Gullit made the initial move, then left it all to Hutchinson. The continental structure represented the new face of Chelsea and the ever-changing world of football. Gullit was unaware of what Vialli negotiated in personal terms. He didn't care. All negotiations, wages, fees and length of contract were left to Hutchinson. 'That is the way Ruud wants things done and it is the way that things have been done on the Continent for some years,' said Hutchinson. 'I enjoy the role and I enjoy the challenge.'

Gullit told Hutchinson who he wanted and it was up to the managing director to do the rest. 'Of course we talk about the value of players and what is the limit we should go to,' said Hutchinson. 'But essentially all the financial matters concerning transfers are down to me. Ruud's job is to look after the players when they get here.'

It was a hectic summer for Hutchinson; he even took a four-day absence from a holiday in Cyprus, much to the chagrin of his wife Linda, to clinch the Vialli deal.

Leboeuf next. 'I had spoken to Ruud about him and he reckoned no more than £2.5m,' said Hutchinson. 'I offered £2.25m knowing that Marseille had offered £2.2m. Strasbourg said they wanted £3m but asked me over for talks. I know from experience that if someone asks you to come for talks, there is the chance of a deal.

I took Graham Rix with me because of his knowledge of the French language and of French football. I went to £2.5m and made it clear I would go no higher. They kept coming back, slightly lower each time. I kept saying no. Eventually we got our man at the price we wanted.'

For Di Matteo the Gullit–Hutchinson valuation was £4.5m. The eventual fee was £4.9m. Had Chelsea paid too much? 'No,' Hutchinson insisted. 'After matches that we have arranged to play, we will re-coup that £400,000, I'm pretty sure about that.' Hutchinson added: 'It is certainly a buoyant time with the players we have here. I mean, I don't think even the most committed fan would have visualised a few years ago that the time would come when Hughes, Vialli, Gullit, Petrescu, Di Matteo and Leboeuf would be at the club. I think we have an international in every position, near enough.'

The feel-good factor also emanated from the outbreak of peace at board room level. The Bates–Harding feud ended. 'It was awkward last season for me, I was the man in the middle of it all,' said Hutchinson. 'But it has all been settled and there is stability at Chelsea. All football clubs need stability to prosper.' Yet a surprisingly pessimistic pre-season prediction came from Alan Hudson in the *Sporting Life*: 'Ruud Gullit, the star of the Euro '96 commentary team, has a very big job on his hands. So much will depend on his repeating the fantastic form of the season just gone. I cannot see him doing so! The player-manager job is an almost impossible one, especially when you are the most influential player in the team. He will find he will have the ball more than ever before. That will cause him a problem, for he will not be able to assess those around him. Playing in that midfield role is tough enough, but manager as well? No! I wouldn't mind taking odds that the Dutch master will not be at Stamford Bridge next May.'

The *Sun* pronounced Wise would be on the way out of Chelsea because Gullit was fed up with his Crazy Gang antics and being called Big Nose! Wise, according to these reports, was about to be stripped of the captaincy which would go to Vialli. David Lee stalled on signing a new contract blaming the influx of foreign stars. 'Seeing all these foreigners coming into the game really affects you as a player. Some clubs have as many as eight foreign players. That makes it almost impossible for lads coming through. People like Muzzy Izzett left Chelsea because they wanted to get a chance. If a player thinks he's not going to get a chance to break through, then he goes. It's happening all the time. I haven't signed a deal with Chelsea because I want better terms. I've shown a lot of loyalty and I want them to show me some.'

THURSDAY, JULY 11

Part of the task of being a footballing superstar is the ever-attendant hordes of journalists, supporters and hangers-on. Gullit had experienced it and coped with it numerous times before. So, his first major press conference in the build-up to the new season, at the club's training ground, held few fears and certainly no inhibitions. It turned into no more than a gentle and amicable alfresco discussion at the Harlington training HQ, not far from Heathrow Airport. There is little to distract here, except the three pitches and club house cordoned off by a wire fence. Stewards are out for press days, and the modernised club house holds an upstairs canteen where the players have lunch after training. Downstairs is a multitude of individual training rooms and a well equipped gym and treatment room.

As the jets thundered out of nearby Heathrow, and the inquisitive punters pushed for pole position along with the reporters, Gullit produced as polished a performance as those he gave when a television panellist during Euro '96. Then, his witty sparring with Des had provided many of the more cerebral duels of the championship. 'It was great fun,' Gullit said. 'You know all the answers, that was not the difficult part. To be clever as well, that is where the difficulty is. I learnt a lot, though, it was enjoyable.' His ease and vast experience under the mike held him in good stead for the rigours ahead in the FA Carling Premiership. He was happy with his triple plunge into the European transfer market and did not envisage any more spending for the time being.

'I have got all the players I want for the moment,' he said. 'I have got the spine of my team and if you have that, you can build around it.' He was particularly optimistic that Vialli would settle in quickly. 'It will be better when he has learnt English. He has to get a house, then he can become a citizen. He can go shopping, buy things and start to pick up the language.'

Vialli, though barely able to convey his true feelings as he grappled with the new language, made a valiant stab at it. He said: 'It is all so different, I feel like a young boy at my first training session, but I am not here to play the star. I am not, how you say, a prima donna. If there is anything I need, I will ask. I don't expect to just be given it.' He, like Gullit, also showed a nice line in humour. When asked by a cameraman to remove his sunglasses, he said: 'Why? Do you like my eyes?'

With his shaven head and piercing stare, he hardly looked likely to be intimidated by Premiership defenders. Vialli is used to the tough world of Italy's Serie A, but he had yet to face the English league's hundred-mile-an-hour physical approach. Vialli said: 'Yes, Ruud has warned me about the tough guys, but I'm ready for anything that is thrown at me in English football. I'm not frightened, I'm here to play my football and that's all I want to do.'

Gullit said: 'Here in England they come in with their studs showing – I will have a word with him about that. In Italy you cannot do that. So here Gianluca is going to have to learn how to protect himself. I do not want Gianluca to get hurt, so he's going to have to learn about it and be able to cope with it.'

Vialli relished the challenge. 'I know Chelsea fans are expecting a big contribution from me. There is a lot of pressure on me, more than there was at Juventus. But I will try to give them success to the best of my ability. Ruud is already here and he's got such experience and is such a big personality that he has already provided an example. I have not come here to be the big star. I'm not going to act like the big man. In Italy I was used to being waited on, to have things brought to me when I needed them. Here I have to be careful to ask for something with manners. I don't want to act like the main man.'

Gullit will not be a 'shouting and raving' boss. 'I'll do it my way. I'll take players aside and privately explain to them what I want.'

MONDAY, JULY 15
Lee agreed a new deal. He looked ready to move, but Gullit persuaded him to accept a three-year contract worth £500,000.

TUESDAY, JULY 16
Gullit sold Paul Furlong. Trevor Francis paid a Birmingham club record, £1.5m. Francis switched to Chelsea's spare striker after failing to meet the 'astronomical' wage demands of Bayern Munich's talented French goalscorer Jean-Pierre Papin who

demanded £25,000 a week. Furlong, a £2.3m Chelsea recruit from Watford in May 1994, moved from the substitutes' bench into Birmingham's promotion campaign. 'Once Ruud Gullit signed Vialli I knew that he and Mark Hughes would be first choices and I would be a squad player,' said Furlong. 'It's also nice to know that I have come here instead of Papin. I won't let anybody down. I always go out confident that I will score goals.'

FRIDAY, JULY 19

Vialli pulled out of his Chelsea debut at Exeter. A sell-out 4,000 crowd turned up to see him in action, but the eager fans had to settle for a brief wave and a few autographs as he sat with fellow new boys Di Matteo and Leboeuf. Dressed in jeans, T-shirts and baseball caps the stars acknowledged their new army of admirers. Under the circumstances, the reception was generous and warm. The absence of Vialli, who celebrated his thirty-second birthday ten days earlier, was explained by a 'slight calf strain' in training. Spencer, Wise, Burley and Kharine were excused duty as they appeared in Euro '96, while Gullit preferred to accustom himself to the surroundings of the dug-out. There was not a murmur of discontent from the paying Chelsea public, who produced welcome receipts of £20,000 for their non-league hosts. A 7–0 scoreline certainly helped, but the real reason for the calm was summed up by Harding, who conceded: 'We're all mad – that's why we keep coming.' There was, though, a new wave of optimism to fuel the supporters' dreams. 'The spending is never over. If a player whom the club wants becomes available then we will be interested,' insisted Harding. 'It's an exciting time – we've made some serious signings and now have the spine of the team in place. It won't be long before we win the Premiership. Hopefully, Ruud can become our greatest manager, somebody has to. He will have our support and I will continue to do everything to help the club fulfil its potential.'

After Harding's half-time thoughts, Vialli, Di Matteo and Leboeuf took their seats in the press box and were all smiles. As were the press until Chelsea officials said that the players were there to watch the game and not to give interviews!

SUNDAY, JULY 28

A sell-out crowd of nearly 14,000 turned up hoping to see the delayed English debut of Vialli at Swindon. But they were disappointed again as Vialli was forced out of the game with a calf injury. However, Di Matteo made his debut – and immediately showed his class. The midfielder played the ninety minutes and treated the crowd to an exhibition of passing. Di Matteo and Leboeuf – also making his debut – were head and shoulders above the rest. Gullit said: 'They've been in training just a week, but settled in well.'

Leboeuf lasted just seventy-seven minutes in the 2–0 defeat of Swindon. He explained: 'It was difficult for me to finish because I was tired. There are a lot of games before the championship starts and the pace of English football is fast compared to France. I watched a lot of Premiership matches on French TV and knew what to expect. David Ginola said it would be difficult. And he was right.'

Hughes volleyed Chelsea into the lead on seventeen minutes, but limped off with a knee injury soon after. Dan Petrescu netted on eighty-five minutes.

WEDNESDAY, JULY 31
A Wise sixty-fifth-minute penalty won this testimonial match for Wolves full-back Andy Thompson before 23,942 fans. Wise scored after Hughes, who had earlier hit the post with an overhead kick, had been brought down. Chelsea were once more without Vialli along with Gullit.

AUGUST

Second in Premiership – Goals from Di Matteo, Vialli & Leboeuf

THURSDAY, AUGUST 1

Gullit kicked out Hoddle's 'Odd Squad' in his transformation plans with a back-to-basics philosophy, after rejecting the new age training methods of England's new coach. Gullit axed the reflexologist, nutritionist and faith-healer used during Hoddle's three-year reign. Instead, Mafe began his task of running the legs off his team of underachievers. Gullit said: 'Every coach has his own ideas and the moment I took charge here I wanted to do it my way. I wanted to be comfortable with the people around me and I've made my choices. I'm not saying that my way is right and Glenn's was wrong. It's just what I believe in. If you look at the statistics last season, there were seventeen games when we went 1–0 up but didn't win. We could score goals but we weren't well prepared and struggled towards the end of games.' A punishing pre-season regime of non-stop running, based on his experiences of Serie A with AC Milan and Sampdoria, improved stamina and ensured his players would not fade in the latter stages of matches.

Rix added: 'There has been a change – we're leaner, fitter and hungrier. Glenn has laid the foundations and we all want to carry on winning in style. But both Ruud and myself believe it's more important just to win. There are a lot of reasons why we were letting 1–0 leads slip last season and we are working very hard on the training ground to put that right.'

Leboeuf, commenting on Gullit's rigorous training programme, admitted: 'It is difficult. In France, we prepare for the season much more technically and tactically. But here we jog around all the time.'

Gullit even banned his Chelsea players from carrying mobile phones on match days! Bob Hoskins might think it's good to talk, Gullit reckons it's even better to listen! All it amounted to was another move to bring a new era of professionalism to the club.

Gullit ordered the entire team to travel to and from games together and banned the team bus from picking players up en route. He brought in the strict new regime in a bid to cut out all the distractions and get his team fully concentrating on the match ahead. Clarke admitted: 'The mobile phones have gone. We're not allowed to bring them with us on match days or on to the team bus. It's common sense really because the calls were getting out of hand and becoming a bit of a problem. Phones would be ringing in the middle of team meetings and all sorts. Ruud obviously felt we were spending too much time arranging tickets and not enough time preparing for the game. As you'd expect with any new manager, there have been a few changes since Ruud took over. Pre-season training was certainly more intense than before. Ruud was used to a very strict regime in Italy and I think he felt we didn't do enough. We worked hard under Glenn Hoddle but there was definitely a more relaxed approach on the training ground.'

Clarke refuted suggestions that Gullit's hard line approach had upset some of the players. 'Ruud wants us all to be as professional as we can, but he's still the most laid-back boss I've ever played for. Of course he's had to change his approach since becoming manager. He's had to distance himself a bit. But he's a very intelligent guy. He's not going to take things too far and suddenly start blanking us all. He still joins in all the jokes and sits down at the back of the bus playing cards with the lads.' Clarke, the longest serving player, conceded: 'The changes I've seen here since 1987 are unbelievable. I really wish I was just starting my career again instead of nearing the end of it. Playing with Gullit, Hoddle, Mark Hughes and now Gianluca Vialli is something I would never have dreamed of when I joined the club from St Mirren.'

SATURDAY, AUGUST 3

Just when he thought it was safe to step up to the penalty spot, Stuart Pearce's Turin nightmare returned to haunt him. Successful in Euro '96 shoot-outs against Spain and Germany, the Forest captain saw his latest penalty saved by Kharine at the end of the goalless Umbro Cup opener at the City Ground. It was Kharine's save from Scot Gemmill, however, which clinched Chelsea a place in the final against Ajax on a 4–3 count, Mark Crossley having saved Mark Nicholls's kick.

SUNDAY, AUGUST 4

Vialli held aloft a trophy in celebration of his long-awaited baptism in English football. In their yellow change strip, Chelsea beat Ajax 2–0 in the final of the Umbro International Tournament; their supporters were cheered as much by the sight of their shaven-headed totem as they were by the unfamiliar glimpse of some silverware.

Vialli recovered from the calf strain with a second-half introduction at the City Ground. His appearance wasn't a welcome sight for Ajax, who last saw him when he raised the European Cup in the Stadio Olimpico. They need not have fretted. Vialli made little impression. An attempted lob and two tame finishes, comfortably saved by Edwin van der Sar, was the sum total of his expensive creative contribution. Not that the Chelsea faithful in the 21,760 crowd were bothered. Their side already had the game won by the break, thanks to the first-half influence of the other Italian in Gullit's cosmopolitan Chelsea set. Di Matteo proved his worth by delivering two perceptive through balls which allowed Wise, in the fifth minute, and Petrescu, in the sixteenth, to shoot past the exposed van der Sar. Chelsea also had to thank Kharine for stopping Ajax with two first-half saves from Nordin Wooter and Kiki Musampa.

The silencing of the Dutch band, which had started the afternoon by striking up a chorus of 'Happy Days Are Here Again', was a confirmation of Chelsea's success. But Gullit maintained: 'This is just the beginning. The only thing that matters is our game against Southampton. Pre-season doesn't count.'

MONDAY, AUGUST 6

Spencer wanted assurances about his future. Gullit told him to challenge Vialli and Hughes. But Spencer wanted to play in the deeper role that Hoddle had persuaded him to consider, which had suited him well. 'The manager says he wants to change the team and the system. But in the Premier League we'll have to get a settled side. I don't like playing up front but that's what I'll have to do to get in the team. I suppose if I score goals, he won't leave me out.'

TUESDAY, AUGUST 7

Ruud was one of the celebrities at the première of the hit film *Independence Day*, with his new girlfriend on his arm, in public gaze for the first time, gorgeous eighteen-year-old Estelle Cruyff. Mick Hucknell was spotted chatting with Ruud. The audience also included Jarvis Cocker, Cher, Zoe Ball, Jonathan Ross, Chris Eubank, Mel Smith, David Baddiel, Martin Clunes and Neil Morrissey, and the film's stars Jeff Goldblum, Bill Pullman and Margaret Colin. Sexy singer Cher drew the biggest cheer from the 3,000 crowd. She joked: 'I love aliens – I've dated a few!'

WEDNESDAY, AUGUST 8

Gullit continued his restructuring, selling defender Anthony Barness back to Charlton for £165,000. The twenty-three-year-old joined Chelsea from Charlton for £350,000 in 1992 but only started sixteen first-team games.

THURSDAY, AUGUST 9

What a blow. A crying shame for the purists wanting more of the Gullit magic of his first season as a player. Ruud missed the start of the new season after his sixth knee operation in recent years. Gullit flew to Antwerp for surgery from the man who saved his career, Dr Marc Martens, while the team journeyed to Genoa for the match with Sampdoria. Chelsea's new player-manager would be out for a minimum of four weeks, but the operation to remove a floating bone was described as 'minor'. Gullit came to English football with fears over his fitness after so many knee operations, but the one time world's number one player confounded his critics with a superlative first season.

Gullit had ominously failed to appear in any pre-season game and felt a reaction just days before the season was about to start. He consulted a surgeon and dashed to Antwerp. Dr Martens felt it was best to remove the troublesome scar tissue immediately. Rix said: 'Ruud looks after himself and is very fit, so we do not anticipate any long-term problems. He was in pain after a training session and decided he wanted the problem sorted out as soon as possible. I have spoken to Ruud and he says the operation has been a complete success.'

The *Rothmans Yearbook* was launched at a champagne breakfast press conference in London with the announcement of the Premiership's best team. When the Football Writers' Association were asked to nominate their finest players of the previous season they came up with seven from Old Trafford. They were, in no particular order, Footballer of the Year Eric Cantona, Peter Schmeichel, Denis Irwin, Ryan Giggs, Roy Keane, Gary Neville and former captain Steve Bruce, now of Birmingham City. The remainder of the side was made up of Gullit, Fowler, Southgate and Shearer. Only Gullit managed to infiltrate the team from the capital's contingent, little consolation as he began his recovery from surgery. But, later that day at his old club Sampdoria, there was more reason for optimism from his emerging team.

Vialli crowned his full debut with a stunning goal as he made a triumphant return to Italy, a five-star display in Chelsea's 2–1 win at the club where he made his name.

Vialli struck in the eighteenth minute with a first-time shot into the top corner from Petrescu's cross. Although the Genoese side hit back when Vincenzo Montella scored from a forty-seventh-minute penalty after Leboeuf tripped Roberto Mancini, Hughes headed the winner ten minutes later from another Petrescu cross. Vialli was substituted in the seventieth minute but had already done enough to send a warning to Premiership defences. He was given a standing ovation by 30,000 adoring Italian fans and threw his shirt into the crowd.

The only disappointment was that Gullit was not there to see it. Even without Gullit, though, Chelsea continued their impressive pre-season form. Vialli said: 'It was a tough match, before a fantastic crowd. I was given a special welcome. It was a good test against a strong Sampdoria side. But we can do much better.'

Vialli celebrated by taking his new team-mates out for a meal in Genoa, but Rix insisted that Vialli had gone out of his way to play down his superstar image. Rix, in charge of the team in Gullit's absence, said: 'Gianluca's attitude has been first-class. He plays for the team and has been very keen to be known as just one of the lads. It was an emotional night for him and it was a great moment when he scored his goal. We took him off after seventy minutes because this was his first start for us but he did enough in that time to show what he can do. He has everything a striker needs to be successful. He has skill, makes intelligent runs, is always aware of other players and has the ability to score amazing goals like that.'

Rix's sentiments were echoed by Sampdoria coach Sven Goran Eriksson, who said: 'Chelsea have signed an excellent player. I wish he was still here with us. If he stays fit, he'll have an excellent season in the Premiership and I expect Chelsea to do very well. He is world-class. It's a compliment to the Italian game that English clubs are paying so much for the players here. But I still believe the Italian league is the strongest in the world. That may alter in the future as English clubs change their style. Glenn Hoddle and Gullit have changed the way of thinking in England. Chelsea do not play a British style; they like to keep the ball, play it on the ground and build their moves slowly in a European fashion.'

Vialli's new strike partner scored Chelsea's winner with a typically powerful header and Rix added: 'Hughes has got better and better in every pre-season game and thoroughly deserved his goal. He has responded very well to Gianluca's arrival and they look like a good partnership.'

SUNDAY, AUGUST 11

It was ironic that Gavin Peacock should be widely quoted in the *Independent on Sunday* regarding his enthusiasm for Gullit's new collection of foreign stars when just a day later he would be asking for a transfer! Peacock had been interviewed during the week extolling the virtues of the elaborately gifted players. 'Technically, they do wonderful things. They are a joy to see and you can only learn from that. We know we can be better players because they're here. Perhaps we can teach each other.'

Peacock was confident that on the pitch the whole multilingual, assorted bunch will speak the same language. 'Ruud has taught us not just about playing the game on the pitch but how to look after yourself off it. Things like diet and general fitness all come into it. He's always worked hard, he's keen to convey those ideas to us.

With his record in the game it's impossible to have anything other than the greatest respect for him. I'm feeling pretty good. I'm moving well and I've got five goals in the pre-season matches so far,' he said. 'I want to be part of this team, which is just developing. The players have all settled in well. It's helped a great deal that we've got to know each other as a squad in the build-up. We've been away and spent a lot of time together. The language on the pitch, as I've said, is the important thing. But all the new lads speak English well. They're getting to grips. There's a comfortable feel to us.'

Peacock was also aware their introduction multiplied the pressure on the side to win something, anything almost. 'Well, we've got to start out thinking of the league obviously. But we've done well in one cup or other for the last two seasons. We've got players here who can challenge and challenge well. There's a good culture here. We've all settled well with each other.'

MONDAY, AUGUST 12

Peacock handed in a transfer request. He wanted to move because he saw no future at the club following the influx of foreign stars. Signed by Hoddle from Newcastle for £1.5m, he feared he would be surplus to requirements. He said: 'At this stage of my career, and as a former skipper of the club, it is not in my interests to be just a squad player. I've had a talk with the manager, who has told me what the position is, so I think it's best I move on. At twenty-seven, my best years are still ahead of me and I know I can do a good job elsewhere. I have notched five goals in limited pre-season appearances and my goal-scoring record from midfield stands comparison with most.'

TUESDAY, AUGUST 13

As the pre-season drew to a close, Rix gave an insight into his new working relationship with 'the boss'. Hoddle gave Rix his first coaching opportunity when he made him youth team manager at Chelsea. Gullit further recognised Rix's promise by appointing him number two following Hoddle's departure. 'I really am excited about the season ahead,' said Rix. 'Who wouldn't be with players of the calibre of Leboeuf, Roberto Di Matteo and Gianluca Vialli in their team?' Chelsea fans were enraptured by Gullit's appointment, but they wondered just how he would cope with the finer points of management in the Premiership. 'Delegation,' answered Rix with emphasis. 'Ruud's not frightened of delegating. He doesn't like sitting on the bench too much and that's not where we want him. Ruud plays and he deals with the media. He will deal with the players also but once that match gets underway, he has to concentrate on playing. I will be on the bench and it will be me doing the half-time talk, Ruud won't have the breath. Ruud puts his trust in me and others like Gwyn Williams, who handles the administrative side. We take as much pressure off Ruud as we can but, at the end of the day, he is the manager. If there are any major decisions to be made, he makes them.'

Gullit is his own man. No reflection on the England coach, as Rix emphasised. 'Glenn improved this club out of all recognition while he was here,' he said. 'People say Vialli, Di Matteo, Leboeuf, they're all here because of Ruud. They shouldn't forget that Ruud is here because of Glenn. If it wasn't for him, none of this would be happening now.' On Guillit's new fitness regime, Rix commented: 'Ruud looks after himself, conducts himself in a professional way and quite rightly wants his players to do the same. The three new signings are an example on and off the pitch.

They're true pros and we don't have to worry about them at all. The other lads have responded well as well. David Lee is an example; he could have gone the other way after seeing the club sign a central defender but he's had the best pre-season he's ever had, a great credit to him.'

The bottom line however, was success. 'We have to make progress,' said Rix. 'We finished eleventh last season and we have to do better than that. I want to see us play the same football as last season but better, with more panache. I also want us to be bloody hard to beat. We took the lead in seventeen matches last season and finished up not winning. We can't let that happen again. We reached a certain level with Glenn. Now we must go higher with Ruud.'

WEDNESDAY, AUGUST 14

The Forte Crest Hotel, near Heathrow, was the venue for Ruud's pre-season lunch to acquaint himself with the country's top football writers, a glass of champagne or bucks fizz to greet each journalist and a Chelsea representative at each of the four tables, alternating so that everyone had an audience with the man himself.

Ruud embarked on a journey to prove that English football doesn't have to be a graveyard for foreign coaches. As Arsenal sought salvation with French coach Arsène Wenger, there was tranquillity and great expectancy across London. Gullit talked of a mixture of fun and hard work as the ingredients for a successful and stress-free season, his first on the management treadmill, but it didn't show any signs of turning those famous dreadlocks grey. No foreign coach has succeeded in the English game but Gullit was smiling as he discussed his plans to bring the continental system of management to English football.

Rinus Michels, Johan Cruyff, Vim van Hanegem, Arrigo Sacchi, Fabio Capello, Sven Goran Eriksson and Hoddle – all of these have coached him. 'I know,' Gullit said. 'I had everything to learn from, but if I don't have the players, I cannot play to a system exactly like any one of them. I will tell you something about systems: at Milan, we had Marco van Basten in a 4–3–3 formation; we lost van Basten, we converted to 4–4–2 and it clicked. Milan became the best team in the world, everyone believed in 4–4–2 and we played it and played it so often that we could do it in our dreams.'

Much was expected from Vialli in terms of goals. Surely he will need to net a Shearer quota of thirty Premiership goals if Chelsea are to win a major trophy, I suggested at a quiet moment during the media gathering. 'No,' smiled Gullit. Not a warm smile, this time. A knowing one. 'I have told Luca that he does not have the burden of goalscoring alone. Fifteen goals would satisfy me because I expect goals to come from a variety of positions.'

Di Matteo, for instance, argued Gullit, is quite capable of scoring many from midfield. Already, Di Matteo had made an impact with his astute passing that brought Chelsea the Umbro Cup. 'It is no surprise,' according to Gullit. 'I give him freedom and the teams against him gave him freedom – and Roberto can pass. But he has his assignment, we all have assignments. You all must do the job assigned and then you can express yourself.'

Rix and Williams mingled purposefully, spreading the Gullit Gospel along with Ruud. Gullit said: 'The players are responding but it takes time. I need a team of twenty players, it's no longer a game of eleven. I want covering players in almost every position, simply because the game has improved and is played so much more powerfully, stronger and faster. Your body is not made for football, no one can play every game in a season, so in every position I'd like two players of the same standard and that's difficult to achieve. But Vialli didn't play every game last season and certainly won't play every game this one.'

Gullit had a clear transfer policy, not dependent on possible acquisitions' salary levels. He detailed how he captured his three summer signings: 'I don't care how much a player earns or what he doesn't earn. All I am interested in is ... is he with me on the training pitch?'

Vialli: 'My best friend, who is a manager and also runs an agency, advised me about Luca being available for free, and it was very good advice. He's a very useful friend!'

Leboeuf: 'During Euro '96 I was praying that Frank wasn't picked. "Don't play him, don't play him, please don't play him." I didn't want anyone to know.'

Di Matteo: 'I made one call each to these players, but I'm not saying they came because it was me, they came because they wanted to play in England. You don't appreciate just how good the standard is over here. I know that we paid £4.9 million for Di Matteo but it cost me less money than I'd have to pay for the same kind of player in England. It would have been double.

Gullit added, 'I accept there are new expectations at Chelsea. Good players don't always become good coaches, there has to be a change of mentality but I think I'm aware tactically and think I have an understanding of the behaviour of players. I now have to hurt the opposition as a coach like I used to as a player. Players also have to decide on the pitch for themselves, it is difficult to feel it out there for them when you are on the bench. I want to give players assignments. The most difficult thing is to keep it simple.

'The changes? Small changes. That's all. Players are allowed a glass of wine or beer after a match or even before it, if they want it, but that's all – they know their limitations.'

THURSDAY, AUGUST 15

Vialli was still the player everyone wanted to see. He was settling in quickly. 'I love London. It is the best city in Europe, if not the world. It's a place where I can relax enough to behave as I want to. London will give me the space I never had in Turin because it's big enough to lose myself in. So I am enjoying myself here very much ... but not the nightlife!' Vialli made it a condition of his move to English football that he wanted to play and live in the capital. 'I'd only visited London on a couple of occasions and was already in love with the place. I spoke to Ruud on the phone and he asked me "What do you want out of life, sporting and non-sporting?" He asked me if I wanted to have some fun again. And, having discussed it, he said, "Chelsea is the place for you. London has everything you want." '

Gullit's presence helped him to make up his mind. 'Ruud is certainly important. He is a friend of mine. We played so many times as opponents and a few years ago went on holiday together in Sardinia. Above all, he has played in Italy and in England and will give me all the help I need to overcome the difficulties of settling into the Premiership.'

Vialli analysed the exodus of Italian players to the Premiership. 'Football continues without me in Italy. Important players are coming to England but others are going to Italy to replace us. There are no problems. I don't think Juventus really wanted me to stay. I could have signed a year's contract but there were signs that the directors didn't really want to deal with me any more. But I left Juve with a smile, there were no bad feelings.'

Vialli was surprised his room-mate Ravanelli was also allowed to leave after the pair had won the European Cup. He was convinced Ravanelli would succeed him as Juve captain. He was even more shocked that he signed for Middlesbrough. Vialli said, 'Middlesbrough are not a well known team in Italy. We only remember it as the ground where Italy lost to [North] Korea in the 1966 World Cup. But Bryan Robson came to Italy to speak to me three or four months ago. Did he try to sign me? I don't know.'

Vialli was honest enough to admit that money talked when it came to moving to Chelsea. 'Of course it did. I will be well paid, yes, and I have no problem with the money side. There is no price tag on my head in terms of a transfer fee and that has got to help. But the money is not as important as it is for me to feel at ease with my new club and I know I will enjoy playing for Chelsea.'

Gianluca was well received by his new team-mates despite his massive pay. 'They have all made me very welcome. But it is important that I quickly learn to speak English. I want to talk to my new friends and be a part of the fun in the locker room. I studied English at school, but not too seriously. I know enough to get by ... enough to read a contract! But I am getting better all the time, even though I have Ruud, Roberto Di Matteo and Dan Petrescu with me who can all speak Italian.'

He relished the new challenge. 'The Chelsea supporters are expecting a big contribution from me and I know how important it is that I give them my best. I am here to play football and I am not afraid of tackles. I can take stick from your defenders and have already learned how to swear at them in English! But football in England is becoming more and more European all the time in the way they play and the signings they are making. And I am sure I will score goals here. I am an attacker and as long as I am in the forward half of the field I have never had a problem playing in any kind of system.'

From European Cup champions to a club that finished eleventh in the Premiership. Can he help bring the much demanded success? 'I am not going to heap extra pressure on the club by promising Chelsea fans the championship. But I do not plan on being out of Europe for more than a season. Winning the European Cup was the best night of my career. I hope for the future I can win something of importance again. I want to come to England and win the Premier League or the FA Cup and score many, many goals. Sometimes I win, sometimes I lose ... this is life. But all the time I must give to the team as much as I can. So my aim is to secure as good a position in the Premier League as we can.' He anticipated a stimulating experience. 'I feel like a young boy starting his first day at a new school. I've not done a lot of travelling around the world and this is the first time I've played out of Italy.'

So why the shaven head? There have been numerous explanations. One of the more exotic was that it was a superstition. 'I cut it off because I wanted a change of luck. Until that luck runs out, my head will remain shaved.'

FRIDAY, AUGUST 16

The massive media attention meant that Chelsea had to make special provisions for journalists at their training headquarters. A table was placed in front of the shooting board and first Ruud, then Vialli, Wise and Rix answered the profusion of questions from the large gathering. Whether Vialli was being serious when he praised Wise for his intelligence, no one was quite sure! However, he did go on to admit that he could not understand a word Dennis said. The mood was convivial. Vialli and Wise even serenaded the media with a line or two of 'Singing in the Rain'. The previous year the media contingent swelled with the arrival of Gullit and Hughes, but now it doubled with the British media joined by TV crews, radio reporters and writers from Italy, Holland, France and Norway on a regular basis. As a consequence, Chelsea faxed the media with advanced notification of specific open days for the press. On this occasion something like fifty turned up.

The training ground is also the venue for Ruud to play host to some deserving causes, usually not on the days the press are on hand. Seven-year-old Tom Mentsmith from Selsey in West Sussex was one such welcome guest. He was on an outing from Great Ormond Street Hospital where he was being treated for a nasty kidney complaint.

SATURDAY, AUGUST 17

First day of the Premiership season, but Chelsea were live on Sky TV the next day. No respite from the training ground. The Dell might be only an hour on the motorway, but Ruud ordered morning training, returning in the afternoon to be closeted away overnight in preparation for the game.

SUNDAY, AUGUST 18

Southampton 0 Chelsea 0

Ruud's first taste of life in the manager's dug-out. It turned into a frustrating, disappointing start for Sky TV's opening live match of the season, kicking off at 4pm. But after all the hype, all the anticipation, the season was finally underway.

Souness and Vialli, team-mates at Sampdoria, met in the corridor near the dressing rooms before kick off and were soon in animated conversation. Did Vialli really smear Deep Heat in Souness's jockstrap when they were team-mates, fill his shoes with shaving cream and cut the legs off his favourite trousers? That's what they say in Italy. Well, Souness thought it was funny when he pushed a fully clothed Vialli into a lake soon after his arrival at Sampdoria. Fate brought them back together in the unlikely setting of the Dell.

Souness emerged to a standing ovation from Southampton fans just before the start and Vialli rushed across to the touchline to give him a kiss on each cheek. Gullit made his first appearance, waving to Chelsea's 1,500 fans in a capacity crowd. He looked relaxed in T-shirt and shorts. Hoddle took his place in the directors' box.

Gullit stretched forward as Le Tissier lifted a shot against the bar. Ruud scratched his dreadlocks with concern as Chelsea wasted their fifth corner. In thirty minutes they had one shot on goal. Gullit grabbed a pen and paper from Rix, and furiously scribbled some notes as Chelsea struggled to find their rhythm. He bowed his head as Leboeuf attempted a 'Beckham' from inside his area. The shot sailed harmlessly wide. At half-time Gullit and Souness left the dug-out on the halfway line, not exchanging words even though they were only a few paces from each other.

Gullit showed signs of frustration leaping from his seat to moan as Petrescu and Clarke failed to break the offside trap. Vialli shot at Beasant and both managers rose from their seats before sitting down again. They both provoked laughter from the crowd as they ducked under a hail of plastic waterbottles thrown back by the players during a break in play.

At the end of a barren game, in terms of goals, Souness and Gullit emerged from the dug-out to shake hands, Souness the more relieved to get a point and Gullit disappointed with his expensively assembled team's opening day show.

Still managing a smile at the after-match press conference, Gullit made few excuses after he twisted and turned at every missed pass and error; animated on the bench discussing the mistakes with Rix, he looked relaxed once it was all over. He moaned: 'Happy? No, I wasn't. We threw it away. Too many of my players were not up to scratch. This was two points dropped. We have not had an easy build-up to the new season, fitting three new players into our system. Vialli has been injured and he is still not ready. Di Matteo has had a back problem and they have found it difficult to find their rhythm. Southampton had no chances at all and we should have built on that and scored at least two goals. We needed to concentrate more when we had the ball but the only positive thing to emerge is that we did create chances. In the last fifteen minutes I was very nervous. We were sloppy. It's a law in football that if you miss a lot of chances you get spanked. I was thinking all the time about that.' He laughed at himself for using the typical colloquial expression 'spanked'. He wished all the journalists a happy Sunday, and left ... still smiling!

Southampton's own debutant manager Souness said: 'Ruud will probably feel a little frustrated at not beating us but it's all part of the managerial learning process. Every manager is searching for perfection but it hardly ever happens.' Souness believed Vialli would become one of the stars of the English game. 'Vialli is going to be an exceptional player in this country. The longer the game went on the more fox-like he became and I have no doubts that he will prove to be a great investment.'

Le Tissier hit the bar in the first minute with a cunning lob which Souness said no other player on the pitch could have executed. But Le Tissier was submerged by the brilliance of Leboeuf. Everyone sweated buckets in the excruciating heat. None more so than Vialli. He even surpassed Le Tissier's first-minute extravagance with a spectacular overhead kick in the seventy-third minute but struck a post and caused mayhem in the Saints' six-yard box. Vialli was also denied a debut goal by Beasant who covered his angles well, not only from the Italian but twice also from his old Wimbledon pal Wise.

In Gullit's foreign legion, Leboeuf stood out. Not even an injury which left him limping and wincing in pain could halt the Frenchman – as effective and crucial in defence for Chelsea as Cantona can be in Manchester United's attack. With relentless accuracy Leboeuf struck right foot passes and then left foot ones sixty-odd yards, arrowing straight to the feet of either wing-back. Nothing in the Premiership can match the cultured central defensive array of talent displayed by Leboeuf.

With eight different nationalities on show, Gullit began the revolution based on his French import, launching attacks from the back and using his intelligence and anticipation to solidify the once suspect defence.

Right from the outset it was plain to see the commitment by Gullit to his managerial role, as one of the most laid-back footballers in the world rose to his feet in frustration after a misplaced pass by Di Matteo. Far too early for any judgements, of course, particularly with the extreme heat, but Gullit demanded a far higher degree of accuracy in his team's passing with only Leboeuf exempt from such criticism.

While Souness insisted his aspirations were far wider than merely avoiding Saints' perennial fight against relegation, realistically that's the best he could hope for. But if Chelsea were to be among the trophy challengers then they would have to do much better than this. Vialli, and indeed Hughes, needed a far greater supply of genuine chances. Di Matteo was a bizarre mixture of the outstanding and the naive.

Ruud reflected on his first experience as 'The Boss': 'It's tougher than playing.' He could not put a date on a comeback. There was a tell-tale sign, a small white dressing on the side of his right knee, to mark the keyhole surgery. 'Next week I shall be visiting the doctor to ask him exactly what I can do. But I hope the team perform so well they don't need me and that will give me more time to come back in a decent way. It is so difficult not playing because you can see what needs changing when things are going wrong. But you cannot do everything and in the end you have to rely on the players on the pitch to work some things out for themselves. You can scream and shout as much as you want but they don't hear you. When you are playing you do not see so many things as you do from the side. In some ways it is good that I have been injured because I have been able to stand at the side and spot where we are going wrong. Being manager is very different and a real challenge.'

Leboeuf, sporting a baseball cap and looking as cool off the field as he did on it, was convinced the manager would get it right. His expansive interview in French was translated by the group of French journalists covering his debut. 'We are still learning to blend and that will take time. Ruud does not want us to play like an English team but we did against Southampton and that is why he was disappointed. Ruud warned those of us who had been playing abroad that it would be quick but it was faster than I expected. That is why Ruud Gullit found his first match so hard. He expected more from us because he knows he has bought some of the world's best players and we did not function. As for Vialli, he has only played in three matches in pre-season because of his leg injury. But he is a star and will cause teams plenty of problems once he has found his feet in English football. We know that every defender is afraid of him as they were in Italy and it is up to the rest of us to help him. We did not do that and that is why he did not play as well as he can. It is true that Vialli wasn't on top form, but I saw challenges on him that were a disgrace. I can see why Eric Cantona sometimes flips his lid playing over here. We had some problems in attack, but it is not a question of making changes. I play football, not karate. The referees should be more strict. It is very dangerous. I am a defender but I never tackle like that.

'People should not judge us too harshly on one display. Ruud is still learning as a manager but he has plenty of ideas and the players must respond by putting them into action. He has assembled too many good players for us not to get it right one day.'

Leboeuf looks back on his debut and reflects: 'This is the best experience for me because it was my first game and the first important game. But all the game is for me beautiful souvenir, can you say that?'

Vialli's first taste of competitive English football brought home to him one big problem: English referees. Martin Bodenham booked Jason Dodd for booting Gianluca into the Hampshire sun, but frequently and happily applied the new instruction to allow offended teams longer to gain an advantage. 'The referee was amusing,' said Vialli tactfully. 'Here they either shoot you down with a machine gun, or the referee doesn't blow his whistle at all! But it makes for a faster game which the crowd enjoy very much. So it must be the way.'

Ruud discovered all the behind-the-scenes problems that go with putting out a team. It was kept secret at the time but Myers was in great distress. 'I slept badly the night before the game and when I woke up my back was in bits. I played through the game but afterwards it felt really sore.' Since then Myers had two scans. 'It keeps flaring up after matches and training and then settles down and flares up again.' One scan showed a slightly bulging 'prolapsed disc'. 'Fortunately there was no fracture, which was good news.'

MONDAY, AUGUST 19

Time for Ruud to sort out his team with some straight talking. There was a time Chelsea would have returned from the south coast happy with a point. No longer. Gullit was decisively unhappy about dropping two. 'We had a team meeting,' said Rix, 'nobody was happy, and I mean nobody.' There were a fair amount of views exchanged between players and management.

It was a surprising, yet stimulating, reaction according to Wise. 'We were all sitting there, totally gutted. It was a good thing. Southampton have a habit of upending clubs like Newcastle and Manchester United – and we'd drawn. The Dell is a tight little ground. Not the best place to play, and not in that heat. To say that we were disappointed with only one point proves how ambitious we intend to be. Now a draw isn't good enough at places like Southampton. That's the best way to feel. Winning becomes a natural thing. Expected.'

Gullit made no secret of his harsh words to the players: 'We will have to play better than we did on Sunday. We have had a team meeting where I told the players what I thought and they told me what they thought. The new signings played well and there were signs that Vialli is adapting to English football.'

The team needed Gullit, despite all its expensive additions. Rix said: 'Of course we could do with Ruud out there but there are compensations. It's a good stage for him, an opportunity to look and make early assessments. It's also been beneficial to me to have him alongside me instead of out there playing, because I need to know what he's thinking, how he's thinking. Fortunately, we think on similar lines and by the time he's fit again I will know exactly what he expects.'

An odd problem cropped up, a complaint from the parents of twelve-year-old James Shipperley, brother of Southampton and former Chelsea forward Neil. The lad's Sky Sports/*Sun* plastic bowler had been used to gather autographs after the game, but Di Matteo had scrawled 'Fuck Off'. Williams said: 'We have resolved the situation internally.' Di Matteo was apologetic and distraught: 'It was a joke, nothing at all. It got twisted by the media and the people involved.'

Inevitably, there were constant rumours that would continue throughout the season that Hughes would go as a result of Vialli's arrival. Bolton were the first to be linked to a move for the Welshman. Ruud informed Bolton boss Colin Todd that he was not prepared to do business. Todd, with the cash from the £4m sale of Sasa Curcic to Aston Villa, refused to give up hope of bringing Hughes back to the north-west. Hughes was a big disappointment in his first Premiership game in partnership with Vialli, which only served to fuel the rumours of his departure.

The Bridge was buzzing with anticipation of the Italian showdown ... Vialli v. Ravanelli. Particularly after Ravanelli's opening day hat trick against Liverpool. 'Lucky' Luca said: 'Of course people will say that's Ravanelli 3, Vialli 0 – that's a fact. But it's a team game – and a long season. It's hard on both me and Roberto because we're coming in after lots of injury problems and without much preparation. Once we get fully fit, then you'll see the best of us. We have shown we are a team that can impose its play on others and we have nobody to fear.' Vialli had whetted the appetite of Chelsea fans with his spectacular overhead kick and he added: 'Maybe in my home debut I'll be luckier.'

Vialli went on: 'I've spoken to him [Ravanelli] a few times and I think he'll do well here – he has the right style to adapt. I'm looking forward to seeing him and congratulating him on his hat-trick – I just hope he doesn't do it against us. I was not happy with my performance on Sunday. But it is not easy to play in the fast and physical Premiership if you are not fully fit.'

Ravanelli was equally looking forward to meeting up with his old pal. 'Vialli and I were together four years at Juventus. Vialli is one of the best strikers in the world. I am sure he will be a success in England. Gianluca and I are good friends off the pitch. I am looking forward to the game, but feeling quite relaxed.' Gullit also insisted that the clash was not just about a personal showdown. 'Of course it is exciting for the fans to have players like these on the same pitch but it is not just about Ravanelli and Vialli.'

Chelsea gave an outstanding performance in beating Middlesbrough 5–0 last season, but Gullit warned: 'They are a different side now, much stronger. They will have learned from that defeat and be much more difficult.'

TUESDAY, AUGUST 20

Ken Bates's annual pre-season media lunch is usually a humdinger for football writers. The bearded one, a stickler for collar, tie and suit, didn't let them down at the newly opened Jimmy's Bar deep in the stand, another carpeted room with a bar, one of several in the new stand complex. The theme was that they were named after legends; this one after Jimmy Greaves. A rip-roaring session of typical Bates banter hit the headlines hard the next day. Gullit and Hoddle were among many subjects. Bates has a voice that can boom for miles but he can be charming when he wants to. Never dull, his comments are usually biting. Everyone lives in dread of inclusion in his infamous programme notes.

Bates wasn't shedding any tears over Hoddle's defection to the FA. He was in typical flamboyant mood as he said: 'Without damning Glenn Hoddle with faint praise, we are even more positive now than before. We know exactly what is expected because Ruud talks to us all the time. He wanted a proper fitness trainer because he felt the players weren't fit enough and brought in Ade Mafe. He didn't want a goalkeeping coach who doubled up as reserve team manager, but instead wanted a goalkeeper coach giving one hundred per cent, so we have invested in a full-time goalkeeping coach and we can already see the sharpness.

'We knew straight away that we wanted Ruud to take over from Glenn. We have made our choice and we don't regret it. We are delighted with Ruud. He didn't need any persuading. From the day Glenn left we knew Ruud Gullit would be our manager. And he had signed the backbone of the team for half the price of Alan Shearer. When you talk to him, it's not like your ordinary footballer, he is an intellectual. You saw his interview after the match at Southampton; he wasn't bland, as most managers are, nor did he make any excuses. He came straight out and said it was not good, the team didn't play well, but should have won. 'The prerequisite of him taking the job was that he had to be protected because he still wanted to concentrate on being a player, and that's why we brought in Gwyn Williams. Ruud has around seven requests a day to open this, that, or the other, or appear on TV. And if he did everything he was asked he would have no life of his own. He's even been asked to turn up on Saturday morning for TV shows. Don't they realise he has a team to run!

It's all ridiculous. We have to shield him from all of that. All we want him to do is run the best team in the country and be part of it as a player. Whenever he's asked about all these aspects of his life and how difficult it is, or how he feels about it, once again he shrugs his shoulders and says, "I don't give a shit." '

WEDNESDAY, AUGUST 21

Chelsea 1 Middlesbrough 0

A fetching Armani dark-blue suit, open-neck blue shirt, and no socks. The fashion police would certainly have swooped on the Bridge. Never has English football seen a manager dressed like this!

Ruud's managerial debut at the Bridge. Gary Lineker and David Platt were among the audience for the opening home game unveiling Chelsea's new array of stars. Platt is an old friend of Luca and former Sampdoria team mate, while Lineker played at Barcelona with Hughes. Ruud's new recruits were introduced to the crowd, and the shirt-sleeved supporters had already forgotten the limp draw at the Dell. It was a night of mixed emotions: frustration at Chelsea's hit and miss football, close to brilliance, and joy at the late winner.

Ultimately Vialli won the Italian showdown with Ravanelli thanks to a wonder goal from Di Matteo, a devastating twenty-five-yard shot into the corner just four minutes from the end. The Chelsea fans spent the entire game chanting 'Vialli, Vialli' and the Italian came close to his first goal for the club with an enticing mixture of trickery and determination. Gullit's anger was directed at the lack of genuine chances provided for his front men, and Vialli was forced to take the initiative himself.

Both Vialli and Ravanelli worked relentlessly, even tackling each other in the early exchanges. But with Leboeuf the master in Chelsea's defence, Ravanelli was restricted to one chance only.

Gullit spent an agonising time on the bench before Di Matteo struck. Gullit admitted: 'It has been a very strange week for him after what happened at Southampton and the story in the newspapers, but he replied like a great player and I was pleased for him. How Di Matteo struck the ball was very, very good. He didn't simply strike it, he wanted to put it in the angle and he did.' Again his collection of foreign stars failed to click and he showed his exasperation sitting on the bench. It was even worse for Robson. 'Robbo' must have felt like pulling Ravanelli's shirt over his own head when Di Matteo struck his winner. He said: 'Mugged! That's exactly how I feel. We were the better side for eighty minutes, we went out and pressurised Chelsea and never let them settle.'

Di Matteo reclined on the Chelsea turf, quickly joined by Wise and the rest of his team-mates in a linking line. It resembled a well rehearsed Roman-inspired goal celebration. 'That's the first time I've done anything like that and I hope to do it a lot in future,' said Di Matteo. 'The other lads just followed my example. I haven't got a name for it but I dedicate it to the team. I think I've begun the year well – my first game at home and I score the winner. They were a tough team, very physical, but in the end I think I came out on top.'

Gullit concluded: 'We were all disappointed after Sunday at not winning that match. But the celebration showed how badly they wanted this victory and how much it meant to them to perform well.'

Vialli outshone and outstyled his former Juventus team-mate in the great Italian shoot-out. The bald-headed maestro was full of tantalising tricks, flicks and expressive football on his Chelsea home debut. After complaining about how the hatchet men 'shot you down with machine guns' after his first experience of Premiership football at Southampton, it was much the same again. Vialli was quickly succeeding Gullit as the player taking the most pounding from opponents. Jason Dodd was booked for a foul against him at the Dell, and it wasn't long before Boro captain Nigel Pearson went into the book. In fact, it was on just twenty-one minutes and he was lucky not to be shown the red card. Di Matteo, although still lacking match sharpness, completely split Robson's defence with an arrow-like fifty-yard pass straight into Vialli's stride. Pearson was guilty of a blatant professional foul, unceremoniously hauling down Vialli. Worthing referee Gary Willard trotted over to the incident with the Chelsea crowd baying for a sending off, but he disappointed them by raising the yellow card.

Emerson had already been booked as early as the tenth minute for chopping down Leboeuf after the central defender had cheekily slipped the ball through his legs. With such an array of attacking talent the crowd were awaiting the first goal. A cross by Wise produced the deftest of touches by Di Matteo but Alan Miller somehow manufactured an instinctive acrobatic save to touch the ball over. Saturday's hat-trick hero Ravanelli had only one genuine chance late on in the first half. The hard working Ravanelli burst clear from almost the halfway line, but ran out of steam with his shot when he got inside the box, hooking wide of the far post.

Di Matteo's winner came from a blunder that needled the Boro boss. A routine throw from Neil Cox was overhit, handing Chelsea the initiative at the throw. Hughes, guilty of a glaring miss moments earlier after being set up by a combination of Vialli and Wise, picked out Di Matteo with a precision pass and he struck with a shot that arrowed into the corner.

Gullit picked out seventeen-year-old Jody Morris for special praise. 'He was not even thinking about playing in this game, he was more concerned about asking for autographs for his friends. Then he saw his name on the board and he said "Go away autograph hunters" and he went to get his boots. In the last fifteen minutes he was tackling, producing good dummies and showing some personality. I said to him, "Don't worry, just play, don't be afraid to make mistakes." All of a sudden he was doing the things that I see him doing during the week.' The miniature England under-21 player was proof that Gullit was just as dedicated to cherishing young home-grown talent as he is to importing expensive foreigners. 'Mouse' Morris – just 5ft 5in tall and not eighteen until December – did not let him down, trading imaginative competition with the equally diminutive Juninho. The teenager, who lives just five minutes from Chelsea's ground, said: 'I'm really pleased. It was a shock because though I came on as substitute at Southampton when Craig [Burley] got a knock, the way things were shaping up in training I didn't expect to start. It was quite tough out there and I was glad to come through the whole ninety minutes. I felt OK from the beginning, but it helps that I've been involved through pre-season. I've played against the likes of Ajax and Sampdoria which was all good experience.'

Already summoned to England under-21 duty, the new kid on the Chelsea block praised Gullit for nurturing young talent in direct contrast to the theory that the imports would block such developments. Morris said: 'He's been very encouraging. He and Graham Rix take me aside a lot and speak to me about the game. Our gaffer's so laid back you feel as if you can talk to him as just one of the players, which he is. It's not as if you feel intimidated by the manager. It's a great atmosphere. I'm loving every minute of it, playing with great players I used to watch.' For such a skilful little player, it was a surprise that, as a Chelsea fan, his idol used to be hard man Graham Roberts. But Morris also has a tough edge to his game which led Gullit to have as much faith in him as Hoddle, who gave him his Chelsea debut as a substitute against Boro at Stamford Bridge the previous February.

'It means we have more good English talent, and it shows that talent gets its chance here,' said Ruud. 'I don't buy and want only stars. I want players who will do what I have in mind and Jody's one of them. We have some other good youngsters behind him too.'

A first win was satisfying in many ways and Gullit was not too perturbed that Vialli and Hughes still had to score. 'They always need time. There's a lot of attention on them, the opposition concentrate on them, so it's going to be hard for them. But it means the others can profit from that and I think they did against Middlesbrough.' For Gullit the overall signs were encouraging: 'We can play better. We only showed a few moments of how we can play but I'm pleased with the way things are going.'

SATURDAY, AUGUST 24
Chelsea 2 Coventry City 0

One of Ruud's new managerial duties was to write the opening notes for the match day programme, a personal message to the committed Chelsea fans. He wrote: 'We have started the season well. But we have to work on all things still. We are not yet near the football I have in mind for the team. But it will only come in stages. I don't think the players realise yet what they can achieve. We need games and we need good results for everyone to believe in themselves. It is unbelievable at the games and at training. So many reporters, and this year a lot of Italian reporters. We are getting good publicity for Chelsea across the world. We have to make it last, yes?'

The thoughts of Ruud rang true as the players left the Bridge following another game which was inconclusive about the team's development. Signs of improvement were there. Vialli illuminated Stamford Bridge with a goal of exquisite quality, but the focal point was the handball horror which cost Big Ron's team the points.

Vialli, in truth, finished with a spectacular strike, taking Clarke's pass in his stride and volleying the ball past Steve Ogrizovic, but it would not rank among his best overall performances. The delight on the Italian's face demonstrated relief as much as ecstasy. Gullit said: 'It was nice for Gianluca to score a goal that everybody was waiting for. And it was a fantastic goal.' But Gullit had not discussed the issues with his players, and with typical humour told the gathered media: 'I won't do that until you have gone, then I can tell no lies.' Ruud prefers to analyse the problems in matches once all the adrenalin has subsided, to discuss the issues rationally, rather than with emotion driving the players' opinions.

Ruud sat relaxed as Chelsea piled on the early chances, Hughes spurning three within nine minutes. By the second half, even though Coventry were reduced to ten men, Ruud was up on his feet screaming at Wise. He cocked his ear. Gullit held up ten fingers and pointed to Gary McAllister. It was the same in any language: someone had to mark the number ten who was running the midfield at that stage, despite Chelsea's numerical advantage. Fortunately, Vialli finally broke his duck with Chelsea's second goal after a frustrating seventy-three minutes; Leboeuf had put the team ahead with a thirty-first-minute controversial goal.

All three of Gullit's spectacular foreign signings had now scored a goal apiece, with Vialli surprisingly the last to make it. He said: 'It was not an obsession for me to score. I was not obsessively after a goal, but I was pleased that I got one to repay all the attention that I had received from everybody at the club. This is a sign I am going to get better. Until now I couldn't train one hundred per cent, so I couldn't adjust to all the continuous running that is needed. But it pleases me that Chelsea are always improving, and that is more important than that I have scored a goal. I was very sad that a player was sent off and it was clear that the Coventry players were incensed.'

Again Chelsea's Man of the Match was Leboeuf. After just three games, he emerged as the Premiership's best and classiest defender. The best move of a relatively disappointing game was a marvellous defensive interception by Leboeuf which he instantly turned into attack, linking with Hughes and Di Matteo, but Vialli's shot was saved. Chelsea relied upon Leboeuf's superlative defensive performance to retain their zero goals against record, but they should have been three Hughes goals up after nine minutes. Instead, despite a Leboeuf-headed opener, ten-man Coventry responded much better and with McAllister dominating midfield the game was always in the balance.

Vialli entered the press room, while Leboeuf was still in full flow. Leboeuf continued to express himself through an interpreter, even though he interposed jokes in English. He explained that although his English was improving, he felt he had been misquoted at times and wanted the comfort of an interpreter. During his extensive interview, Leboeuf paid tribute to Gullit. 'He makes me feel that I can play and he encourages me without actually saying anything specific. In that way we can see that he trusts us and we respond by wanting to repay that trust. It is very important to be given such trust and you appreciate when someone gives you that freedom. It makes you want to do your best to repay that confidence and trust placed in you.'

Gullit was delighted with his keeper, 'Dimmi', as he called him, also praising the contribution of Niedzwiecki, switching from part-time goalkeeping coach and reserve team coach to a full-time post concentrating on the keepers. 'I was especially pleased about the one save Dimmi had to make in the last minute. It is very difficult going the whole game with nothing to do. He has to be concentrated, tuned in all the time.'

There was still plenty of room for improvement. 'In a way we had too many chances, real chances. The game could have been finished in the first ten minutes, when we had three good chances. We made it difficult for ourselves by not scoring enough goals, and that gave them hope. It took a long time to get the second. We must be more accurate, more hungry for goals. But we have created so many chances and that is very positive.'

Ruud felt the sending off worked against Chelsea. 'I was not pleased about the sending off. It is more difficult against ten men than eleven. We were all over them when they had a full team, and they played better when they had ten. However, I am very pleased because we would normally have drawn this type of game last season, we did that far too often. Now the team plays more for the result. What pleased me was the way we handled the game. If you want to do well in the championship you have to do well against teams like these. We lost two points at Southampton and it's a mental attitude in these games where you find yourself against ten men. There is more space, you tend to flick the ball here, try a lovely curly ball there and think it's easy. But the opposition work hard for each other and it's strange. It's just a mental thing. I hammer it home, we must be concentrated and the team must be in super shape. Everything depends on detail. But you cannot make it perfect. No team is perfect. It is a good period for me, even though it is frustrating that I am not playing, because I can see how things are going from the bench and see where I must work on several players.'

Liam Daish failed to curtail his fury at the referee who had shown him the red card following the controversial moment which led to the decisive first goal by Leboeuf. The goal should never have been allowed, argued Ron Atkinson, Coventry's manager, because of a blatant handball by Petrescu early in the movement – and Daish made his feelings known to referee Paul Danson.

Vialli was furious with the way English football was being portrayed in Italy. Vialli's midweek confrontation with Ravanelli was condemned as part of the substandard English game. Vialli rounded on his critics when he said: 'I am very annoyed about what has been written about the English after the Middlesbrough match. The English football league has been described as if it is something minor, something inferior to Serie A. That is not so. English football has no reason to be envious of Italian football. I am an intense type of player and that is why I enjoy the English game because effectively I am involved for seventy-five minutes as opposed to sixty-five minutes.'

After two blanks his first goal was extremely welcome. He felt that it wasn't the real Vialli in the first two-and-a-half games – but his brother! 'I think in the first half you saw my brother; the real Luca Vialli has arrived now. His brother has played in the first two matches against Middlesbrough and Southampton. Anyway, I'm very happy because this is my first goal at Chelsea and of course I hope it's not the last.'

It's a tradition in Italy to 'dedicate' a goal, or an honour, to somebody or something. Vialli went on: 'I want to split my first goal with all the fans and all the players, everybody. Because they always helped me, in this, my first period in London. I missed some chances earlier on, but I think my accuracy is coming back now. I am getting better, I am not one hundred per cent fit yet, but I think I can play now like I want. More goals will come when I'm fit. I can help the team, I can score and I'm very happy because I can help Chelsea to go into the first position of the Premiership. I think the crowd enjoyed my goal and I have to say thanks to the crowds, to everybody. The atmosphere was fantastic for me.'

Chelsea had yet to concede a goal and, up front, Vialli believed his fledgling partnership with Hughes would develop. 'I play very well with Mark because he's a very generous player. He touches the ball off very well and sees how I want the ball, sometimes to my feet, sometimes deep, so we play well together. That's because we play for the team, for ourselves and for the other striker. Frank and Roberto have also settled in well, they are great players.'

Despite the euphoria, there was caution from Vialli. Demonstrating his new expertise in English, he said: 'We have to keep our feet on the floor because it will be a long and winding road!'

MONDAY, AUGUST 26

Gullit took the opportunity of the forthcoming free Saturday, due to international games, to give his players three days off. 'Sometimes it is better to rest. The body needs that also. You can gain new energy from being with your family or whoever it is, while you are relaxing.' Gullit had the chance to visit the surgeon in Antwerp for an update on his operation, and Leboeuf had plans. 'My mother and children are coming over here and then I shall be going to Strasbourg to play in a friendly against Mexico.'

Time to reflect on a start that left Chelsea second in the Premiership even though their players had yet to be fully integrated and Gullit was still recuperating from surgery. But Gullit was not deceived into believing that everything would click without even more hard work. No doubt Wise had taught him yet another dressing room colloquialism to sum it all up. Asked about Chelsea's league position, Gullit smiled: 'Good . . . but it's early doors!'

TUESDAY, AUGUST 27

Ruud brought his attractive girlfriend to the clubs Player of the Year dinner-dance at the Novotel in Hammersmith. A regular at the Bridge, the smiling face of Estelle was never far from Ruud after home matches. Estelle is the niece of Dutch legend Johan Cruyff. Estelle's father approved of the relationship. Estelle and Ruud were inseparable, living together in swish Cadogan Square, just behind Peter Jones. Bates announced that Ruud was last season's Player of the Year, with Spencer second, Duberry third.

THURSDAY, AUGUST 29

Bad news for Ruud! Press reports stated that his doctor insisted Gullit won't kick a ball in anger until December at the earliest. Ruud said: 'It's true I am not getting any younger, and with these things [the knee problems] you have to take things as they come. I can't put a date on it, but if it takes six months then that's what it has to be. The good thing is that as manager I can give my full attention to the business of management.'

Speaking from his Brussels clinic, Dr Martens was more realistic. He said: 'It is difficult to pin a date down when he will play again, but I would suggest a minimum of three months. It is not a virgin knee. It's true I have operated on it in the past, but Ruud takes care of himself and this is important. Otherwise this could slow down the healing process. But I am optimistic he will make a full recovery. I was happy when I looked inside the knee at how little scar tissue remained from the previous operations. We have cleaned it up well, and there look to be no complications.'

Ruud was privately optimistic; he had started running again as he gradually and carefully stepped up his training schedule.

SEPTEMBER

Best Dressed Man and a Winning Team

SUNDAY, SEPTEMBER 1

Ruud was named the Best Dressed Man in Britain. He impressed the judges with his fashion choice for appearances as a BBC pundit during Euro '96. He was the first foreigner to win the award. Gullit was praised for his 'ultimate blend of style and substance'. Tony Blair was one of the runners-up. The award was presented by the organisers of an annual trade fair for the fashion industry at Olympia, and a spokeswoman said: 'Ruud was delighted. He said he was interested in clothes and would wander around the exhibition.' Continental footballers did the double, with Newcastle United's French heart-throb David Ginola a runner-up.

It was not such a happy day for Leboeuf. Sent off during France's 2–0 win over Mexico for his second offence, a high tackle on Ricardo Pelaez, Leboeuf fumed: 'I've been with Chelsea for less than two months, but I've already come to appreciate that in England, football is a game played by real men – and not by cheats. I was an idiot to let myself be conned, as were the referee and linesman. I had already been kicked in the thigh and punched in my stomach, and when Pelaez elbowed me in the face it was the last straw. We squared up to each other, and when I raised my knee to push him away he threw himself onto the ground like a rag doll.'

TUESDAY, SEPTEMBER 3

So, can Chelsea win the championship? Only three games into the season the question was already given a serious airing.

Wise was genuinely surprised when told it was forty-one years since Chelsea's one and only league championship. 'London have made a few challenges for the title but you need a bit more quality in the squad. Ruud has done that with three top-class signings and now we have seventeen or eighteen players who are all good enough to do a job. No one is getting carried away after three games but our aim this season is to qualify for Europe ... then push a bit higher.'

Gullit knew his team were not yet championship material, but they were determined to mount a challenge. 'I've been in Manchester United's position when I played in Italy for Milan. Now I am in a different situation. I'm not here because I thought I was joining a team which was automatically going to win something. I've never been like that. I like to do something with a team that has not been a success for a while. When I came to Chelsea I let my heart speak for once. The first impression is usually right and my first impression was very sharp. I needed a new challenge. I loved many aspects of Italy and could have stayed for another couple of years, but you have to know when enough is enough. I'd won everything with

Milan and Sampdoria. Now my concern is not to win a whole lot of cups, but just to face a new challenge. I don't even think of winning the Championship. I am so focused on our next game that many times I don't even know who the match afterwards is against. You don't win the league by beating Manchester United, Liverpool and Newcastle. You win it by beating the so-called smaller teams. No team has scored against us so far and that has been good. Decent teams build from the back. We have to defend without being negative. But we have also created a real lot of chances at the other end. At Milan we calculated we'd get four good goalscoring opportunities every game and had to take at least one of them. At Chelsea this season it has been more like ten to fifteen chances and we have to concentrate more on converting them.' We will carry on with the style which Glenn Hoddle introduced at Chelsea but I want players to realise that it's not just about passing the ball. If we got a point for every ten passes we'd win the Championship. But it's winning the game which is important and we have to play more for the result. It's not always possible to play beautiful football. I want them to be more efficient.'

Gullit still declined to put a date on his Premiership return. 'I am now starting my own fitness programme but first I have to look after the team. After they have finished training, I do my own routine by myself. I go into the gym with Ade Mafe, and the specialists have given me a special set of exercises to do. I will start running again but I want to be sure I am completely fit before I start playing again.' Initially, he found his enforced lay-off frustrating. 'You see things happening on the pitch and there's very little you can do to influence the play from the sidelines. It's much more difficult to see what is going on from the dug-out, but if you sit in the stands you cannot communicate with your team.'

Ruud faced his toughest assignment as new manager the next day at Highbury, despite all of Arsenal's problems, with the controversial sacking of Bruce Rioch and the fight to hang on to caretaker boss Stewart Houston until Arsène Wenger's arrival. When Graham was dismissed, Houston was in temporary charge, steering the Gunners away from relegation trouble as well as into the final of the European Cup-winners Cup with superb wins against French champions Auxerre and Italy's Sampdoria. Now he had taken Arsenal to third place in the Premiership with two wins in the first three games – achieved without the injured Adams and with Wright only a substitute. Gullit argued: 'Current positions in the league are irrelevant. Maybe after seven or eight games you will begin to see which teams will be up there at the end of the season, but three games is not a realistic time to measure a team's quality.'

Houston was not underestimating Gullit's team. 'Chelsea have caught the imagination with their summer signings all of whom seem to have settled in quickly. I watched them in their opening game at Southampton and Vialli, Leboeuf and Di Matteo have given them a great strength.'

WEDNESDAY, SEPTEMBER 4
Arsenal 3 Chelsea 3

The fashion-conscious Ruud wore a fetching tracksuit for the dug-out but later, for the TV and media interviews, he donned the dark blue Italian suit and bright yellow tie that was the new look for the entire team courtesy of club sponsors Lubiam 1911.

It was certainly a smart start for Chelsea, quietly earning the tag as 'the most fashionable side in London'. The capital confrontation between second and third in the Premiership was also going to be something special – and it fully lived up to its billing.

Chelsea looked more like AC Milan in the first half. Breathtaking. Leboeuf's display of defensive mastery confirmed his instant impact in the Premiership. Locked in a fascinating duel with Bergkamp, Leboeuf was not only the master in the heart of Chelsea's defence: he opened the scoring from the penalty spot after just five minutes. Steve Bould was adjudged to have brought down Wise just inside the penalty area. That stunned the Arsenal fans and immediately made referee Keith Burge a target for their anger. But Leboeuf coolly sent Lukic the wrong way. He enjoyed the experience of his first London derby and explained how he came to usurp penalty-taker Wise. 'Yes. I know Dennis Wise shoot penalty last year, but when there was a penalty he told me "Okay, shoot it." No problem. I shoot, I score, and it was good. But if Dennis want to shoot we can speak, it's not a problem. It's not very important for me. I know I can shoot very well penalty, I don't miss penalty since three years. I have big confidence about it.'

John Lukic, making his Highbury return on a free transfer from Leeds, picked the ball out of the net for the second time after just thirty minutes after he made a complete hash of a wicked Vialli shot. Vialli let fly from inside the penalty area but the angled drive was well covered at his near post by Lukic, only for the giant keeper to completely fumble the ball through his hands and over the line. Once Chelsea sprang ahead from a penalty there was no holding Gullit's team of foreign allsorts.

Arsenal supporters' fury with the ref intensified when he turned down their penalty claim after Ray Parlour was bundled over by Myers.

The poor Arsenal keeper made one outstanding save from a Vialli shot before his dreadful fumble. Chelsea fans gave Lukic a sarcastic cheer the next time he touched the ball after conceding the second goal. Lukic was clearly affected and from a close range Hughes header, where he opted to stay on the line for a cross, he just about got one hand to it. When he cleanly caught the Wise corner both sets of fans cheered him!

It isn't often that Arsenal are outplayed at Highbury, but they did manage one moment of magic of their own. A delightful Merson lob left Bergkamp clear in the penalty area and the Dutchman took his time to get the ball under control, but then fired wide across the face of the goal.

Chelsea's supercharged side gave Arsenal a footballing lesson in the first half, but then suffered two setbacks which turned the game. After 315 minutes without conceding a goal Paul Merson, ironically a Chelsea fan, plundered the first and brought Arsenal back to life for a resounding comeback in the second half. Almost five minutes into injury time Merson struck. A lovely sidefoot flick by Bergkamp from John Hartson's header set up Merson for a low shot into the corner. Chelsea were second best at two challenges from a routine Bould free kick that left Gullit dismayed at the lack of concentration.

Platt began his season with a second half appearance to be greeted by his former Sampdoria team-mate Vialli. The turning point was the moment Leboeuf was stretchered off, clutching his side in agony. Chelsea's defence collapsed along with him. Duberry was Chelsea's discovery of last season but not even this outstanding young talent could replace the Frenchman.

From a short corner movement, Platt to Merson, and the latter fired in a deep cross to the far post where Keown headed the sixty-fifth-minute equaliser. Ten minutes later, Wright bounced off the bench with only fifteen minutes to go and surely his goal was destined to be the winner. After just four minutes on the pitch, Wright scored. The lightning reflexes were still there as he brushed off Clarke and beat Kharine to the ball at the edge of the box, flicking it into the corner.

Of course, it wouldn't be Ian Wright if he didn't explode. Held back by Clarke, he shoulder charged the defender in the chest and just under the chin. The linesman spotted it, drew referee Keith Burge's attention to the flashpoint, and out came the obligatory yellow card. Clarke laughed off the last-minute lunge. 'I've been playing against Wrighty for ten years now and I think he was just introducing himself to me again! I don't have a major problem with him – in fact the fifteen minutes he was on the pitch was Wrighty all over. A goal, a booking, giving his marker a good chasing ... that sums him up. Take that spark out of his game and he wouldn't be the same player; something is always liable to happen when he's on the park. He's some player to have on the bench – it must be like having a nuclear deterrent in reserve. We thought the Arsenal whirlwind had just about blown itself out – and then we saw him stripping off on the touchline.'

Amazingly, three minutes into injury time Wise plundered the equaliser. Wise had the final say to protect Gullit's unbeaten record, leaving Chelsea just ahead of Arsenal in the capital's challenge for the championship, although they dropped one place, with Aston Villa moving into second behind Sheffield Wednesday.

For Wright there was an extra special final moment of magic: a smile, a handshake and a hug on the touchline at the end of the match from his hero Ruud Gullit.

Clarke admitted Chelsea trooped away dismayed at letting a 2–0 lead slip rather than relieved by Wise's ninety-third-minute equaliser. 'It shows the measure of our own expectations when we can come away from Highbury with a 3–3 draw and feel disappointed. That should tell everyone what we are about this season. But at least we have the perfect opportunity to iron out the creases on Saturday by getting a result at Sheffield Wednesday and ending their one hundred per cent record.'

Gullit walked into the luxurious Arsenal interview room. He looked shocked at the massed media turn-out sitting in their plush red seats. 'What is this? A cinema?' smiled Ruud, as he looked for the silver screen but spotted the giant cannon as the backstop to the media room. Gullit was 'disappointed' at the way his side succumbed under Arsenal's desperate second-half onslaught. 'This game should be an example to us for the rest of the season. Not many teams will come to Highbury and control the game the way we did. But you have to be disappointed when you have been in control of the game. It's normal when you are 2–0 down to try and do something about it and I'm not happy about the mistakes we made, especially from dead-ball situations. But I suppose I've got to be happy that we showed pride. I have to compliment my team on the way they fought back right to the last minute.' We've got to learn how to control a game like this and maybe it will serve as a lesson for the rest of the season.'

Ruud refused to use the loss of Leboeuf as 'an excuse'. He explained that he had twenty players of good enough standard but added significantly: 'Some players can give a little more in terms of skill.' Leboeuf is one. Gullit, of course, is another. One of the contingent of Italian journalists suggested the player the Chelsea team needed most was Ruud Gullit. 'I'm already ahead of my schedule. But there are too many examples of players returning too early from injury and they struggle for the rest of the season, and that's a pity. After an operation there is always trauma to your body. Your posture is not right as you try to compensate and there are changes to your body and muscles. It goes in a circle, and you have to come out of that circle, but you have to be careful. We shall just have to see, but I hope it will be quick.'

'Where will you play?'

Ruud responded: 'If selected!' Even the hardened hacks enjoyed his sense of humour. He is one of the precious few managers guaranteed to bring a smile to their seen-it-all, heard-it-all-before faces.

While he waited to play again, Ruud was grasping the qualities necessary to become a successful manager. 'I am happy, but unhappy. But I am not angry with the team, not at all. To come to Highbury and play this way, even for the first half, I must be happy. In reality you cannot win a game on quality alone, there has to be something more. We have the quality and showed it, but it was not enough.' But he was philosophical. 'Defensive mistakes are part and parcel of football. Without them it would be rather boring, wouldn't it? Our new foreign stars were very happy, they said they were so excited about the pace, crowd and atmosphere. That's great for me because it was one of the things I told them about when they joined.'

Most managers consider after-match interviews an ordeal, still wrapped up in the emotions of whatever cross words might have escaped in the dressing rooms. Ruud prefers to air his views once the adrenalin has ceased to pump a day or so later, with a far greater degree of rationality. He always appears relaxed as he sits answering endless questions; he quickly became one of the most listened-to managers in the Premiership.

THURSDAY, SEPTEMBER 5

Ruud starts running at last. Newton returned to full training with the youth team, contact activity for the first time since his broken leg.

The Coca-Cola Cup draw. Chelsea against Blackpool, first leg at the seaside town. Blackpool manager Gary Megson was delighted to have landed a glamour tie, evoking memories of the club's famous past. 'It is great for the town to be able to see some of the game's finest players back at Bloomfield Road. The game will put us in the spotlight. Players like Vialli may never have heard of us – until now.' Blackpool had four players with Premiership experience – assistant manager Mike Phelan, defender Dave Linighan, full-back Andy Barlow and striker Andy Preece. It was five years since Tottenham became the last Premiership club to play at Bloomfield Road when they beat the Seasiders 1–0 in the FA Cup, and two decades since Blackpool and Chelsea last met. The gate limit was fixed at 9,000 for safety reasons. The tie was immediately nominated the 'live' TV game.

But Chelsea's next assignment was at surprise table-toppers Sheffield Wednesday, where manager David Pleat was rewarded for his one hundred per cent start to the season by securing the Carling Manager of the Month for August. Wednesday were tipped to struggle, but answered their critics with wins over Aston Villa, Leeds, Newcastle and Leicester.

Pleat recruited Shreeves when Gullit left him out of his backroom staff. Shreeves was suitably impressed by the club he left. 'I saw them at Arsenal and I was very impressed, they have some excellent players.' The league table suggested Shreeves was making an impact, notably with wins over Aston Villa and Newcastle. 'Tremendous results for us, those,' said Shreeves. 'But no one is getting carried away. At the moment we are just pleased to have got a good start. That is so important these days. That has been achieved with a set of hard-working players and no superstars.'

The Chelsea line-up depended on the fitness of Leboeuf. 'It was certainly a lot better yesterday morning and we are optimistic he will be fit,' said Rix. Bates treated the office staff to a night out at the theatre to see 'Ferry Cross The Mersey'. Harding donated £1m to the Labour Party, to steal all the national and international news headlines.

FRIDAY, SEPTEMBER 6

Another huge media gathering at the training ground for the *Match of the Day* clash between first-placed Sheffield Wednesday and third in the table Chelsea. Around twenty reporters gathered for every Ruud word. 'Having been in demand as a player in Italy with people always wanting to talk and write about me, all this is not really anything new to myself. It's different of course for many of the guys here who have been at the club a long time. This is something that may be new to them.' The range of questions fired at Ruud covered anything from whether the team can sustain a championship challenge to Harding's Labour Party gifts. Every question politely answered – as usual – and with a smile whenever possible.

It would have been easy for Chelsea's laid-back manager to indulge in a rethink after his side threw away a 2–0 lead at Highbury – but that isn't the Gullit way. He recognised the defensive shortcomings and was working on ways to rectify them, but he stuck by his attacking philosophy. That was his pledge as he took Chelsea to pace-setters Sheffield Wednesday. He enjoyed the full backing of his talented imports who were thrilled by the passion in the London derby. He said: 'All my new overseas players were very happy after the Arsenal game. They were so excited by it all. And from what I've heard and seen from the fans on the street, they are just as happy with the Europeans who have come into the club. They clearly feel the players have brought something extra and I can tell that just by the noise the crowd are making. It's such a positive sign. We need to concentrate harder at certain times and must try and avoid defensive lapses. I know the way I want to play and overall I am pleased with our start to the season.'

Gullit's crowd-pleasers had the bookies worried. Chelsea's odds for the title dropped to 10–1 with Stan James after being available at 25–1 early in the season, though you could still get 14–1 from Ladbrokes.

So far Gullit had had to do little shouting and gesticulating. 'All managers have their own ways of letting out their frustration. But I won't jump up and down if things are going wrong. I just sit there because it really means I haven't done my homework right. To be honest, what else can you do if the preparation is wrong. It's something that you just have to accept. I can't scream and shout from the touchline and anyway I don't see the point because you can't make yourself heard with all the noise from the crowd. They clearly feel the players have brought something extra and I can tell that at Chelsea just by the noise they are making. It's such a positive sign.' Well, so far little need to jump up and down. Would it last?

SATURDAY, SEPTEMBER 7

Sheffield Wednesday 0 Chelsea 2
A triumph for Ruud. Chelsea's first league win at Hillsborough in more than a quarter of a century, his Euro stars prepared to fuse steel with undoubted style to wreck Wednesday's perfect start to the season. As Gullit put it succinctly: 'I'm a very demanding person, but even I know it's not always possible to play beautiful football.'

Could Chelsea be mentioned in the same breath as Manchester United or Liverpool? 'I don't know yet,' said Gullit, 'but we have to start somewhere and keep trying to build and grow. We came here with a team far from completely fit. Injuries, colds and sickness. Against opponents who had won all their games we needed to play in a certain way.'

Leboeuf was stretchered off in midweek and needed pain-killing injections to start. Gullit revealed: 'He wanted to come off after twenty minutes because of his damaged hip but we told him to stay calm, and he saw it through.' When Kharine was carried off, Hitchcock performed heroics. Gullit emerged for his TV interview. 'We have two almost world-class goalkeepers.' Steady, Ruud. But it was typical of how Gullit built up his players' confidence, notably the so-called 'players making up the numbers' around the superstar foreigners.

Pleat questioned whether foreign superstars can be relied on to roll their sleeves up and get stuck into their Premiership rivals. But Vialli, Di Matteo and the excellent Leboeuf left Chelsea fans in no doubt that they were all prepared to sweat for their millionaire pay packets. Goal hero Burley observed: 'When these foreign guys come here, you do think "Good players, but are they prepared to work?" Well, the three we've signed are all huge names but they all want to get stuck in and do their share. Nobody at this club thinks they are better than anyone else. Everyone has got to muck in because it's as much about hard work as it is about ability. I did wonder if Ruud Gullit was still up for it when he came here and it was the same with Vialli. But they've both showed they've only got where they are because they've got the right attitude. We've got a long, hard season ahead but if we don't do well, it won't be for lack of effort. The management wouldn't stand for that. I've been here eight years and this is the best squad we've ever had.'

Burley had to prove he was worthy of a place with competition growing and with Gullit still recovering. His prospects were boosted with his clinical twenty-eighth-minute goal to put Chelsea in control. Charging down defender Dejan Stefanovic's attempted clearance, he kept his nerve to race from the halfway line and shoot beyond Kevin Pressman. 'I had a lot of time to think about it and they are often the worse ones to take. If Ruud is going to drop me, he will. But if I'm doing well and scoring goals I don't see why I shouldn't keep my place in the side.'

Burley also teed up Myers for the late second to put the result beyond doubt. Gullit was brimming with pride at the victory. 'The way the team is playing gives me more time before I need to make my return. I'm in no hurry. I'm very pleased with the way we defended. Even Vialli was back in his own box. It proves we have the spirit to win in a different way.'

Pleat refused to be despondent after watching his team's attacking efforts blunted by the superb Leboeuf and substitute keeper Hitchcock. The Frenchman was once again Man of the Match and Hitchcock came on after just twenty minutes to make a string of vital saves. The only sour point of yet another exhilarating match was the constant barracking of Wednesday old boy Dan Petrescu by the Hillsborough fans.

A measure of Chelsea's emerging force was yet another appearance on BBC's *Match of the Day*. Gary Lineker, anchor man of the show, and guests Alan Hansen and Trevor Brooking were again full of praise for Gullit's team.

MONDAY, SEPTEMBER 9
Bad news for Kharine. He punched a ball and landed awkwardly, twisting his knee. It looked as though it would keep him out for some time and probably need an exploratory operation.

TUESDAY, SEPTEMBER 10

First night out for Ruud at Langan's Brasserie in Stratton Street, Mayfair, famous for its celebrity clientele. An appropriate location for Ruud with the walls adorned by giant old oil paintings of Stamford Bridge when the Shed was the centrepiece of the stadium. The floor manager, Michael Henry, is one of Chelsea's biggest fans. Ruud was accompanied by his Wembley-based agents Jon and Phil Smith. Jon Smith said: 'Ruud liked it, but then again he enjoys going to all the top restaurants. The only problem was that he was plagued by autograph hunters; he must have had about twenty people come up to the table. But you know Ruud, he signed them all with a typical warm smile.'

The King's Road, the Fulham Road, Knightsbridge and Kensington boast wall-to-wall high-profile, where-to-be-seen restaurants, the centre of London's swish and in-crowd. San Lorenzo, in Beauchamp Place behind Harrods, a long-established haunt of Princess Di, was instantly established as Vialli's favourite eaterie. A chauffeur car would transport him directly from the Heathrow training ground to San Lorenzo for lunch. In the evenings, it was just a short stroll from the Cadogan Hotel, the temporary accommodation which became more permanent by the month. He would be spotted at a corner table with his girlfriend, casually attired in lime-green pullover, and smoking! He looked so much at home, he might as well have been in his own dining room. Ruud's favourite haunts were Italian restaurants close to home, the highly fashionable L'Incontro and Sarbinis, both owned by Gino Sarbin, who acted as the middleman in the transfer of Gazza from Spurs to Lazio for £5.5 million. Ruud's ideal meal would be either pasta or risotto. Only grape juice, strictly no beer or even wine.

Naturally, the best Italian restaurants became a magnet for the Chelsea set. Scallini's in Walton Street displays photographs of Vialli, Di Matteo and Leboeuf on its white walls, alongside Gary Lineker and his wife Michelle, and Liverpool stars Jamie Redknapp and Steve McManaman. San Frediano's in the Fulham Road, recently refurbished in bright yellows, used to be frequented by the sixties set from the Bridge and was enjoying a renaissance with occasional appearances of the Italian players accompanied by Leboeuf, who said: 'The other night Gianluca and I went out for a quiet meal in town at a pavement restaurant, and all evening only one person asked for an autograph. Obviously there happened to be an Italian tourist passing at the time!' So far Leboeuf has failed to persuade Vialli about the virtues of French cooking. 'We often go out together, above all to Italian restaurants. At the beginning he ordered for me, he is a connoisseur, but soon I will teach him something about French cuisine. He doesn't like it too much, he says there is too much sauce.'

Vialli had no trouble discovering the best pasta in town, but his priority was finding his ideal flat. Gianluca searched for the right rental accommodation, a flat valued around the £1.5m mark, close to Ruud who lives just off Sloane Square. House-hunting with fiancée Giovanna was one of Vialli's main concerns. Vialli, whose family home is an imposing mansion outside Cremona, said: 'Living in hotels is not the right lifestyle for me. It is very important I find the right apartment. I can't settle and enjoy London, the theatres, shops, restaurants and cinemas, until I find a permanent base. I love the freedom of London, I can walk around without being mobbed all the time, like I was in Italy.' Vialli's agent Athol Still, who represented John Barnes, said: 'Gianluca is chasing his dream apartment and he won't stop until he finds it. I'll be delighted when he finally says yes, because it will be a weight off my shoulders.' A spokesman for west London estate agents Hamptons said: 'There are only a few properties in the area which match up to Gianluca's requirements.' House and flat prices have risen faster in this area of London than anywhere else in the country, and rents in some flats were £1000 a week.

WEDNESDAY, SEPTEMBER 11

Bates was so keen to keep up with his suave manager that he was starting to learn Dutch, with pocket dictionary to hand. So is his Dutch as good as Gullit's English? 'Not yet, but my Afrikaans isn't bad,' Bates tells me.

THURSDAY, SEPTEMBER 12

The post-mortem on Manchester United's failure against Juventus in the opening Champions League match inevitably included the thoughts of Juve's former captain, Vialli. 'Juventus played much better than Manchester United and created more chances. But Italian sides like Juventus do their homework on teams and go into games knowing far more than the opposition know about them. In England, they don't think the same, they just want to show everyone that they are better. If they plan for games better, they can qualify with Juventus. They have the talent, they just need to think more like Europeans.'

FRIDAY, SEPTEMBER 13

Not the right day for optimistic predictions. But the mood in the training camp was high. Sky high. With another Sky appearance scheduled for Sunday and the possibility of going top of the Premiership, Chelsea were enjoying the heady, rarified atmosphere of life at the top, something special for the domestic stars. Wise summed it up: 'I've never been so high after five games. When I was with Wimbledon in about 1988 I scored the winner against Charlton that took us top after four, but this is different – I'm getting nose-bleeds.'

Vialli was full of self-belief. 'Currently we are one of the best sides in the Premiership. We are growing in confidence as a team with every game and I think we can only get better. We beat Sheffield Wednesday, now we must build on that.'

No one within the Chelsea camp was getting carried away with talk about the title. 'No, no way,' said Wise. 'We are thrilled with the start we have made but that's all it is, a start. We have to maintain it and it will be anything but easy against Villa. We haven't done as well in the league as we should have over the years. I think the highest we have finished is eleventh in the last three seasons. That's not good enough. Our first target this season is to qualify for Europe. We will see how it goes after that. Obviously, having three quality players arrive has helped us.' The Wise forecast for the Villa match? 'I think there will certainly be a couple of goals.' Not so extravagant there, Dennis.

Villa were hyped up to dampen the Chelsea surge. Steve Staunton said: 'Gullit has finally assembled a Chelsea side that looks as if it has the ability to win something. And that is bad news for any team going to west London. Chelsea now look as if they have the makings of a great side. And that is down in almost complete measure to the influence of Gullit as their chief coach. He is typical of the new generation of manager, a business that seems to attract younger incumbents by the season. Thanks to his continental training he has his players far more aware of things like diet, physique and aerobic culture. Thanks to his skills, his experience in Italy and the Bosman ruling he has been able to persuade the likes of Vialli, Di Matteo and

Leboeuf to come here. And thanks to Vialli, one of the best strikers in the game, he has managed to get the best out of Mark Hughes. Sparky has been overlooked by the pundits in all their analysis of Chelsea this season but believe me we will not overlook him. He is the one player in England who really knows how to lead a line. With Vialli alongside him it is a potential recipe for disaster for any opposition. We have taken note of that already.'

SUNDAY, SEPTEMBER 15
Chelsea 1 Aston Villa 1
The game was a mirror image of everything in Ruud's pre-match message to the fans, hard work, some good football, but still not quite right – notably in the attacking third.

Leboeuf preserved Gullit's unbeaten run, leaving Chelsea poised in third place, with an exquisite goal. He said: 'I very much enjoy to score like this because it's very difficult. The ball fell just in front of me and I can touch the ball with my inferior foot and just turn around the goalkeeper, and come down very slowly. It was for me very beautiful goal. It's my goal.'

But title contenders? No. Not according to Leboeuf, even though Chelsea could have gone top of the table for the first time in seven years, had they won. 'I discovered it will be very difficult for us to win the championship. I found it a hard game, I knew it would be and there are seven or eight more teams like this for us to play. They put nine men behind the ball and we could not get round them, it was a problem for us. We ended up going around instead of going forward – it was like handball game in the end. We don't press Aston Villa very well and they can play easy.'

Highly rated Villa paid Gullit's new-look side the highest compliment with a well-organised and sound team performance to hold them to a battling draw, but it was Leboeuf who not only mastered the Villa attack, but popped up with the vital equaliser to become Chelsea's top scorer with three goals. The name of Leboeuf resounded around the stadium: the fans had taken the Frenchman to their hearts. In contrast, the more publicised arrival of Vialli had produced just two goals for the Italian.

Indicative of Chelsea's slumbering giant status was the fact that they hadn't been top of the table for six years, since Bobby Campbell was manager. They would have managed the top billing on alphabetical superiority to Liverpool had they won 3–1 after Liverpool beat Leicester 3–0. It didn't happen, as Villa proved tough to crack.

Leboeuf was the first to show any sign of a goal with a cheeky chip after just twelve minutes when he launched into one of his forward forages. The effort was tipped over by keeper Michael Oakes. Old boy Andy Townsend almost unlocked the Chelsea defence with a diving header from Staunton's cross as early as the seventh minute, bringing a save from Hitchcock. After eighteen minutes Townsend stunned the Blues. Burley was guilty of a foul on Sasa Curcic and Villa worked a clever free kick manoeuvre as Dwight Yorke slipped the ball to Townsend, who curled the ball round the wall and beyond the lunge of Hitchcock. The irreverent Wise was not happy that the ball took a deflection off Vialli. He told him: 'If you still had your hair, if you had your 1987 cut, that shot would have gone for a corner!'

Villa might have scored a second, putting the game beyond Chelsea, when Curcic carved a path through the middle after a one-two with Mark Draper, but his shot was superbly saved by Hitchcock. With the outstanding Ugo Ehiogu completely subduing Vialli, and Hughes closely marked and complaining constantly about the referee, Chelsea were continually frustrated until Leboeuf made his mark again. Two minutes over time at the end of the first half, Petrescu was off the field injured, only to come back on unmarked to collect a throw-in and weave a passage across the area until he crossed to the far post where Leboeuf's delicate touch was enough to beat Oakes. Suddenly Chelsea were in the ascendancy, but there was another scare when wing-back Fernando Nelson let fly from twenty yards and Hitchcock couldn't hold it and had to make a second save at the feet of Savo Milosevic. The giant Slav centre-forward couldn't believe it when his manager Brian Little hauled him off after sixty-eight minutes to replace him with Tommy Johnson. 'Why me?' was Milosevic's reaction as he turned away from Little and walked disconsolately down the tunnel.

A far post header by Hughes brought a good save, but the game inevitably ended in stalemate. Gullit's first real problem was to discover a more productive partnership between Vialli and Hughes in terms of goals. Significantly, Gullit changed his strategy after the interval. Johnsen, injured before the interval, came off and in his place Gullit boldly sent on Jody Morris whose confidence was growing game by game despite his tender years. Switching his team's formation from 3–5–2 to 4–4–2, Gullit encouragingly showed that, unlike his predecessor, he makes neither a fetish nor a panacea of tactics. Little, for his part, told his own team: 'It may be a compliment that the team said to be better than you at the system you're playing had to change their system.' Gullit explained that he forced Johnsen to suffer through the last eight minutes before making the tactical switch. 'He wanted to come off but he had to wait. I wanted to talk to the team first so I wanted to wait until half-time.' Whether Johnsen had been injured or not, Gullit planned the change. He felt it worked, that Chelsea then took control. Gullit took some consolation out of this result. 'Last season we were losing games like that. To come back and score showed that we can lift this team up in difficult situations.'

In the after-match press conference Ruud was too shrewd to be drawn into a row with the referee, Jeff Winter. Gullit laughed: 'I would like to say a lot of things, but I don't say anything.' Clearly, Gullit was upset by the lack of protection offered to Hughes. Gullit said: 'He controlled himself very well, but it was not easy. He's in a battle, everybody's in a battle, it was a typical English game but both teams did everything to make it attractive. I'd be more worried if we didn't create anything, but I know we can play much better than we did today. But the opposition are very good. We are still collecting points, and that is important.'

Ruud was asked again about a comeback date. 'I am asked that every time.' He was getting closer. 'I've had a lot of operations and I know exactly when my body is ready. I'm working very hard and when the moment comes that I can play I'll be happy.' Physio Mike Banks reported: 'He has been running well and working excellently in the gym and swimming pool. I'm very pleased with his progress. I'm hoping he'll rejoin training very soon. It's just as well because he'll never make a swimmer!'

The weekend tabloid speculation centred around Rix becoming Wenger's assistant when he arrived at Arsenal from Grampus Eight in Japan. Arsenal wanted Rix as Wenger's deputy when it became clear Houston was being chased by QPR and Leeds. Wenger knew Rix from their days together in French football but Rix wanted to stay at Stamford Bridge and work alongside Gullit. Rix said: 'I'm happy here. There's no point going anywhere else. The team is playing well and I'm happy to be working with Ruud.' Gullit laughed off Arsenal's approaches. He said: 'It's been a great source of jokes. We were going to have a picture taken in our new suits and I asked him if he wanted to be in the picture.' Rix was in the frame with Chelsea, and out of the picture with Arsenal. Gullit said: 'It's only his concern and he doesn't want to leave, so I don't even take it into consideration what is being said.'

The only Frenchman on Gullit's mind was his own. Leboeuf was again Chelsea's star performer and Gullit enthused: 'He played very well and got a goal. We are very happy with him! A friend who is a manager recommended Leboeuf. At first I went for Laurent Blanc, but the day after Barcelona came in. I called him again and I understood when he told me about Barcelona, so I had to change my tactics. I saw Leboeuf on video but it was difficult during the European championships because I could not get into the French training camp. I was just hoping no one would notice him.'

Leboeuf had plenty to Le Beef about after the Villa match. He accused the referee of letting potential leg-breaking tackles go unpunished. He moaned: 'I thought the rules of football were the same the world over but they're not, it seems, with this referee. Those rules say it is forbidden to tackle from behind because it is dangerous. But the referee seemed to forget that I am a defender and I can't accept this. It is not professional. He is very lucky to be refereeing in England. I talked to Luca Vialli. If the ref was doing what he did in France and Italy he would not be able to go out at night.' Leboeuf was also incensed by a kick on the head against Andy Myers. 'I told Villa's Dwight Yorke that the way things were going, we may as well play Australian rules. When I said something to the referee, he just smiled. When you play football in France and Italy there is a lot of acting among the players. They react like they are diving into a swimming pool. It does make it difficult because you don't need to touch a forward and he will jump and fall over and the referee will give a free kick. But that is not dangerous. You don't stand the risk of having a broken leg.'

The most bizarre episode involved 'Dirty' Diego Maradona. The Argentinian turned up in T-shirt and jeans and was denied access to the Directors' Box where four seats had been bought for him and his entourage at £250 a time. Then he was escorted to the Executive Club where hundreds of fans mobbed him. He tried to escape to the stairway where he crouched demanding to leave. Bates said: 'I didn't know anything about it until I was leaving the ground, but his sponsors Puma should have known about the dress code throughout the Premier League that collar, tie and jacket are worn in the Directors' Box. Diego turned up in casual attire and was taken down to the Executive Club. That's no snub, as our Executive Club is full of extremely rich members who prefer to be casually dressed. Unfortunately Diego was mobbed by fans seeking his autograph. All I can say is the time to start worrying is when you're not mobbed!' Maradona ordered a cab to escape from the fans.

Maradona and Gullit played in Serie A, and Gullit succeeded the Argentinian as the world's number one player. Maradona was in London to promote a street football campaign that was launched in Battersea that morning. He then went to the Bridge to see Gullit's team. At one point, it was announced over the tannoy that Maradona was present at the Bridge. Fortunately for Maradona he had already left – he was booed.

TUESDAY, SEPTEMBER 17
Ruud's backroom staff were in full swing, organising a signing and arranging press conferences. Chelsea signed Norway's first-choice international keeper Forde Grodas on loan from Lillestrom until the end of the year. Chelsea needed to bring in cover

with Kharine out. Grodas, aged thirty-one, had conceded only thirteen goals in twenty-five internationals. He added to the growing contingent of foreign talent. With Hitchcock taking Kharine's place, youngster Nick Colgan had been promoted to the bench.

On the domestic front, the prospect of Ruud and his boys in Blackpool was setting the old seaside town alight. Chairwoman Vicki Oyston had been excited from the moment the draw took place, as she explained: 'More importantly, it means Ruud Gullit's coming here. I used to have a life-sized cardboard cut-out of him in the kitchen at home. I picked it up from a sports shop in Thurrock. We're all so excited he's coming, it's pathetic.'

Sponsors Coca-Cola, always keen to whip up some interest in their competition, dispatched a huge red and black beach ball emblazoned with their name for the ideal publicity-seeking photocall with Di Matteo, Leboeuf and Petrescu only too eager to oblige. Pity there was no picture of Rix boarding the coach in shorts and dark glasses as if he was heading straight for the beach.

WEDNESDAY, SEPTEMBER 18
Blackpool 1 Chelsea 4
Ruud's touchline laugh-in was the star TV turn. Gullit was captured on the Sky 'live' transmission, repeated later on Carlton Sport, laughing his head off as Wise and Hughes both conspired to miss open goals in the same move at the end of his Cup debut as manager. The most laid-back boss in football was in fits when, with the game well and truly won, in injury time Hughes missed the chance of the match. Wise should have scored but as he fell he managed to poke the ball through a sea of legs to Hughes, who let the ball bounce off his shin. Hughes tumbled in a comical heap with keeper Steve Banks out of his goal as he tried to deal with Wise, who had also fallen over! Gullit pulled his tracksuit over his dreadlocks as if to say 'I can't watch this, it's too funny.'

Gullit said: 'I was pretty relaxed even when they scored so early because it helped us tune in better. The crowd got right behind Blackpool – it was spooky. But in the end we had a good laugh especially when Dennis Wise missed in the last minute. He had a fight with a football and fell over before Hughes missed.'

Ruud's first trip to Blackpool ended with a smile as wide as the golden mile. Blackpool's state of the ark stadium, with its crumbling corrugated roofs, had all the makings of another burial ground for the Premiership club with a grim history of being giantkilling victims. Nine times in the last sixteen years Chelsea had embarrassingly fallen to lowly opponents in the League Cup. But in the land of 'Squeeze Me Slowly' hats there was no way Gullit's gang would be fall guys.

It wasn't that funny, though, when Blackpool, assembled for barely £1.1m, rocked the Chelsea aristocrats with an opening goal after fifty-three seconds. Mark Bonner fed to Andy Preece and as he went tumbling in the box he was clearly seen to handle the ball twice as David Lee appealed for a penalty. But as Chelsea hesitated James Quinn cracked the ball into the bottom corner. Bloomfield Road exploded with nearly ten thousand fans shaking the whole ground by stamping on the dilapidated terracing.

The celebrations were cut short in the sixteenth minute when Chelsea unveiled a hero of their own in Jody Morris. In only his second senior game, the Chelsea kid showed electric pace to race on to an immaculate defence-splitting Di Matteo pass and clip the ball beyond keeper Banks. The game finally slipped away from Blackpool with the second half just one minute old. Chelsea were awarded a corner – the TV cameras proved the keeper did not touch the ball. Spencer eluded Ben Dixon and played short to Petrescu whose darting run across goal culminated in a shot into the far corner. Hughes was next to find his goal touch as he cracked a first-time shot into the corner, meeting a cross from substitute teenager Mark Nicholls. At last, Hughes was off the mark for the season.

Butler, Blackpool's biggest buy at £245,000, failed to cut out the cross as Hughes scored, and was in more distress in the seventy-first minute when he pulled down Hughes on a clear run at goal and was shown his second yellow card to be sent off. It hardly made a difference. Chelsea were far too hot and Blackpool surrendered the fourth as Spencer's accurate shot looked too easy. His unusual and extravagant bump of chests in a bizarre goal celebration with Morris brought even more smiles from the Chelsea bench in one of those laugh-a-minute nights that showed that Gullit was in total control.

But it wasn't all happiness for Ruud. He was outspoken in his after-match views on TV and to the written press. He was angered by Blackpool's tough tactics and called for a protection act for Hughes, victim of some bone-jarring tackles. Gullit said: 'I was pleased for Mark Hughes because he got his reward with his goal for staying calm. He was definitely kicked. He does not get the protection and then gets frustrated about it. You tell him to stay calm but it's difficult. I was pleased he did and he got his reward for keeping faith in his skills. We don't want any favouritism. We just want him to be protected a little bit more.' Hughes said: 'Maybe I'm mellowing a bit! I am going to get kicked about because of the role I play. But I have been a little bad-tempered with what's happened to me this season in some games. I have been a little hard done by. Perhaps it's my own fault because I've been moaning and groaning at referees for donkey's years. Maybe now they are getting their own back. It was hard out there. They had three big centre-backs and they made it difficult. I have been trying to stay calm. I should do that at my age. But now and again I lose my temper.'

Vialli was left behind in London to get himself into a superior physical condition, and, together with his fiancée, had a workout session in the evening at Holmes Place club in the Fulham Road, a quarter of a mile from Stamford Bridge.

Gullit shrewdly utilised his squad for a first-leg cup tie, with Johnson and Myers omitted, Leboeuf on the bench. A chance for Lee at the back, together with Duberry. With Clarke injured in the first half, there was a debut for Nicholls.

For the record books, ten different Chelsea players had already got on the score-sheet. Even though Spencer was among them, it was clear that the Scot had become disillusioned with his exile from the starting line-up. 'I'm going nowhere fast at the moment, but it seems like I'll be held to my contract.' Spencer had eighteen months left, but had been interesting Celtic. In contrast Burley was proud to establish himself as a regular. With that change of status he sought a pay rise.

THURSDAY, SEPTEMBER 19

Former top referee Clive Thomas backed Gullit's plea that players like Hughes be afforded more protection. Thomas said: 'Ruud is right to want something done. Referees are being brought in at the top level without enough experience. That is the root cause of the problem. Our referees are honest but are badly trained and badly managed.'

Hughes has been involved in many physical battles over the years. Thomas said:

'Say what you like about Hughes, but he does not cheat and he is not sneaky. He is always up front and out in the open. You have to stamp out the tackle from behind and the jersey-pulling, which has become part of our game. The problems at Blackpool should have been stamped out early on by giving the offending player a rollicking in front of Hughes. I think the message would have got through, but once again a referee's role has been brought into question. The Football Association has got to look at the whole subject because there is a breakdown at the moment between clubs and referees. I am concerned at how matches are being refereed and so should the FA be.'

FRIDAY, SEPTEMBER 20

Roy Evans set the tone for the showdown at table-topping Liverpool. Despite their going top for the first time under his command, Evans felt his unbeaten team had not been at their peak. But he hoped the visit of Gullit's purists would bring the best out of his multi-talented stars. He said: 'Chelsea have a similar philosophy to ours. They play the same system and play a possession game. I'm not at all surprised by Chelsea's form. They showed signs last year of what they are trying to do and have improved since then. From what I've seen of them so far they have gone past being dark horses to genuine title contenders. The three teams we've played at home so far have gone out to stop us. I'm sure Chelsea will try to do their own thing. It will be a game of possession and it will hinge on which team does best when they've got possession. It's certainly going to be a different game to what we've seen so far this season at Anfield. We've had to grind results out so far but I've been pleased with our patience and resilience. We know our football has not been brilliant and we haven't had good press reviews. But we know what we are capable of and we know we can improve.'

Gullit re-called Leboeuf and Vialli after resting them for the midweek win at Blackpool, while on-loan Grodas was on the beach with Kharine facing a second make-or-break knee operation that would force him out for the rest of the season. Specialists were not happy with his progress. The news stunned Gullit. 'Dimmi had one operation, now he needs another to see what is actually wrong. It shows how important it was we signed a keeper.' Grodas said: 'If I was honest I would say in my country we knew more about Liverpool than Chelsea – until Ruud arrived. I have played twenty-five matches for Norway, and am strong and big. I like pressure. I heard from Chelsea only a week ago and the plan is I am on loan – but things can change.'

Gullit's priority was to continue the unbeaten run. 'Surprisingly, I have never played at Liverpool, but with them also not losing so far it should be a good game. But we have improved. People say I played reserves in midweek, but I say we never have reserves at Chelsea, just squad players. You've got to have at least twenty to choose from. Everyone is playing well, as people saw at Blackpool. But Liverpool is a different test, it will show how far we have come.'

SATURDAY, SEPTEMBER 21

Liverpool 5 Chelsea 1

Gullit and his team dashed away from Anfield – they had a plane to catch. But it was feet firmly back on the ground for Chelsea.

The first taste of defeat in his managerial career was a bitter disappointment. And with it, Chelsea's proud unbeaten record came to an ignominious end. But it didn't prevent Ruud breezing into the after-match conference with a chirpy 'Everybody okay, can I help you?' He spoke for as long as he could answering all the awkward questions about his tactics and his players' performances, before the coach left Anfield for Manchester Airport and an early flight back to London.

From the moment they arrived at Anfield, Chelsea knew where they stood when they read the match day programme. 'Chelsea, founded in 1905 and a music hall joke for much of their existence...'

After some comical errors and self-inflicted wounds it was hard to disagree. Chelsea arrived with championship pretensions – and left as pretenders. Both Gullit and Evans were brutal in appraisal of their teams. Evans wasn't satisfied! Goodness knows how formidable Liverpool would be once they hit their peak. Evans explained: 'I was reasonably satisfied but we can do better, and I don't mean that in a flash sense.' For Chelsea, defeat brought the realisation to the club's supporters that the team must walk before it can run. Gullit said: 'The positive aspect is that everybody now knows where Chelsea are. It has been an exaggeration to suggest that we are going to battle for the title. I never said we would challenge for it. This team is very young, we have new players and it takes time to settle. You can see today why we have not settled, so perhaps this game came at the right moment. We now have to work very hard, but already this season we have shown some good stuff. But this game was not our game. We gave four goals away and that was a pity. We were too generous ... Santa Claus is later.'

Gullit changed tactics to deploy three forwards against Liverpool's three central defenders and in the opening ten minutes Liverpool were outclassed by Chelsea's slick passing movements. Gullit refused to be fazed when questioned about his tactics. 'The game plan was okay. We have to play these games in a different way. In other games we have given chances like these away and got away with them. This time we slipped back with individual mistakes and we must avoid these things.'

The game plan fell apart when Chelsea's defence was caught out by a Bjornebye cross to the far post after just fourteen minutes and unmarked Fowler plundered the opening goal with a devastating header.

Hughes, Chelsea's best player, almost took advantage of a Mark Wright error but his attempted lob was saved by David James. Gullit observed: 'We played some very good football and were near 1–1 with that lob by Mark Hughes, and we were pressing and pressing. But the second goal maybe broke something there.' When Morris was robbed by Dominic Matteo, Berger made no mistake with the second after forty-two minutes, and on the stroke of half-time Myers hopelessly headed past his own keeper when there was no danger from another Bjornebye cross.

Gullit dismantled the flat back four formation to revert to the tried and trusted three central defenders and wing-backs as he took off both Morris and Myers and sent on Spencer and Duberry. Myers had pain-killing injections before the game, and clearly it backfired. Within three minutes Wise was badly caught in possession by McManaman to allow Berger the luxury of grabbing his second. The fifth arrived after fifty-six minutes when a Barnes volley wickedly deflected off Leboeuf sending Hitchcock the wrong way. At least Chelsea showed some pride and Leboeuf scored his fourth goal of the season from the penalty spot five minutes from the end after Matteo fouled Hughes.

'We want two!' was the sarcastic, yet highly amusing, cry from the Chelsea fans. At least they had a sense of humour. They needed to. Liverpool supporters applauded them. But for Vialli the frustration got the better of him as he shouted 'F— off' at the coaches on the Liverpool bench. He received his first yellow card in English football from referee Steve Dunn and might even have been sent off after throwing the ball high in the air after another offside decision went against him. Earlier Hitchcock might have been shown the red card after upending Fowler a foot outside of the box. Vialli, booed throughout after over-elaborate 'dives', stomped off first at the final whistle. Gullit pushed him back by the chest, had a word with him before wrapping his arms around him, and led him back to the dressing room before any more confrontations with Evans and his coaching staff.

Hoddle might have discovered a key to England's future as he watched his old club destroyed by the new title favourites. It was a player with Italian ancestry that caught the new England manager's eye, but he wasn't one of the foreign stars recruited by his Stamford Bridge successor. Vialli and Di Matteo were swamped in their most humiliating defeat in English football as Dominic Matteo was a revelation in the centre of Liverpool's defence. Born in Dumfries with an Italian grandfather he had already committed himself to England's cause in a competitive under-21 match. Berger received a standing ovation when substituted late in the game, but it was the development of Matteo that interested Hoddle, and that was a forecast of Matteo's England call up five days later with Hoddle saying: 'He did extremely well against Vialli and Hughes.'

Leboeuf was nowhere near as effective in the orthodox English-style flat back four, the tactic Gullit deployed at the start for this game. Leboeuf said: 'I like to stay free. I think it's better for me to stay in three at the back and you know I like to give the long ball. I want to forget this game. I watch on my TV Moenchengladbach against Dortmund and it was the same game! Dortmund lost 5–1, and they are a very good team. They won the championship twice and I think Dortmund was great club. Maybe Chelsea is a great club and we can lose once – but only once like this.'

MONDAY, SEPTEMBER 23

Ruud was delighted with his fitness programme, and recovery from surgery. 'Before the second leg with Blackpool I had trained three times with the first team as a player. So I still have a long way to go. I feel okay mechanically, but it will take me time to get back physically, and it's hard, I tell you, it's very hard. I've had three training sessions, which have been good, but there is still a lot of work to do. We have a two-week break coming up and that means I will miss less games but it doesn't mean I'll be fit to play after it. I can't put a date on when I'll be back. It's very frustrating to watch games like that from the bench because you can't do anything. You can try to make changes as manager but that doesn't always work.'

Fitness and conditioning coach Ade Mafe drew two lines twenty yards apart, placed a ghetto blaster behind one of the lines, and pressed 'play'. Bleep. Off they set. They paced themselves perfectly, reaching the line as another bleep sounded. Back and forth, constantly, the bleep maintaining the steady rhythm of each length … until, suddenly the ghetto blaster announced a new level. The pace intensified; timing still remained intact.

Ruud attracted plenty of banter. Chief culprit … mischievous Dennis 'The Menace' Wise. 'Come on Yeti!' he yelled as the pace stepped up. 'Lovely, lovely lovely, lovely boyyyy!' Mocking Ruud's favourite phrase.

Some players were not laughing at the new hard-line regime, notably in the treatment room. A notice was pinned up at the training ground:

TREATMENT OF INJURIES
As from Monday 23 September 1996, and until further notice, the timetable for reporting and managing injuries/rehabilitation will change to the following schedule:

Report	9.30am	Train until	12.30pm
Report	1.45pm	Train until	3.00pm
Report	3.30pm	Train until	5.00pm.

Under no circumstances are times negotiable.
The club doctor, Mr Millington, will also be in attendance each Monday 12.00 noon to 2.00pm to oversee the long term injuries and to assess fresh injuries each week.

Mike Banks.

Gullit explained: 'There is a new harder regime in the treatment areas with Mike Banks. This is good. If you are injured you have to get fit. It's no good just coming in and going home. If you have an injury in the foot you must go training the upper body, go swimming. You must have the feeling of it not being pleasant to be injured. You must want to be fit again as soon as possible.'

Clarke observed: 'I was in there after Liverpool. Who wasn't? Everyone was there. Andy Myers, Dennis Wise, Dan Petrescu, Erland Johnsen, Frank Sinclair, Scott Minto, Gavin Peacock, Jakob Kjeldbjerg, Dmitri Kharine, Mark Stein. But not "Phelo", he'd been sent away to Lillishall. The new regime is designed to get people fit quicker. It's a long day and harder work. There's a lot of complaints from the players because of the longer time involved. It's a little bit different for those with long term injuries, they can become depressed doing the same routine day in day out. Maybe they're more likely to get time off, an hour earlier away here and there as you can't push a long term injury, you have to let treatment takes its course. It's the ones who pick up a knock on Saturday and want to be fit for the following Saturday who need to spend as long there as possible.'

It was soon recognised that players who reported at 9.30 had to wait until 11.00 as players training that day had preference early on rubbings, strappings etc. That took the physio's first hour. So, the physio revised the time. Clarke continued: 'The power of the players' union was put into action, and the players not training don't have to start now until 10.30. Common sense did prevail.' However, the players' appreciation of the new regime eventually hit home. Clarke again: 'In some ways I have to admit that all this new stuff is working. I did a circuit with Wisey and Erland. Ade was taking it. It was made even harder by the fact that the gaffer was sitting watching, laughing and taking the mick as we did our press-ups. But you can guess the results. After the first day of this Steve Clarke, Dan Petrescu and Scott Minto all returned to training. We couldn't take it any more.'

TUESDAY, SEPTEMBER 24
Ruud dismissed newspaper tittle-tattle that he had blasted his players after defeat at Liverpool. He never makes much of a fuss of those sort of stories. The article was based on comments from Gwyn Williams, who had said on Club Call the previous day that the manager had to 'dig a few people out'. Williams said: 'There was major disappointment. It was the reality of it all. We had been beaten badly and it could have been worse. One or two heads had gone down and Ruud said his piece. He dug a few people out and said what needed to be said. We know we've got to work hard

in training and put it right.' Gullit was actually getting worked up! It was clear from Ruud's demeanour as he approached Vialli, even before the Italian had left the field, that he was bitterly upset by most players' performances.

Gullit concentrated on building up morale, even though their next match was the second leg of a cup tie with a three-goal advantage that was theoretically already won. 'You saw during training that they want to get rid of it. We all want a good performance, especially after that setback. We have nothing to prove, but we must get back our shape and our focus on the game. I don't believe there will be a big crowd, but we need the crowd to support us. I only know what I want us to do, and I am happy with this team. One week you are not a bad team, a good team the next, and then a bad team.'

Gullit prepared a tribute to the Chelsea fans in his programme notes. 'Even though it was a difficult time you were still backing the team. Afterwards, the players talked about that and were very happy at your performance. You sent positive vibes, which in difficult moments can help us as a team and individuals as players. You can certainly help in bad moments, and we will be stronger to put things right as a result.'

Gullit planned a debut for Grodas. 'I have seen him when Norway have played Holland in a lot of games and now is an opportunity to see what he can do for us. He is on loan for three months, but it might be longer depending on the injury to Dimmi.' The knock-on effects of injuries had taken their toll, contributing to the extent of the Liverpool defeat, but Gullit stressed: 'I will not moan about that, it is not my style. I know what I have seen, I know what is wrong and I will correct it.'

At least, that was the Gullit game plan . . .

WEDNESDAY, SEPTEMBER 25

Chelsea 1 Blackpool 3 (Chelsea win 5–4 on aggregate)

'There can be no fooling around,' warned Ruud in his programme notes. 'If you have a certain standard you must always perform to it.' Worse than fooling around, this was sub-standard. Gullit tore into his players after they embarrassingly scraped into a third-round tie at Bolton. Gullit was furious and mystified by the lack of 'passion'. After the match he said: 'Class is not enough if you don't have any passion. We have enough quality, but we have to show we have passion too and combine it with the will to win. Blackpool could smell our lack of concentration and sensed they could do something better for themselves – that's exactly what they did. I felt so frustrated sitting on the bench because I wanted to go out there and change things, but I couldn't. In a game like that you never know what's going to happen. We did well in the end, but I'm not happy. You begin the game 4–1, not much crowd, don't have the same concentration as you have on a Saturday. I'm not surprised about the goals that we let in. I think it was our punishment for the lack of concentration.'

It started well enough. Gullit added: 'We passed the ball about well, missed one or two chances, should have been in front, they scored a good goal, but that's no excuse for the way we played. All of a sudden it was a difficult game. It was a difficult last twenty minutes, I can assure you. The crowd had a growl-up at the end and they were entitled to.' Gullit failed to get a positive reaction to defeat at Liverpool. He also discovered what every previous Blues boss has felt like in recent years. When the going gets rough – Chelsea don't get tough and fall victim to cup minnows. Fortunately it wasn't a humiliating cup knock-out.

Ruud was concerned that this dismal display lacked any professionalism; his star-studded side thought they could stroll through, but ended up walking right to the end of the plank and so nearly fell off.

Only a Spencer goal spared them from crashing out against a side that had not won in their four previous games. A Tony Ellis wonder goal breathed life into the seemingly dead tie when he fired Blackpool into a thirty-fifth-minute lead. Burley lost possession on the edge of the box and Ellis took full advantage, controlled the loose ball and drove left-footed into the top corner from twenty-five yards to leave no chance for debutante Grodas. He had not touched the ball before then and did not get near Ellis's power drive. Poor finishing let down sloppy Chelsea. Vialli was the first culprit when he lobbed over the bar, with only the keeper to beat, in the fourth minute. Spencer, in the side for Hughes who was a substitute, was guilty of the miss of the match. A sixteenth-minute Vialli shot bounced kindly to the Scot, who somehow managed to screw the ball wide from within four yards of an empty goal.

After the Ellis thunderbolt Blackpool sensed more blood and James Quinn cracked their second goal two minutes after the break. Leboeuf casually passed straight to Ellis, who put Quinn clear on goal but it still needed an excellent finish to beat Grodas. Spencer appeared to kill off the tie when he rounded Banks to score in the fifty-fifth minute, but still Megson's men refused to lie down. Ellis hit his second in the sixty-first minute after Quinn nodded down a Ben Dixon cross. Megson then made a triple substitution in search of a goal that would take the tie into extra time. At long last, Chelsea found the will to compete and Clarke could easily have scored in the closing minutes. But the damage was done by then and the poor 11,732 crowd wondered why they had bothered – apart from the vocal visiting fans.

FRIDAY, SEPTEMBER 27

Gullit, hurt and wounded as his side conceded eight goals in five terrible days, demanded a vast improvement. He warned: 'We must get back our pride. There were a lot of fingers pointed at each other this week and that was only right. Even now I can't understand what happened. I'll just put it down to the fact these situations occur in soccer. I've played for Milan when we suffered a similar fate. It proves a point, however, that you can't go into matches with sixty per cent concentration. It's got to be everything. I'm not the type of person who rants and raves because I know players are aware when they haven't played well. We've had a lot to talk about and I feel a lot better at the moment. I said at the beginning things like this might happen but it was a shock when it did. What we've got to do is make it up to ourselves, and the crowd. But I noticed something very special in training and it made me feel good at last. Everyone criticised each other and that was important. The fingers were pointed and that was also good. We spoke long and hard about what went wrong, although I was unhappy with certain unnecessary criticism about us. It was weird, every time Liverpool shot the ball seemed to go in the goal and it was the same with Blackpool. If you had seen the players in the dressing room after that match you would have noticed they realised enough was enough. They were very angry with themselves. Nottingham Forest will be a great test of pride for them. I couldn't shout at the players because you know your words get lost in the screaming. But what is the point anyway, it's best to talk sensibly. I only hope we'll learn by these errors and it will not happen again. But I'm confident there is no danger of that.'

Gullit was deeply upset at the degree of Chelsea's capitulation at Anfield, but was more concerned with the shock performance against Blackpool. 'I hope it happens only once. We don't talk too much of this game. We just go on now having learnt from it. We have had some tough games and we look well. I am happy with the way we have dealt with our one defeat. After the second leg with Blackpool I was much more frustrated with our attitude and performance than against Liverpool.'

SATURDAY, SEPTEMBER 28
Chelsea 1 Nottingham Forest 1

Some managers might go home and kick the cat. Not Ruud Gullit. A manager who attends a press conference in jeans does it his way. With a twinkle in his eye and a broad grin Ruud made it perfectly clear what he had in mind when after a week of undiluted frustration he said: 'I'll do something to keep my mind occupied and not think about this . . . you may guess what it is!' With gorgeous Estelle to escort around town you don't have to guess very hard!

Vialli might have scored four, Hughes at least a couple, but Chelsea missed glorious chance after chance and were caught by a wicked Jason Lee equaliser at least two minutes over time. After a week of setbacks, Gullit described Lee's goal as 'like a slap in the face'. Mark Crossley finished up Man of the Match. His best save came from a spectacular scissor kick by Hughes: the keeper got down to the foot of the post, pushing the ball away before Vialli could get to it.

Vialli cracked a thunderous shot against the underside of the bar before finally converting a low shot into the corner for only his third goal of the season. Gullit still had every confidence that the Vialli–Hughes combination would eventually strike gold. 'If they take their chances everybody will be happy. If they'd scored goals there would be nothing to say. But both played well and Vialli was there for his chance, they did everything they could, and they worked very hard. The chances are there and they will go in. I'm enjoying it as a manager, but it has been a difficult week. But we played well in this game so what can I say? It's different sitting there on the bench to playing. It's all there inside and you can't get rid of it.'

The big debate centred on whether Vialli could score enough goals to make the club serious championship contenders. Crossley was given one of his busiest afternoons, and said: 'I think they work superbly well together. They could be a forty-goal partnership, let's see what happens by the end of the season.'

But Vialli had to produce more; so, too, did Hughes. Leboeuf was top scorer with four, including two penalties. Hughes had only one goal, but he said: 'I've never been a prolific, twenty-five goals a season man. I got twenty-five in my first season at United, then defenders got wise. I'm certainly not worried about lack of goals. I know Vialli believes he should score more and I've no doubt that he eventually will.'

Lee was taken more seriously since cutting off the dreadlocks for which he was taunted so mercilessly on *Fantasy Football*. No longer the Pineapple Head, he had sharpened up his game. His lob over Hitchcock sent Forest away with a point they hardly deserved.

Frank Clark described a contest with Gullit's team as 'cerebral'. 'It's not like most Premier games, it's more low key and we've been working hard all week in trying to stop them from doing what they want to do. Their front two are not prolific, but they create a lot of chances for other players. Ruud might feel that in time they will start scoring enough goals. They are difficult to play against. They are such good players: they create for others, and you don't know where they are coming from.'

Gullit abandoned any post-mortem. He explained: 'There is nothing to blame my players for, they worked hard, it is just an anti-climax. We must just go on and it will pay off. There is a law in football that if you don't take those chances you get punished. For them, it was a big surprise they got a point. We have to forget it as quickly as possible. It was just so frustrating, but there is nothing you can do about it – it was a new feeling for me.'

Gullit shook his head in disbelief at the end, looking as though the job had finally got to him. But his demeanour changed very quickly. 'I've seen friends who made me smile after the game.' He was still smiling as he left the press room. 'At least you will have a nice weekend!'

SUNDAY, SEPTEMBER 29

Vialli was heading back to Italy and was thinking of not coming back according to a Sunday newspaper? True or false? The facts were that Vialli left the Bridge without stopping to say a word to waiting journalists. Unusual. But that hardly constituted a walk out. Rix said: 'Gianluca loves it here, and he's just had one of his best games. He doesn't feel fit, but he is getting sharper and stronger at the end of games. Ruud has given all the players time off until Wednesday, and Vialli will be returning on Tuesday night. He is adapting to the particular demands of the English game, not just the pace of it but the mentality of the teams and players.' At the same time Rix buried the persistent rumours that Hughes would be sold. 'Not at all,' said Rix, 'he's happy as well and if anything he is playing better this season than last. We are not selling him. Ruud thinks the world of him and that is showing in his play.'

OCTOBER

Farewell Matthew RIP

FRIDAY, OCTOBER 4

Interviewed on Channel 4's *TFI Friday* by Chris Evans. Fellow guest Dani Behr gave Ruud the big build-up...

'Now normally football managers equal thick coats and hoarse voices. How cool, then, when one turns up with dreadlocked hair, drop-dead nonchalance, and plays like a god. He is and always will be Ruud Gullit...'

Enter Ruud, dressed all in black with even a black V-neck T-shirt. Evans suggested that this managing lark wasn't as easy as it's cracked up to be after losing at Liverpool 5–1! 'No, it's not,' said Ruud, 'it is very different than I thought it would be.' Evans pointed out that it might be easier if he played. 'I'm busy trying to come back and I have to be careful what happens with the team.' Clips of Ruud in the dug-out at Anfield were shown as Evans told him that he was showing signs of stress. But the clips were taken from the Blackpool game. Naughty. And he was laughing! So, where's the stress? Evans playfully ticked off one of the backroom boys for the deception.

'Expectations are very high,' said Ruud, 'at the moment too high, but we're working very hard. Maybe other teams want to take the pressure off themselves and put it on Chelsea. But I am enjoying it. But I cannot do anything when I am sitting there.' Ruud completely refuted that he was in contention for the job with England. He shook his head about questions of how he has changed players' diets and training schedules. That was not the key issue. 'What I have done that is important is that the apprentices, the young boys, sit with the big boys and chat to each other. That builds team spirit.'

There was also a clip of Ruud singing with his reggae band Revelations Time. 'Oh no!' Ruud was embarrassed. Longer dreadlocks and what about that moustache? Ruud: 'You made a mistake, that was my older brother. He's now in New Zealand, he had a sheep farm there.'

Evans, who had been cutting up objects with a saw, spread dust all over himself, and nearly over Ruud. Evans asked: 'You never divulge how often, or not, you wash your hair.' Ruud: 'I wash my hair regularly. I have to.' Waving away the dust, he added: 'After this show for sure.' Hilarious TV. But there was actually another serious insight as Ruud said: 'I'm not as cool as everybody thinks I am. I am a very, very warm person.'

MONDAY, OCTOBER 7

A Channel Tunnel journey to Brussels then on to Antwerp to obtain the all-clear from the specialist who carried out his knee operation. Plenty of time for thought about the Chelsea team. The early season hype hit a rocky week with a touch of realism. A letter published in the *Daily Mirror* suggested Chelsea needed more teeth up front if they were to make an impression in the Premiership. The fans knew the deficiencies as well as the manager. The Vialli–Hughes partnership, while pleasing on the eye, produced insufficient goals.

TUESDAY, OCTOBER 8

Gullit shocked quite a few people who had been drooling over England's fabulous thrashing of the Dutch in the European Championships. Ruud gave Holland a vote of confidence despite their Euro '96 flop. In the build-up to Holland's World Cup campaign, he said: 'The players think what happened against England was just an accident and that if they had had to play another game against them they would have beaten them. That shows that they are very confident about themselves, which is good.'

Outspoken, controversial and unique when it came to handling frustrated players left out of the first team, Gullit symbolically shrugged his shoulders at mounting pressure from disillusioned Chelsea players. Up to ten of the squad Gullit inherited from Hoddle were considering their futures. His insistence on a twenty-man first-team squad and his brutal honesty off the pitch provoked a growing threat of a players' revolt. Peacock delivered an official transfer request, while Johnsen, Lee, Spencer, Minto, Stein and Rocastle were all concerned about their lack of first-team opportunities.

Johnsen was upset about his failure to win back his place after returning from injury, and critical comments in Norwegian papers leaked back into the national press in this country. Johnsen complained that he had been informed by Rix just before the kick off against Forest that he wouldn't be included. He said: 'I want an explanation of why I didn't play. Let's be sure about this, I will definitely want a meeting with Gullit. Obviously I must look at my situation when I am not selected, especially after the way Chelsea have played without me in the team.' Gullit preferred Duberry despite eight goals conceded in a week and another against Villa. Rix responded: 'Yes, I suppose he has a point! I understand how he feels. I like that – when a player is left out you want him to feel aggrieved, it shows he wants to play. But Ruud wants a strong squad and so there are bound to be people unhappy when they don't make the team. That's life.'

Johnsen knew the consequences of rocking the Gullit boat. He said: 'You are not allowed to moan at Chelsea, if you do, you get punished. John Spencer has been told that if he doesn't keep quiet, he will be training with the juniors for the next eighteen months.' Gullit made it clear to dissatisfied players that they are regarded as important squad players. But with sidelined stars, notably Gullit himself, on the verge of returning, there was going to be further disappointment ahead.

A number of the unsettled players blamed Gullit's inaccessibility as the cause of their problems. While Gullit had been concentrating on getting fit again, Rix and Williams handled the running of the club.

Reports that Spencer was about to leave after a training ground row with Gullit were dismissed by Williams. 'There has been no argument between John and Ruud. Naturally John is frustrated not to be playing more often but he knows there is competition for places.' Spencer said: 'I'm in the reserves when I want first-team football. When I was with Rangers I was in the reserves competing with big first-team names like Mo Johnston, Ally McCoist and Mark Hateley. I know being in the reserves at Chelsea doesn't help me with the international team. I'm not happy and come Christmas I will have to take a hard look at the situation. I've made only two starts this season and both were in the Coca-Cola Cup. No player is happy with reserve team football. It comes as a bit of a shock to go from the excitement of Euro '96 in the summer to playing in front of a couple of hundred people for the reserves on a Monday night.'

Spencer knew there was no point trying to knock down Gullit's door demanding a transfer. 'That doesn't do any good. I've got eighteen months of my contract left and I'll spend that time trying to get back into the team. Things can change very quickly in football. The team can have a couple of bad results or there can be a run of injuries and suddenly I'm back in. I've got no doubts that when I get back into the Chelsea team, I'll show the manager I'm good enough to stay in it. But it's obviously a problem for me – and if I don't get back into the first team it could harm my Scotland chances.' He was told that Celtic's Pierre van Hooydonk was linked with Chelsea, but Spencer added: 'That doesn't worry me. I know my own ability and that counts.'

Hughes, constantly linked with top clubs in the north, aired his views in the club programme. Speculation was fuelled by his family moving back north, but Hughes said: 'People are putting two and two together and making five all the time. I'm very happy here, I'm in one of the top sides in the country, so why would I want to leave? My family going back is nothing to do with my football. My son passed some exams a year early and we had the chance to get him settled to go to the school he'll be attending for the next few years. We don't want him changing again. And that is not anyone else's business.'

Minto was another who feared for his place. 'It's getting to the stage when I will have to ask some hard questions about where I stand here. It's no use everyone telling me how well I played – I'm willing to bet I won't be in the team for the next game. Both Andy Myers and Terry Phelan will be fit by then and I must get a run of games somehow. I don't want to burn my boats but will have to see what side Ruud picks against Leicester. There is no row or anything like that. I get on well with Ruud. Everybody does.' Lee had spoken to Gullit about his situation. Rarely on the bench and only once in the starting line-up, he said: 'I'm not happy and I'm not prepared to spend the next three years in the reserves. I realise you've got to have a big squad but I'm twenty-six now and reserve team football's no good to me. Don't get me wrong, I don't want to leave the club. I want to get back in the team. I haven't been given that chance so far.'

Duberry was looking forward to a chance with England under-21s, until the game fell victim to a bomb scare at Molineux. They eventually kicked off two hours late. Duberry recounted the scene in the dressing rooms. 'We were about to go out for the warm-up and Dave Sexton, who is Peter Taylor's assistant, said we weren't allowed to go. Everyone was wondering why, and then Ben Thatcher said it was a bomb. Everyone thought he was joking. We turned on the television in the dressing room, Sky were covering the game, and Richard Keys said it was a bomb. So we asked Peter Taylor and he said we had to wait ten minutes for the Army to come. Then we were told another fifteen minutes, and it kept going on like that. There was talk of the Poles wanting to play next day, but everyone wanted to play that night and get home. We got some biscuits and cake in 'cause everyone was getting hungry, and started playing head tennis, things like that, to keep active. We even watched *EastEnders*. We wanted to get in a McDonald's but they wouldn't let us do that. We knew the bomb was the other side of the ground, so there was nothing to worry about for ourselves. Dave Thompson of Liverpool was the funniest guy as we all messed about. Ben Thatcher was up to his normal pranks. So we knew they were going to defuse the bomb, and just kept watching the television until they did. And then we had zero minutes to warm up and kick off at ten o'clock.' It finished 0–0.

WEDNESDAY, OCTOBER 9

Footballers must be among the best customers in the cellular phone revolution. The pocket mobile is a godsend for worried managers when their players are far away on international duty. Petrescu was in Iceland with Romania where the weather was so bad there were fears that the game would be delayed twenty-four hours. Fortunately the match went ahead, Romania won 4–0, and Petrescu scored. Minutes after the final whistle the Chelsea star was on the mobile to confirm he was free from injury. Around the same time Di Matteo was dialling his mobile to report no injury worries after Italy's 1–0 win over Georgia in Perugia.

No doubt Chelsea had a deal with British Telecom! It didn't need a telephone call from Burley to say that he was okay after Scotland's match with Estonia.

Spencer was injured in the previous Scottish match in Latvia, while Duberry was hurt in the England under-21 game with Poland.

THURSDAY, OCTOBER 10

Ruud embarked on his first tentative steps towards a comeback, his first game for five months. It was by far the smallest crowd of the season at the Bridge, but the press box was packed for the Gullit Return. Ruud managed the first forty-five minutes of a specially arranged reserve team outing against Nottingham Forest. Although he came off at half-time, he insisted: 'My knee is fine. I have not played any football since the final game of last season in May so the plan was always for me only to play the first half. I have had a message and now I'll just have to wait and see whether there is any reaction tomorrow.' Although he was clearly short of match fitness, he still found the time and class to set up Chelsea's first goal with a superb defence-splitting pass to Stein. Stein and Phelan, both playing their first games of the season, were replaced at half-time as Rocastle and Newton also found the target in a 3–1 win. Transfer-listed Peacock, watched by QPR chief scout Steve Burtenshaw, was also withdrawn as a precautionary measure after taking a knock on his ankle.

FRIDAY, OCTOBER 11

Time to act. Gullit gathered his first-team squad together. He made it clear he was unhappy about the fitness problems among his players. He told them that too many players were on the treatment table instead of the training ground. He said that if a player was not fit enough to train then he would not be considered fit enough to play. There would be no exceptions and to underline the latest measure, Vialli was the first victim. The highest earner at the club was relegated to substitute.

It was the perfect riposte by Gullit to all moaners and rebels. Mark Nicholls, at nineteen, was selected to make his Premiership debut alongside Hughes in attack at Leicester. If ever there was a message for those whingeing players who had been protesting about their lack of first-team opportunity because of the Italian imports, then this was their answer. No favouritism. No one was exempt from Ruud's Rules, not even Vialli.

Vialli hadn't found a home and spent most of his spare time returning to Italy consulting specialists, anxious about his fitness. 'He's had a scan, and that has shown everything is all right, but it's what the player feels. The scan just proved there is no medical damage but if the player is still feeling it then he obviously cannot be right to play,' said Gullit.

Gullit wanted Vialli to play against a side he personally picked in a full-scale training ground workout. He was due to play for the 'Oranges', but ended up watching Hughes and Nicholls in action for the 'Greens'. Vialli trooped off and laid out cones and practised alone. 'Gianluca is injured, he has lost fitness,' said Gullit unconvincingly.

'So why is he in your squad?'

'He needs time. He looked fit? Yes, but not the fitness I require. He's in the squad and available but that doesn't necessarily mean he is fit.'

The Italian scored Chelsea's goal against Forest, and looked sharper, but not sharp enough to save him from being benched. Vialli admitted: 'In the last two games I've had ten chances, missed nine and scored only one. That's not good enough for Chelsea. I have to score more and if I do then we will win more matches. I mustn't be too angry with myself as it seems whenever I get a shot on target the goalkeeper makes an amazing save. But my time will come.'

Gullit had been stung by recent results. 'I have been happy with the chances we have created, but we also need a killer touch. I am happy being a coach, I am happy being a player, but it's hard being both. I want to continue being a player, but while I am out I need to look at things more closely. I was more animated in training today, I accept I was, but I needed to get things over to the players. Gianluca has found it difficult finding a house, but I understand he might have one in mind now. It's important you find the right one.'

Without a win in three games, discontent among the shadow squad was mounting. Gullit shrugged it off: 'I would be unhappy if they were happy not playing, but I don't want them moaning. I'm not surprised if they moan, but what they mustn't do is moan in public. Things like that only upset the fans and they turn against the player. If a player has a problem then they should go out on the pitch and show it. Things like this happen at clubs, and sometimes it is not the player who says them. It's perhaps others who are making it known they are available. I am a disciplinarian, but I won't tell you what I have done about it. It's a private matter.'

Newton was also back in the squad after breaking his leg. 'When it happened I did think I might not play again, but the club were superb, offering me a new contract straight away. It was heart-breaking because I thought I was playing well and might make England's Euro '96 squad. Now I've got to start all over again.' Newton played just one full game since declaring his fitness. 'I knew I was going to be all right when a young player clattered into me and I didn't feel anything. He had heard of me and wanted to make a name for himself.'

In North London another foreign coach prepared for his first Premiership match in charge at Arsenal, with a daunting trip to Blackburn. Arsène Wenger discussed the failure rate of foreign coaches, convinced he could be successful. The Frenchman said: 'There is, of course, Ruud Gullit at Chelsea, but his case is a bit special. He benefits from his aura as a player. I don't have that. In England they don't know me. Arsenal are taking a big chance. I can open the way for others if I succeed, but here it will be considerably harder to convince people than it was in Japan.'

SATURDAY, OCTOBER 12
Leicester City 1 Chelsea 3

Bates knew he was on his way to a significant fixture as he travelled by coach to the Midlands. 'This will be a test of whether we are going to be the same as under Glenn Hoddle or real contenders for honours.'

Gullit made two man-management and tactical decisions, and they both worked. First he decided to bring on Vialli for the second half, and also take off Wise and bring back Newton. It transformed the team. Vialli came off the subs' bench to destroy Leicester; then he shot down rumours that he's unhappy in England. Cult figure Vialli pledged himself to the club and aimed to show he had settled by stepping up his search for a permanent London pad. The extrovert Italian stressed: 'There are no problems between me and the club or Ruud – I'm very happy at Chelsea. My problem is trying to be fit. But I love to play football for Chelsea and I love to live in London. If someone writes or says some different thing then it's not true. There have been stories about me going back to Italy, but I've been in Italy for fifteen years, it's such a long time. Now I'm happier, I'm very happy here. I'm looking every day for my place but it's difficult because I'm hard to please. In Italy we have a different style. I don't know if it's better but I'm looking for an apartment with an Italian style. It's difficult, but I think in a week everything will be OK.'

While Luca had not yet found his 'des res', he was beginning to feel at home on the pitch. Gullit decided his recent hamstring trouble wouldn't last the whole ninety minutes, and it proved an inspirational move bringing on Vialli for the second half.

Within two minutes of his arrival Vialli held off marker Spencer Prior, turned on a sixpence and shot low to level Julian Watts's forty-third-minute opener. He then teased and tormented Leicester before opening up their defence with an exquisite pass with the outside of his right foot to send countryman Di Matteo clear for the second on sixty-four minutes. Finally, ten minutes from time Vialli set up Hughes for a neatly finished third, getting Chelsea back on course after three sticky results.

Vialli said: 'I was a bit disappointed not to start but I haven't trained much this week and I had to be careful because of hamstring trouble. Everyone likes to play from the start but that's not possible, since we have twenty-five players in our squad. The manager has to make the decisions and we have to respect them. The team always comes first, the player second – and I'm happy because the team won. But football is so strange. In the last two matches I've had ten chances and scored just one. Now one finish, one goal – football is unbelievable. It was a very good result because it means we can now start again and aim for that top position in the league.' Gullit added that Vialli had not been happy about being dropped: 'Gianluca was disappointed. But I expected that. I would be disappointed if he wasn't disappointed.' Equally, it had not been preordained that he would come on at the start of the second half.

Gullit made another brave decision in taking off Wise at half-time and replacing him with Newton – who sparkled in his first senior appearance after eight months. Gullit said: 'As a manager you have to do what's best for the team. It was a very difficult decision for me, but it's one I had to make and the result says it all. We missed Eddie last year. He's as important to us as Roy Keane is to Manchester United because he allows others to play. When I played for Holland we had Jan Wouters. Every team needs a player like Eddie.'

Consolidated in sixth place Chelsea laid the foundations for a push up the table with renewed confidence after Vialli's fourth goal and super second-half show. Leboeuf was impressive again at the back, along with Di Matteo, Myers and Clarke. The game ended Leicester's run of four straight league and Cup victories.

Leicester's own highly rated teenage striker, Emile Heskey, was left counting his bruises after a busy week. Three players were cautioned for fouls on the new England under-21 cap and Heskey admitted: 'Yes, I've got quite a few bruises. I'm getting more attention now, more or less two people are on me in every game. That's quite hard but I think I'm coping pretty well with it and it also allows the team more space elsewhere. It's all good experience for me and when you can watch players like Vialli, Mark Hughes and Alan Shearer you can really learn from them.'

MONDAY, OCTOBER 14
Fulham brought a side to Harlington and Gullit managed seventy minutes in his recovery programme. Phelan and Stein played the entire game. Thanks to the Fulham keeper they held on to a goalless draw.

TUESDAY, OCTOBER 15
Arsenal winger Glenn Helder implored Gullit to sign him and save his career. The Dutch international had failed to fully establish himself at Highbury since his £2m transfer and feared for his future under the new Gunners manager. 'I want to play for Ruud,' Helder insisted. 'He's a good manager and I love what he's done at Chelsea. I'd love him to give me a call and ask me to play for him. If he did, I'd go. I suppose I could also give him a call, but I haven't got his number.' Unfortunately, the call never came.

THURSDAY, OCTOBER 17
A third outing for Gullit to prove his fitness level as Chelsea travelled to Crystal Palace's training ground. Frank Sinclair played his first forty-five minutes.

FRIDAY, OCTOBER 18
Wise was dropped for the encounter with his former Wimbledon pals. As Vinnie Jones and the Crazy Gang prepared to get stuck into Chelsea's foreign stars, Gullit again displayed his ruthless streak. Just a week after leaving out Vialli, he made another controversial selection. Vialli was back for the starting line-up, with Wise feeling the sharpness of Gullit's axe. Wise was dragged off at half-time when Chelsea turned a 1–0 deficit into a 3–1 win at Leicester. Wise, in the programme notes for the Wimbledon match, wrote: 'Flippin' 'eck! I wasn't a happy bunny last week when I got pulled off at Leicester, I can tell you. But we're a big club now and everyone is likely to suffer a kick up the backside at some time. Luca was hoping to start but had to make do with a place on the bench, and he responded really well when he came on. I've got to do the same today if selected.' Well, he wasn't picked. And his reaction would have been stronger than 'flippin' 'eck'. Wise was stuck on the subs' bench for the first time this season.

Gullit was forthright. 'My job is to win games for Chelsea so I have to make decisions that are right for the club, not to make me popular. If I can't make those tough decisions then I am not the right man for the job.'

Ruud forgave Vinnie Jones for the 'foreign squealer' jibes in his first season in English football, and promised the Wimbledon tough guy one hell of a battle. Jones was fined £2,000 by the FA for his amazing verbal attack on Gullit after being sent off for fouling him at Stamford Bridge. Gullit laughed off the comments and said: 'Of course they didn't hurt me. I know Vinnie and off the pitch he is a nice guy.' The two men buried the hatchet in April when they met in Amsterdam while making an address to the Council of Europe.

With Wimbledon seeking their seventh straight win in the Premiership, Gullit was the unlikely leader of the Jones fan club. 'What I admire about Vinnie is the great influence he has on his team. He has great desire, shows the others how to battle and they follow him. Wimbledon's style is obvious and I admire their spirit. It's good for the Premier League to have a side so different to everyone else. Maybe in the past they had too much foul play, now they have more good players. But I'm not going to change my tactics. The English game is all about passion. It's important to have technique to finish the game off, but first you must show guts to win the battle.'

Newton started his first game since a collision with Hitchcock left him with a snapped tibia. 'I never worry about getting injured and if the tackle is to be made I'll go flying in.' Wise knew his former club would be on the prowl for a big upset at the Bridge. Again, in his programme notes, he wrote: 'Let's be honest, we haven't played that many good sides yet. Liverpool was one and that's our only defeat in the league. Arsenal were another but we played our best forty-five minutes of the season so far at Highbury. Yet we only got the draw. Middlesbrough were pretty good here. That was a very good performance in a well-balanced game. And Aston Villa are a strong side, and again we had to be happy with a draw. We've done okay so far, but now we need to step up a gear.'

A culture shock awaited Vialli as he encountered the awesome Jones. Hero and anti-hero. Face to face as highly paid columnists in a tabloid. They shared a drink in the old world surroundings of Vialli's Knightsbridge hotel, tucked away just behind Harrods. The Victorian actress and royal mistress Lillie Langtry used to entertain the future King Edward VII there. But they'd never seen the likes of Vinnie Jones before! 'Well it certainly beats the Watford Hilton,' said Vinnie, as he came bursting through the revolving doors in T-shirt and tracksuit bottoms. What did Gianluca know of 'Vinnie'? 'Dennis Wise has told me about him. Wisey says he loves him ... Vinnie is what we would call in Italy "Un Duro" – a hard man. He plays like Roy Keane with blood in his veins.' Did Luca know how many times Vinnie had been sent off? 'I read in the paper but I can't remember. I think nineteen ... or was it eighteen?' Jones: 'Just twelve – a nice round dozen.' Vialli: 'Not so bad, then.' Had Vialli been sent off? 'Of course – six or seven times. Three at Sampdoria, I think, three at Cremonese and once for the national side.'

It was going to be a physical battle. Vialli: 'I don't think of things like that. But Dennis has said they are the best team in England at set pieces. Sure, they don't have a fine style but they are solid. Sophisticated? I don't think so.'

When Vialli and Ravanelli arrived in England, Jones said they must have been laughing all the way to the bank. Jones said: 'They're still laughing. But these guys haven't had the big test. Wait for the wet Wednesday night in February at Sunderland and Southampton. At the moment it's lovely. In February they will be thinking "What the hell am I doing here?"'

SATURDAY, OCTOBER 19

Chelsea 2 Wimbledon 4

A comeback, a hug from arch-foe Jones before the start, and a crushing defeat. Some day.

It all started with a smile from Jones as he warmed up along the touchline. Ruud caught his eye and the lingering embrace was the first public 'all is forgiven' after the war of words from the previous season.

Despite Wimbledon's new-found success, it was still a touch of their old ways and attitudes towards foreign players that laid the foundations of this emphatic win. The opening goal was a combination of blocking the keeper from the Jones long throw and then the charge on the line with all the sophistication of the bulldozers behind the goal on the building site. Leboeuf was left with a memory of the day he first faced Wimbledon, a huge painful swelling on his temple, dubbed by Gullit Le Bump! It was also an eye opener for Vialli and Di Matteo.

The Crazy Gang felt Leboeuf qualified as one of those foreigners who 'fanny on the ball'. They sorted him out at the opening goal after just four minutes. The Chelsea defence made the mistake of allowing a specialist Jones long throw to bounce and Earle stole between both Hitchcock and the polished Leboeuf – both the ball and Frenchman landed up in the back of the net. After some time the groggy Leboeuf regained full consciousness with his left temple the size of a tennis ball and his vision blurred in his right eye. Swathed in bandages for the start of the second half, he threw them off in disgust by the time his error cost Chelsea a fourth goal and he was then booked by David Elleray for catching Jones in the guts. Not only Jones, but the entire Wimbledon team have plenty of that commodity.

By the time Gullit warmed up as the second half began, the damage had been done. The home fans paid homage to Ruud, and his emergence for the first time as both player and manager. His presence back as a player visibly lifted both the fans and his team. A disallowed goal, a well-struck shot pushed out, and two delightfully accurate crosses as Gullit patrolled the right, and then the left, flank set the pulses racing. But Wimbledon had the last laugh. Chelsea believed they ought to be pushing for the title. Instead it was Wimbledon!

Joe Kinnear was honest enough to admit that he didn't believe in his wildest dreams that Wimbledon would be in such lofty company. Nor did Gullit. As a master of the beautiful art of football Gullit was shocked that Wimbledon were ahead of his own multi-talented Foreign Legion. Politically correct Gullit stopped short of slagging off the Dons. Gullit said: 'They were excellent in the things they do. It's just frustrating that the better team can't win against them. If you're not a team who can pass the ball, then you don't play it that way, but it's not right to say bad things about them simply because they work hard. It's about details and if you're not alert and concentrating on the small details it makes it difficult for you. Wimbledon were excellent at those details, free kicks, throw-ins, and they worked their guts out every minute. But the key was that we couldn't handle their centre-forwards. They made it difficult for us and it put us in trouble.'

Should Elleray have allowed the opening goal? Gullit said: 'If the ref didn't give a foul I'm not going to complain.' Leboeuf certainly did complain. He did well to stay on the pitch. Gullit said: 'He decided to stay on and the doctor allowed it but he was clearly dizzy after a smack around the head.' Jones, naturally, had a different version. 'Some of the goalkeepers can't deal with it,' Jones said, 'and I see the big man Leboeuf in the zone and they try to keep him free, so I tried to throw it over his head, and I did.'

Joe Kinnear didn't even know if there was any bonus money to come from his club owner Sam Hammam for being in the top three! Kinnear said: 'We have a collective bonus for staying the Premiership. Top three! I've no idea. It's nice to be up there, it's better than being down at the bottom and we deserve it, we're there on merit. All I know is that we have a £500 win bonus, which must be the lowest in the league, but as all the players have individual contracts I don't know about bonuses for being in the top three. But now we've won seven on the trot Sam will have to get his hand in his pocket, and it's about time too.'

Gullit could hardly believe the 'ridiculous' goals Chelsea conceded. He asserted that 'they got the goals out of nothing'. After Hughes was held back, a free kick movement on the edge of the box set up a ninth-minute equaliser with Minto's drive finding the corner. But Hitchcock was deceived by Neil Ardley's long-range shot and Gullit was hoping it took a deflection for the keeper's sake. He went home with the video bulging out of his right-hand jacket pocket to find out for himself. Jones shouted at him: 'Shoot, shoot!' More in hope, perhaps, than expectation, Ardley did shoot, from more than thirty yards. Hitchcock dived into space.

As Kinnear accurately suggested, Efan Ekoku and Marcus Gayle terrorised Chelsea's defence. Gayle cracked a shot against the post after eighteen minutes and Ekoku might have scored but his chip was saved by Hitchcock. Kinnear said: 'We frighten the life out of most of the defenders in this league. Gayle? Two hundred grand up front and he looked like a giant. He's getting better.'

Chelsea fans marked Gullit's return with a standing ovation. Gullit and Spencer came on to rapturous applause, taking over from Minto and Burley. 'When Gullit came on,' Jones said, 'it was like the Zulu charge. There was players everywhere. I thought Charlie Cooke was going to come on, and Ray Wilkins.'

Immediately Gullit delivered a pinpoint cross to the far post and suddenly brought the ineffective Vialli to life; the ball just knocked off his bald head. Then Gayle collected a long ball in the sixty-fourth minute, turned and shot into the top corner to end any hopes of a Gullit-inspired revival. When a Gullit goal was disallowed in the seventy-fifth minute and Ekoku embarrassed Leboeuf four minutes later for the fourth, it was clearly not Chelsea's day.

Wise came on for the final ten minutes in place of Newton. 'To be honest,' Jones said, 'we were pleased that Wisey wasn't playing. It was a bit of a bonus for us. He's a terrific player. When he came on, he was dictating it.' But Gullit was unrepentant at leaving out Wise. 'You can reflect on the game and talk about Wise, but that wasn't the reason we lost.'

Vialli was brought down for a late penalty. He picked up the ball and dashed to the spot, usurping Leboeuf's job. But what an extraordinary penalty kick! A cheeky lob that Neil Sullivan caught, but it crossed the line by inches. A great deal of urgency getting the ball out of the net, but time had run out for any revival. One surging burst by Leboeuf culminating in a fierce shot from Gullit pushed out by the keeper was all that Chelsea could manage. Vialli was again the first to leave the field on another bitterly disappointing experience in English football.

Gullit did not turn on Wimbledon's style to look for any hard luck excuses. He said: 'We had seventy-five per cent of possession and they scored their goals out of nothing. The first I've never seen before and the second one you don't normally take. But I always say who wins is always right.' Little wonder Kinnear could hardly stop laughing. 'Someone asked me what Sam Hammam was doing on the track. He was saying: "For God's sake, Joe, tell them not to score any more goals: I can't afford the bonus!"'

Traditionally, rival managers share a drink and a chat after the match. Kinnear was stunned by Ruud's laid-back approach. 'I just couldn't believe it. I'd seen managers burying their heads, red-faced with worry and moaning. "Oh Joe, what am I going to do, you've got such a good team, but we're going down." We've just given Chelsea a beating but Ruud was sitting there with his feet up and I asked him "Why is it that all the managers are stressed out in defeat, apart from you?" I'll never forget what he said ... "I will go out tonight with my gorgeous girlfriend, we shall go to a wonderful restaurant, have a lovely meal, and then we shall make love ... and then on to the next game."'

SUNDAY, OCTOBER 20

The Italian press speculated that Gullit was about to raid Serie A again, planning a £5m double swoop for Inter Milan's Nicola Berti and Roma's Francesco Moriero. Who would go and who might arrive was a constant guessing game. Most of the speculation was way off the mark, but Gullit clearly wanted to improve his attack. Wise suffered a turbulent week, and Phelan was upset when he was not even among the substitutes against Wimbledon.

MONDAY, OCTOBER 21

Gullit's team faced Bolton in the Coca-Cola Cup, English football's leading scorers, thirty-one goals in thirteen league games. Colin Todd, so often linked with bids for Hughes, said: 'At this moment I don't think any side would relish coming to our ground. I always felt our two strikers, John McGinlay and Nathan Blake, would score goals this season and they were both called up by their countries for the last internationals, which is a testimony to them and the rest of the team. Chelsea are a cosmopolitan side packed with internationals but we move the ball as well as any team. It is a good test for us to pit our wits against them. Over the seasons we have tasted a lot of giant-killing success in the cups and we want to continue in that vein.' Newton knew Chelsea were in for a hard time at Bolton – because his friend Nathan Blake had told him so. The First Division's top scorer with ten goals, Blake was an apprentice alongside Newton at Chelsea but never played a first-team game and was released as a teenager to join Cardiff on a free transfer. He was reunited with Newton when the Chelsea man was on loan at Cardiff five years ago, and they remained close friends. Newton said: 'I spoke to Nathan last week and he told me that we are in for a hard time. Bolton are going great guns at the top of the First Division and are the leading scorers in the league. Nathan said they are a really good passing side, like us, and will make it tough for us. I can see what he means.' Newton had yet to complete ninety minutes in a game. 'I'm pleased that the boss rates me so high – it has done wonders for my confidence,' said Newton. 'I'm playing slightly out of my usual position as a holding midfielder, but that gives me the chance to get forward and have a go at goal.'

TUESDAY, OCTOBER 22

Bolton 2 Chelsea 1

Gullit's expression told the story in full. Shock, anger, frustration. All those emotions were clearly visible. A cup knock-out had not been on his impressive CV – until now.

Demolished by Wimbledon, crashing out to Bolton ... it was crisis point. It reached the stage for searching questions about whether or not this side were good enough for honours.

Gullit pulled no punches as he accused his players of 'silly' mistakes. Typically, Gullit also remained upbeat. He said: 'Fundamentally, there is nothing wrong with the team. We controlled the game and I was waiting for us to score the equaliser. I'm not happy about the way we give games away, especially when we've started well and are in control. If we were beaten by the better side I could have understood it. I think in the second half we did everything to win the game. But we conceded two goals at corner kicks. Until we start defending set pieces properly we're going nowhere. Sometimes you have one of those nights – tonight it wasn't our night. We gave silly goals out of nothing at Wimbledon and now it's corner kicks. That makes it silly again. The team worked hard but once again I must say we were punished by two corner kicks and that followed us through the whole game. We did everything we could.'

Hughes was devastated and claimed that the whole team should shoulder the blame. 'It's a big disappointment. Yet again we haven't defended at set pieces. It was the same thing against Wimbledon. And until we get it right we are always going to be up against it. But I'm not pointing fingers. We are all in this together. It's a team game and the blame has got to be taken collectively. But by giving away silly goals we're giving ourselves a mountain to climb in every game. We're falling down on our defending. You could see, though, why Bolton are top of their league. They work hard. But we all knew what to expect. We dominated in the second half without creating clear cut chances. If we don't sort ourselves out quickly, what should be a decent season is going to disappear. We have the players to be successful, but at this stage we are not doing it.'

Chelsea were added to the scalps of Liverpool, Everton, Aston Villa and Arsenal, as Todd said: 'Anybody coming here in a cup tie must fear us now. People always talk about the Wimbledon spirit. But what we have here in our dressing room is something special.'

Gullit's team fell to pieces. The first sucker punch came in the twenty-second minute when McGinlay stepped ahead of the Chelsea boss, playing his first full game of the season. Scott Sellars whipped in a wicked corner and McGinlay somehow nudged the ball home as Hitchcock went missing. As early as the forty-third minute Sellars was again the provider of a venomous corner which completely bamboozled Chelsea. This time Man of the Match Per Frandsen did the damage with a clever flick and there was Blake ghosting in at the far post to nod into the bottom corner.

Gullit missed Vialli, out with a hamstring, and Petrescu, who suffered a calf injury. Yet Chelsea had streaked into a second-minute lead. Minto embarked on a forty-yard run and just didn't stop until he finally ran out of breath on the edge of the area. There seemed nothing on, but somehow Minto found inspiration to scoop the ball with his right foot into the top corner as keeper Keith Branagan flapped his gloves in the cold night air.

Bolton's best effort at this stage was a shot by Frandsen which amazingly landed on the nearby Co-op store roof. There was even more potential trouble for Bolton when Spencer claimed that he had been brought down unfairly by Jimmy Phillips in the box, but to Todd's relief no spot kick was given.

Blake continually ripped apart Chelsea's back four. Leboeuf was unable to stamp his class and authority on the game. At times Chelsea's frustration boiled over with Sellars paying the price for nutmegging Wise. A split second later he got his own back with a cruel but crushing challenge from behind. Hughes was booked for a heavy foul on Michael Johansen with McGinlay pointing accusing fingers as tempers flared. In the dying minutes Clarke followed Hughes and Johnsen into the book for a clumsy foul on McGinlay.

Before that, Di Matteo saw a twenty-five yarder palmed away by Branagan. That was virtually Chelsea's last hope. Gullit, playing behind the front two of Hughes and Spencer, had struck the woodwork twice, and Wise, restored to midfield, was in control alongside Di Matteo. The final whistle brought celebrations both on and off the pitch from the Bolton contingent, but for Chelsea it was a long and thoughtful journey home.

Di Matteo admitted: 'My form is average – perhaps only so-so. I have had some good games, but could play better. The thing that would help most would be if the team could put together a run which would help everyone's confidence. But I have yet to show fans my best form. Why? I wish I knew. These things take time and maybe it will appear next week – who knows?' He had just paid out £300,000 for a luxury flat in Kensington – but he was far from happy with it! 'It's okay, but just that,' he moaned. 'I have discovered how expensive it is to live in London.'

Hitchcock, deep in the players' tunnel, offered words of hope even in defeat. 'We are all working really hard to win honours for this club. We're striving to go forward. The foundations have been laid at Stamford Bridge and now we have to put more belief in ourselves. We just have to work harder and keep searching for consistency. We have to be more professional in our play. But I have a message for the fans and that's "Yes, we can definitely win something for this club in the future." Ruud Gullit has been great for us. He came in against Bolton for his first game of the season and looked as though he had never been away. He's a winner. I'm a winner. We are all winners in the blue shirts of Chelsea. There are plenty of winners at this club.'

Final word with Gullit. 'Now we're out of this, maybe we can say that at least we will play less matches – that's the only positive thing I can think of.'

WEDNESDAY, OCTOBER 23

The Press Association sent out this 'news flash' to the national and provincial press: '03:31 Soccer Harding Snap ['snap' is PA jargon for the latest news item]: Chelsea vice-chairman Matthew Harding killed in helicopter crash.'

The shock of the tragedy first became apparent at 2am as the Chelsea team bus headed south from Burnden Park. Reporters telephoned Rix on his mobile. He informed Gullit. A clearly distressed Gullit said: 'It's strange when someone calls you and tells you about bad news. You don't know what you are being told is really the truth, so I didn't say anything to the players. The only one who knew was Dennis Wise because he was the captain. The management wanted to wait for everything to be confirmed.' Wise recalled: 'As we got off the coach at Harlington, Ruud told me what he had just heard. He said there had been a helicopter crash and he wasn't sure but Matthew Harding might have been in it. Well, you just feel shocked, don't you? I just hoped it wasn't him. I tried Teletext when I got home but there was nothing on there, so I went to bed hoping and praying it wasn't him. But in the morning the radio confirmed it was true. Theresa, our receptionist, phoned and told me not to go into training, it was called off. She said it wouldn't be right to be carrying on as usual in the circumstances, and anyway there were loads of press around and it would be impossible to do anything down there.'

During an emotionally charged press conference at Drakes restaurant at the Bridge starting at 4.30pm, after hours of coming to terms with the tragedy and piecing together the events of the previous night, Bates and Hutchinson looked at each other, perplexed, as Gullit tried to explain his 'strange' feelings. His voice breaking with emotion, Gullit said: 'It has been a strange week. I have felt strange in myself. I have felt depressed and have not slept for two nights. I could not work out why I had not slept the first night. Perhaps I now know. All this is so hard to take in.' Gullit's agent, Phil Smith, explained that Ruud had told him in a telephone call of 'a strange feeling the day before the match'. Smith explained: 'He said he had a strange feeling in the days before the match, then a strange feeling during the match. He believed the result was strange and he had had a bad feeling on the way back. He could not explain it. He was very upset.'

As Ruud stood alone, away from the press conference, he said: 'No, I don't think it was a premonition. No I don't think so. You know it has happened to me before when I was at Sampdoria; the president Paolo Montovani ...' The Godfather of Sampdoria died of heart failure after years of illness, and the shock waves were the same. Montovani's will left the club to his four sons and daughters, with his eldest son inheriting power within the board room.

Gullit was deeply moved as he paid his own tribute to Harding, who died at the age of just forty-two. 'He was a guy who wanted to be a player, he wanted to be one of us. He was more like a supporter than a director. His reaction if we won was more like a supporter. I've only known him for a short, short time but I will remember his laugh, his happiness after a game, his enthusiasm about the club, he was really a Chelsea fan and that is something I would like to treasure.'

Outside, the fans transformed the Bridge into a shrine.

The fans idolised a man they recognised as one of their own. They turned the blue gates that mark the entrance to the Bridge into a moving floral tribute. In their own way the ordinary people paid their respects. It was a touching sight. Dozens of bouquets, messages of love and devotion attached to shirts, scarves and even a tiny teddy bear. A nine-year-old supporter had pinned his beloved Chelsea shirt to the gate with his own message: 'RIP Matthew Harding'. Fittingly, the board named the North Stand after him, and from now on, just like the Shankly Gates, the entrance to the Bridge will forever be the Harding Gates. Bates said: 'You can see from the floral tributes that started coming in early this morning that he means such a great deal to the fans of this club. He was the same as any other supporter, it was just that he had a high profile. They identified with him.'

The mood was sombre as officials and players arrived for work. Fans shook their heads in disbelief as they walked past the stadium shortly after learning of Matthew's death. Supporter Nicky Nakrja, forty-two, summed up the feelings of many when he said: 'To us fans, Matthew Harding was like a godfather. He gave us hope and spirit in the team, which he built up with his money. The new stand that is being built is down to him, too. I'm so upset, it's really personal. He was a real Chelsea fan and would talk to anyone. It's such a tragedy as he was so young and had a lot of life ahead of him.' Thoughts at the Premiership club instantly turned to who else had been on the fatal flight. Reserve team player Neil Clement said: 'We're just worried who else may have been involved and we're trying to find out. We just can't believe it. Mr Harding has invested so much money and time in the club and this new stand is down to him. I'm just so shocked.' The building work continued on Chelsea's new stand. Doug Johnson, the stadium manager, said: 'Everyone working here is so sad and we have great sympathy for Mr Harding's family.' Con O'Grady, owner of the Imperial Arms in the King's Road, said: 'At the moment everyone is still in shock. The impact hasn't hit home yet. Everybody knew Matthew, from the smallest supporter to the big power people. They all knew him. It's going to be a rather sombre day for us.' The multi-millionaire would go to the Imperial before matches, wearing his Chelsea shirt, to meet friends for a Guinness. O'Grady said: 'He always came in before the game and had a drink with the boys, and he'd come back after the game with his girlfriend, Vicky, and sometimes his children and his father. They were all here last Saturday. Midweek he would often come here for lunch with Ken Bates or a journalist. We've had many board room battles fought here.' He heard the news of Matthew's death from one of his staff who had seen the report on Teletext. 'I turned on the TV and saw it on the news. They named Matthew as one of the victims, but I don't know who the others are. I'm just wondering if Vicky was with him.'

Supporters began arriving at the club's ground early in the morning to lay floral tributes at the gates and attach scarves. Hannah James, twenty-three, and Paul Diggins, twenty-nine, both wearing Chelsea shirts, brought flowers in the club's colours – blue, white and yellow. The note attached to them read: 'Chelsea will not be the same without you. Blue is the colour.' Ms James explained: 'Matthew Harding was this club. He built the team and the new stand. When we heard about his death this morning, we came straight round. We just wanted to do something as a tribute to him because he meant so much to the club and its supporters.' Another fan, Mark, tied his Chelsea scarf to another bunch of flowers and attached a note saying: 'You did the club proud, CFC supporter.' Brian Sargeant, fifty, who has supported Chelsea since he was a boy, said: 'It is such a great loss. He was a Chelsea fan through and through. It wasn't just the money he put into the club but it was also the fact that his heart was in it too. He gave our club respect and glamour. It would be a great idea if they had a memorial to him like naming the new stand after him.' Another supporter added: 'Matthew Harding was really popular with ordinary fans. It's such a sad day. He had the common touch as well as putting so much money into the club.'

Bates announced that the North Stand, built using part of Harding's £170m personal fortune, would be named after the vice-chairman. Bates said: 'We will build a world-class team and a world-class stadium and the board believe that Matthew Harding's memory will be best served by achieving these objectives.' Bates confided that 'somebody close to him' had informed the board that his greatest wish was for the North Stand to be named after him. It was to the North Stand that Harding retreated when Bates banned him from the board room when their row escalated to incredible heights. It was the North Stand that began the Harding story when he loaned the club £5m to build it. Bates said: 'It is fitting that the stand should be named after him. It was what he always wanted. It was a unanimous decision of the board that it will be called the Matthew Harding Stand in his memory and rec- ognition for what he has done for the club. Matthew Harding was the catalyst for rebuilding Stamford Bridge. His £5m was the seed capital that started it all.'

Bates explained the extent of Harding's financial commitment to his love of Chelsea. 'He had £15m in shares and guaranteed a new £5m loan for the next ten years.' Harding also negotiated a deal with the Royal Bank of Scotland for the ownership of Stamford Bridge, taking over its £16.5m debts for which he received an annual rent from the club. Bates added: 'In our board meeting it was clear that all the things he had promised have been done. His death does not and will not affect our future plans. The promise of financial commitment is in place and evidence of this is the South Stand complex under construction.' The £30m South Stand complex includes a 6,800-seater stand, 160-bedroom hotel, forty-six-apartment block of flats, four restaurants, megastore, Galleria, executive club and three floors of offices. Bates said: 'We have spent, or are spending, £46m on the ground and in three years £20m on players.' That is part of the Harding legacy.

The worlds of football, finance and politics mourned. Listed as Britain's eighty-ninth richest man, he was one of five people killed. The Eurocopter Twin Squirrel helicopter – used to ferry Tony Blair from the Labour conference in Blackpool – was heading for London when it crashed into a field in Middlewich, Cheshire. A Chelsea fan since the 'sixties, he became a director three years previously at the invitation of Bates, who recruited Harding through a chance conversation with a club employee who told the chairman she knew a very wealthy man who wanted to become involved at Stamford Bridge. Bates rang Harding and later invited him to join the board after a promise of £5m to rebuild the club's North Stand.

Tony Blair was one of the first to pay tribute and express his shock. Hoddle was also 'deeply shocked'. Harding's commitment to Chelsea was total. 'He could recount the names of every Chelsea team down the years, the goals they scored, who provided the pass,' his wife Ruth once recounted. He tagged his son Luke 'Greavsie' (after former Chelsea star Jimmy Greaves) and his £1m seven-bedroomed mansion in East Sussex inevitably included a miniature soccer pitch to go with the swimming pool.

Spencer spoke of the grief. 'It's an absolute tragedy – nobody can take it in. Everybody is devastated because we all knew Matthew and his family well. He was about the club all the time and was a Chelsea fanatic. He never missed a match and his wife and family attend most of them as well. Matthew knew all the players and used to ask us about our families. He was a fantastic fellow and to think he's passed away is unbelievable. He put a lot of money into the club but nobody is even thinking about that today. All our thoughts are with his family, who must be absolutely devastated.'

The news sent shares in Chelsea Village, the public company which owns Chelsea Football Club and in which he was a major backer, diving 9p to 80p. Harding's death raised serious questions about what would happen to his Chelsea stake, and the direction the club would take.

It was no surprise to those who knew him that Harding had hired a helicopter for the trip to Bolton. When the odds were stacked against his seeing a midweek fixture because he was attending to business two continents away, nobody pulled out the stops harder to be in the Directors Box before kick off. Harding was in Morocco sponsoring Richard Branson's abortive round-the-world balloon flight the day of Chelsea's FA Cup replay at Newcastle last January. On the spur of the moment, he summoned a private jet for the return trip to Tyneside. Cost: £27,000. He would never have forgiven himself had he missed that penalty shoot-out thriller.

Tributes to Matthew Harding came flooding forwards. Among the first was that of Glen Hoddle, a close friend who worked with him on the first stages of the rebuilding of Chelsea, who said: 'It is almost unbelievable that the game should lose somebody who had so much to offer, so young and in such circumstances.' Hoddle added that his thoughts were with Harding's family and friends. When Hoddle was offered the opportunity to succeed Venables, Harding unsuccessfully tried to persuade him not to take the England job. Even his powers of persuasion failed to work but Hoddle remained close. Hoddle added: 'Matthew was a friend of mine and he had made a considerable contribution to football and to Chelsea in particular. He still had a huge contribution to make in the future and it is a very big loss for us all.' FA chief executive Graham Kelly paid tribute on behalf of Lancaster Gate. 'Everybody at the Football Association is deeply shocked at the news of Matthew's death. Matthew had an infectious enthusiasm for football which touched everyone he met. He is a sad loss to the game he loved. Our deepest condolences go to his family and friends.' For the Chelsea fans, many of whom saw Harding as the knight in shining armour whose cash would bring the glory days back to Stamford Bridge, his death was also a savage blow.

While Harding's political backing for Labour had shown that red as well as blue was his colour, Chelsea fans from across the political spectrum spoke of their loss. Tony Banks, Labour MP for Newham North West and a fervent Chelsea supporter, said: 'It is terrible news. He was such a nice guy, warm and generous. He was a total Chelsea nut and a good friend of the Labour Party. Both the club and the party are going to miss this guy. He was larger than life. The impact of his loss is going to be very extensive across a range of areas; he was a successful businessman and a lot of people will have reason to mourn him.' From the Tory side, MP, radio presenter and Chelsea fan David Mellor said: 'It is a dreadful tragedy for all of us at the Bridge. Matthew was a major figure at the club. It puts the footballing side of things into perspective. He was a passionate Chelsea fan. He lived, ate, breathed and slept Chelsea. Although occasionally there was a controversial aspect to his relationship with Ken Bates, they had mostly got over their differences and were working together for the good of the club. He was a life-enhancing figure. He went down there on the Saturday and he'd be very cheery and convivial.'

Bolton manager Colin Todd, who watched the game with Harding, said: 'It's a terrible tragedy. Matthew was very well-respected in life. He was a great football supporter and he'd done an awful lot for the club. My heart just goes out to his family and the families of the others. It takes a bit of the gloss off our performance last night.' Wimbledon midfielder Vinnie Jones, a former Chelsea player, said he was 'chilled to the bone' at the news. Jones, in the Dons side which beat Chelsea the previous Saturday, said: 'He was a friend to all football players and supporters. It is absolutely frightening to think that such a young man with so much energy could die in this way. I heard about the crash this morning – and I just knew right away it was Matthew.' Jones revealed that the Wimbledon players used to enjoy banter with Harding when he visited their changing room before Chelsea games. 'The last time Chelsea played at Wimbledon he came into our changing room and shouted "Where's Jones?" I was on the treatment table and we had a bit of a crack and a wrestle. He was great fun. He used to enjoy coming into the changing room and having a laugh with the boys. He was such a warm man and his energy was infectious. He will be sadly missed by everybody.' Wimbledon owner Sam Hammam was one of those who went to Stamford Bridge to lay his floral tribute. The tribute read: 'A football tragedy, a Chelsea catastrophe. You were full of life. Goodbye my friend. Sam.' And Hammam added as he went into the ground: 'This was such a shock. This is a tragedy for Chelsea and for football in general.'

Chelsea's scheduled reserve game at Crystal Palace was cancelled as a mark of respect, while the first-team players were called and asked to stay at home.

Alan Sugar, whose Tottenham team were to play Chelsea at Stamford Bridge the following Saturday, said that Harding was a loss to the soccer industry as well as to Chelsea. The Spurs supremo paid his personal tribute to Harding. 'He was one of the new wave of men coming into football bringing into it big finance that was necessary to bolster a big club such as Chelsea. He will be a loss to the industry as well as to Chelsea.' On a more personal level, the Spurs chairman added: 'I've only met him a few times but he always struck me as a jovial character. One thing was always crystal clear, he was very passionate about his club. Outside of football he was a very charitable man. I know that because I met him on a number of occasions when he was raising money for charity. He was a family man and that must come as a terrible blow to them. In fact it's a shock to the whole football world and everybody else.'

I must say that I liked Matthew – even though I knew him very little and had reported a number of Bates's typically icy blasts against his board room adversary at the height of their squabble. Matthew spotted me in the corridor that separated the press room from the dressing room after one match the previous season. He strode up and shook me by the hand and said: 'I'd like to thank you for all your help!' He had all the other journalists in fits of laughter. I must admit I laughed too. He had a sense of fun. I admired him for that. Whatever his faults, he had blue blood in his veins, a true fan.

Although his greatest exposure came on the sports pages, reflecting his growing influence at ever-fashionable Chelsea FC, his fortune was based on a meteoric rise in business. His career was a remarkable story. He progressed from office junior to company chairman, accruing a £150m fortune by his early forties. He enjoyed a private education as a boarder at Abingdon School, Oxfordshire, emerging with ten O-levels and an A-level in Latin, which was followed by a brief career in merchant banks in the City. Family connections came into play when his father, a cargo underwriter, introduced him to Ted Benfield, who was starting up a reinsurance brokerage – Benfield, Lovick and Rees. The nineteen-year-old Harding was hired as the company's most junior employee. He swiftly mastered the business and by 1982 had a seat on the board. By 1988 he had organised a management buy-out, becoming chairman and renaming the new company Benfield Group. Of his passions – for Bob Dylan, Wagner, the writings of J. D. Salinger and Chelsea FC – Chelsea was the greatest.

With the money to do anything he wanted, he realised his biggest dream by investing in Chelsea FC and their Stamford Bridge home. When, in September, he pledged £1m to the Labour Party, he declared: 'I believe that Tony Blair is the best leader for our country and new Labour the best party to prepare our country for the future.' The irony was that John Major is a Chelsea fan. In a statement at the time, Harding said: 'It is unhealthy for our political life that one party should be supported by business and the other not. I have never believed that being wealthy means being Tory, and I think new Labour has a far greater understanding of the enterprise economy than many people in the Tory party do. I want to put something back into this country. I hope that with this personal donation I can show people that it is possible to get on and be wealthy, but still believe in the things I always believed in, and to help the party that wants all the people to get on and do well.'

His company thrived under his leadership. In 1995, it made a profit of £32m, with Harding paying his sixty-six staff £11m. Harding himself collected £3.2m in salary and £2.4m in dividends. Six years after he joined the Benfield board, he bought out

Mr Benfield, borrowing £160,000 to buy a thirty-two per cent stake, now worth £150m.

Rick Parry, chief executive of the Premier League, announced that clubs were asked to observe a minute's silence at the weekend's Premiership matches.

THURSDAY, OCTOBER 24

Chelsea's players, mourning the death of their beloved vice-chairman, kept their grief private as they arrived at the training ground. They drove straight into the Imperial College sports ground without speaking to reporters, photographers and camera crews. Gwyn Williams emerged to inform the media: 'This is private, there are no press allowed. We've got to work, we've got a big game on Saturday.' A handful of security guards manned the gates to make sure no one got inside. Among those arriving were Wise, who had a mobile phone to his ear as he turned into the grounds, and Gullit, almost immediately afterwards, looking grim-faced. Vialli was driven into the grounds, closely followed by his compatriot, Di Matteo. Hughes arrived by black taxi.

Before training Ruud addressed the players in a ten-minute talk. Minto painted a vivid picture: 'Everyone was very subdued. Ruud was the only person who spoke. He did not cry, but he got quite emotional. He said Matthew would have liked us to carry on. You can be as professional as you like, but when something like this happens, it is devastating. To say it doesn't affect you is a lie. Training was a release, but then you shower and it hits you again. It is going to be very awkward leading up to the Tottenham game. We're dedicating that match and the rest of the season to him. It would be lovely to win three points in front of the Matthew Harding stand. It still hasn't sunk in fully yet. It makes you realise how important health and happiness is.'

About 200 fans turned out. One of them, Mick McGeown, forty-four, was keeping a promise to take a neighbour's son, Marc Woodward, ten, to watch the players train. He said: 'Sometimes we have a chance to have a word with them inside, but that's not going to be the case today. That's up to the club, I quite understand. I am shattered. He was a great guy. He was a supporter, he drank in the pub with the fans. He was always happy to chat with anyone.' The civil servant, from Northolt, west London, has been watching Chelsea since 1968 and is a club member. 'Saturday's match against Spurs is going to be a very sad occasion,' he said. Later the fans were allowed in to watch the players train, but the press were asked to leave the entire area so the training session could be private.

David Beckham called Stamford Bridge to pass on his own 'thank you' to Harding personally. The switchboard was jammed, but the receptionists were surprised when the Manchester United and England star called. Hutchinson said: 'We have received calls from all over the world, and the club has been inundated with faxes. But the receptionist told me that David Beckham personally passed on his condolences to the club.' Leytonstone-born Beckham has close links with Chelsea – for a surprising reason. Hutchinson explained: 'His father is an engineer who has serviced a lot of our kitchen equipment in the summer, and young David had been there with him.'

FRIDAY, OCTOBER 25

Ruud's own suffering was related in a voice that barely rose above a whisper. 'I am not a Christian, not a Catholic, Methodist or Buddhist. But I believe in God. This week I needed him. I found a church near where I live and prayed. My thoughts at

Above A Chelsea legend in the making. Gullit heads Chelsea ahead against Manchester United in the 1996 F.A. Cup semi-final at Villa Park.

Below Just another face in the crowd. One of the last training sessions before Hoddle's departure in May.

Above A grim Gullit watches Chelsea's defeat at Liverpool, September 21.

Below Chelsea pay tribute to Matthew Harding before the Tottenham game, October 26. From left to right; Burley, Clarke, Phelan, Vialli, Gullit, Minto, Johnsen.

Above Di Matteo congratulates Duberry on his goal against Manchester United, November 2.

Right Tomorrow's man taking control.

Di Matteo's first goal of the season, against Middlesbrough, August 21.
From left to right; Johnsen, Leboeuf, Morris, Di Matteo, Wise, Petrescu.

Above Di Matteo scores against Leicester in the 5th round of the F.A. Cup, February 16.

Below Zola hands over the Evening Standard Player of the Month Award for February to Di Matteo.

Above left Gullit conducts from the sidelines before bringing himself on against Derby, March 1.

Above right A painful coda. Gullit in agony with his broken ankle, later in the same game.

Below Ken Bates (without the horns) at the F.A. Cup quarter-final against Portsmouth, March 9.

Above Vialli in action against Middlesborough, March 22.

Far left Celebrating Mark Hughes' goal against Portsmouth. Chelsea on their way to a 4-1 win.

Left Leboeuf cuts a certain dash, arriving at Chelsea for the Sunderland game, March 16.

Above Zola turns away in delight after playing his part in the 6-2 demolition of Sunderland.

Left Gullit at the training ground with his two children, April 4.

Right What more could a team ask? Chelsea supporters provide a riot of colour for their team in the F.A. Cup semi-final against Wimbledon, April 13.

Above left Zola standing tall against Wimbledon.

Above right And celebrating scoring Chelsea's second goal.

Below Wise and the rest of the team join in.

bove After celebrations on the pitch, Leboeuf partakes of a little liquid refreshment in the changing room.

Below At least Mark Hughes and Zola are prepared to use a cup.

Above May 17 1997, history in the making. After just 42 seconds Di Matteo lets fly, one second later the ball is in the net and Chelsea have scored the fastest goal in the history of the Cup Final at Wembley.

Below Zola and Wise celebrating.

Above The Season comes good for the Ruud Boys.　　　*Below* 'We're gonna make it a blue day'.

The first foreign manager to lead his side out in an F.A. Cup Final takes the prize.
Not bad after just one season in charge.

that time had no meaning at all, I needed to know more. I've done this before occasionally when I needed help. I believe God gave me a talent and I've asked why. This time I asked him other questions. God is everywhere. I never ask for what I will get. I prayed for Matthew's soul and I hoped someone would listen. What happened to him is part of life. We all know we are born to die, but it still comes as a dreadful shock. I've been through some very bad periods of my life, very bad, this is another one. Now we've got to carry on. For the fans, Matthew will live through the game. For me it's a different kind of emotion. I went for walks and eventually to church to work something out. I felt I needed it. I believe in God. I wanted him to help me. I've done it before and taken my kids, although they weren't keen. When I was young, I didn't believe in God. But the older you get, the more you understand about life. I have suffered many bad things in my life but when you have a belief in God, it helps you appreciate the good things. I suppose it's best in the long run that this game is played so everyone can reveal their suffering. It will be a very emotional occasion – a lot of people wanted the game postponed. I understand that, but we've all got to get our suffering out in the open. I wasn't keen at first, but I realise now it's the best thing otherwise it'll be the next game, or the one after that. To be honest, I really don't care about the result. I'm sure our supporters feel the same. It's the time we can show our personal grief. But I still think it's right for us to play this game. The match will enable everyone, the players, directors, staff and the fans, to express their emotions in memory of Matthew. Had it been postponed, we would still have found a situation with the game next week where it would have been the first since Matthew's death. So it's better we play now. It was something we discussed at the club and we all felt it was what Matthew would have wanted. Hopefully, we can go out and give a performance worthy of his memory but, to be honest, for once I don't see the result of a football game as important. What is important is for everyone to face up to what has happened and do what they feel is right, to express their emotions in the way they believe is appropriate. Only after this weekend can we start thinking about results again, although I know what Matthew's wish would be. He would have wanted us to go out and win the game. So that's what we must strive to do. The players know how they feel inside, they won't need me to make any speeches. Matthew used to come into our dressing room and say "let's win it". I hope we can do it for him. But really, it doesn't matter. It's only at times like this when you realise how lucky you are. It's been very difficult for us all to think about football in the past few days. And just because I am the manager it doesn't mean that I am unable to take a detached view.

'Three years ago when I was at Sampdoria, the president of the club, Paolo Montovani, died. He had been at the club for a very long time to the point where he was the club. The players were even required to carry the coffin. It took me and others some time to get over it all but the one thing my belief in God has taught me is that death is part of life. We're all born to die and in the end you have to face up to reality. I have told the players that but at the same time they must deal with the situation in the way each of them sees fit.'

Clarke said: 'The game will be secondary, it's certainly the most difficult I've ever prepared for. I think it is important we play so we can all have collective grief and start living again.' Spurs chairman Alan Sugar said: 'It is going to be a very difficult time for everybody under these tragic circumstances. I'm sure that based upon the respect demonstrated by our fans at White Hart Lane last Wednesday that they will once again react in the most gentlemanly and sporting manner during the minute's silence.' Sugar was delighted with the reaction of the Spurs fans during the minute's silence before the Coca-Cola Cup tie with Sunderland, anticipating the same reaction at the Bridge. Spurs full-back Clive Wilson, a Chelsea player for three years, said: 'It is sure to be an emotionally charged atmosphere. Matthew Harding was not like the average football director – he was a true fan and that's why the supporters all identified with him. He was Mr Chelsea. While we at Spurs were not affected by his death directly, you cannot help but feel sad because he was a true football person like all of us. But we have to put sentiment at the back of our minds and be professional about our approach.'

In such terrible circumstances, Gullit prepared to play his first full home game of the season. He welcomed back Vialli; Duberry returned to the centre of the defence where he partnered David Lee in place of the injured Leboeuf. Johnsen, Spencer and Burley were all axed.

Ruud's original programme notes were scrapped and in their place, he wrote: 'I don't want to talk about any football at all this week. I had a feeling that Matthew had a dream and he was really fired up on that dream. He was also a supporter who wanted to be first of all a supporter. Only secondly did he want to be one of the board. I think I can say on behalf of the team that Matthew was one of us. In many ways he was like one of the players. There was always a warm heart there for him and from him. But he was not the type that wanted to be in the locker room, nothing like that. He would rather have been in the North Stand cheering us on. It is always difficult to talk about things like this. The bad thing is that he started to build on his dream, but couldn't have the opportunity to see it come true. Everybody now at Chelsea, especially the players, wants to do everything to make Matthew's dream come true. We, as players, will I am sure remember him as the man who would be in the North Stand, cheering, shouting, singing. I know that all you supporters will remember him like that. A very nice person has passed away, but his spirit will always be a part of Chelsea. May God have your soul, Matthew. In peace.'

SATURDAY, OCTOBER 26
Chelsea 3 Spurs 1
They placed a symbolic pint of Guinness in the centre circle ... they all wanted to turn it into a trophy. The best tribute to Matthew Harding was to transform his dream of bringing silverware to Stamford Bridge into reality. Replace the pint of Guinness with the FA Cup, or even the championship. Gullit knew Harding's fantasy. 'He had a dream and the best way we can preserve his memory is by fulfilling that dream. He didn't say what that dream was. But we can only guess. If you have a dream, you don't talk about it, because it no longer becomes a dream. I can guess what that dream was and I hope to take the team close to that.'

An emotional Ruud organised a bonding of the players in the dressing room to help everyone cope with the trauma of the match. They gathered close in a circle and held hands, and then when skipper Dennis Wise, goalkeeper Kevin Hitchcock and defender Steve Clarke emerged from the tunnel holding the players' tribute, a giant wreath with the message 'Matthew RIP', they took it to where his personal fortune helped to build the North Stand, now dedicated to his name, and they stood in the goal mouth facing the fans occupying the Matthew Harding Stand. Gullit said: 'The most difficult part was that minute, the minute's silence ... it was so loud. That's when it really hits you. We joined hands in the dressing room and again when we stood for that minute's silence. It was so emotional the only way that everybody could cope with it was to bond together. By holding each other's hands it became one emotion, a shared emotion, and that was the way we could rid ourselves of it and get on with the match.' It was also an emotional moment for Ruud. 'I'm also human, I also have feelings, so it will be very difficult. I've been through a period like this before at Sampdoria, so I know how difficult it is. It is a period when people must have an opportunity also to express their feelings. As a manager, I want a good performance from everyone but I think everybody, in moments of grief, needs to express themself in their own way and their own time. I can't make demands on players, it would be egocentric to ask them to perform well.'

Wise, in a low voice, described the electricity within the dressing room. Not one of the game's most articulate, Dennis suddenly found himself discovering the appropriate words to vividly depict his innermost emotions. 'Ruud told us in the dressing room to form a circle and hold hands. It geed us up, it brought us all together, it was a very emotional experience. Yes, it really hit us during that minute's silence and we all held hands again, we all felt united. It was Clarke's and my idea to take the wreath close to the fans and face them. We didn't want to be just like any other minute's silence where you stand in the centre circle with black armbands. We owed the man a lot more than that. We wanted to take the wreath where the fans could see it and we wanted to face those people in the stand ... they were his people and we saw them looking down on Matthew and we all wanted to show him great respect. He was not just a normal director, he was part of Chelsea, he always has been and he always will be.'

Matthew's two seats in the Directors Box remained poignantly empty. Only blue and white flowers adorned the seats that would have been occupied by Matthew and his guest. And, the sign was up ... 'The Matthew Harding Stand'. Hutchinson said: 'At one stage we didn't think it possible but there was a firm where the people worked night and day to have the sign ready.' The cost was irrelevant. Hutchinson explained: 'Normal policy is to seek quotes for any type of work. Not this time. We never asked the price. It was not possible to place it at the top of the stand for the time being, so we shifted adverts to place in the centre. If the sign wasn't perfect, we shall have it re-made if necessary, but we wanted it in place in time.' Hutchinson worried that the match and the players would become a mere side event. 'The match day programme has been re-jigged, the sign was in place, Matthew's seats were covered with flowers, and there was a minute's silence, not just for Matthew but also for the others who died. But we had to say no when someone rang wanting to sponsor a military band to play Abide With Me. It was reaching the stage where it would have become difficult for the players; we have to be very mindful that they are only human and they have to go out and play. Matthew would not have wanted anything to have interfered with the game...'

As the fans, from both Spurs and Chelsea, filed in their thousands past the floral tributes that stood almost a foot deep at the entrance to the Bridge, there was an eerie atmosphere. Not a single soccer chant for more than an hour before the game. Gullit, who has put on public display all of his vulnerable innermost thoughts, paid his own tribute to Harding as no other footballer or manager could. He said: 'You think it over, how strange life is. You can think about that in church, but also at home. I had a feeling that I needed to go to church and I prayed for good health for myself and good health for my fellow human beings. I have a vision of life that it is strange, strange that life can change so dramatically from one day to another. It keeps you thinking. Everyone has their own dimensions, Matthew Harding in the business world, and football has its own world. Sometimes it seems like a world of glamour, but sometimes it can be a hard world. It makes you think "Hey, look how lucky we are." You realise sometimes that you are doing something that is nice to do and that can be the case with every professional.'

The game didn't really matter, just the result, and Gerry Francis's team could feel the force of an inevitable Chelsea win. That's why Francis wanted the game postponed, and his club approached Chelsea with the offer to postpone the fixture. He said: 'This is a game I'll remember, not with any happy memories. Whoever came here in these circumstances would have found it difficult. Perhaps football is not the right thing to be talking about. You could feel the emotion throughout the ground. It was a sad day for a lot of people.' But Gullit had no doubt the game had to go on. 'Everybody would still have the same feelings when we would first play our game. There was no point in waiting a week. It was better to play immediately; it was right to do that. Everybody in the stadium participated in a special feeling, even the Tottenham supporters. I want to thank them, also. There were special vibes throughout the whole place, even people not playing felt it. Everybody is just happy the way we played, nothing to do with the three points, just that we won for him.'

On the touchline Rix wept as he was consoled by Mafe during the minute's silence. The game seemed superfluous to the proceedings. But there was a game. It was a vital result for Chelsea.

Hoddle paid his respects to his old friend and witnessed a vision of England's defensive future. Campbell and Duberry were in opposition; one day they might be partners in an England back line. Campbell was ahead in the race for a World Cup place having earlier been called up.

Di Matteo ensured a fitting tribute to Harding's memory with the third, decisive goal. The Italian connection finally clicked in the eighty-second minute when Vialli slid a precision low cross into Di Matteo's path and the finish was perfect. Di Matteo said: 'My understanding with Vialli is getting better and better. When foreign players came to Italy it took them at least four months to adapt and it's clearly taking time for us here. But having Gullit playing, we can feel his presence, it's important to have him in midfield. The atmosphere in the past few days has been quite heavy, not only within the team but you feel everybody around you is in a sad mood. I'm delighted about the outcome, particularly pleased we could offer this as a tribute to Matthew. But it is more important that we keep on doing this for him and for the club. It was a very important goal for me because it settled the game but I must point out that Tottenham never really had many chances. We have been vulnerable at throw-ins, but the defence played exceptionally well, particularly as we were missing Leboeuf.'

Man of the Match Gullit opened the scoring only for his defence to fall victim to a Wimbledon-style long throw with Hitchcock receiving some wicked verbal criticism from the player-boss after flapping at the first attack and then again at Chris Armstrong's header. Lee restored the lead from the penalty spot after a trip on Petrescu by Campbell. A touch of Gullit magic, scintillating one-touch passes from Hughes and Vialli, a curling cross from Hughes, Minto's shot struck the bar – how did Hughes miss the open goal? With Gullit tiring and then Lee carried off with a broken leg, that wasted chance might have proved costly until Di Matteo struck just eight minutes from the end. Chelsea recovered from a slide to emerge five points behind the leaders.

Gullit came to English football accused in some quarters of being one of many of the foreign mercenaries. He dispelled that illusion after just one season of breath-taking skills, and in his first start back in the Premiership after injury he scored the opening goal and talked about his affinity with Chelsea. 'I was pleased to score. It was good to be busy all the time during the ninety minutes. Yeah, I think I am closer to the club. If you don't have feelings for a club you can be more distant from what happened. But it struck me so much. It hasn't changed me, because I knew what was coming having experienced it when the president died at Sampdoria. We have dedicated this victory to Matthew in style, the perfect tribute. Matthew Harding realised he was a lucky man, realised he had made a lot of money, but he never wanted to show it; he was one of the boys who wanted to have fun like anybody else, that's what people admired in him. After every game, whether we had won or lost, he was like a fan, emotionally involved; that is the memory I will hold of the man.' Who thought of the pint of Guinness? 'There were so many ideas, so many thoughts, but there are things you can do and things the FA wouldn't let you do. This was one of the ways we could do something.'

Gullit was so drained by the emotional experience that he could only last for seventy-four minutes. He limped off and had a bag of ice strapped to his troublesome right knee. But he said: 'No problem with the knee. I was just tired. I have played two matches in a week and it was better that I came off. But on a day like this the difficulty is how to cope with all your emotions. Everybody was exhausted, not just physically but mentally as well. You can't talk about tactics, just their strengths and how they score. All you can do is ask your players to give whatever they have. Everybody gave more than they had, and that was important. I have to forget my goal because we have to go on, and we hope to go on like this, and if we can to the end I will be very pleased.'

No predictions about winning trophies from Ruud, but his skipper said: 'Winning the FA Cup, or something like that, would be the ideal dedication to Matthew Harding. We can't rule out the title when we're only five points behind and we certainly showed more passion in this game, because we knew we had to win it, it was as simple as that. Now we have to show that kind of passion in every game.'

If Matthew was looking down on his beloved Bridge he would have been happy with what unfolded on this unforgettable day. The players said it all with the wreath . . . Matthew RIP.

MONDAY, OCTOBER 28

Ken Bates appeared on TV informing supporters that the club's future was 'totally assured'. He made it clear that Gullit's future was not in doubt, either. Bates insisted he would sanction more money for new signings to strengthen Gullit's team. 'We have the money to get them but that is not the problem. We are now looking only for world-class players and, of course, their clubs are reluctant to let them go.'

The chairman ridiculed newspaper claims that Gullit would switch to Ajax alongside Johan Cruyff when coach Louis van Gaal left at the end of the season. Considering Gullit's past conflict with Ajax and their stars, such a suggestion seemed ridiculous. Bates said: 'I'm not even going to deny stories about Ruud Gullit leaving this club because that would give them credibility. Ruud has a three-year contract and he's staying here. I regard suggestions to the contrary as part of a malicious rumour-mongering campaign coming from people with a hidden agenda.'

And the future of the club? 'The club is well financed, the development is continuing and we have no financial problems,' Bates told Carlton Television's *London Tonight* following what he described as 'ill-informed, somewhat ghoulish, press speculation' that Harding had left his fortune in trust to the Benfield Group, for dispersal at their discretion. Bates declared: 'I am aware of the contents of Matthew's will. It is totally supportive of Chelsea and it asks his executors to do all that they may need to do to help us. But, without diminishing Matthew's contribution in any way, I should point out that we are already ahead of schedule in our rebuilding at Chelsea. We have spent over £66m in completed works and contracts since 1992 and Matthew's valuable contribution is £15m. That means we have raised over £50m from other sources, including our own cash generation. That puts it in perspective. We do have other loans, we do have other shareholders and we are continuing to talk to other people who want to be part of the Chelsea story. I'm very sorry that Matthew will not be here to see it, but if he is looking down from above he will have the satisfaction of seeing it completed.' Bates laid plans for a ten-storey hotel and appartments at the Bridge as part of a £25m redevelopment. The first part of a package of five projects, Chelsea's new South Stand will house 6,500 fans and include a 2,500-capacity Family Centre. Harding engaged in a famous falling-out with Bates about how Chelsea's finances were being channelled. Harding wanted to see more of the money spent on strengthening the team. An uneasy peace was agreed. Bates said: 'There has been speculation over the last few days over the chairmanship of Chelsea Village plc, but under the articles of association of the company it is for the directors to elect the chairman. I have the unanimous support of the rest of the board to complete what I want to do.'

THURSDAY, OCTOBER 31

Among early mourners to arrive at Matthew's funeral were Labour's deputy leader John Prescott, Hoddle, Bates and Gullit. Dark storm clouds hung over the picturesque thirteenth century St Margaret's Church in Ditchling, the tiny East Sussex village where he lived, reflecting the sombre mood of the 100-strong congregation. The light oak coffin was brought to the church an hour before the service, but the five pallbearers were delayed for a few minutes as the doors could not be opened. The two women in his life were united in grief. Estranged wife Ruth and girlfriend Vicky Jaramillo came together for the first time at the service. But they did not sit together or speak to one another, and Vicky slipped away from the church in tears minutes before the service ended, leaving widow Ruth, her four children and Harding's father Paul to accompany his coffin to the cremation. Miss Jaramillo, wearing a black double-breasted jacket, arrived at the church twenty minutes before the service began, supported by Harding's best friend Peter Wood, the founder of the Direct Line insurance group. Mrs Harding and her four children arrived moments before the twenty-five-minute service began. Dressed in a blue and black checked suit, Mrs Harding clutched eleven-year-old twins Patrick and Joel for comfort. Their faces, like those of daughter Hannah, eighteen, and son Luke, fourteen, were drawn with sorrow. After a twenty-year marriage, Harding moved out of the family home in Ditchling that summer to live with lover of four years Vicky and their child Ella, two, in Wimbledon, south-west London.

His love of the London club was much in evidence, with the blue and white wreath first displayed at Chelsea's match against Tottenham placed outside the church and the coffin draped in the club's colours. It was suggested Harding's ashes were to be scattered at Stamford Bridge.

NOVEMBER

Benvenuto Zola . . . 'He's fat, he's bald, he's always got a cold, Vi-ah-lli, Vi-ah-lli!'

FRIDAY, NOVEMBER 1

Devastated, Ruud left himself out of the game at Old Trafford feeling physically and emotionally drained. He was still affected. 'I am glad it is all over,' Gullit admitted. 'I feel better after doing these things but Matthew will always be in my memory.' He missed training to attend Harding's funeral and had already made the decision by then not to play against Manchester United. 'The team played very well against Tottenham but I didn't put any pressure on the players because of the circumstances surrounding that game. We've built on that performance in training this week and now we're going to Old Trafford with the attention on United. They have something to prove to their supporters and will want to do better than they did in midweek.'

SATURDAY, NOVEMBER 2

Manchester United 1 Chelsea 2

Gullit masterminded Manchester United's first Premiership defeat at Old Trafford for two years, stretching back over thirty-five matches. The atmosphere was electric, particularly for the handful of Chelsea fans able to get tickets for the restricted away support allowed at Old Trafford. The home fans were stunned into silence. Ruud stood at the entrance to the tunnel to congratulate each and every player before they left the field. Ruud's replacement, Burley, was outstanding and only Hughes's superlative performance and a wonder goal by Vialli robbed him of the Man of the Match nomination.

Manchester United, considered almost unbeatable, had been trounced *four* times on the trot, conceding *fourteen* goals. David Mellor, at the start of his 6.06 radio show, made no secret of the fact that he was 'ecstatic'.

Three successive Premiership defeats and thirteen goals conceded to Newcastle, Southampton and Chelsea. Sandwiched in between that the Fenerbahce embarrassment. And what happened to Cantona? From the moment he took a fresh air swipe, missing the ball, when he overhit a pass out of play, you could see it wasn't going to be a good day. Frustrated. Angry. Near to boiling point with three successive Premiership bookings. His latest came after a collision with Duberry, the Chelsea defender complaining he'd been head butted in the 'unmentionables'.

Wise, with his track record, was an obvious candidate to judge an X-rated character like Cantona. 'He's not losing it. Mark my words. All he's guilty of is being a winner. He got frustrated against us because United were losing 2–0.'

Leboeuf was on the receiving end of a few French expletives from his fellow countryman and calmed Cantona down after the confrontation with Duberry. Leboeuf said: 'I spoke with Eric on the pitch because I had a problem with Ole Gunnar Solskjaer. I said a bad word to him because he kicked me on my knee. Eric told me to stop. I said OK. No problem. You don't argue with Eric. I have played against him once, played with him once in the national team and we were born in the same town. But I don't really know him that well. All I can say is that English people must have forgotten that he was a big, big man last year. He played very well when he came back and I think he will be better after Christmas. It's not only Cantona, though. It's not just about him. Maybe you should look at the whole team.'

Leboeuf was grateful to Cantona for raising the profile of French players in English football. 'I am only in England because Eric Cantona has played so well. A lot of managers are now interested in French football because of him. Eric isn't as big a star in France as he is here. I have the same problem. But, like me, he loves being in England. I love living in London and the only thing I can now ask is health for my family and myself. There is no passion in French football, just spectators. Going to a football match is like going to the theatre. When you're a defender nobody applauds you when you make a tackle or a good pass. They are only interested in goals. After eight years in the French league, playing in front of 10,000 people is not my dream any longer. It is playing for Chelsea against Manchester United with 55,000 there. I want to be in the limelight and playing with such great emotion all the time. That is why I like English football so much.'

Wise revealed Gullit's game plan was simple: stop Cantona. 'The only way to stop Manchester United is to stop Eric Cantona. We played tighter and we didn't give him time on the ball. We managed to push him deeper into midfield. But we had a game plan for the whole team as well. We saw what happened to them during the week and we decided to sit back, take all the pressure, soak it up and just play our football. The initiative was with United and we expected them to come flying at us. We just passed the ball better and played better than them.'

Duberry and Vialli did the damage with the goals but huge praise was heaped on Wise and Hughes for outstanding performances. Hughes's he-man show, shrugging off anyone who dared to wrestle with him for the ball, highlighted just what kind of player United were missing. But Wise predicted that wasn't the end of United in the title stakes. 'This defeat means nothing. They were twelve points behind Newcastle last year and that meant nothing then. OK, they have had a little hiccup but I'm sure they will get over it. Simple as that. Everyone goes through this kind of stage and they would rather it happened now than at the end of the season. I didn't really see a lack of confidence out there.'

Ferguson axed Jordi Cruyff and Karel Poborsky in favour of Paul Scholes and young Norwegian Ole Solskjaer. Poborsky, however, made a late entry in place of Scholes, his volley deflecting off May in the eighty-first minute to provide a flurry at the end more in hope than expectation. By then Chelsea's cultured passing game had put the champions firmly in their place.

From a Wise corner, Duberry's towering header squeezed past a shattered Schmeichel on the half hour. When Leboeuf launched a pinpoint sixty-yard pass, Vialli timed his run to perfection to beat the offside trap, and his finesse in beating Schmeichel, a precise shot through the Dane's legs, was even more embarrassment for the keeper than in previous games. Was Vialli mocking the stricken keeper? Di Matteo suggested not. 'It wasn't aimed at Schmeichel, he was saying to Frank "It's your goal, it's your goal."' Di Matteo added: 'I think, when you win a game at Man. United, the whole team has to play well. So maybe some players played better than others, but the whole team played well.'

Gullit was kept waiting as Ferguson held his press conference and then politely passed on his regrets that he had to rush off with his team to catch the 7pm Manchester shuttle back to London. He stopped briefly for a chat to Club Call to agree that that 'was the best performance of the season' and he praised Duberry: 'That was a great header. It's difficult to head the ball when there is a crowd like that.' What about that Vialli goal? 'I said to him he had to be patient and it will come. And it did.'

Vialli's best goal in English football created frenzy back in Italy. He was still on the coach crawling away from Old Trafford to Manchester Airport when his mobile was rung by *Gazzetta dello Sport*'s Sloane Square-based journalist Giancarlo Gallavotti. Vialli told him: 'It was a great performance by the whole team and we could have scored even more goals. But we are getting there. Now the only thing we have to bring to perfection is the final ball. We know that in terms of level of quality of play and individual talent we are second to none in this league. But United is a team that didn't allow for any mistakes. Anyway we could beat them because our defence and midfield was exceptional.' Gullit's instructions were to allow them to take the initiative. Vialli explained: 'Gullit asked us to wait for them. They are a team that has problems in handling the initiative. Our pressing game was very effective and we could keep them under pressure with counter attacks. Once they went a goal down all their problems emerged. They obviously miss the qualities of Pallister. Cantona wandered all over the pitch as he does normally and is always capable of doing damage to you in a fraction of a second. We didn't allow him any chance.'

It's traditional in Italy to 'dedicate' a goal or a win to someone or something. Vialli said: 'I dedicate my goal to Chelsea and I hope it stops all these rumours that I want to go back to Italy and not being happy at this club. I enjoy being at Chelsea tremendously. I find it exhilarating to play for them and I like living in London. It is very important that we get results like this and the one at Tottenham because we have to be in the top places in the league come December if we want to have a serious chance in the second part of the season.'

Ferguson had to swallow hard to admit: 'Chelsea deserved to win, no doubt about that.'

On the shuttle back to Heathrow, Gullit sat alongside Wise and Vialli. The players bought refreshments in the Manchester lounge, mixing freely with the fans who could afford the British Airways ticket, £190 return. Few fans hassled them, merely one or two asking for autographs. They talked animatedly the whole journey. With so many foreign stars, as a group they are less rowdy than the average squad of players. His players, naturally, were in buoyant mood. None more so than Leboeuf, sporting his 'Ice' baseball cap. Leboeuf echoed the determination to win a trophy to dedicate to Harding. 'Ruud Gullit has told us all that Matthew had a dream and if we can win something at the end of the season it will be for him. I only met him twice but I felt there was something between us. He was a great supporter and a great person. A lot of teams have been scoring against us and we have got to find a solution to that. We played very bad against Liverpool and the mood was very poor after that. People ask how we can win the championship when we lose 5–1 to Liverpool. But we have the quality and personality to succeed and if we concentrate more then I do think we can win the title. It will be a big surprise, but it is possible.'

For the record ... Duberry's goal brought the tally to fourteen different players scoring that season. Recent goals from Lee and Gullit plus Duberry's equalled the number of three years ago. Two seasons before there were fifteen and sixteen. So, there had to be a goal from Clarke ... or any more signings!

The match was beamed back 'live' at the Bridge. Just under 1,100 fans, paying £10 a head, were at the screening at Drake's, Tambling's, Dixon's and Jimmy's bars. The closed-circuit viewing generated a marvellous atmosphere.

Leboeuf was naturally delighted with the adulation from the fans, and also the recognition from critics like Alan Hansen who picked him out as a potential star of the season. 'They began to say that. Sure, it's good. It's nice to come to another country and have people say good things about you. But for two months I've had a problem with my groin and it's difficult to play like I played at the start of the season. But I hope that will finish soon.' The win at Old Trafford was something special. 'This was a big game for me. I played for the national team in Senegal and 60,000 were there. But I never played for my club before in front of 55,000. I have never known an atmosphere like it. We won, it was beautiful. It was a very great souvenir for me.'

MONDAY, NOVEMBER 4
With England on World Cup duty and the Premiership weekend closed down, the first team had a day off. Ruud took a trip to Holland, Vialli flew back to Italy. Grodas, Duberry, Leboeuf, Di Matteo, Burley and Spencer were all away on international duty.

Shares in Chelsea Village broke through the £1 barrier for the first time on the back of the glorious success at Old Trafford. The price, first listed at 55p, hit £1.20p within hours of the Stock Exchange opening, but when it was disclosed that director Stewart Thompson had sold 75,000 shares the day after Harding's funeral, the price steadied at £1.13.5p; even the value of the company soared by nearly £15m!

TUESDAY, NOVEMBER 5
Gullit stepped up his pursuit of Gianfranco Zola.

Sardinian-born Zola, who replaced Diego Maradona at Napoli and Roberto Baggio in the Italian national side, was a key figure in Italy's Euro '96 challenge. His Old Trafford penalty miss against Germany led to his country's shock first round elimination. He spoke a little English and had always said he wanted to move abroad at some stage of his career. Zola, thirty, wanted to quit the Serie A giants following a series of rows with new coach Carlo Ancelotti. He was unhappy about being played out of position and had been assured by Gullit he would either be used in attack or directly behind the front two.

WEDNESDAY, NOVEMBER 6
Hutchinson spent the evening with Parma's sports director and general manager Riccardo Sogliano in London. Talks finished at 1am. A fee of £4.5m was agreed by chairman Giorgio Pedranaschi.

Gullit wanted Zola as his first Chelsea signing, but Parma refused to sell at the time. His persistence paid off after getting the go-ahead from Bates to spend big again. It took his spending to over £12m. Parma coach Ancelotti said: 'If he has been able to get a good deal, that's good for us. We're both happy.'

A sparkling new foreign acquisition, but Morris also signed a new two-year contract. Morris made the breakthrough to the first team under Gullit and had also been part of the England under-21 set-up. His progress caught the imagination of everyone at Stamford Bridge.

Hitchcock had an operation on an elbow to remove three floating pieces of bone.

THURSDAY, NOVEMBER 7

Hutchinson flew to Italy, spent two hours with the Parma president. Zola finally sealed the deal with Hutchinson at 3.30am after all-day negotiations. Zola agreed a four-year contract worth £25,000 a week. He would get a basic £16,000 a week, but with bonuses and signing on fees that figure soared to £1.25m a year. It was the first signing since the death of Harding, proof that the dramatic rise of Chelsea continued.

Zola was grateful for an escape route from his Parma misery. He said: 'I will be able to play in my proper role in England, whereas Parma could no longer find a place for me. At the start of the season I was shattered after my penalty miss against Germany. I tried to recapture my best form but the atmosphere at the club had changed. I kept reading claims that I was an egotist, or that I had failed to work with the other strikers Parma had signed and later sold – such as Faustino Asprilla or Hristo Stoichkov. I was being made scapegoat for all the team's problems and I couldn't face staying to put up with all those lies.'

He became totally disillusioned. 'During the last few months I hated it, I didn't want to play football any more. I was expected to play wide on the right. I was very unhappy and my football suffered. I decided to join Chelsea because I wanted to be happy at my club.' Vialli predicted Zola's arrival would improve Chelsea's disappointing strike rate. 'Zola is one of those players who bring strikers good fortune. He is a great character and a winner.'

Zola's arrival placed a huge question mark over the futures of Hughes, Wise and Spencer. After lavish spending, Gullit would begin to claw some of it back. Bates told me: 'Ruud said that Zola was the best striker in the world and that he wanted him. A lot has been made of his age, but as Ruud pointed out Ian Wright was going to play for England again at the age of thirty-three. That was good enough. Colin was due to fly over on Wednesday morning, but there was a strike at Milan so he flew from Stansted on Thursday and got to Milan at 9pm. We had to act fast as we knew that Arsenal were interested. He finally agreed the deal at 3.30am on Friday morning and got home late on Friday afternoon. 'I know everyone is thinking "How can they afford it?" Well, we are up to 35,000 capacity next year. If we are sold out every game that is worth £2.8m and playing in Europe is worth £1m. I feel we have to start qualifying for Europe, and don't forget every place up the Premiership ladder is worth another £100,000.

'Also, buying players from Italy we can spread the money over three years. We are taking advantage of the big TV money that kicks in from next season and that we will have over the next few years. I suppose we are taking a risk, but it's a risk worth taking.' Bates also felt that, as the season progressed, clubs would be in difficulties and come to Chelsea to make realistic bids for their surplus players.

FRIDAY, NOVEMBER 8

Ruud left the training ground by motorbike for the GQ Magazine Awards, presenting a lifelong award to football-loving Rod Stewart.

In faraway Georgia, Duberry scored the winner for the England under-21s, nine minutes from time, in just his third international appearance. He'll never forget the half-hour plane journey. 'This plane was smelling of gasoline and petrol, my seat belt was broken and the seat was wobbly like it would collapse any minute. The tyres on the aeroplane were bald. Otherwise, outside the thing it hadn't been that bad. But inside! The pilot's cockpit didn't have a window. I don't know how he flew it. It was like one of those planes where you expect goats and chickens on board. I was wetting myself. I was sitting next to Emile Heskey and we were dead worried. We felt really sick. We had our tops over our noses, and to top it off the air hostess looked like Bea Smith out of *Cell Block H*. But we got there and I scored the winner near the end. I stayed up after a free kick and the ball was played back to me and I lashed it in the corner. And I thought, oh no, we've got to get back on that plane. It was delayed at first. We just wanted to get on board, we all tried to sleep the whole experience off. It hadn't been a great team performance, but I was told well done on my goal. I was just pleased, really pleased to get out alive!'

SATURDAY, NOVEMBER 9

At Clarke's House of Commons Benefit Dinner, Vialli paid £1,100 into the night's takings when he won the bidding for a specially made Chelsea chair in glorious pale blue stripes and the CFC crest. The auction, presented by auctioneer-host Tony Banks MP, was so successful that at the end of the evening Steve announced a donation of £1,000 to a charity of the diners' choice.

Performing 'YMCA' was punishment for latecomers. Although only two minutes late, Vialli, physio Mike Banks and his wife Judith, Geraldine Lennon and her boyfriend Dennis Wise found no escape from the indignity of the dance. Neither did Luca escape the mad waiter who rubbed whipped cream into his scalp. One surprise diner was Wimbledon striker Efan Ekoku who, three weeks earlier, had done so much damage to Chelsea at the Bridge. He was taken by his brother-in-law, a keen Chelsea fan.

SUNDAY, NOVEMBER 10

Andy Gray, a big fan of Gullit's, praised him for bringing another Italian superstar to the Premiership. In his *Sunday Express* column he wrote: 'Zola's arrival from Italy tells me that manager Ruud Gullit is here to stay and that can only be good for Chelsea, the Premiership and the rest of English football. I'm not surprised that Gullit's return to the transfer market should take him to Italy. That is the market he knows best, having spent most of his career in Serie A with AC Milan and Sampdoria. At Milan they had three Dutchmen, Gullit, Marco van Basten and Frank Rijkaard, as the core of the side and that formula is repeating itself at Stamford Bridge with Zola, Gianluca Vialli and Roberto Di Matteo ... Zola is the latest piece in the jigsaw for Gullit, who is gradually introducing a more flexible, European system to the English game. But he ought to know that his place in the side is not just a matter of turning up. Gullit has shown with his treatment of Vialli that he is quite prepared to make difficult decisions and leave out star names for the benefit of the team. There are a lot of other managers who would not have had the courage to do that.'

Could Zola have signed for Spurs? Sugar refused to break the club's wage structure; top players like Sheringham earned £12,000 a week, the level on which they recruited John Scales, Steffan Iversen and Ramon Vega. Big signings, but not the biggest wages in the Premiership. In contrast, Chelsea were prepared to gamble next year's Sky cash on recruiting top overseas players. Sports lawyer Mel Goldberg contacted Spurs about Zola three weeks before he signed for Chelsea. Goldberg insisted: 'We offered him to Spurs. They could have had him for the same price and same wages. I was told by Sugar's people "We are not paying that sort of money for a player." Zola wanted to come to London because he saw that the other Italians had settled well. It is their choice and they missed out.'

Burley played central midfield for Scotland as they beat Sweden 1–0 at Ibrox in a World Cup qualifier. He switched to right-back in the second half. Grodas was outstanding for Norway as they beat Switzerland 1–0 to keep their third successive qualifying clean sheet.

MONDAY, NOVEMBER 11

Zola flew into Heathrow Airport from Milan with his wife Franca. As soon as he stepped off the plane on English soil, one of the Chelsea officials' mobile phones rang. It was for Gianfranco. Vialli was on the line. They spoke in English! Vialli invited him to his favourite restaurant, San Lorenzo, that evening for a more detailed run-down on English football and his new team-mates.

Wearing a blue baseball cap and black leather jacket Zola was confronted with his first of many interviews of the day at the airport. He said: 'I decided to come here because I wanted another experience in football. This will be a good experience for my life and for my career.' It had been a tough decision. 'It was not easy to leave Italy and Italian football which is very important in the world and important for me. But I decided to have another experience and I hope to have many satisfactory seasons here.' He said the fact that two of his close Italian friends, Vialli and Di Matteo, were playing for Chelsea was an important factor in his choice. 'To have two friends in the same team is important so you can learn things the right way. I hope to settle in quickly and I'm sure I can adapt, and I plan to stay here until my contract expires in 2000.'

Zola was taken straight to central London for a medical. Gullit welcomed his new player at a packed news conference in Drake's restaurant. Gullit felt that Zola would be the final piece in the jigsaw to make Matthew Harding's dreams come true. Gullit said: 'This is what Matthew would have wanted. He had a dream for Chelsea and now we can help deliver that dream. Matthew's hope was that we could keep on improving as a club. This is another big step along that trail and I know he would have enjoyed today; he would have been very happy.'

Gullit was delighted to have persuaded Zola to join the Italian exodus into the Premiership. Hoddle was first quoted £10m when he tried to buy him eighteen months earlier and Zola's capture at less than half that stands in stark comparison to the exorbitant fees demanded for home-grown talent. 'I think with Gianfranco that his qualities are obvious,' said Gullit. 'He has great technical ability and he sees the game very well. I think it's vital for us that he is the sort of player who can decide a game with his vision, technique and ability to open it up from even ordinary situations. At Parma this season he has been a victim of a change in the playing style. If Parma didn't want to use his quality I knew I'd like to have it. You don't get an opportunity like this every day and when I heard he might be available I knew that I wanted him to come to Chelsea.'

Zola paid tribute to Gullit's influence as a player in Italy with both Milan and Sampdoria. 'I came to Chelsea because they believed in me. This is a great opportunity for my career and I decided I wanted to play in this team and play in this country. It was important for me to have this opportunity. Conditions at Parma haven't been ideal for me. I've had a lot of problems but now I want to do the best

I can for Chelsea. I have spoken to Roberto and to Fabrizio Ravanelli and they told me that English football is good. They say it's hard and strong but that the football is good, that I can play well and live well here. Perhaps there will be some problems in adapting at the start but I think I can overcome them. The thing I love about English football is the atmosphere in the grounds and I want to be part of that.

'It made a difference that Ruud wanted me. I played against him in Italy, knew what he could do, and have strong memories of him as a player.' He laughed when he recalled one encounter with Ruud in an Italian Cup semifinal 'when he played us a trick; he scored against us just when we were playing well'. Zola insisted in conducting a cheerful interview in English to give him practice for his new life ahead. He thought long and hard before he answered each question.

Zola played just once with Vialli, for Italy against Cyprus in 1994, but he believed the pair could hit it off. 'I think we can play well together and we won't have any problems. I believe I can help him to score goals and that with him I can help the team to reach our aims. If Chelsea want to win the league then I want to be part of that. I certainly think that this team will be in Europe next season and perhaps even better than that. We are fifth now and I am sure we can progress from there.' Gullit's aim was to play Zola in an attacking formation with Vialli and Hughes.

Zola doubted last summer that his 5ft 5in frame would be sufficient to withstand the rigours and physical demands of the Premiership. Five months on, Gullit had no doubt that he would be able to cope. 'Look at Nick Barmby and Dennis Wise, they are not so big.' Zola showed he had a sense of humour. 'I may have said that in the summer,' he said. 'But I have grown a lot since then!'

As for life in the capital, he said: 'I have only been in London once before and all I saw was Big Ben, so there is a lot to be happy about. I understand that Chelsea is a very beautiful area and I've just learnt that there are some excellent Sardinian restaurants.'

While a debate raged about the motives of the big name foreign stars, Zola's attractive wife Franca insisted that unlike Mrs Andrea Emerson, who was homesick and simply sick of the north-east, her husband was not making a fleeting visit to England. 'We are here to stay. I come from Sardinia and compared to that, London is a great and wonderful city, one of the best in the world to live in. It is very exciting for the whole family to be here and there is a big Italian community for us and that will help us to settle in. I don't know anyone here yet, but I understand that the other wives are friendly too. We will be here for four years so it is important to be happy but it is an exciting experience.' The Zolas have two children, Andrea, five, and four-year-old Martina. 'They will join us shortly and we will try to find a house to live in as soon as possible.'

Zola spoke to Vialli about life on and off the pitch. 'Gianluca has described situations to me in the Premiership that I find incredible, such as when Frank Leboeuf scored Chelsea's only goal in their 5–1 defeat at Liverpool – the fans wanted him to score again with only minutes to go. Also after each game the two teams meet up for half an hour at the bar and every nasty tackle gets forgotten. In Italy people look at me very strangely if I go up to congratulate an opponent.'

Vialli knew Zola's pedigree intimately, and knew he would click in the new-look attack. 'He is one of those players who can make the fortune of any striker. The way he puts the ball onto your feet is unbelievable. And he can change the course of a game with just one touch of invention. Skill. He makes me look ordinary. You will see, and quickly. He will emerge as a revelation in this country. I have a feeling he will prove himself the best Italian player to come here.'

Gullit was equally convinced that Zola would prove a runaway success. 'It's important for Gianfranco that he tries to cope with the different situation here in England. You have to adapt yourself to a new environment, and everybody knows that. I'm sure Gianfranco will adapt, but we'll see later in the week if he can play, at Blackburn.' Zola was sure to run out in his new number twenty-five shirt at Ewood Park, although Gullit was giving nothing away. Gullit added: 'I believe that he can take us up a level from where we are now. Things are getting better all the time, but we know there is more to come and I think he can give us that. I knew he was the player I wanted, and when the opportunity came up I had to take it. I knew other clubs would want him, but we were first when we had to be. I told Luca and Roberto about the signing and they were happy. I think he will give us something extra, and they will make it easier for him to settle here.'

Gullit's spending was on hold. But he refused to rule out further signings in the future. He indicated that those signings were again most likely to come from the other side of the Channel. 'Everything over here has gone out of proportion, and class foreign players cost less than class English ones. We would love to have some English players, but when you have to pay £15m for players like Alan Shearer that takes them out of the reach of even most of the top clubs. But it's not for me to say it's ridiculous.' No one will worry about the overload of foreign stars at the Bridge if they are successful. Gullit joked: 'We had a foreign legion before I arrived . . . there were Scots, Welsh and Irish.'

Zola had the credentials: an Italian championship with Napoli in 1990, European Cup Winners Cup finalist with Parma in 1994 and a UEFA Cup Final the following year. At Napoli he scored thirty-four goals in 131 appearances and sixty-three goals in 136 games for Parma. In twenty-six internationals he scored seven goals. His arrival inevitably intensified speculation about players being sold off. But Gullit promised: 'Nobody has to go. If you look at our last few games Mark Hughes has been outstanding, a great help to the team. What's been better for him is that he's been playing with better players and finding that fun, and we've now got even more better players with Gianfranco here.'

Nationwide First Division leaders Bolton confirmed an interest in Hughes as soon as the ink was dry on Zola's contract. Todd said: 'The situation is just as it was. We enquired about the player in the summer only to be told he wasn't available. If and when that changes we would be interested as we would with any good players.' Hughes wanted Zola to enhance his career at the Bridge, not end it. He argued: 'I don't know what this means for my future. Nothing stops in football and you expect a club like Chelsea to be in the market whenever big name players become available. It shows how far the club has come in a short space of time. I just hope my situation does not change. Hopefully, it will not, this is a great place for me at the moment.'

Spencer's future was more likely to be on the line; he wanted first-team football to keep his place in the Scotland squad. He was not even on the bench for the Sweden match and his position was at risk.

Zola made an immediate impression scoring *five* goals in his first practice match for the Blues. But would Chelsea win the title? Bookies slashed their odds from 14–1 to 10–1. William Hill spokesman Graham Sharpe said: 'Chelsea are now the most heavily backed team in the Premiership. It could cost us £400,000 if they win the championship.'

TUESDAY, NOVEMBER 12

At the training ground, Zola entertained half a dozen Italian journalists, escorted to the large white-walled canteen on the second floor of the clubhouse for an audience with the new signing. After the interviews, Jody Morris was called over. Zola and Morris lined up side by side. Yes, Zola was the new shortest player at the club. Only by half an inch. Wicked mickey taking as Wise called him the 'fairground freak'. Quite a cheek coming from Wise!

Juventus striker Alessandro Del Piero joined the queue of Italian stars wanting to play in the Premiership, as Zola became the Premiership's fifth major Italian import this season. Del Piero, regarded as one of Italian football's hottest properties, declared: 'I wouldn't be at all surprised if an English club was to make a bid for me right now. Their league is currently the richest in Europe. It has undergone vast expansion both in terms of finance and skill levels. What's more, it is far less stressful to play in than Serie A. I wish Zola all the best – he is a fantastic player and a great guy.' Del Piero's Juventus team-mate Attilio Lombardo turned down Sheffield Wednesday. 'I wasn't interested in going to England, despite all the money on offer,' said the bald-headed midfielder. 'I would not have gained anything from it either as a person or as a player. Had I been in Zola's shoes, I would have stayed put in Italy.'

Gullit resolved his goalkeeping crisis after losing Hitchcock, who went into hospital for an elbow operation. Gullit had a fortnight to decide whether to keep Grodas, on loan from Austrian club Sturm Graz, on a permanent basis. Grodas had to be pitched into the side at Blackburn. Williams saw Grodas perform heroically for Norway in their 1–0 World Cup qualifying win in Switzerland at the weekend. And Gullit was so impressed by the video he had virtually made up his mind to sign him.

THURSDAY, NOVEMBER 14

Showdown, confrontation, and bust-up are tabloidese for Gullit and Wise exchanging words at the training ground. In reality, Wise was not happy with his situation. The fall-out was the talk of the dressing room. However, Gullit was hardly likely to become agitated about anything. Wise feared he would be substituted at Blackburn rather than any of the millionaire foreigners. Yes, Wise was right. He was replaced by Gullit after an hour. Gullit was aware of the growing discontent but was adamant that there was no players' revolt as suggested in the papers. Instead, Ruud saw his job was to win games by making decisions that were right for the club, not to make him popular. There was no personality clash with Wise, and Gullit just laughed off reports that he had taken offence at being called 'big nose'. But relations were strained since Wise was substituted at Leicester then axed for the game against his former Wimbledon team-mates. The signing of Zola brought matters to a head. Wise still had nineteen months of his contract to run, but was becoming increasingly concerned about his long term prospects.

Footballers are easy to understand. In the team equals contentment and appearance money; out of the side represents misery, loss of earnings and itchy feet. Gullit wanted a big squad for ultimate success. He preached the squad system, and that took time to sink in. Those who lost patience were sold off. Gullit's priority was to prepare for the Blackburn game with a practice match against the reserves acting out the opposition's tactics.

FRIDAY, NOVEMBER 15

Zola would take the English game by storm and become a major influence. Gullit just knew it as he set off for Blackburn. 'Gianfranco was a vital man for Napoli and Parma and now he will be just as important to us because he's the sort of player who can decide a game. His quality is obvious. He has great technical ability, vision and the skill to change a match which is so desperately needed today.'

Vialli felt Zola would love the easy-going camaraderie within the Gullit camp, compared with the more rigid regimes in Italian. 'There is a problem in Italy now because it is getting more difficult for the good players to perform well. It seems there is a negative atmosphere in the Italian game and that is not helping. I have settled in very well at this club and I'm sure Zola will do the same. The atmosphere is tremendous here, better than in Italy where players are more independent.' Vialli was impressed with the formidable squad assembled by Gullit, and the willingness to utilise it to the full – even if Vialli himself was the victim. 'Things are changing in this country. No longer is it a question of selecting eleven players from fifteen. Now there are twenty good players at a manager's disposal. While this is fine for Ruud Gullit, it is not so good for the players. Sure, they get angry when they are out of the team but it is a bad mentality. If you want to win something, you have to have more than just eleven players. You must accept it. If you want to play every week then it may be better to join another team. Milan is a tremendous example. For the first time an Italian side had something like twenty-two great players. From that moment they won everything. That is what Ruudi is trying to do at Chelsea. He wants the best and he wants lots of them.'

Gullit moved Burley from midfield to sweeper for the injured Leboeuf, and also to accommodate Zola. Grodas made his Premiership debut.

SATURDAY, NOVEMBER 16

Blackburn Rovers 1 Chelsea 1

Only a goal could have bettered Zola's introduction, and that almost came, spectacularly, deep in the second half, when he volleyed Gullit's cross into the side-netting. To appreciate the skill involved it should be pointed out that many decent players, presented with a ball at comparable angle and height, would have propelled it into row Z. 'It was always my intention to play him from the start,' Gullit said, dismissing the notion of a more gentle introduction. 'It is important that he gets to know us and we get to know him as quickly as possible. There is no point in leaving him on the bench. And, as you can see, he is very fit and has no problems with the pace. He told me he enjoyed the game.

'He made a very nice debut and will get even better. It was nice to see how he played. He got better and better as the game went on and ended up playing very well. He is tired, but physically he will have no problems with the Premiership.'

Gullit, having started on the bench, took the field for the final thirty minutes, and under his guidance Chelsea subjected Blackburn's goal to sustained attack. Zola was thwarted in the box by Henning Berg's last-ditch tackle and was then felled by McKinlay at the edge of the area. Two saves by Grodas denied first McKinlay and then Gallacher in the home side's quest for a late winner.

Zola struck a hefty blow for foreign football, providing the perfect response to the growing army of Little Englanders questioning the motives of the Premiership's overseas recruits. Emerson's disappearing act and the constant jibes of Sugar called into question the character of the international stars. But on a wet weekend in

Blackburn, Zola showed character and bottle to match his undoubted skill. Even when his first game in England was threatening to completely pass him by, the little man with a big heart refused to hide. Parkes admitted: 'I didn't even mention Zola in my team talk. He scared me to death and I knew he'd do the same to my players. What can you say about Zola, Vialli and Gullit except sing their praises? I'd rather not talk about them at all. I was hoping they'd stick with the side which won their last game at Manchester United. When I saw Zola was playing I weren't right happy. So I told my team to hound them, to put the pressure on and see how they reacted to that. It was possible that they might not fancy it. But we never got a chance to test them, because they hit it all long to Vialli and made it difficult to crowd them out in midfield.'

Zola grew more influential in a hard, muscular, unmistakably English match. His willingness to learn impressed his new player-manager, who wanted Zola to acclimatise before the encounter with Newcastle. By the later stages Zola linked promisingly with Vialli and Di Matteo – and with Gullit. It must have helped to receive instructions in his own language, but intelligence also played a part.

Gullit acknowledged that it was not until he replaced Wise for the last half-hour that his team dominated. Gullit intended to resume his playing role as more than just a bit part player.

How do you assemble a large squad and keep all the players imported and home-grown happy? 'You can't,' Gullit said. 'But I have been there and the most important thing I learned from Milan was that you have to create a situation in which, no matter what they think of the coach's decisions, all the players have only one goal, which is for the team to achieve something. I don't mind if they don't like me sometimes as long as they have a common goal. At Milan, I hated the coach's guts when he left me out but in the end I realised what he did was right for the team. As for myself I feel that I am now nearly one hundred per cent fit and now I just need to find my rhythm.'

Parkes believed Chelsea enjoyed the advantage of playing their foreigners because they were in the top half of the table. He relied on more domestic virtues to ease his side's problems, having already axed Georgios Donis and Lars Bohinen. 'In our position we need battlers to get us a result. Foreign players are the icing on the cake when things are going well. We can't afford the luxury of guys who are only interested in attacking. We've got to tackle, get close and get a foot in. It's what the crowd expect of us, because they know it's the only way we're going to get off the bottom of the table. We never used to have trouble attracting the biggest stars in the game to Ewood Park when Kenny Dalglish was in charge. But things have changed now and someone like Zola would have taken one look at our league position and gone somewhere else.'

At least Rovers had the consolation of climbing off the foot of the table for the first time in two months thanks to Kevin Gallacher's well-worked fifty-fifth-minute goal. Yet Chelsea, who finished this game with just two Englishmen, still showed enough commitment to deserve Petrescu's deflected equaliser off Billy McKinlay.

Vialli produced one of his best all-round performances. Grodas was warned after just four minutes and booked in the twelfth for time wasting – as he waited for his manager to get across his messages from the touchline! Burley's tackle and pass to Vialli who worked his way round the back to set up Hughes for a shooting chance which he should have buried in the thirty-first minute was the move of the match and deserved a goal.

Minto, one of those rare Englishmen in the Chelsea camp, laughed: 'I've got to learn Italian to get on with everyone now! But there isn't really a communication problem, even if Ruud has to speak a bit slowly at times. All the foreign lads understand English and that's very important. They've come over here and are getting paid a lot of money. But they've realised the English league is very hard physically and we are prepared to put the effort in. Luca and Dennis Wise are always playing little pranks on each other and there's a good banter in the camp. No one says "I'm on twenty-five grand a week so I'm not talking to you." There was a lot of pressure on Zola today and this was probably a bit of a culture shock for him after living in Parma. But I've already seen a great deal to suggest he'll be a big success. He's only tiny, but he's very strong and his low centre of gravity means he can twist and turn past big defenders. All the Italians are bringing great technique and tactical awareness. But they're also prepared to dig in the English way.'

Norwegian stopper Henning Berg claimed: 'Chelsea are great going forward, but not too many of their players want to defend. It was very difficult for Zola, because it was his first game and he was playing in a position he's not used to. But he wasn't a big threat.'

Zola said: 'It was a physical game, very tiring but I like that incredible aggression in the English game. For a first match I was pleased, but I know I will have to get better. I've never felt so tired in my life, yet I'm already looking forward to playing Newcastle; I wish it were tomorrow, that's how exciting it is to play in English football. The atmosphere is simply unbelievable. I've never enjoyed a match so much in my life. It took me a while to adjust but I think in the second half I started to get going. Vialli was simply magnificent. We only played twice together for Italy but I'm looking forward to a great partnership. I'm pleased and satisfied with my performance because I've only been here five days. Parma is a chapter in my life that is closed for good. I can only say it is exhilarating to play football like this.'

The early play passed him by, but he was more influential as the game progressed. 'I'm not a novice, I know something about English football. But I still have a lot to learn. I've started on the right foot and for the first match I'm quite satisfied. You play for the first to the very last minute. The aggression was incredible, there were a lot of tackles, but none that were cruel. One of the things that struck me was the intensity and the amazing public all around the pitch. The game was hard. They scored when we were playing our best. But Dan scored an important goal for us. I kick just one free kick for goal but I kicked too high. Next time, okay. I hope.'

Zola was asked what he could 'call' if he wanted the ball. 'I only know "Hello!"'

'I can tell you, I felt knackered.' No, it wasn't Wise. It was Vialli. 'We had to fight for a result but in the end we got it and I'm told Chelsea haven't won in Blackburn for several years so it was even more important that we came away with a point. I can see good things coming from myself playing with Zola.'

The coach sped away from Ewood Park so the team could catch the last shuttle from Manchester to Heathrow. In the airport departure lounge was Hoddle, on a mission to watch his England players at Old Trafford, Manchester United against Arsenal. The perfect chance for Ruud and Glenn to chat as they queued to board the shuttle. Zola and Di Matteo, who had shared rooms, were joined by *Gazzetto dello Sport* correspondent Giancarlo Galavotti, who translated their conversation...

Di Matteo: What would you like?
Zola: No, it's okay, I'll pay.
Di Matteo: You'd better, if I have to listen to certain figures in the press you are being paid.
Zola: Well, actually these figures are not exactly true.

MONDAY, NOVEMBER 18

Gullit, on the prowl for more foreign signings, was linked with German keeper Georg Koch, but there was no intention to go ahead with any deal for the Fortuna Dusseldorf player; whose surname meant 'cock'. Perhaps it was simply a tabloid newspaper cock-up!

Williams put Chelsea's interest in perspective: 'Somebody recommended him. We've had various agents recommending players. We have watched him once, and it wasn't a good performance. But he is not the only one in that position we have looked at. It doesn't mean we are not happy with Froda. He's on trial as well. This is a big club and we are always looking. It is our job to look and look. We have nineteen scouts out each Saturday.'

Gullit could recoup millions with the sale of unhappy squad members. Spencer led the dissatisfied section. 'All I want is to be treated like an adult. Ruud Gullit hasn't spoken to me for eight weeks. I don't know what my situation is. I don't even know if I'll be here at the end of the week. I'm obviously not happy with the playing side of things because we are paid to play and I have had only eighty minutes in the first team all season. The club have neither said I can go but they haven't said I'm not for sale either. If I'm not for sale then the club should say so. If Ruud Gullit was linked with another club they would do that.' Leading scorer last season, he feared for his World Cup place with Scotland. 'I didn't train with the first team today because the reserves have a big game at Borehamwood on Tuesday. I've sixteen months left on my deal here and I would be the happiest man in London if I was playing regularly, because I don't want to leave.' He ruled out a move back to his native Scotland, where Celtic were keen on signing him. 'I like it in London. Perhaps when I'm thirty-five I'll be ready to go back to Scotland. I have to thank Scotland manager Craig Brown for still picking me at international level although he can't keep doing that if I'm not playing for my club. Every time I pick up a paper I seem to be linked with yet another club but we'll just need to wait and see. Clearly at this stage of my career I'm not interested in reserve football. I've already picked up thirteen caps for Scotland and with the World Cup finals now looking a distinct possibility, I want to be involved. And I cannot expect Craig Brown to pick me if I'm not playing at the highest level. Actually the huge influx of foreign players to British football is a worrying thing. And I don't mean at the top end of the market. There is a flood of cheap labour coming in which could swamp our own emerging youngsters. I know that the PFA are worried about it and chairman Pat Nevin has already come up with some constructive proposals. As far as the youngsters are concerned it throws the onus on parents to make sure their kids make the right choice when it comes to joining a club. And big bucks shouldn't be the deciding factor!'

TUESDAY, NOVEMBER 19

The Chairman's Revenge! Bates drove his giant Bentley into the ground on match day to discover Ruud's top of the range Audi sports car in his car parking space. Bates told Gullit precisely what he thought of such impertinence! 'I love you dearly,

I admire you greatly, you can have anything you want at this football club – except my car parking space!'

Three days later at the training ground, the chairman drove down to have a look around. Bates said: 'I saw a spot reserved for a "R. Gullit". I parked in his spot and went into his office and sat down behind his desk.' 'Just trying it for size,' he told his manager. 'You put your car in my parking space and I'm just making a point by sitting in your chair!' Ruud just loved the banter with the club owner. 'No problem, Mr President!' said Ruud. And the pair laughed together.

Ruud's training ground office isn't lavishly furnished, a simple desk and chair, TV set and stack of videos, photos on the wall, charts and a book shelf. One picture catches the eye, a nude shot of Vialli with his hands over his private parts. It's signed by Vialli: 'I love you, Gwyn.'

On another occasion, Bates knocked on Ruud's office door. 'I always knock on his door,' said Bates. 'He was sitting there with his feet up on the table reading an Italian paper. I said "Hallo", and then I thought for a moment. I told him "I've just worked it out how much I am paying you in the time its taking you to read that paper."' Again Ruud saw the joke.

Bates's office at Stamford Bridge overlooks the massive hotel and flats development on the first floor, with lavish desk and chairs, room for a sofa with cartoons on the wall and filled with private photographs. Gullit's office is tiny by comparison, but hardly used. Ruud is still a player and his coaching and training is done on a daily basis at the Harlington training ground. His office at the Bridge is used by Rix and Williams.

Another day with the Crazy Gang for Vialli. A downpour produced huge puddles at the training ground; Vialli was the victim as the players searched for someone to push into one of the murky wet spots. Once fully clothed and on his mobile the Italian superstar was drenched with a bucket of cold water. Could Wise be the instigator? Of course not. Wise said: 'It was a terrible day and we just asked Luca if it was his birthday, and he said it was which was his worst mistake. Especially as it wasn't. There was a very big puddle in the middle of the pitch. We were going to strip him, but knowing Luca he would have caught a cold. So we left his clothes on, threw him in and wished him a happy birthday. Then, when he was on the phone standing outside under the canteen, someone did him with a bucket of water. I won't say who it was 'cause I'm not a grass. But Luca didn't look too happy. He'll have wrapped himself up for the rest of the week to save himself getting a cold.'

Luca was a practical joker of some repute himself. He enjoyed the banter. 'We joke a lot in the dressing room, after the training, before the training. Never during the training because we are always concentrating on what we are doing. Ruudi's our manager, but he's also our player, so it's normal we take the **** out of him.'

Ruudi gives as good as he gets. He can be heard singing this little ditty in the corridor outside Luca's changing room ... 'He's fat, he's bald, he's always got a cold, Vi-ah-lli, Vi-ah-lli!'

Later Ruud was diverted from his analytical duties in the BBC studios during the Metz–Newcastle UEFA Cup tie to be asked by Des Lynam 'whether he was still enjoying management'. Gullit was less than enthusiastic about his task of 'having to put players on the bench, or not even on the bench'. He hoped 'they were all professional' about it. He went on: 'I have to make tough decisions. There is no point in making decisions just to make yourself popular. You have to do the things you think are best for the team.'

No players would be leaving on the cheap, Gwyn Williams said: 'No one will leave unless it is best for Chelsea, and for the right money. Men like Spencer and Erland Johnsen are valuable members of our squad.' Then Williams made his way to Metz. 'Ruud might have come with me, but he had another job with the BBC – it would be warmer in the studios.'

WEDNESDAY, NOVEMBER 20
Morris was ruled out for eight weeks after breaking his jaw in an incident outside a nightclub. He was taken to Charing Cross Hospital to have it wired up. Gullit had singled out the youngster as a great prospect, throwing him into the side ahead of more experienced players.

THURSDAY, NOVEMBER 21
The Spencer saga finally concluded; a £2.5m move to Queens Park Rangers, to become the Loftus Road club's record signing. 'I'm just glad to get this chance with a club that has faith in me.' Linked to Strasbourg and Lens, Sunderland had a record £1.5m turned down, with Leeds United, Derby County and Leicester City also desperate to buy Spencer. But he opted for Loftus Road after long discussions with QPR boss Stewart Houston and his assistant Bruce Rioch. His main objective was to get the First Division club back to the Premiership. Spencer joined Glasgow Rangers in 1986, but it took him five years and a loan spell to Morton before he played his first league game. He even had a spell at Hong Kong outfit Lisbung. He moved to Chelsea in 1992 for £450,000 and became a favourite with the fans. He was Chelsea's top scorer with thirteen Premiership goals in the previous season, having been joint top scorer a year earlier. But he was frozen out following the Gullit revamp up front. He made just three starts, all in the Coca-Cola Cup, with just four Premiership appearances from the bench. The 5ft 6in Scot made clear his displeasure at the start of the season, and while Gullit had gone on record as saying that nobody would have to leave to balance the books, the arrival of a third Italian tipped the balance.

Spencer insisted that Gullit was wrong. 'I don't care what big names they have signed or where they have come from, I felt I was good enough to be in the side. But I wasn't going to hang around in the reserves. At twenty-six, I needed first-team football, especially as I have international ambitions. It was a difficult decision to leave. I got on well with the other players, but it was frustrating not being picked. Now I have to forget about it because Chelsea is finished for me and I have to think about QPR.' Spencer signed a four-and-a-half-year contract. He had no regrets about dropping down to the First Division. 'QPR offered me first-team football. Just speaking to Stewart Houston for ten minutes made me realise it was the right decision. He is ambitious and QPR won't be in Division One for very long. I wasn't in the first team at Chelsea and I'm not the kind of person to sit on my backside and take the money for playing in the reserves.'

Houston said: 'When I knew he was available I moved quickly, because John has the quality we need and I'm very hopeful he is going to be our main goalscorer. His scoring record at Chelsea was very good and he is also very adaptable – somebody who can slot into other positions. That makes him the kind of player every club wants and if he performs well in this division he'll still get the attention. We lost Kevin Gallen with a bad injury right at the start of the season and that severely reduced our options up front, but I'm confident John is going to do a great job for us. I call John my little big man. It's not just his goals – it's his character, too. He is a bubbly man and very enthusiastic. Already I've noticed a difference in training from the other players. He has given us a boost.'

Houston also snapped up Peacock, on loan, pending a permanent transfer. Next out the door was Stein, who rejoined his former club, Stoke, on a month's loan. The South African-born thirty-year-old cost £1.5m from the Potteries club in October 1993. QPR went back for Burley but baulked at the same asking price as Spencer.

Shearer was given the green light to make his Newcastle comeback against Chelsea. The England skipper came through a training session and would be back just one month after his groin operation. Shearer had his first full Newcastle training session on Tuesday morning ahead of the UEFA Cup third-round first-leg tie in Metz. Shearer's return was a timely one for the Premiership leaders with strike partner Les Ferdinand several weeks away from a return. Ferdinand had suffered a depressed cheekbone and was recovering from an operation.

If Shearer needed any extra incentive, it came from Gullit himself, who had reflected on the world-record £15m transfer before the start of the season. 'Shearer's price is crazy and a waste of money in my opinion. I look abroad for players of the same or better quality – and I manage to sign them for a lot less. People were asking questions about Shearer before Euro '96. But he was on a roll once he got that first goal, and his price shot up. He went for all that money in the summer because of post-Euro '96 hype, in my view. Newcastle have bought a player who has the knack of scoring, and that is valuable. He is an out-and-out goalscorer, but he has no tricks and does not seem to get any joy from the game if he fails to hit the target. I prefer players who contribute in other areas and have a sense of fun. Someone like Gianluca Vialli, who certainly fits into that category. My ideal striker will get fifteen or so goals a season, with another dozen spread across others in the team. That way, no one knows where our main threat is coming from.'

Shearer grinned. 'He said *what* about me? Hey, I'm not going to let something like that get to me. He's entitled to his opinion. It may not exactly coincide with mine, but it's certainly not a problem. People can say what they want, and I'll just get on with things like I normally do.' Shearer had an impressive career tally of seven goals against Chelsea – and was bookies' favourite to open the scoring. He was 5–4 with William Hill to mark his Newcastle comeback with a goal. 'I've lived with high expectations for years and it has never worried me,' he said. 'I'm just glad to be playing again so soon after my operation. I always had this match pencilled in for my comeback but was reluctant to say so because I didn't want to pile on any extra pressure. I always get a real buzz before a match, and I'm looking forward to getting that same feeling at Stamford Bridge. We've got three games coming up in seven days. It's a busy period that's going to test me, but I'm confident I'll be all right. When I'm fit, I really am one hundred per cent and you won't find me picking and choosing games.'

Shearer relished his head-to-head with Zola, saying: 'I know what he's all about after watching him on TV several times. He's another example of the exciting players Gullit has brought into the club. Ruud's done extremely well, and if we are to get anything out of the game, we're going to have to be at our best.'

Shearer scored four goals in four games before his surgery and, inevitably, comparisons were made between him and Vialli. Shearer said: 'Vialli has got winners' medals. I haven't. I would be delighted to be able to achieve what he has done. If we are to get anything at Chelsea we will have to be at our best. I know I will get a bit of pain in this first game back but there will be no time to rest because we've got three important games coming up in the next seven days. I'm hoping to be able to pick up where I left off.'

Batty played with a black eye after having four stitches in a wound, a punch from Metz midfielder Isaias. Leboeuf was back after missing a game with a groin strain.

FRIDAY, NOVEMBER 22

Ruud's old pal Marco van Basten turned up at the training ground, fuelling speculation that he could become the club's new coach! The world-class striker, forced to quit because of an ankle injury, trained with the players for two hours. He even played against the first team for the reserves, who took the shape of the Newcastle side. Marco was probably Shearer! Gullit said: 'He is a great friend. He wanted to see what I was doing here. I can't say whether he wants to get back. Read into it what you want.' The thirty-two-year-old former Dutch international was the surprise sight that greeted supporters at the club's training ground. Van Basten, who hit a hat-trick against England when he led the Netherlands to their triumph in the 1988 European Championships, looked as fit as ever. His last game was in the 1993 European Cup Final against Marseille. Ruud said that he popped in to say 'hello'. 'Marco just came to visit us,' Gullit said. 'It was good for us to have him, the excitement it generated was OK, and it was nice for him to have contact with football again. It's been a long time since he has played, and he was quite satisfied with his performance, but he just came to visit me, to join in.'

At the end of a week when Spencer, Peacock and Stein left with rumblings about other players, Gullit was in no mood for compromise. 'Chelsea is changing, like all the top clubs. That means a lot of players in the squad, and that nobody is guaranteed a place in the team. That's the reality. Some players can cope with it, but if they don't want to they've made that decision. Of course, there will be consequences for those who are not happy.' With ten foreigners at the club, he added: 'I listen to the players and I can honestly say that accusations of me being arrogant are not true. I speak to everyone individually. I hear what they say but then I tell them I pick the team and I make the decisions. I pick certain players for certain games and no longer will they have an automatic right to be in the side. If British players don't accept that, then it's best they go. Manchester United have a similar situation with Poborsky and Cruyff while Newcastle often have problems with Asprilla and cannot accommodate Gillespie in the side.

'Sometimes, English players don't want to listen. They want to be cuddled every day. Reality is not like that, and I do not have time to do it, anyway. I was hurt many times playing for Milan by similar tactics. I had to learn to get on with it and realise it was club policy. If the players don't like what I'm doing then they know what to do. The majority are changing. Some have come to me and said now they want to be part of our future. That is good. My relationship with Dennis Wise is outstanding. Ask him.'

Wise said: 'Ruud has asked you to ask me, has he? Let's say everything is sweet.'

Gullit carried on his crusade, and featured on BBC *Grandstand*'s Football Focus. 'A year ago Chelsea were not mentioned in the first five in the table. Now Chelsea is on that table. A whole lot of things have changed, how we see the game, how we approach them. The consequences are that if they don't want to cope with this mentality, because they are not used to it, it says more about them.' Vialli was also on the Saturday midday programme. 'I want to become a Chelsea legend. I want to score a lot for Chelsea. I will try. It is not important if you don't speak English very well; on the pitch the language is always the same. I will try to put Chelsea on the top and do my best for the team.'

Gullit would have been more worried had his team faced van Basten in his prime, rather than Shearer in a Newcastle shirt. 'Marco now plays golf and swaps his life between homes in Holland, Italy and Monte Carlo. I will say that Marco was the world's greatest striker at every level. Alan Shearer is without doubt a wonderful player but he's yet to do it at the same level as Marco. Yes, he had a very good European Championship, but until he performs and succeeds on all the biggest stages – the World Cup finals and the Champions Cup – he will not be able to claim the title Marco held at his peak when he was widely regarded as the best striker around. Van Basten proved himself for both Holland and AC Milan at the highest level. It is the only way to be regarded as a truly world-class player. George Best had a huge reputation here in Britain but he was not considered as big in Europe because he was never able to perform in the big tournaments at international level. That was not necessarily his fault and must have been a big frustration for him. Shearer did well in Euro '96 and that has helped him become acknowledged on the continent because, until then, his reputation was not so big in Europe. But now it depends on whether the potential they have at Newcastle is fulfilled so that he has a bigger stage on which to prove himself as one of the best strikers on the world scene. That was always the gamble he took when he decided to go back home rather than to other clubs who might have wanted him.' Shearer ignored overtures from Barcelona and Manchester United in the summer in the belief he could spearhead Newcastle's emergence as a genuine force both at home and abroad.

Zola – already nicknamed 'Gorgon' – prepared for his home debut with an unusual problem. What about his number twenty-five shirt? 'I need a "M", not "XL". I told them this at Blackpool.' He meant, of course, Blackburn, the venue for his debut. Zola mockingly rolled up his sleeves. It brought hoots of laughter during the press conference, and was screened on Football Focus where Ferdinand was the guest with Lineker. The dry-cleaners opposite the Bridge completed the necessary shortening alterations to Zola's shirt. Kit suppliers Umbro promised one that fitted in time for the next game at Elland Road.

Ferdinand supported Gullit's quest to build a powerful squad. 'Like Ruud says, at any top Premier League club it is difficult to keep everyone happy week in and week out. Winning eases the pressure, you don't change a winning side. But it's a very delicate situation, different managers cope with it in different ways.' With pictures of Shearer training in the snowbound north, Ferdinand was glad to be back in London, the only consolation for being injured.

Bates, in his programme notes, publicly backed his manager's stance. 'When a player signs for Chelsea he gets well paid. In return he undertakes to give his best, never bad mouth the club and to put the team first. Chelsea looks after the player's well-being, provides the finest medical attention, helps him with any problems off the field and of course keeps him on full pay whether sick or injured. Chelsea does not guarantee anyone a first-team place, as Vialli found out, and he took it like a man. If any player is unhappy at not being picked then perhaps he should try a little harder in training next week to prove that the coach made a mistake.'

SATURDAY, NOVEMBER 23

Chelsea 1 Newcastle United 1

Gullit hailed this spectacle as 'a good promotion for English football'. Less than twenty-four hours after the new Arsenal manager, Arsène Wenger, foresaw Premiership sides containing seven or eight foreigners, Zola raised Chelsea's continental complement to six. Gullit, anticipating that a third Italian would attract sceptical comment, drew the parallel in his programme notes with the arrival of himself and two fellow Dutchmen at Milan. 'It looks here now a bit like Milan was when I was there. Milan suddenly had three foreigners, three Dutchmen. Nobody called it in that moment Milan-Dutch. Or called the training ground Hollandello instead of Milanello. Or Milamsterdamo! Everything does need some time to get used to. But everybody will not be talking Italian here. The team is now under more pressure with Zola coming. There is more competition. Players are aware they have to perform each week. And you supporters will be demanding it of them. It's a new situation for everyone. I know you supporters don't accept complaints from players. We all have one goal, the same goal, winning something. I think you feel something good is coming and players aren't expected to act for themselves. I want everyone acting professionally and trying to get into the team.'

While Rijkaard and van Basten lent moral support from the stand, was it stretching the symbolic point to expect Chelsea's Italian contingent to make a comparable impact? When Gullit and his compatriots exploded on Serie A, they were still approaching the peak of their powers, the catalysts for a team already brimming with world-class talent.

Gullit received his Player of the Year award, took it back to the dressing room, and then resumed his place on the bench. Vialli and Asprilla exchanged kisses on the cheek and Ginola shook the Italian's hand before the kick off.

Zola made an instant impact on his home debut. Keegan joked: 'I liked him better in their half than our half! He was a bundle of tricks and he's always going to be dangerous from any free kick.' It was from Zola's free kick in the twenty-third minute that Vialli claimed the deftest of touches. Even after watching the replays half a dozen times it was hard to tell whether he actually did get a touch. 'Maybe it went in off his hair!' said Gullit. 'He has got one!' Zola whipped in one of his famous free kicks and Vialli insisted, 'I definitely headed the ball. I would never deprive my old friend of a goal on his debut unless I was sure about it.' It was suggested that Vialli's motive was a clause in his contract worth £3,000 a goal. 'Not so,' said Hutchinson. Zola was happy to accept Vialli's word for it. 'If Gianluca says he touched it, I believe him. It's no problem, even though I was actually trying to score as I have done so many times from similar situations in Italy.'

Vialli answered the burning question in English football. Are the foreigners good for our game? He delivered an emphatic 'yes' but with a very essential proviso. 'It is important when you buy foreign players that they are the best, they must be very clever, strong mentally as well as physically and they have to be a teacher. If you choose well England can improve, if you don't choose well English football will go down.' On view was £30m worth of some of the most glamorous of the foreign imports, intriguing confrontations: the French connection of Leboeuf and Ginola, the Parma connection between Zola and Asprilla, and the Italian job lot acquired by the Dutch boss.

The occasion was spoilt by the sending off of David Batty, forcing Keegan's hand in withdrawing his flair players Ginola and Asprilla. Keegan explained: 'There is no great magic to this game, it would just have been crazy to carry on with ten men as if it was Roy of the Rovers when real life is not like that. There was still a lot to be written in this game. People think I'm a bit cavalier, and perhaps I am, but it would have been suicide to have left on Ginola and Asprilla when we were one man short.' Keegan threw a consoling arm around Ginola when he brought him off soon after Batty's dismissal and there was also a cuddle for his Colombian later in the game as he opted to send on first Watson and then Lee Clark. Keegan moaned that the spectators were the losers by his pragmatic approach of putting ten men behind the ball to protect the point, keeping Newcastle at the top of the Premiership. 'Sadly the game was spoilt but I had to take the flair players off. Ruud had a very good side here and they gave us a lot of problems but I felt at half-time that if we kept possession we could win the match. When you see this result on Teletext – 1–1 – you would think it was not very interesting. The truth was both sides wanted to entertain. Please God we do better than them.'

Batty had swung his elbow and caught Hughes full in the face. Batty was full of remorse, Keegan full of recriminations. Batty couldn't apologise enough. 'I went over to Mark on the floor to tell him that I was sorry I didn't mean to catch him. I just felt his presence behind me and I've caught him but not meant to do it. So, I deserve to go. I felt bad, I'd let everyone down and said so. It was the first time I've been sent off in my career but there was no intent to harm Mark Hughes at all.' Keegan had no complaint about the referee's decision but felt Hughes should have been punished, if only a yellow card. 'Obviously something happened to make David Batty react in that way. One guy is sent off but the other guy goes scot free.' Hughes was not impressed with Keegan's view. 'Mr Keegan's player accepted that he shouldn't have done what he did, so I don't know why the manager can't as well. If I don't challenge for every ball I get stick off my manager.' Gullit sounded like a typical English manager when he professed that he didn't see it! 'I was warming up. But I saw his nose. I saw a little bit of blood coming out, and Mark is not a guy who moans a lot!' Are you sure about that one, Ruud?

At times Shearer was the last man in defence, a backs-to-the-wall display that gave Keegan more satisfaction than some of his glorious attacking successes. Srnicek had given Keegan nightmares at times; on this occasion he was outstanding. Keegan said: 'The keeper answered some of his critics with great saves.'

Wenger had predicted Hoddle would be deprived of international talent as foreign stars swamped the top Premiership sides. It was appropriate that the England coach should be at the Bridge as Keegan delivered his verdict. 'I'm not one of these Englishmen out to protect jobs because they believe that is to the benefit of English football. I've no qualms about the top foreign players coming to these shores and I believe it will make English players better. We should not be scared to learn and our game will benefit by having top quality stars to learn from.'

Shearer (who else?) grabbed the equaliser with persistence, concentration and calmness that marked him down as world-class. Shearer was thwarted first by Grodas but kept his composure to weave backwards past Duberry and shoot into the corner before Wise could tackle, Clarke getting his head to the ball but only helping it into the corner in the forty-second minute. Shearer is one of the few English players on the same level as Gullit's recruits from Serie A. Vialli had nothing but admiration for Shearer, back after just thirty days from a hernia operation. 'He's a great player, very strong, but our keeper was very good to stop him, but then he showed unbelievable ability in the middle of three or four of our defenders to score. Congratulations to him.'

No one questioned Shearer's long term commitment, those are the sort of accusations levelled at the Italians. But Vialli doesn't plan to be a 'Herr today gone tomorrow' Klinsmann! 'I am working to put Chelsea on top. I want to become an important player for the club. I don't know if I can, but I want to become a Chelsea legend. I am staying here three years to do that. I plan to enjoy myself here and win something with Chelsea and I think it's looking good. Chelsea played better than Newcastle, we had eight to ten chances in front of goal and we were unlucky. Newcastle are a very good team, Liverpool the same. I'm happy and Mark is happy, we may not score like Ferdinand and Shearer or Ravanelli, but we work hard for the team and as a result sometimes our team-mates score maybe because of us.'

Vialli's verdict on Zola's home debut: 'He's a great player, the best player in the world to deliver to you a pass.' Gullit agreed: 'Everyone is very happy with him. He created so many things, he improved our team performance. Overall I'm happy about everyone's performance. It was a good game tactically and technically, an open game with little excitement. I was disappointed when we drew against Nottingham Forest, especially the way we played, but this was a really good game with both sides wanting to play exciting football, so I'm quite happy about the way we played. Of course it was always difficult against ten men, very difficult. But everyone worked very hard, I have nothing to complain about – only the result.'

Gullit made his entry in the sixty-first minute, Di Matteo's turn to be substituted for the first time. Again no favouritism. Di Matteo said, 'Okay, we have now good players in this team and it can happen that you go substituted, yes? And I hope to play the next game and I hope to play maybe better than this game or maybe he choose somebody else!' Gullit gave no guarantees the three Italians would all play every game together. Di Matteo wasn't sure it was such an advantage being all of the same nationality. 'I don't know, I don't know. We can help each other if we are three Italians. Maybe Franco can help Luca and Luca can help me. But I don't know if we can bring a new style to the Premier League. It depends on the whole team. Because you play with eleven players, not three. So if everybody does what he has to do I think we can have a good season.'

In the final frenzy, when Chelsea might easily have grabbed the winner against the ten men on the retreat, Wise struck a marvellous long-range shot that whacked against the bar, bringing the fans to their feet. Wise recalled: 'I said to Alan Shearer at one point "In a minute I'll hit a thirty-yarder in the top corner." He said "If you do it I'll give you a hundred quid." So what happened? I hit the flippin' crossbar from thirty yards. He turned round and muttered "Unlucky, I nearly had to pay up there." I bet he couldn't have afforded it anyway!'

Ruud was answering one question from an Italian journalist, rapidly followed by a Dutch writer, then an Italian TV interviewer, interspersed with questions from the English press. Impressive? Well, someone suggested: 'What about the Norwegian journalists?' Another said: 'There's one in Greek!' A smiling Gullit departed the interview room. 'A night out,' he announced with van Basten and Rijkaard. Together with Vialli, Di Matteo and Petrescu they all dined at the Cafe de Paris off Leicester Square.

Rodney Marsh was spotted on Sky TV suggesting that if Vialli was claiming the goal he was a liar. Luca's response: 'Rodney March (sic) is a ******.'

MONDAY, NOVEMBER 25

Golf with van Basten in a tournament at Wentworth. Gullit delighted with the extra development of his team with the arrival of Zola. 'He's made a big impact on the crowd at Blackburn and against Newcastle. It's not easy to adapt yourself quickly, but he has. He can play midfield or up front, he has freedom during a game to do what he wants as long as he remembers the responsibilities he must carry out tactically. His arrival was followed by John Spencer leaving. We had a whole lot of players who I didn't want to leave. The policy of this club is we want them to stay and battle for a place. But if someone only wants to play, if he says, "I don't want to stay if I'm not in the team", then the coach cannot motivate him. If he wants to go somewhere else then he must go, and I truly hope that he finds that luck. Good luck, Spenny! It is the same for Gavin and "Steino". With "Steino", perhaps it is a little different. He's had a lot of injuries for some time, he was having difficulties getting in the squad last year and maybe it is best for him after nearly two years of that, and of training with the reserves, to go on loan. Gavin is another who didn't want to wait for his chance, who wanted to get away. I regret it, but we can't have people to stay here if they don't want to. Again, I hope he finds his luck. Wisey played very well in his 250th Chelsea game at Manchester United. He's played very well for the last few games. It has been up to him to adapt to the new situation, and he is handling it very well. That's because he is a good professional. He is playing well, better than before. He understands now that we can't assure him or anyone of a place. You have to play well every week. I see players playing better than before, now. Of course, this brings pressure. Good! It makes it easier for the staff. It is difficult with the crowd, too, now. The crowd demands that you do everything in order to win, and if they can see that the team is doing everything in their power, then it doesn't matter so much if sometimes it doesn't go for you. Like against Newcastle, we didn't win but the crowd was very happy with the performance. The team gave what everybody expected. The staff was happy too.'

TUESDAY, NOVEMBER 26

Hitchcock returned to training as the club owned up to a secret about the extent of his injuries ... he played with a broken finger while waiting for an operation on his elbow. Chelsea feared Hitchcock would be targeted if it had been known he was carrying such a serious injury. He was already nursing his injured elbow when he broke the small finger of his left hand during the warm-up against Nottingham Forest. He played the next five matches in pain until finally undergoing an operation on his elbow during the break for international matches. Goalkeeping coach Eddie Niedzwiecki said: 'For four weeks after his break he couldn't train with me until Friday. Kevin was in a lot of discomfort. He wanted to play, the manager wanted him to play. He's a brave lad and did well during the period. Unfortunately during that time we had one or two minor hiccups and Kevin is the type of player who needs to be training all the time. He had bits of bone floating around in his elbow as well and every time he straightened his arm or landed on it, it caused him a lot of grief. So when we had international week it was decided he'd go in for a small operation which needed twelve staples inserted and it just goes to show the bravery of him to play through such pain. Kevin is a quality man, a daft east Londoner, and I can't speak highly enough of him.'

Regrettably, Danish international defender Jakob Kjeldbjerg, twenty-seven, was forced to retire, losing his eighteen-month battle after two operations to try to clear up his knee cartilage damage. Gullit 'felt' for him. There was empathy, as Ruud had fought back from a number of knee operations. 'I've been close to that so I have some idea of how he must be feeling. It's a very difficult moment for anyone. I wish him good luck for the rest of his life. He is talking of taking up physiotherapy, and if he wants any guinea pigs he can always come here. He'll always be welcome to work on our boys!' The players bought him a Rolex watch, and organised a night out, starting at Covent Garden's TGI Friday's. They'll remember his piano playing and singing!

WEDNESDAY, NOVEMBER 27

Rix was annoyed at the suggestion the importing of foreign stars would hold back the youngsters at the club. 'It's untrue and I think we have disproved it. Even with all the foreign players who have come in, we have had Jody Morris and Mark Nicholls, at seventeen and nineteen, making their full debuts this season. By bringing in the best, we have set our standards high. Young lads are thinking "I've got to be a bit special to get in this team", and that's how it should be. We shouldn't settle for mediocrity. On the Tuesday after Zola signed, we were playing an eight-a-side possession game and his technique and the zip in his passing just took your breath away. The next day we did it again and all the home-grown players were trying things as well, to show him what they could do.'

There were casualties. As well as Spencer and Peacock, Phelan expressed his disillusionment. He spoke to Rix and Williams about his personal grievances. 'Since Ruud took over I've had a terrible time, been made to feel I am completely out in the cold. There have been times when he has simply walked past me in the corridor, not even acknowledged my existence. I have had a few injuries.' Phelan wanted to make it at the club, but didn't believe it would happen. 'I am fit now, yet haven't started a game. I've told the club if they don't want me, they should let me go.'

But British players did thrive in the new set-up. Rix cited Clarke, ten years with the club, as Chelsea's most consistent player. 'We've told him not just to kick it, that he's better than that. Most players are.' Duberry, he added, was keeping out overseas defenders, having blossomed in the 3–5–2 regime of 'keep the ball, pass it, show good imagination' established by Hoddle and skills work that filters down to under-12 level.

Was there a danger in buying expensive, fading, though talented, footballing tourists, especially in London, with no resale value? 'All the boys have been selected carefully for their character and adaptability, on the field and off,' said Rix. His experiences as an overseas player with Caen helped in dealing with players, notably Leboeuf, although 'at work' English is the only tongue encouraged.

None adapted better than Gullit, first as player, now as coach. 'It helped our relationship that he was injured for the first two months,' said Rix. 'I could pick his brains and know what he was thinking. We are on a similar wavelength, notice the same things in a game, and he trusts me. Sometimes Ruudi needs calming down a bit. Now he is playing again, he is thinking as a player. That's great during the game but at half-time you have to be cool. He's not complicated. His team talks last two or three minutes. His attitude is low-key: play with a smile on your face. He concentrates on what we do well rather than the opposition because he believes that we will give anybody a good game.'

Rix accepted there was still a problem, the capacity for defeat by the lower orders, as Bolton illustrated. 'We are trying to instil it into them that if you do not have the right mental approach in the Premiership, you can get beaten by anybody. It's as simple as that.' How close were Chelsea to muscling in on the elite of the north? Rix pinpointed the coaching at the pre-season Umbro tournament. 'As an experiment, Ruud had us man-for-man all over the pitch against Ajax and we slaughtered them. The players started believing how good they could be. Also, for me, the signing of Zola was interesting. Coming shortly after Matthew Harding's tragic death, it sent out a statement that we mean business. We are building a team, a club, a stadium to compete with the best. That was the legacy Matthew would have wanted.'

FRIDAY, NOVEMBER 29

Gullit was even more relaxed than normal. 'These are the happiest days of my football life. The job gives me a lot of pleasure, more than I ever expected. My first five months in charge of Chelsea have been the most fulfilling of my career. When I first took over at the start of the season, I didn't know what to expect. I thought I would have to play, whereas now I think I can enjoy and savour the good moments better from the bench. I am still not sure what to do, whether to be a player or coach. I know it is impossible to do both well. Sitting on the side means it is easier to see what's going on. Although I still love playing, I'm even happier if the team are doing too well for me to be in the starting line-up. That's what has happened. The players have earned my trust so I'm content to let them play without me. I think the very best time is the relief of scoring a goal, and watching the celebrations of the players after scoring. One of those moments came when Gianluca Vialli scored at Leicester. It meant so much to everyone. The enjoyment comes from watching and seeing the pleasure on the players' faces, knowing there is harmony throughout the club and that the players can handle the responsibility.'

The future of the team was in the hands of youngsters like Duberry as well as the big name signings. Gullit gave a new six-year contract to Duberry, a four-year extension, tying him to the club until the year 2002. The England under-21 star, linked to Manchester United as a replacement for Steve Bruce, said: 'This is one of the top clubs in the country and when you are offered the chance to stay here, you're going to want to take it. You've only got to look around to see the direction the club is going, especially when players like Vialli and Di Matteo are signed. All I can do is learn off them. If I do then, hopefully, by the time I'm twenty-four or twenty-five, I can be a full international. But I've got to keep listening and learning. The foundations are set, now we've just got to build on them.' It was the second pay rise for Duberry in nine months and elevated the youngster into the £6,000-a-week bracket.

Grodas signed a two-year contract, with a free transfer under the Bosman ruling. He rejected a two-year deal with Austrian club Linz which would have taken effect once his loan period expired at the end of the month. The thirty-year-old Grodas cost a £60,000 loan fee when he arrived from Lillestrom. Gullit twice had German goalkeeper Georg Koch watched but baulked at the £2m fee. Gullit said: 'It's a great sign that Frode wanted to join the club. He's an international keeper and it shows that world-class players want to be a part of Chelsea. It's now very easy for us to get these sorts of players and attract them. That's something I've always wanted to do and, by changing a few things, we are now more professional in every department. I want us to feel we are one of the big clubs and to think like one. I don't know how far down the road we are to getting there. Life's an adventure. You find out your limits and what you can achieve. So here we just take it week by week and see what happens.'

Kharine was out for the rest of the season and although Hitchcock had resumed training, he wasn't quite ready to be risked. Kharine suffered a rupture of his cruciate ligament for the second time in his career. The club had known for some time but had kept quiet about the devastating damage while they searched for a new keeper. After three clean sheets at the start of the season he recalled: 'I went for a cross and my knee did a twist. I felt very hurt, much pain. I had to wait two weeks for the arthroscopy because the knee was so swollen. Then on October 2 I had the main operation.' The same knee he injured when he was twenty. Improved technology made a big difference. 'I feel much better than after my last operation. I can bend my knee, walk and do exercises. I didn't do anything for three months last time.' Niedzwiecki twice ruptured cruciate ligaments. Kharine added: 'Russian people have saying: if you have everything then you wait for trouble. This is life. It is not possible to have everything.'

One alternative had been to sign Bobby Mimms, the much-travelled thirty-three-year-old at Preston. Mimms said: 'Yes, I had a chance to join Chelsea. They wanted cover for Kevin Hitchcock as Dmitri Kharine had got injured. But it was only going to be for twelve months. I was at Preston at the time and told them the situation and they sorted out a three-year contract which gave me more security. It was good of Chelsea to offer me the chance but I'm based in the north anyway and I've got absolutely no regrets about the decision.'

Gullit kept himself on the bench, naming an unchanged side for the Leeds game. Vialli missed training with a slight knock but Gullit said he would be fit. Burley, ruled out of the previous week's draw with Newcastle with a calf injury, was named in the seventeen-man squad but would probably have to be content with a place on the bench.

Few fixtures encompassed the feel for the seventies more than this one – those flying wingers, silly sideburns and colourful characters. The cultures of Elland Road and the King's Road were more than the World's End apart. 'They hated each other, kicked lumps out of each other, didn't they?' said Rix, a Yorkshireman, and then an Arsenal player. Little changed. 'Leeds will be steaming in, tackling for everything, the crowd will be booing Gianfranco Zola and Luca Vialli, calling us southern softies and all that,' said Rix.

Chelsea prevailed after a replay in a spiteful FA Cup Final between the two clubs in 1970, when Leeds finished second in the old First Division, Chelsea third. It was a prelude to the championship for one, in 1974; decline for the other, leading to relegation in 1975. Now Leeds looked at life from the drop zone as George Graham sought to arrest a decline of their own. Their 5–1 defeat at Anfield obscured it, but Chelsea's away form had been the basis of their recent ascent. Before that weekend's matches, their record of twelve points from seven matches was bettered only by Newcastle United and Liverpool.

'There are two kinds of courage in football,' said Rix. 'There is putting your head or foot in and there is sticking to your principles, playing with the pressure, not getting carried away by the taunts of the public. The likes of Zola, Vialli and Frank Leboeuf have the character and belief in themselves that comes from having seen it all. They have a mental toughness that maybe this club has lacked at times.'

Leeds hard man Mark Ford warned Gullit's football aristocrats to expect a rough ride. 'Gullit has assembled some great players, but hopefully we can knock them off their perch. We've got to get stuck in and deny them the space they need. No matter how good players are they need time on the ball, and we must make sure we don't allow them that time.' Powerful Duberry wasn't going to wilt but what about the rest of the team? The strapping centre-back said: 'If we can match Leeds for bottle, our football can win us this game. We get pumped up for matches against the likes of Manchester United and Newcastle, but we must also meet the challenge of a team lower down in the division. We have got to be up to meeting Leeds's enthusiasm and we must compete with them. People say we have no bottle, but we came back from a goal down against Blackburn Rovers and could have sneaked a win, so we can compete.'

Graham, with Deane, Rush, Wallace and Yeboah to call upon, said: 'I like to spring a surprise or two.' Would Yeboah return? Would it matter? Gullit said: 'He has suffered a long time. I know what it means to be out a long time – it is hard, physically and mentally. I'm happy he's back again, for his sake.' Gullit added: 'The Leeds game is more important to me than the Newcastle match. I know how George managed at Arsenal, and I expect the same at Leeds. But I don't talk about how other coaches interpret the game. You have to have your own vision. Games such as Newcastle are easy to get motivated for because they inspire players. It's when you play the so-called lesser or struggling sides that you are really tested.'

Gullit was sure his side were shaping up. 'We are doing well. With a third of the season gone, however, we can still improve a lot of aspects. But that is normal. I expected improvement by this stage, and it has come. But we are not yet where we want to be. Everybody, I am pleased to say, is aware of this which makes it easier for the management. You can see it in people in training, not going home immediately they've finished work together, but maybe going in the gym or staying on the pitch doing exercises. They are aware of how to improve themselves by themselves. The management doesn't have to tell them any more. In other words their awareness of being professional is much greater now.'

DECEMBER

Ruud Wear, M&M TV ad, computer contract. Gullit joins sporting elite. But away day blues at Roker Park and Elland Road.

SUNDAY, DECEMBER 1
Leeds United 2 Chelsea 0

Mark Hughes was lucky not to have his leg broken, stretchered off after being pole-axed by a high tackle from striker Brian Deane. Six stitches in an ugly four-inch gash above his ankle left him grimacing as he hobbled away. 'He came in high and when someone does that, you know you're going to be in real trouble. I feared the worst. I'm lucky. I think I got away with it. Once a challenge comes in higher than the level of your boot, you know there's a chance of serious injury.' Graham countered: 'Brian has some nasty scratch marks down his shins. That is part and parcel of the game. You don't want to take away the sport's physical nature.' Physio Mike Banks said: 'Mark's sock over his right shin was in tatters when I got to him and the pad was broken underneath. As usual, Sparky made light of it all, but there was an extremely deep gash which was impossible to repair.'

Referee Steve Dunn clocked up seven bookings but somehow managed to miss the horror tackle. Hughes had already felled Beesley with an assault from behind when Deane dished out retribution. Deane's studs crashed into Hughes's shin and left him crumpled in a heap near the touchline. He was eventually helped on to a stretcher and carried down the tunnel as a bemused Dunn looked in vain for help from his linesman. The Bristol official didn't have the best of afternoons with feuds breaking out around him. Beesley jabbed an angry finger at Vialli and Clarke for what he saw as blatant play-acting. Even Rush got involved and had a slanging match with Leboeuf, himself public enemy number one after playing a part in Deane's first-half booking. Gullit was bitterly upset. 'People always seem to be getting away with doing damage to Mark. I'm getting a bit fed up with it. I don't know if it's something to do with his past reputation. But I see things that amaze me at times. I could tell from the reaction of the crowd that it was a bad tackle on Mark and that he was in trouble. Mark is no angel on the field himself. He isn't the sweetest of players. It strikes me he has to pay the price for that but I don't want Chelsea to have to pay as well. I always thought the English attitude was that you love the physical side of the game. But it seems to go against Mark. The way things are at the moment, players don't know where they stand. They don't know which foul or offence will be punished.' Gullit was frustrated that players were confused and upset by inconsistent referees. 'A player doesn't know where he stands. He doesn't know which tackle will be punished and which one will be allowed to go. It is a big issue and we have to discuss this with the whole of the Premiership.'

Gullit's European Union came across a touch of Yorkshire grit. At a wet and windy

Elland Road, from the opening minutes when Vialli fell to the ground clutching his face following the merest nudge from Lee Bowyer, it was suspected that the foreign legion didn't fancy this one. Leboeuf was once again subjected to the rough stuff. Wimbledon gave him a major battering, and Deane carried on where the Crazy Gang left off. At least Di Matteo tried to get involved in the midfield war of attrition; but he was so much out of his depth he was withdrawn at half-time with the battle already lost. Petrescu was given the run-around from Lee Sharpe. Vialli managed one shot ... in the eighty-ninth minute. Zola managed a couple of tasty corner kicks, but he was completely snuffed out by South African defender Lucas Radebe. At least Grodas earned his corn – he had to!

Chelsea hadn't lost often on their travels, but when they did, it was normally pretty comprehensive. Gullit arrived with fifth place in his sights and left fortunate to have conceded only two goals. Instead of marvelling at the skills of Zola and Leboeuf, the more prosaic talents of Deane and Beesley were dominant. It was hard to remember when Leeds last played so well. A tetchy match of seven bookings was reminiscent of their meetings in the 1970s. The bookings for Leeds: Kelly, Deane, Ford, Beesley; Chelsea: Leboeuf, Hughes, Gullit. Gullit said: 'The game was maybe too hard. I believe the referee allowed too much.'

The match was won and lost in the first ten minutes. 'We threw the game away in ten minutes with two soft goals,' groaned Gullit. 'It was not a very good Chelsea performance, but I was pleased with the way everybody worked hard to get back into the game.' Deane put Leeds ahead, Rush got the second, his first goal since moving from Liverpool. After seven minutes, Beesley arched a ball down the left that ought to have pushed Deane too wide to be of any real threat. Grodas came for the ball and when he was second to it, Deane had an empty net to aim at, albeit from a narrow angle. Two minutes later it was 2–0. Gary Kelly crossed from the right, Petrescu was sufficiently hampered by Sharpe's challenge as the ball ricocheted to Rush eight yards out. For Liverpool he would have had the ball bulging in the net in a flash; after fifteen goalless matches for Leeds, you couldn't be sure. To his huge relief he scooped the ball in. 'Our tactics were spot on,' Graham said. 'We knew they would want to slow the game down and it was our duty to impose the pace of our game on them. We denied them time and space to show their ability. Zola is one of my favourite players but we gave Radebe a job to do and he was up to the task. Their defence looked a bit suspect.'

Chelsea had little option but to take risks, but their defence was given a fearful mauling by Deane in particular. He won virtually every ball in the air and his ungainly runs spread panic. Gullit tried to stem the flow by introducing himself and Newton at half-time; in a double switch, Di Matteo and Wise made way. Chelsea had to wait until the final twenty minutes before they could assume any authority. Clarke should have had a penalty when he was brought down by Carlton Palmer, and Sinclair headed powerfully against the bar from Zola's corner. Gullit observed: 'If we had been given the penalty it may have been a different game. I don't want any favours. We knew it would be physical and that we had to take care of the first twenty minutes. In spite of that we were two goals down in no time and then we were always chasing the game.' Deane had the final word in the closing minutes, hitting a shot from twenty yards against the bar.

Life was suddenly grand, at least for Rush. He was £1,000 richer and back on the goal trail. The grand-a-goal bonus was part of a lucrative contract thrashed out with previous manager Howard Wilkinson. Rush registered his first Leeds goal after the longest drought of his career. The thirty-five-year-old insisted all along that months of mental anguish in front of goal were not bothering him. Don't you believe it! An explosion of relief and elation when the magic moment arrived told a different story. 'I just knew it would come right if I kept battling away and kept looking for the openings. Three or four came my way today. That's the first time I've had anything like that many. I've kept believing that I'd score if I just got the chances. They finally came today and I was proved right. It's a great feeling to get my first goal in a Leeds shirt and hopefully there'll be plenty more to come.'

Graham concluded: 'Chelsea have to start winning things soon. With the players they have at the club now, they have got to win trophies. Me? I'm just going to enjoy this victory before catching up on my homework.'

After the match former Juventus legend John Charles was in the dressing room area collecting autographs from the Italians. 'Gentle John' was the first major Italian signing from the Football League, joining Juve from Leeds in 1956, returning to Elland Road after six highly successful years. He spoke to Vialli and Rush – three former Juve centre-forwards together!

Chelsea's dismal defeat prompted bookmakers to lengthen title odds from 14–1 to 20–1. Liverpool were 2–1 favourites, with Newcastle at 5–2, Manchester United at 3–1, and Arsenal at 7–2.

MONDAY, DECEMBER 2

Wise had either been substitute or substituted four times in the last eight matches, after being pulled off at half-time at Elland Road. Phelan was also closely monitoring events after failing to establish himself after injury. Johnsen wanted out, and so too did Burley, who said: 'I'm very disappointed in the way things have gone at Chelsea. It would appear that home-grown players are having to make way for the foreigners that have come into the club. I played in the first twelve matches of the season and was told I was doing a good job by the management themselves. Since then I have been out in the cold. I spoke to Graham Rix and Gwyn Williams about how I feel so I'm pretty certain Ruud also knows. I am aware that Wimbledon have already made enquiries and Bolton, too. I may get back in after the 2–0 defeat at Leeds but there have been a number of things I have been unhappy about at Chelsea over the last few months.'

Johnsen's patience snapped after four months stuck in the reserves. He could go for free when his contract ran out at the end of the season. 'I'm done with reserve team football. It is really good to know Rosenborg are interested in me. There's no doubt I'd like to go if it was right.' Johnsen cost £300,000 from Bayern Munich four years previously. He was a first-team regular until Gullit signed Leboeuf.

Vialli hoped for an international recall to face England in the World Cup. Coach Arrigo Sacchi resigned, leaving the way open for Vialli's return. Vialli, capped fifty-nine times scoring sixteen goals, had given up hope of playing for his country again, four years after rows with Sacchi saw him dropped from consideration. Even at the age of thirty-two Chelsea's top scorer with seven goals was hopeful about the Wembley clash. 'If I was called up to play for Italy now, I would go. When Sacchi was manager lots of people turned against him, regardless of how they played or the results.'

Vialli was enthusiastic about his new life and career in London. 'In Italy, I had a lot less freedom as there it was so difficult, both for me and Gianfranco. Italian supporters are very different from English fans, which is one of the big advantages for me of living and playing here. When I go out in London the fans don't make such a big thing of it. I can go out where I want to: museums, theatres, restaurants, cinemas, walk in Hyde Park or to Piccadilly, the Trocadero ... If the fans see me in the street they come up to me, shake my hand, say "Congratulations", "All the best" or "Well done" but then let me go on. Italian supporters are around you all the time, always on your shoulder, never leaving you alone. That gets very difficult.'

As for the football: 'The passion here and the love of the game are the same. But football in Italy is like a war. That makes it very difficult for you, your friends and your wife and children. Here in England I'm able to express myself more as a person, to be Luca Vialli the man, not just Luca Vialli the footballer. I've even started to change my personality. I've been here for five months but I feel more free, a lot less nervous. In Italy, I was nervous all the time as football is just so important there. If you lose a game, it seems to mean absolutely everything to the fans. Here it means a lot, but not everything.'

MONDAY, DECEMBER 2
Hughes went 'home' for a few days to rest the injured leg. Rix said: 'The injury is in a position where it could be padded and he could play, but the final decision will be left to him.'

TUESDAY, DECEMBER 3
Gullit was offered Israeli star Avi Nimni. Israel champions Maccabi Tel Aviv wanted £1.5m for the stylish midfielder. Nimni was so keen to move to London his advisers agreed to pay all his travel and hotel costs. A persistent Israeli agent sent a video of Nimni in action against Russia to Williams, but Chelsea decided not to proceed.

THURSDAY, DECEMBER 5
Gullit signed a £250,000 deal to produce a line of 'urban street' clothes – Ruud Wear. The potential royalties are worth millions. Under the brand name Admiral, which dominated the football strip market in the seventies and eighties, 'Ruud Wear' planned to launch a forty-piece range to coincide with next season. The deal with British company Hay & Robertson was the first of its kind involving a British soccer player, although Michael Jordan, Bjorn Borg and Greg Norman had all put their names to leisure clothes. Jon Smith said: 'The deal had been discussed for some time and actually sealed a few weeks back, but the company wanted to announce it through the *Financial Times*.'

The result of signing up Ruud was a Stock Exchange boom. Within weeks Hay & Robertson shares rose 201 per cent to 132.5p, the market's nineteenth best performer of the year. Jon Smith said: 'The contract has the potential for a seven-figure royalty payment.' Smith signed only major deals for Gullit: a new BBC contract to continue the Lynam–Hansen connection, a series of TV adverts with M&Ms, and a 'mega' computer deal. Gullit also coached world stars in Cyberspace in a computer game for kids, Striker '98.

But how much of Ruud's fashion sense was down to his girlfriend? Irascible Wise revealed the problems Ruud caused with the club suits. 'Ruud picked the first tie, the yellow one, and I think he's got himself out of it a little bit now because Estelle picked the second one and we look much better!' Ruud's turn for some internal leg pulling. 'Gwyn Williams will be my cat-walk model.'

Ruud joined the ever-swelling throng of football stars featuring in TV commercials with a deal with Mars to advertise M&Ms in a pan-European campaign, starting in March. It was suggested that the £600,000 deal included an agreement that Gullit would keep his trademark dreadlocks for a year after the ad goes on air, and wouldn't appear in any other sweet or ice cream shoot for two years.

The thirty-second ad produced for Mars by agency Abbot Mead Vickers is part of a world-wide campaign and as Ruud is fluent in four languages, he recorded the commercial in English, French, Italian and Dutch. A spokesman for the company said: 'Ruud is fun, young and successful. He combines this with being slightly irreverent and has a great personality. He's his own man.'

Jon Smith said: 'Ruud is in the same bracket as the world's top tennis and golf stars. His off-the-field earnings are enormous. The computer deal will be mega, so too will the designer wear. Ruud has been working for the BBC this season, we knew he would continue with them even though ITV were desperate to win him over. Ruud feels he is still learning the trade in front of the cameras and feels very comfortable with Des Lynam and Alan Hansen, and wanted to stay with them. We have been inundated with offers from the media, but have restricted Ruud to only a handful of appearances. Frank Skinner was desperate for him to appear on his new talk show; first a call from the producer and then one from Frank himself. If we do set up the occasional interview for a national newspaper, we do it based on the journalist and the paper and we don't charge.'

Venables, the new Aussie boss, was also signed up on the back of the expected success of the Ruud Wear, to market El Tel leisure. Lance Yates, Hay & Robertson chief executive, said: 'We were attracted to Ruud Gullit for his charisma and street cred. Terry Venables is loved by the public. Our strategy to promote the Admiral brand is pretty much in place although we are in discussions with some Premier and First Division clubs.'

FRIDAY, DECEMBER 6

Wise signed a £4m new contract to end any lingering rumours of a rift. It took Wise into the £15,000-plus-a-week category for the next five years. The one-year extension on his current four-year deal meant the thirty-year-old finishing his career at Stamford Bridge. Wise made his peace with Gullit. 'I'm very happy. Ruud showed me he wanted me to be part of his new regime so I signed the new deal. I did have doubts about my future and that's why I spoke to Ruud. There was no bust-up or storming out of rooms. Everyone has to find out where they stand and talk to the boss. If you're part of the plans you stay – if not you go. I'll be thirty-four when this deal ends in 2001 and my playing days will be numbered then. I've effectively tied myself to Chelsea for the rest of my career. But it wasn't a big step for me because I was always going to stay here. I've always liked it here. People said I had a bust-up with Ruud but when you have a conversation with someone it doesn't mean you've had a fight with them. We talked about a few things and everything's lovely. He explained that he needed a squad of eighteen to twenty players to win anything and he needed to use them. I wasn't happy at being taken off, got the hump, and he expected that. He expects you to show you care. But I never said I wanted to leave. Because I've never wanted to leave. Never.

'It was always an easy decision and I just needed to know from Ruud that he wanted me. It's nice to be part of his way of things and I'm glad to be involved. You sometimes need to sit down with the manager and sort a few things out. When people come in they do their own things. Ruud explained what he does, now I know and that is nice. I understand you have to be taken off sometimes for tactical reasons. You need certain players for certain games. That's the way it has to be. The game is about the squad and not just individuals. It's a team game and you win when everyone is involved. If you're out of the team then you have to fight to get back in. You can't sulk or moan. If you're not playing well you don't get back in the side. If I'm out of the side I have the hunger to get back in. I've always been like that.' Ever since Gullit took charge there was constant press speculation that Wise would be shown the door. 'It didn't unsettle me. Nothing unsettled me. But I couldn't understand why it was being said I would be out of the door before we'd even started.

'My main object is to win something now. That's very important. We still all enjoy it, but enjoyment, money, nothing comes into it. I want to win something. I don't want someone to say he had great times here but he never won anything. I want my photo up on the wall, and punters saying, "Yeah, we won this with him, we won that." I want it to be like it is with Peter Osgood, people remembering him for what he won. We've got great players here now. Over the years we've always just missed out. Now we have to fulfil our potential.

Wise spotted the difference between Hoddle and Gullit. 'Glenn and Ruudi have their ways of discipline, which are different. Players can't be complacent any more. There used not to be the squad here, so there were always a number of people who were certain of their place. Now you have one or two bad games and you're not playing.'

Gullit said: 'I'm glad Dennis was unhappy being on the bench – it's not normal to like that situation. Every week a story comes out that a player is unhappy, but they must prove me wrong to leave them out. It's not a bad thing that players are unhappy if they are left out. The big clubs have top players and if someone moans that he cannot cope with being left out, maybe he is not ready for a top team and should go to a smaller club.'

Gullit rewarded two more in-form players with new three-and-a-half-year contracts, Petrescu and Clarke.

Now Gullit wanted some old-fashioned English spirit after coming second-best in the physical stakes at Leeds. Rix said: 'The first twenty minutes cost us the game. Sometimes you have to earn the right to play your football by having a battle early on. Everton won't be that different from Leeds. They have big Duncan Ferguson and could well start with him. They push up and don't give you a moment's peace. We have been talking about it this week and the players will be prepared.' Gullit agreed: 'People know now that we can play good football. So people will want to try to stop us doing it. They will try and pressure us. You expect to be pressured but if you don't get the right protection you won't have a game. If you don't have the right attitude you won't have a game. We know we have another battle. We know we must be prepared for it.'

SATURDAY, DECEMBER 7
Chelsea 2 Everton 2
Zola's wonder free kick had Gullit drooling over the virtues of Italian imports. Vialli headed his eighth goal in the league as Gullit said: 'We had the same discussion in Italy when the foreign players arrived ... is it good for the national team? Now, a lot of discussion is about the Italians that have come to Chelsea and are pushing out the British players. But they are having a major impact on

the Premiership, they are bringing something special to Premiership football; everybody is very happy to see them play. I don't really understand what the discussion is all about. These players have brought something extra to the Premier League and they are talked about all the time, but for some reason they only talk about Italians.'

Little Zola's first goal in English football was a gem. A thirty-yarder, mesmerising Earl Barrett and Neville Southall after clearing the wall. Gullit said: 'I couldn't have done that, my feet are too big! I knew he could do things like that, that's why I bought him. He's small, but he is still strong.'

Zola is a free-kick specialist who sharpened his art by watching Diego Maradona at close quarters. He has a list of dead-ball experts he admires. 'Yes, Maradona, Platini, Zico and others. I always like to play football when I was young, always liked it. I watched television and could see great players shooting free kicks. For me this was very important. I had an example to follow. Maradona was my favourite because I played with him and I think he was the best player of all time. Every day I saw him kicking, so I could learn other things to improve my technique. Usually I train at free kicks once a week for thirty minutes, or maybe twenty minutes now. Before when I played for Naples I used to train more, maybe for an hour. I have to train my quality. When you train yourself you improve a lot. The important thing is to believe in it. Nothing is impossible. Everybody can do it. It is most important to try, try, try. You have to understand yourself. I am very happy to have a free kick. It is important when I have the ball in a game that I believe I can do it. Very important.'

Zola might have scored a second from another free kick, much closer, just outside the penalty area. Gullit's quick turn and right-wing cross left Vialli grounded and Barrett complaining to referee Paul Durkin. Zola's free kick clipped the top of the defensive wall, and from the corner Vialli chased, produced a delightful back heel and from Duberry's cross Gullit, of all people, headed just over from two yards – kicking the post in frustration.

Despite all the attention showered on the Serie A stars Royle picked out Gullit as the superior foreign player on show. 'He is probably still their best player. No disrespect to the others but he looked terrific. Up front or in midfield or wherever. Only he will tell you how often his legs will take him there. But he was terrific ... I just wish he'd stayed in the dug-out!' A smile of sheer modesty broke on Ruud's features when told of Royle's accolade. 'No!' He said modestly. Yet, to his own incredibly high standards probably he didn't play well enough.

Gullit played in attack in place of the injured Hughes and missed three chances, all of them headers. 'I could have scored in the first half. I feel I don't have my rhythm yet, especially in the second half when I made three runs. After that my tongue was on my shins! You compensate by trying to play it easy.'

Would next season be his last? He was already pacing himself. 'If things are going well with my team then I will not be playing. That was my first striker's role of the season because of the injury we have with Mark Hughes. When I was offered the job as manager here I thought hard and then hesitated to take it because I wanted to carry on playing. At this stage in my career, every game is precious to me. I must make the most of every time I play. It's a lot easier to stay on the sidelines and watch the match, only then can you see what you need to see. It's difficult for me because, of course, I want to be out there but sometimes you have to do what is right for others, not for yourself but for the team and for the club. Now that I have experienced playing and managing together, I have realised it's hard to do both and that's why I may not play so much.'

Gullit refused to risk Hughes. 'We spoke about whether he should play but because of the extent of the wound, especially on the shin, there was a danger of it opening up and being infected. So I played up front.'

With the increasingly impressive Vialli pulling up in the last few minutes with a hamstring Gullit was poised for an extended run in the side. In fact Gullit had problems for the next match at Sunderland with Vialli ruled out. Hughes would be back, but first he had a World Cup assignment with Wales against Turkey at Cardiff, then would have to travel north for the Roker Park clash twenty-four hours later. Even more problematical was Petrescu who faced Macedonia in Skopje on Saturday with the club trying to work out how to fly him back in time. On top of all that Leboeuf was suspended. Maybe the Frenchman would enjoy a rest. In the last minute he got in the way of a Wise clearance and Grodas made his best save of the match to save Chelsea from defeat. Maybe Gullit would have to play sweeper as well as striker.

How long would Vialli be out? Gullit smiled. 'Well, if I say four weeks, then anything less will be a bonus.'

Gullit's presence from the start certainly lifted Chelsea but another draw did not truly satisfy either manager. Royle was upset Zola was allowed the free kick in the twelfth minute after the Italian dispossessed Barrett and while taking up possession was brushed off the ball by Joe Parkinson. Just six minutes later the ever-dangerous Duncan Ferguson touched on Andy Hinchcliffe's cross, Leboeuf was beaten to the bouncing ball, and young Michael Branch equalised. A magnificent pass by Ferguson over Clarke into the stride of Andrei Kanchelskis culminated in a comfortable goal in the twenty-eighth minute but emphasised Everton's growing dominance of the first half, and Chelsea's frailties at the back.

It changed after the interval, with Gullit making tactical adjustments, reverting to a flat back four. At the end Chelsea were unfortunate not to win. But what about those defensive blunders? Was it the defence at fault? Gullit brushed aside suggestions that he needed to do something drastic, similar to Keegan employing Mark Lawrenson as a defensive guru. 'When I started the second half with a back four, three in midfield and three up front, that was something drastic. You make it hard for the opposition because they don't know how we will play.' Minto came off and Burley took his place. Royle conceded: 'They put on an extra offensive player but they already had a dozen of those!'

Gullit conceded his side gave away 'two sloppy goals' and 'in a strange way'. But he added: 'Ten minutes into the second half we scored an equaliser that gave us enough time to win and we dominated.' Gullit did not share Keegan's philosophy that his team would outscore the opposition, irrespective of how many goals were conceded. He was intent on cutting down the mistakes and eliminating the goals against.

Zola was the inspiration behind Chelsea's equaliser, winning the ball in his own half, then a sharp passing interchange with Gullit and his chip to the near post was finished off by Vialli in the fifty-fifth minute. When Gullit took a throw to Leboeuf, the Frenchman produced a magnificent pass to Zola whose shot was cleared off the line by David Unsworth; somehow Southall saved the rebound from Vialli. Zola also clipped the top of the bar from a corner in an all-round outstanding display. Zola said: 'I was happy because it was my first goal in England. But we made little mistakes and the other team scored. That is the problem. In the second half we played well but we did not win, and we have to think about that.' Zola's interview in the press room was interrupted by his son Andrea. For a while the yellow teddy with the headscarf over his eye occupied him, but soon boredom set in!

Down to seventh place, Chelsea needed a winning run to re-establish title aspirations. Royle branded Chelsea and Everton as 'wannabes' ... they are better than their position on the fringe of the championship. How do 'wannabes' become canbes? Gullit's instincts told him Chelsea were not that far away. 'Everybody was really amazed the ball didn't want to go in for the winning goal. Twice off the line, incredible it didn't want to go in. We have to win these games, but instead we've lost four points. We hope we can still win them back, but of course they have gone already. We hope to break that one day but with all those efforts that don't want to go in, you can't coach against that.' While Gullit sought divine intervention Royle was more basic. 'We've got to start keeping clean sheets. They've played very well but Arsenal will tell you how to win things, and so will Manchester United, and that's the answer. We've beaten all the top sides in the last two years, we don't fear anybody in this league. There are six or even seven sides capable of winning the title, not one team has stamped themselves as the one. We have ten points to make up and I hope we can.'

Royle had no objections to the foreign revolution. 'The problem arises when someone arrives from Eastern Europe with four Cs and two Zs in his name but is no better than those we have here. But Zola was different class.'

It wasn't all glory for the Italian boys. Di Matteo was dropped for the first time to the subs' bench. Gullit explained: 'There's no problem. For two weeks he has been a little bit out of form. I want him in the team but he has to work hard to get back. He understands. It's nothing bad, a lot of players have this kind of period. As a coach you pick the ones who are fit and doing well; Craig Burley came in and did very well for the team. It shows the choices made by the staff are right. It's only a matter of time before he is back.'

Gullit concluded: 'It's a very open championship, a very good championship. There is not one weak or very strong team in it. Everybody can challenge. We have a good team but we need to win these games and it was a pity that we didn't. I was satisfied how the team reacted in the second half, much more effort, much more of everything, and that was shown by the reaction of the crowd, they were very happy the way the team played in the second half. Still it's a very interesting race.'

SUNDAY, DECEMBER 8

Thugs clubbed Phelan and Norwich's Mike Milligan with champagne bottles after releasing CS gas. The Republic of Ireland internationals needed stitches. Phelan spent four hours in Manchester's Withington Hospital. Neither player spoke to police about the attack early on Sunday morning at the Four Seasons hotel near Manchester Airport. A police spokesman said: 'There were no arrests because there were no complaints made.' Leeds star Lee Sharpe was praised by a partygoer sprayed in the face with CS gas during the fracas. Sharpe said: 'A gang of lads went over to Terry's group. The next thing Terry was being carted into an ambulance.' Later Phelan said: 'Because I was in such a state of shock it didn't really dawn on me how lucky I had been. At the time none of us had any inkling there would be trouble. But the next thing I knew I was in an ambulance with blood pouring from a wound at the centre of my forehead.' It was to cause a problem in training later with the wound opening up after he headed the ball. It only hindered his crusade to get back in the team.

MONDAY, DECEMBER 9

The FA Cup third-round draw live on BBC 2 at 10.15pm with Hoddle pulling out the black balls for the home side and former England boss Bobby Robson the away balls. Hoddle pulled out a home draw for Chelsea against West Brom … David Baddiel against Frank Skinner! Hoddle reminded millions of TV viewers that Chelsea's biggest scare en route to the 1994 final was in the third round against Barnet, when the Third Division side came so close to snatching victory with a late chance. Liverpool were 5–1 favourites, with Manchester United and Newcastle 6–1.

An ultra-scan suggested Vialli's hamstring was not as severe as first feared, and Luca dashed off to Italy, seeking an early cure with a week of non-stop treatment from Sampdoria master healer Sergio Vigano. Vialli wanted to take him to Juventus when he left Sampdoria, but Roberto Mancini objected and so did the club. Vigano treated Vialli on numerous occasions and got him through some difficult injuries. Gullit consulted his own injury guru when he needed surgery on his knee. It is custom and practice on the continent for top stars to consult specialist physio-therapists. A hamstring was routine, but Vialli's Italian mission highlighted how badly he wanted to play for his club.

It caused a stir in Italy; he was bundled out of the club's training ground in a clothes basket to avoid waiting journalists! Italy's most famous footballer covered himself with smelly rags and was carried to his car to avoid the paparazzi besieging the club. Reporters wanted to quiz him on his treatment. One journalist said: 'All the press were waiting. No one noticed when two boot room men carried a clothes basket to the car park. It was only later everyone realised how he had escaped speaking to us.' Williams said: 'I spoke to Luca on the telephone and he is a lot better. It's not a question of him being unhappy with our injury treatment. It's just he has known Vigano for a long time and has great faith in him. Luca paid out of his own pocket for the treatment and it's fine with us.'

TUESDAY, DECEMBER 10

The players attended a packed Christmas dinner-dance at the Novotel, Hammersmith. Vialli, Petrescu and Hughes were abroad.

WEDNESDAY, DECEMBER 11

Hughes joined the Wales squad in Newport where national team doctor Graham Jones assessed his injury. Hughes had not given up hope of playing in the World Cup qualifier against Turkey. Chelsea physio Mike Banks predicted Hughes would be determined to defy the injury and declare himself available. 'He should be available but the stitches will still be in on Saturday and if Mark gets a whack on the injury it will really hurt him. It's a case of getting it well padded up and protected and seeing how that feels. The injury will be reviewed by the Wales doctor but I think the final decision will be Mark's and knowing him he'll be up for it.' Rix said: 'If there is a chance of Mark playing for us after the Wales game we would obviously want him to be involved. Unfortunately for us, we will definitely be without Dan Petrescu. There is no chance of him getting to Sunderland in time to play.'

Hughes said: 'The medical advice is to keep the stitches in until after the game, so I will be guided by that. That shouldn't be a problem, although the cut is still a little inflamed and there's quite a bit of fluid around it. But I don't want to miss this match if at all possible. We need to put in a big performance after the Holland defeat. Everyone in the squad was bitterly disappointed after that display. But I am sure we can put it behind us.'

THURSDAY, DECEMBER 12

Gullit ordered his stars to cut out the fancy stuff and get back to basics, fed up with the number of goals his team were leaking. Chelsea hadn't kept a clean sheet in their previous fourteen games, since Kharine suffered a serious knee injury at Sheffield Wednesday three months earlier. Rix said: 'We need a change of attitude when the other team have got the ball. Everyone wants to play nice football but first of all we've got to defend properly. We're not winning because we're letting in too many goals. We're creating so many chances and really dominating games and we just can't keep going on like this without winning more. Our first four or five games of the season were based on keeping a clean sheet but now the emphasis seems to have shifted and we've got to get that back. It's not as if the opposition have been scoring wonder goals against us. We're just making too many individual errors and you can't legislate for that on the training ground. It seems that every time a defender makes a wrong decision the ball ends up in the back of our net. We've got more than enough players to create opportunities and we're always more than capable of scoring goals. So if we can get things right at the other end of the pitch we won't be too far away at the end of the season.'

FRIDAY, DECEMBER 13

Gullit insisted he was not too hasty disbanding the strike force inherited from Hoddle, despite being forced to travel to Sunderland with a scratch attack – himself! Gullit was not yet match fit, and Hughes would be on international duty twenty-four hours earlier. Chelsea would need all the striker resources they could muster with five games in fifteen days. Gullit had sold Spencer, loaned Peacock and Stein, sold Furlong. Gullit said: 'I am not nervous about it at all. We will cope. People say: "This will test them, can they handle this?" But no one here feels they are being tested.' Gullit planned to review the Hughes situation at the last moment. 'I will see how Sparky is when he arrives and then decide. But I want him to be with the squad. It is a matter of keeping spirits up. Mark at least is in the country. We will see whether he is fit enough to cope with two matches in twenty-four hours. But he is tough. I am slowly coming back to fitness and if I am needed to play, I will play. We have twenty-two players and each has different skills. Every skill is useful.' Gullit ruled out any further forays into the transfer market. 'I am happy with the players I have. There is no problem.' Gullit named Zola among the greatest dead–ball specialists in the modern game. 'Sometimes when he is doing his exercises it is amazing how the ball is curving. I don't know how he does it. I only know I could never do it.'

Zola was sure Gullit would find a successful team plan. 'Chelsea are working hard to play the European way under Ruud Gullit. We need to improve, and I think we will with time. But the style of play was important to me. Sunderland will be a difficult game. But we are looking forward to this match with victory in mind.'

Sinclair, yet to start a match, replaced the suspended Leboeuf. Sinclair said: 'I'm fit and raring to go. I'm just waiting for my chance to get back into the side and then it's down to me to play well.' Hitchcock was included in the squad and Di Matteo travelled despite missing training with a cold.

SATURDAY, DECEMBER 14

Training at Harlington before jetting off to Sunderland. Hughes played in a 0–0 with Turkey, the watching Niedzwiecki drove him straight back to Heathrow to catch a flight to Newcastle, then he was driven to the team hotel. Petrescu had an even more hectic schedule: played in Skopje where Romania beat Macedonia 3–0 in a World Cup tie, flew to Vienna, caught another flight to Heathrow, arriving Sunday morning, telephoned Williams and was told it was not necessary to fly north straight away. He watched the match on TV.

SUNDAY, DECEMBER 15

Sunderland 3 Chelsea 0

The Gullit championship dream turned from a swagger to a stagger, title odds tumbling from 16–1 to 33–1 long shots.

Gullit was in despair after another humiliating defeat. Five games without a win! Zola yet to finish on the winning side! Gullit was not happy. 'There were strong words afterwards. We didn't deserve anything. I know we haven't won for five games, but I'm not worried about that. We didn't play well against Leeds and Sunderland but we certainly had the other games there in our hand.'

Without Leboeuf – suspended – and Vialli injured, while Petrescu didn't make it back on time, and Hughes was only risked after an hour; flu victim Di Matteo didn't go on until after half-time. Sunderland's opener was the turning point. Craig Russell's shot was diverted in by Duberry. Gullit complained: 'Until Sunderland's first goal we'd played some good football. We went in at half-time and said we had to be solid, then went out and gave them a goal straight away. It was incredible. And that has happened to us in our last five matches. People call it bad luck and I only hope it ends as soon as possible. What worries me most is we keep giving away stupid goals. I had hoped we'd got rid of that aspect of our game. You pay the price if you don't pick up the man. From that point we were chasing the game after what I felt was an open match. We had some good chances. We were unfortunate.' Talking about his attacking role, Gullit said: 'I had to play in this position. I don't think it was mentally or physically right to ask Mark Hughes to start as he could have picked up something like a hamstring injury.'

A shimmy and turn by Gullit shook off two close markers in one moment of blinding brilliance; but that was a rare moment of magic to savour for the Chelsea travelling fans. Wise was clean through on the stroke of half-time but gave keeper Lionel Perez the chance to come out and block at his feet.

Sunderland defender Andy Melville reflected on two emphatic away defeats for Gullit in front of the live TV cameras, and said: 'Other teams will have noted that Chelsea can be hustled out of their stride and are bound to try it themselves. There's no doubt about it – they're going to have to cope with that side of the game if they're to challenge for honours.' Leeds showed raw-boned aggression can triumph over finesse. Sunderland took that as their cue. Melville added: 'They've got so many players who are top quality and who can do brilliant things on the ball. Gianfranco Zola, for instance, is a class act with an exceptional first touch. But we were determined they weren't going to have the space and time to start showing everyone what they can do. Sit back and let them play, and you're in trouble. But if you get your tackles in and work hard at closing them down, it's a different matter. That was the key for Leeds, and it was the same for us. Maybe I expected a bit more from Chelsea, but, to be fair, we didn't let them play any better. They've got great individuals, but we worked so hard as a team that they had no answer to it. Other teams are going to learn from this. They're bound to. It was live on TV, and teams due to face Chelsea are sure to set their stall out to do exactly the same as we did. Chelsea like to play to a pattern, but we didn't give them a second to settle on the ball. Now the big question is whether they can cope with that sort of close attention.'

Gullit was anxious to reinstate the work ethic. Grodas said: 'He told us that Sunderland had worked harder and wanted to win more. He said football was simple. We did join the battle but I don't think we battled hard enough. Some players were working, others were looking. That was the problem. We have to stick together and work together as a team. We did not have the luck for the first goal when a shot hit Michael Duberry's back. At half-time Ruud told us to stay calm but we did the opposite, losing a goal shortly after the break. I don't think we should worry too much about our formation but perhaps we should look at how little work we put in against Sunderland.'

Chelsea were the great under-achievers and Gullit knew the sniggering and the sniping was beginning to start again. Sunderland, hardly the most prolific scorers in the Premiership, could have had half a dozen. Brian Little was at Roker to spy on Chelsea in preparation for the Boxing Day match at Villa Park. He came away a happy man! The Roker fans roared: 'Can we play you every week?'

A booking for Clarke took the season's tally to forty-three yellow cards, on a par with worst offenders Middlesbrough, who also had one red card to their name. Next came both Arsenal and Leeds with forty-two yellow each and one red card.

No video of this game on the coach journey home. That came later in the week when the defeat was analysed. Wise said: 'We tried to forget it for a while and watched a video Scott Minto brought: *Toy Story*. It went off after ten minutes.'

MONDAY, DECEMBER 16

Chelsea slumped to eighth in the Premiership – a dozen points behind leaders Liverpool – their lowest since the second game of the season. Hughes declared: 'At Chelsea we play brilliant football one day, and then fail to win matches we should have done the next. I think it takes time for a side with new players to settle down. At the moment we are not producing the goods week in, week out, which the sides who finish top do.' Sparky shot down suggestions he did not get on with the Italians. 'It's great to play with Luca. He's so quick, and you always think things are going to happen when he gets the ball. I get knocks and all kinds of bruises, including my current shin injury. But they don't bother me, and I have a good injury record. I shall play until I'm thirty-six at least.'

TUESDAY, DECEMBER 17

Hoddle made his playing comeback and was carried off after scoring. The England boss turned out in the annual Christmas fixture between club staff and the youth team. 'We packed the midfield, with Glenn slightly overweight it has to be said,' joked Rix. But Hoddle hit the second goal in the staff's 4–2 win and was carried back to the dressing rooms in the traditional piggy-back style. Gullit refereed and left the losers bleating about some of his lop-sided decisions! Hoddle joked: 'Some things never change at this club – that's three years running the staff have won this fixture. But you know your career is going downhill when you are called away from the England job to earn a late call-up for this game! I can tell you something – when I'm sixty-four, I'm not coming back to play here.'

WEDNESDAY, DECEMBER 18

Gullit's staff targeted Stockport's Luis Cavaco, the twenty-two-year-old Portuguese winger. 'Chelsea saw Luis score a wonder goal at Brentford, they were also at West Ham and then took another look at him in our league game at Walsall,' said chairman Brendan Elwood. 'But we are not interested in selling any of our players.'

Lee had the plaster removed; Hitchcock and Johnsen made comebacks in the reserves. Harding left £200m in his will; the cash split between wife Ruth and girlfriend Vicky. His children and Vicky's daughter Jessica also got a share. Harding left instructions that his fortune should continue to support Chelsea. The will, drawn up in May, was witnessed by Hoddle, a mark of the closeness that grew between the two men. The High Court granted two of Harding's friends – Mark Killick and Margaret Nugent – power to invest his fortune for the good of the beneficiaries. The club might be left with a financial headache if the trustees of his estate decided to sell his £50m shares in Chelsea Village.

THURSDAY, DECEMBER 19

The players' Christmas lunch at the training ground, with their tradition of the staff acting and dressing as waiters in their wing-collared white shirts and bow ties. Quite an experience for the foreign imports. Ruud claimed he was still a player and sat at the back enjoying the hilarious proceedings as the youth team and all the new players sang for their meal.

Leboeuf was the star turn with a rendition of 'My Way' in French. There were cheers for the Italian trio, Vialli and Di Matteo on lead vocals and Zola doing some sort of soft shoe song and dance routine. Grodas performed a Norwegian folk song which included jumping on a table. Leboeuf said: 'The new players must sing, that's what we were told. But it was a lie. It was just the young players who have to do that. But they wanted us to perform. I only knew two hours beforehand. Yes, I enjoyed it. I liked the three tenors, Pavarotti, Domingo and Carreras.'

Kharine flew off to Spain for a two-week break in his rehabilitation programme.

FRIDAY, DECEMBER 20

Mike Newell arrived at West Ham on a month's loan with a view to a permanent move, after the Hammers were dumped out of the Coca-Cola Cup by Second Division Stockport. Ian Dowie had the nation in stitches as his bizarre, headed own goal helped the Hammers to a 2–1 defeat, then broke a bone in his ankle. 'No crisis,' said Harry Redknapp. 'The fans are not going to be happy with what has happened but it is up to me to lift the players now. And I am sure Ruud Gullit will be doing the same after Chelsea lost against Sunderland.'

Gullit re-called Di Matteo, explaining why he had been rested. 'He has not been up to the level I would expect from him for the past few weeks. His form has gone down a little bit and he has suffered more with the winter months, although I expected it to some extent. I wanted to save Roberto a little. I've told him which are the tough games and told him to rest, train and get settled again. But he will play against West Ham.'

Newton, groomed by Hoddle for a 'holding' role in midfield, was playing the best football of his life when he broke his leg in a collision with his own goalkeeper – Hitchcock – against West Ham. Ten months on, Newton re-established himself in the side. 'It was a freak accident. I was running towards my own goal with Dani, got in front and guided the ball back to Kevin. But then Dani gave me a little shove in the back and Kevin's knee connected with my shin. I remember Kevin was crying for me as I was carried off. The worst part was in the ambulance when, even though I was having gas, I could feel every bump in the road. They told me it was the best of breaks, very clean, but it's been hard.'

As time stood still for the Chelsea youth team graduate, he witnessed a procession of continental signings arrive. For all the flamboyance of Di Matteo and Co., Newton never doubted his importance to the side taken over by Gullit. Newton, twenty-five the previous Friday, said: 'You're working on regaining your fitness as Vialli signs, Leboeuf joins, Di Matteo comes in and then Zola. You desperately want to be in there, proving yourself. But you know there's nothing to do but keep concentrating on getting fit. If you're playing at the top level, you can't expect not to have competition. I've had to prove myself with four different managers, all with different ideas. When they came in they may try something different; you bite your tongue, buckle down, prove them wrong and get back in the side.'

Gullit bought Di Matteo for the anchor role but Newton was confident of keeping his place. Coming on at Leicester to turn a 1–0 deficit into a 3–1 win, he replaced Di Matteo. The former England under-21 cap said: 'This won't be the last time I'll have to fight for my place, but that's OK.' Newton added: 'They've all come in and got on with the boys. Their English is improving, and they're enjoying London. When they see all the trouble at Middlesbrough, they say: "London's the place to be." They understand our humour.'

The promotion to the England job for Hoddle had not brought with it an influx of Chelsea stars to the World Cup squad. Newton said: 'He pulled me aside one day and told me: "You can tackle, you can head, you can pass, you've got the skill when you're in trouble. In the system I want to play, you're the man for the holding position." Glenn had seen it on the continent and he showed me the way. It worked.' Newton believed that in this position only Ince and Batty were ahead of him in the international pecking order before his clash with Hitchcock. He set his sights on France '98. 'It is a burning ambition for me to play in the World Cup Finals. Glenn knows my qualities,' he said with a grin. 'But I might have to slip a few notes in with the Christmas card.'

In contrast Phelan, Hoddle's last signing who hadn't started a Chelsea game, was handing out an ultimatum if he was left out again. 'I've had enough. I'll be in my car driving back to Salford if I'm not playing. I am totally frustrated. I was signed as number one left-back, yet I can't get my place. It's not as if I've had a bad spell. I've been injured. What is going on? If I'm not good enough then surely Ruud should tell me. I want to play for Ireland, but manager Mick McCarthy has told me he can only pick players who are actually playing. I enjoyed every minute of returning to London and playing for Chelsea with Glenn. He made me feel wanted. Now, all I know is that if anyone is picked ahead of me on Saturday, then that's it. I'm off.'

Phelan became Britain's most expensive left-back, leaving Wimbledon for Manchester City for £2.5m. Hoddle signed him for £700,000 and he became an instant hit with fans because of his aggression and pace. He added: 'I was injured and accepted being out and others coming in. But I've been fit for weeks. I just ask for Ruud to be fair. I want him to pick me or let me go. It's as simple as that.' First

Minto, then Myers leapt ahead, and there was another shock. Gullit called up eighteen-year-old Neil Clement and told him on the morning of the match that he would be making his debut. Leboeuf and Wise were suspended, Vialli still had a hamstring injury but Petrescu returned. Clarke captained the side, and Gullit was primed for yet another role, back to sweeper with Zola up front alongside Hughes. Chelsea were twelve points behind leaders Liverpool . . .

Gullit turned on the critics still sniping away at his foreign captures. 'This whole thing has exploded because of what has happened with Emerson at Middlesbrough. It has given attention to the foreign players, especially ours. It is not fair to say every foreign player can be compared with what is happening at Middlesbrough. I am happy with the commitment of my players. The fans are also happy. When I was at Milan, we were not given any favours because we were so good. We had to fight jealousy from so many people. Everyone wants to beat Chelsea now, that is natural. I have told my players this and advised them to stick together and carry on working hard. I am not looking to build a side completely of foreign players, but people should ask themselves "What do we want, what are we creating?" We have been going up this season and now we have levelled out a bit. But that is natural. The trouble is, some people do not like change. Some clubs look into their wallet and do not want to spend or cannot. Because of the Bosman ruling, foreign players are coming here. It seems you want to be part of Europe in this country, but not football. My team keep playing right to the end and we never give up. I can do nothing about goals that go in off one of my players' backsides. I never see these kind of things happening in our favour. One day the luck will change. I would like to see us play badly and win. We have played some very good matches; we have deserved more than draws. I'm pleased at how we have handled the games. It is disappointing that we've lost points, but everyone is convinced by the way we're playing. It's a very good sign. I am sure our results will change. I believe it is just a matter of results now. My players know they can do better and there is a lot of hard work for us to do yet. My team have adapted well and there is a very good atmosphere here. They all get on very well.'

SATURDAY, DECEMBER 21
Chelsea 3 West Ham United 1

'Gorgon' Zola become a *grand fromage* among the foreign legion in English football with a world-class goal and dazzling display in his first win in the Premiership. Zola was as amusing off the field as he was devastating on it in giving terminator Julian Dicks the run-around in a way that nobody else would dare contemplate. Zola dribbled one way then the other, leaving Dicks embarrassed and searching for revenge, before scoring his goal – and when the Hammers hard man targeted Zola his tiny feet were just too quick. Was it bravery or sheer stupidity to take on the shaven-haired assassin from the East End? Had he heard of Dicks's formidable psycho reputation? In his broken English, Zola joked: 'I think they could have told me about him before the game! Had they done that I'd have played for the other side.' Zola knew the importance of this result. 'Yeah, if we didn't win today maybe I would have needed a ticket to go back to Parma . . . I am only joking.' He added: 'It was not only my goal it was my overall performance for the team. I could have scored more and I can do better, but the most important thing is that today we played a very good game and everybody is happy.'

Gullit assembled the highest level of overseas stars other than West Ham. The

Hammers had the most non-British players in the Premiership, ten, reduced from eleven after the loss of Paulo Futre. Chelsea had nine, followed by Man. United with seven, Southampton six, and Arsenal, Aston Villa, Coventry, Derby, Middlesbrough and Sheffield Wednesday with five apiece in a Premiership that shared ninety-seven foreigners among its twenty clubs. Zola was up there among the elite already. He said: 'I can be more effective for the team, that's my target. We all have to work a lot to improve but it helps to have an intelligent person like myself!' Zola asked, when he was handed a glass of Coke, 'Is it wine?' The press steward duly ran off to fetch a glass of white wine to put before him. 'I was only joking,' he said again.

Still finding it difficult with his pronunciation, grammar and sentences he called his new team 'Chels'. He tried to explain the fluctuating fortunes of his team's frustrating away form compared to its successes at the Bridge. 'It's not only a problem for Chels, it's a problem for other teams. At times English football is very physique [physical], aggressive, but if you are organised you can win. It is a small margin between winning or losing and I think we can still win away.'

Zola expressed his utmost admiration for Gullit. 'He's a good coach because he knows the football, he knows how the football must be played. I don't have a problem with his ideas. I think he will give Chelsea a lot of satisfaction. Football is different here but I see good things from the coach and it's very interesting.'

A cheeky back heel and Zola set up Hughes for the opening goal after five minutes, the Premiership's fastest of the weekend. Then, Gullit started the move that ended with Zola twisting Dicks in all directions for the second after just nine minutes. Gullit demonstrated his remarkable versatility. From emergency centre-forward, to the wing, or midfield. Now sweeper, where he started in his first six matches the previous season. 'It's a different role; I had to adapt myself a little bit at the beginning. The first half was so-so, but in the second half I felt more solid. You have to get used to new positions.' He could have fooled me!

Gullit's priority was to tighten up at the back. 'If you feel solid behind everybody you feel comfortable. Frode had to make a good save before half-time, but everybody was tuned in.'

As I put it to Ruud, 'You've not played in goal yet!'

It was a Gullit tackle that gave Hugo Porfirio the shooting chance to haul the Hammers back after eleven minutes. But from a Burley break and Petrescu cross, Hughes headed Chelsea back into a commanding lead after thirty-five minutes. Two minutes later, from a Gullit pass, Hughes's shot was deflected off the line by Dicks and on to the post. Hughes might have scored more but it was a triumph of courage surviving the entire game with his ankle heavily padded, despite taking some nasty whacks. Di Matteo struck the post eight minutes from the end after a move from Gullit, Zola and Hughes, leaving Redknapp moaning about defensive frailties. 'We started two goals down in only ten minutes. We played three centre-halves but can't defend and we can't give away goals as we've done today and expect to win matches. We had a fair amount of the ball but the difference was that when they had the ball they looked like scoring. I didn't try to man-mark Zola because we haven't a marker – neither, on today's showing, have we defenders who can pick up Mark Hughes.'

Southern softies? Gullit shrugged. In all probability he hadn't the slightest idea what that meant. He didn't let on. 'Everyone can say whatever they like. Criticism and compliments are part of the game and you have to accept it. This was a good solid performance, I never had the feeling we'd throw this game away. Zola's goal was world-class, both strikers were world-class. I'm happy about every foreigner who has come to this club and Zola has brought something in particular. His skills have stolen the hearts of everyone; the crowd like him. The players we have brought have given something extra to the Premiership and I am very happy for Franco, this was his best performance.'

Gullit's purchasing policy was based on a simple philosophy of recruiting the right player for the right role, not of creating an exclusive overseas club. He wanted good players who could adapt. 'You must understand the first thing you say when you talk to them, it is a different ball game. But I know exactly what I want. I don't buy a foreign player because he is foreign and I must go with the fashion. I buy players I need. I think, "I need a midfielder, what skills do I want from him? Who can do that? Then, is he available?" It is incredible the phone calls I get. Really great players are offered. I think "That's not possible", but you have to check everything. But it must also be someone I can use. If I already have three strikers why buy a fourth?'

How will Gullit accommodate Vialli? 'It's nice to have that problem, especially now that Gianfranco Zola has stolen the crowd's heart.' Gullit himself planned to drop out when Leboeuf's suspension was over. 'I am comfortable with the players I have to do a job. There is always somebody who can create in this team, there are a lot of options.'

Naturally the questions concentrated on the big names, but Gullit also had a word for the new boy. Although he substituted debutant Clement after fifty-nine minutes to bring on Myers, Gullit said: 'I was quite happy with him. I didn't say anything to him, maybe he couldn't sleep. He was totally surprised when I told him he was playing at 1.30. We were all very happy for him.' The boy's debut was a source of great pride and joy for his mother Pat and brother Paul. Fifteen years ago his father Dave Clement, the England full-back, committed suicide. Neil followed in his father's footsteps as an England junior. Dave, a stylish right-back, won five England caps, helping QPR finish second to Liverpool in 1976.

Neil recalled: 'I was only three when dad died, yet I feel I know him really well. I was choked up, especially when our assistant physio Terry Byrne said that dad would have been proud of me. Dad was a very stylish player and I'd like to think I could be half as good as he was. People see similarities in us, but I'm left-footed, he was a right-footer. QPR showed an interest in me but, as I was told people would always compare me with my dad, I did the next best thing. He was a Battersea boy and a Chelsea fan, so what better club could I join than the one he supported as a lad?'

As for the debut: 'Ruud Gullit told me ninety minutes before kick-off that I was playing. I couldn't believe it. There was a team meeting called by Ruud at half-past one and I was thinking of getting my coat with Nick Colgan to go and sit in the stand, and Ruud's come in, everyone's gone quiet, and he's come up and whispered in my ear: "Oh and by the way, you're playing today." My stomach was just in my mouth. I was really nervous, but they all started taking the mickey out of me, and that made me feel really confident. When I went for the warm-up I just wanted to stay out there as the crowd built up. When I went out for the game the crowd was just so loud. It felt great because they were all on my side. My brother was gutted. He was in Birmingham collecting his girlfriend for Christmas.'

Why didn't he play Phelan? 'Good question,' Gullit said with a smile. But he didn't actually answer the question, except to say: 'I could have played Andy Myers. Every decision I make is for Chelsea, not myself. Di Matteo found it physical so I left him out for a rest and he accepted it.'

MONDAY, DECEMBER 23

Peacock completed a permanent move to QPR, signing a three-and-a-half-year deal with an initial fee of £800,000 rising to £1m after a certain number of appearances. Peacock was also linked with clubs in France and Spain. 'I had options to move abroad on a free transfer at the end of the season but I'm glad that it has been finally sorted out with QPR. It's like coming full circle. This is where I started and learned my trade, and I feel very positive about our promotion chances. The management team of Stewart Houston and Bruce Rioch have worked at the highest level and want players who match their drive and ambition for the club.' Peacock was Chelsea captain and played in the 1994 FA Cup Final, but had not played under Gullit. 'I felt it was time to move on. I had some great times at Chelsea and I like to think I had a good relationship with the fans. But now I am one hundred per cent committed to QPR and I believe we have all the ingredients we need for success.'

WEDNESDAY, DECEMBER 25

'Christmas is a family day,' said Gullit, 'but in England it's a bit different. I must admit I wish we were off this Christmas. It still should be a family day for everyone. Unfortunately the rules are different in England to elsewhere. Elsewhere we would be off. They have a break in Italy, Holland, and Belgium, everywhere has a break apart from England. We have to play so many games now, it is like a mini-marathon and we will have to divide our forces to get through it. There are a lot of points to be won and lost. I've heard the FA are thinking about introducing a break, so that's okay.'

An overnight stay in a Midlands hotel to prepare for the Boxing Day match at Villa Park, after training at the Bridge at 6pm on the heated turf. Gullit said: 'I shall allow the players to stay as long as possible with their families and we shall only go away in the evening.' Ruud trusted his 'professionals' to 'take care of their bodies'. He did not expect them to 'eat or drink a lot'. Zola was aware of the concentration of fixtures, five games in fifteen days. 'We shall need a lot of ... how you say ... strength. We hope to give our supporters good games, so they can have a good Christmas, that will be our present. I shall spend Christmas with my family and some friends from Italy. We know we are going to play a lot of games.' He had no problem if he had been asked to switch roles. 'If you buy Zola you want Zola to play the way Zola knows. I am not in a situation to say I want to play here or play there. My coach will decide this for me. If he thinks Zola can play better forward I'll play there. The important thing is the team. I came here to play because I want to give all my possibilities to Chelsea. I don't want to create problems.'

Even Wise, seeing out the final game of a two-match ban, trained in the evening after lunch at his mum's. Veteran of the holiday programmes, Wise stressed: 'It's the period when it shows what you can do in the second half of the season. Have a good Christmas and you can be pushing. Have a bad one and you're always catching up.' Vialli and Leboeuf needed more rest and training before they would be back. Gullit explained: 'We're getting there in terms of injuries and most of the players are almost fit. We're looking forward to playing Villa having looked so sharp against West Ham. People are saying Villa are a championship side but the same can be said of a lot of sides at this stage of the season.'

Villa were brimming with championship confidence after their 5–0 demolition of Wimbledon. Staunton was hyped up for the Christmas run, against Chelsea, Arsenal and Manchester United. 'Our season has really turned in the last few weeks. There are few teams in the Premiership with better recent form than Villa. From what I've seen of the teams immediately above and below us in the table there's nothing to frighten us.'

With Boxing Day off, Wise settled down to listening to the lads play at Villa Park on Capital Gold. The team trained on the Villa pitch on Boxing Day morning.

THURSDAY, DECEMBER 26

Aston Villa 0 Chelsea 2

Zola added Villa to his growing list of victims with a devastating display of finishing, a decisive two-goal burst in the space of just four minutes, his first Premiership double since his arrival, enough to shatter Villa's five-match winning streak. For Gullit, making his fiftieth Chelsea appearance, the most pleasing aspect was the first clean sheet in seventeen matches. 'At last,' as he put it.

All the title talk was directed at Gullit's revitalised side. It was the perfect introduction for Zola to festive football by Villa's generous defence. First he was allowed to cut across from the right before delivering a low sixty-fifth-minute shot to beat Bosnich with the aid of a slight deflection off Ehiogu. Four minutes later, Zola was first to react to another Bosnich blunder when the Australian keeper hesitated and missed as he came out to collect a back-header from Fernando Nelson. Left all on his own at an acute angle, Zola *didn't* hesitate before squeezing his shot inside the near post for his fourth goal in seven games.

Little complained: 'Bosnich could have done better with both goals. The first was slightly deflected but he certainly should have dealt with the second goal long before there was any danger.'

Gullit was full of praise for Zola again. 'The rest of the team have been supplying the bullets and he's our big gun to finish them off. His first couple of weeks were always going to be difficult, but now he has moved into a house, has settled in and is beginning to feel appreciated by everyone else here. The other players like the fact that even though he is such a very good player technically, he is still prepared to work hard, run back and do his fair share of defending.'

Just as crucial was Gullit's own role in the middle of a three-man defence. Deputising again for the suspended Leboeuf, Gullit showed the class to blunt Villa's previously rampant attack. He said: 'Our defence was very good and very disciplined. We didn't give away many chances, that was the key to us playing well. Having got that right we could rely on the talent in our team. When we have the ball we can do so many good things.'

Villa, looking to establish a club record sixth successive Premiership victory, managed one real effort, just seconds before Zola's breakthrough, when Dwight Yorke's header was blocked by Clarke before Ian Taylor miskicked in the six-yard box. By comparison, Chelsea could have won by a much greater margin, with Bosnich making amends for his blunders by defying Newton and Zola. Little refused to condemn his side, insisting it was the presence of Gullit which made all the difference. 'Whenever he is at the back for them, he keeps things very tight. He doesn't lose possession and tactically he is so aware of everything going on around him.'

Gullit warned absent stars Vialli, Leboeuf, Wise and Minto there would be no quick return. 'I'm glad that my players are all available again because it gives us greater competition. It's not so good for the players themselves but it is for me as a manager. Zola and Hughes are playing very well as a pair together up front. It's unfortunate for Luca but he will have to start on the bench when he comes back, not because he's not a good player, but he has to be aware what is happening and happy for the team to be playing so well.'

Chelsea were level on points with Newcastle in the championship race and Gullit refused to discuss the possibility of a challenge. Bates, dressed in an outrageous wolf-skin coat and matching hat, would settle for a place in Europe. Clarke's harsh booking meant a two-match ban after the FA Cup third round.

In the dressing room after the game Ruud spoke to the players about the New Year's Eve arrangements. The players were unanimous that they wanted to stay at home. The manager decided to trust them again. There would be training on New Year's Eve morning, then the players reported to the Bridge on New Year's Day for the same routine as a normal Saturday match.

FRIDAY, DECEMBER 27

Would master strategist, David Pleat, put the shackles on Zola? The Sheffield Wednesday boss used his skipper, Peter Atherton, as an occasional man-marker and contemplated a similar role on Zola. 'I hope he does,' said Gullit. 'It will mean he will have one less player playing for his side and give us more space. Franco is used to it in Italy and so was I. I loved to be man-marked, it was a compliment to me.' Atherton, normally a centre-back, was used to stop McManaman; it worked so well that Wednesday won 1–0 at Anfield.

Pleat staged a 'Stop London' campaign in Christmas week, denying Tottenham a win at White Hart Lane, frustrating Arsenal in a 0–0 draw on Boxing Day. Gullit has the utmost respect for Pleat and his tactics. 'Everyone thought Wednesday were down last season but they recovered and you have to give him credit for that and also for the way they have played this season,' said Gullit.

Ruud believed the team had turned the corner defensively, after their first shut-out in seventeen games on Boxing Day. 'We've worked very hard on our defending to make sure everyone does his job when we're not in possession. If the team feels solid it brings the best out of the strikers, who can concentrate on attacking instead of tackling back.'

Newton, retaining his place despite the return of Wise from suspension, said: 'We've sorted out a few problems at the back and the result has been there for all to see in our last couple of games. It's no coincidence we've done so well with Ruud in defence. He's got so much talent and a great brain when he's on the ball.'

Vialli, Leboeuf and Wise on the bench! That signalled a powerful squad. Not so good for Vialli's bid to return to World Cup football. New Italian coach Cesare Maldini went to the Bridge to check on the four Italian players. Gullit insisted: 'I'm happy to have Luca back and it's good he wants to be in the team, but we'll have to see. I must do what is best for Chelsea and the players understand that. It is not personal and I would never let personal business harm what is good for the team.' Instead, Maldini watched Zola and Di Matteo as well as Sheffield Wednesday's Benito Carbone before moving on to Highbury to check on Ravanelli.

For Vialli, being stuck on the bench with Maldini in town did not help his mood.

Carbone might have considered himself a rival to Zola, but the Chelsea man was in outstanding form. Gullit said: 'It wasn't easy for Franco at the start, because he was living in a hotel rather than his own home and couldn't get his rhythm. Now he is at home, feels appreciated and the team appreciates him, and that is what he needs.' Zola's swift acclimatisation to English football pleased Gullit more than anything. His goals and his skill enraptured the fans. 'Don't worry about him playing too much. Or that it is cold. It is cold in Italy now. It is no different for him than playing two matches a week in Italy. If you play a lot of games and maybe one of them is a not so good a game, you have the chance to forget about it because another game comes along so quickly. But if you are winning these games, you can jump three or four places and that is good for confidence. But we must aim for consistency and not lose matches we should win.'

Gullit refused to talk of titles or UEFA Cup qualification. 'It is vital we just concentrate on our next match, no more. The Boxing Day result at Aston Villa was good and I am particularly pleased with the way the team is rolling, with the players sharing the responsibility for trying to score goals. That is good because if only one player is scoring most of the goals, he can be stopped. I am also pleased with the way Roberto Di Matteo has returned to the side and done well.'

Gullit reckoned the foreign legion made the Premiership the envy of the world; even the Italians were jealous at the cash and glamour generated by English soccer. He was convinced Vialli, Zola, Ravanelli, Vieira and Cantona had improved the quality of our game. 'I've a feeling the Premier League is becoming better all the time and more teams than ever can now challenge for the title. It is a very open championship because there are more foreigners bringing extra quality here while the Englishmen have gained confidence because of the performances of the national team at Euro '96. The attention the Premiership gets from abroad has boosted all the players here and the standard is so much better. There is now a whole page every day in the Italian papers about English football. The Fiorentina president Vittorio Cecchi Gori has just been complaining about the number of Premiership games being transmitted on Italian TV.'

Zola's two-goal blast at Villa Park made the front page of the Italian sports pages.

SATURDAY, DECEMBER 28
Chelsea 2 Sheffield Wednesday 2

Not a trace of grey in those famous dreadlocks. There won't be any despite all the frustrations of the embryonic stage of piecing together a side capable of winning trophies. While Pleat talked of managerial suicide, Gullit said: 'Stressed! Why should I be stressed? I'm not stressed about it. All these people don't understand why. I have already won everything in the game, I'm a happy man, I have everything I want. They insisted that I do the job so I take it how it comes.'

Two up with Zola scoring another brilliant goal only to squander two points. Surely that was enough to reach for the Grecian 2000? Gullit was totally frustrated: 'We gave chances away to them; that's sloppy. We were losing the ball in midfield, that's stupid. For me, they were no threat to us yet they scored two incredible goals from thirty yards.' An error several minutes over time by Grodas, but Ruud refused to apportion blame. 'It has nothing to do with who makes the mistakes, we were in control of the match. No one gets the blame. It was just unfortunate. It was such an anti-climax. The way we played deserved more. We lost two points we thought we had in our pocket. You can't train or coach against two incredible goals from that distance.'

Enough to make you want to pull those dreadlocks out. Not so! No worries, man. 'No stress but of course I'm ambitious. I can lose nothing but I want to win at this club and the first step is to put a system in place that is good for the team.'

Despite all the lavish praise attracted by the Italian trio that brought Maldini to the Bridge, Gullit had no illusions. The previous season Chelsea were ahead no fewer than nineteen times but failed to win. They suffered again from a lack of killer instinct in Gullit's first season as coach. 'It has to be step by step and we're only at the second step. The first step is to bring more stability in the team and that means week in and week out. The first step is how aware the players are of each other and the team building. You can't make them all happy but they have to be aware of team spirit. It's a slow process. It's no good people thinking we have good players so off we go. It's not like that. You have to work very hard for the team. There are a lot of steps and we are still building to create something. Even when you win something the most difficult part is the season after that. All of a sudden you can go down. Why? I'll never know. Only big clubs stay there. Blackburn won the championship and then go down. Even if we win something we are still not there. We have to learn to be better than we were in the last game. We did well against Aston Villa and then there was no reason why we should draw this match. It was an anti-climax, especially as we've conceded two long-range goals. It's frustrating.'

A goal was disallowed after only seven minutes when Burley's shot was just touched onto the upright by Pressman, Petrescu, following up, converting with a stooping header. There were few complaints about the offside decision and a minute later Phelan, in his first full game of the season, was instrumental in linking with Hughes whose low cross was slid in by Zola lurking at the far post. In the twenty-second minute Gullit stepped forward to make the perfect defensive interception, and Di Matteo launched a brilliant pass to Zola whose cross was headed into the corner by Hughes, marking his fiftieth league appearance for Chelsea. Within seconds, a routine clearance was struck from thirty yards into the top corner by Pembridge. Pleat, in his haste to move down from the stands to the dug-out, got stuck in the lift and missed it. 'I nearly fell off the roof of the stand. It was suicide stuff because I thought it would be nasty for us as Chelsea were superb. It's splendid for the game the way they played. I love their movement, it was superb. I was glad I was here today, it was a very good game. With ten minutes to go and 2–1 down I'd have had no complaints if we'd have lost because we were playing such a good side. I'll take the video of this one – Zola was superb.'

Pembridge struck a post and Grodas produced his best save to thwart Andy Booth from the rebound. Then came the Norwegian's horrendous error when he caught Dejan Stefanovic's long-range effort above his head only to fumble it over the line in injury time. That came a minute after Di Matteo was celebrating a goal only for the referee to belatedly spot a linesman's flag. Substitute Wise had to be dragged away from the referee Paul Durkin at the end as Chelsea vented their fury at the referee's decisions. 'A very alert linesman,' was Ruud's unique way of criticising the official. Substitute Donaldson followed up to make sure of the equaliser although the goal was credited to Stefanovic as Pleat pointed out: 'I'm glad he put it in the net because you could imagine the controversy if he hadn't.'

Pleat had the honesty to admit: 'We were nil-two down and going nowhere at a quarter past three. It was like trying to deal with an avalanche; they were coming from all directions. If you'd have had a sweep nobody would have had 2–2.' Five points clear in September, Pleat's side were back in ninth place, with a run of eleven games unbeaten, nine drawn. 'We played very passionately for a team that had been chasing the game for long periods. We played with strong hearts for the last fifteen minutes,' added Pleat.

Atherton was praised for subduing Zola in a man-marking role, only assigned the task after Zola scored. Personally, I felt Zola came out on top by some distance. Pleat said: 'A journalist rang me to say that Zola ran the game against West Ham. Did I plan to man-mark him? I had another plan – it didn't work!' Atherton got tighter on Zola, but he was hardly fazed by the experience. He even joked that he would have 'preferred his wife' to the close attentions of his marker. He added significantly: 'I know that I'm preparing myself well and I'm improving, running better than before. It is not a problem to find a player marks me like that, I had it all the time in Italy. But by the second half I was getting tired after playing in a match two days earlier. I'm not used to that ... now I'm going home to bed.' However, he would be 'watching *Match of the Day* first'.

Pleat was enthusiastic about the way Zola had been marked. He said: 'Atherton was splendid. He's a rarity in our game. He can tackle and mark but doesn't do it in a dirty way. Zola was superb, but not so superb when Atherton went onto him.'

Zola was cheered every time he went to take a corner. It was the sort of adulation he had never experienced before. 'I am very, very pleased, the people are important; they are very, how do you say, keen. Very supportive.' In just a few weeks he'd become the idol of the Bridge. Gullit said: 'The fans need someone to identify with, especially the youngsters, and he's growing with every game.' At 5ft 4in I suggested to Gullit that he needed to grow! Gullit laughed. 'It's very good to see great footballers in general. People come especially to see him and you have that with players like Shearer and McManaman. It's the same with the good foreigners who come to the Premiership. When we go to other stadiums they want to see us.'

The Italians were shocked by the extent of the passion in the crowd. Even Vialli, overcoming his disappointment at being on the bench in the presence of the new Italian coach, had to laugh when he spotted the famous Sheffield Wednesday fan – The Tango Man. Wearing any number of sweat tops and sporting a woollen hat and gloves, Vialli couldn't believe the bare-chested bald-headed fan chanting throughout the game yards behind the dug-out.

Maldini was content with Zola and Di Matteo, less so with the substituted Carbone. Gullit said: 'I've been speaking to Mr Maldini and he is very impressed about the way people here deal with the game in a different way. He was not basing anything on one match, he had come to see the players and to talk to them after the game, that's normal. It was very nice for him to see this game. There is a good atmosphere around the Premiership, everyone is trying to promote it in a good way and give it a good image. When I was in Italy the image of England was always about the fans making a hassle. Now the talk is more about the football. That's what you have created yourself. There is a high expectancy level here among the game – that's good. More pressure on the players, but that's how it should be.

'We shall forget this game very easily. The players can think about what they did in this game in the first half. They know they have the quality and they were unlucky. But we don't have the time to worry about it, the next game is very soon and it's very important.'

Gullit never shirks a questions, irrespective of how provocative, awkward or downright silly. 'What did you learn from this game?' Answer: 'To score more goals than them!' If only the game was that simple. 'I hope we can do well, I'm very pleased how the team is performing, but I don't know what will happen every week. Before the game I think "They'll win the game." ' And, would Ruud carry on playing? 'If the team needs me I will have to be there. They needed me today because of suspensions and injuries. But I hope everybody comes back.'

But would Vialli be back? That was certainly the big talking point for the regular, large contingent of Italian journalists. Di Matteo said: 'I'd rather have him on the pitch, but that's up to the manager and I have to accept it.' Zola also felt for his fellow countryman. 'It's very hard for him sitting on the bench and he has to be a very strong man. But he's overcome more difficult circumstances and will do so again.' Gullit defended his decision. 'Vialli has been injured and he has to work hard to get back in the team. I asked him if he was ready to sit on the bench and he said "Yes". Everybody has to work hard to get in the team. Somebody plays good, he will stay there. It's not my concern what the national coach of Italy thinks.' Maldini, who arranged a friendly with Northern Ireland, said that he knew Gianluca well 'so I didn't have to see him today, but I will be back to take another look'. He added: 'When I see him I will embrace him.' But there were no clues to his selection for the clash with England. 'All roads are open,' he said, 'I didn't come to find anything new, just to see what form they were in.' But he was impressed with Zola. 'I know him very well. I thought he was in very good form. I was pleased with the reaction of the public toward him whenever he touched the ball.' He was also pleased with Di Matteo. 'He was good in the second part of the game.'

Chelsea's next assignment was against championship favourites Liverpool. Gullit would discover whether stage three, a tilt at the title, was a reality. Pleat said: 'I enjoy Liverpool because the way they play is patient, passing, working; chess-like, not too direct. Chelsea are becoming like them, a very good team too. People automatically think that because it's close at the top the quality isn't so good. They think it would be better if one team was streaking away. I don't follow that argument at all.'

Di Matteo, back in form, was in optimistic mood. 'I hope we play better and better and get more points to go on top of this championship. It will be very difficult. The next few games, particularly with Liverpool, will tell us the truth whether we can win the title or go into second place. It is very interesting. Manchester United, Arsenal, Chelsea, Aston Villa, there are many teams.'

Zola would be a key figure. 'I saw Liverpool a little in action but I will see them on TV. We have possibility to do it, I don't think it will be easy, but we will try. It was not easy to accept the result today. I am very, very angry.' The title? 'I don't know. We are a team improving; we're getting better. But we have to work more, it is not easy to win the title. Chelsea are a very, very good team.' English improving. He's got his tongue around 'Chelsea', and relying a little less on the interpreter. 'We can win the Premier League but we have to work hard getting results. There are a lot of teams like Chelsea [in the same position], about four who can win the Premier League the same. The difference will be the work done in training, that is the key issue.'

Could he keep on scoring? 'I'll try to score in every game, but it is impossible to say whether I will. I'll try to score ten, twenty, thirty. I'd like to score thirty but it is not likely. The best I have managed in one season, excluding the national side, has been nineteen with Parma.'

SUNDAY, DECEMBER 29

Ruud was still attracting accolades despite his infrequent appearances. The *Independent on Sunday* placed Gullit in their top twenty performers of the year, albeit at number eighteen. 'It was the footballing cliche of '96. No matter how long the lay-off, or how short the appearance as a substitute, Gullit was the best player on the field. One of the greats in his prime, he remains a delight in his dotage, apparently playing the game in a different time zone. Would be far higher, and his Chelsea team more successful, were he able to play more frequently.'

Liverpool won at the Dell even though it was an unconvincing performance with an error from keeper Dave Beasant punished with a forty-yard first-time shot from John Barnes. Liverpool went five points clear at the turn of the year – ten points ahead of Chelsea having played one game more.

Chelsea Old Boys, including Langley, Stanley, Finnieston, Fillery, Chivers, and Graham Wilkins, beat Chelsea Supporters 4–2 at Carshalton FC, followed by Chelsea Ladies losing 2–1 to National Premier League Wimbledon in a memorial match for Matthew Harding, which raised nearly £3,000 for the NSPCC.

MONDAY, DECEMBER 30

The year ended with a transfer turnover up to £17m, selling Phelan to Everton. Phelan played his first full game – and his last – under Gullit against Sheffield Wednesday. Phelan's £850,000 switch to Everton was set in motion just two hours after that game. Gullit said: 'My assistant Gwyn Williams took a call from Joe Royle at about seven in the evening after our draw with Sheffield Wednesday, and we worked out the deal on the Sunday. Terry wanted to play for us, but with competition from Scott Minto and Andy Myers I couldn't guarantee that. Terry was always a real pro for us and in the end a move was the best solution all round.'

Williams elaborated: 'I got home on the Saturday night and Joe had telephoned me asking about Terry Phelan. I phoned Ruudi and Ricco to discuss his offer. We knew of Phelo's domestic problems and were aware that if a chance to go back to see more of his kids came along, he'd like to take it. Colin Hutchinson did the negotiations with their financial director.'

Despite outbursts in the press on his departure, Phelan thanked the man who froze him out at Chelsea. He was grateful Gullit quickly agreed to the deal to take him back north. 'I wouldn't say I was a flop at Chelsea. I just had a few injuries and whenever a new manager comes in he has his own ideas. When I was fit again I found myself third choice left-back. But Ruud was great to me. He knew I had one or two domestic problems and needed to move back up north. I've left a big club for an even bigger one. Once they are over their current injury problems, Everton are going places. I've started only one Premiership game this season and I've lost my Republic of Ireland place. I know if I do well here I can win it back because I want to play in the 1998 World Cup finals.'

Gullit elaborated on Phelan's domestic plight: 'I was surprised when Terry moved so quickly. He had been out this season but then had his chance when he played against Sheffield Wednesday. I thought he played well. Then Everton came in with an offer for him on the night of the game. He has split up from his wife and his kids live in Manchester so he had domestic reasons, as well, for leaving. But we have lost a quality player, although he knew I couldn't guarantee him a first-team place. He takes with him the best wishes from us all at the Bridge and he has only good memories from his time at Chelsea.'

Phelan added: 'I had to return to the north-west for the sake of my children. Now I'm with Everton I can be close to them again. Even though I had just got back into the Chelsea side, I was delighted when Joe Royle came in for me. I signed within twenty minutes of meeting him. But everyone at Chelsea was great too. Gwyn Williams was very helpful, as was Ruud, and the rest of the coaching staff. They were always available for a chat and Ruud was very understanding about my problems. He told me I'd get through it all and let me have the day off when I needed to see my kids. People think footballers have a wonderful life but it can put a great strain on family life when you are often moving around the country.

'I couldn't wait to get into a Chelsea team that looked to be on its way to the top. But I got injured in the FA Cup and from that point things went from bad to worse for me. At times I didn't see eye to eye with Ruud. I was missing my family back in Manchester and there was even a time when I thought I would be better off out of the game. Missing out on Ireland's games at the start of the season didn't help. But I knew I had to quit Chelsea and get myself back up north.'

Vialli goes down with the flu!

TUESDAY, DECEMBER 31

Gullit played down talk of a £6m move for Tottenham and England striker Teddy Sheringham. While he discounted the possibility of landing the thirty-year-old Spurs skipper, he was not in any way disgruntled at seeing the idea floated. 'I have enough strikers and I'm quite happy with the ones I've got. But you have to see what is happening. I get so many players offered to me, from abroad and from English clubs, and you have to consider what you want to do. In the past few weeks I've been linked with so many players, first Jurgen Klinsmann and now Teddy Sheringham. But, as far as I'm concerned, that's a positive thing for Chelsea. These sort of players just wouldn't have been linked with the club two or three years ago. If you want the best strikers, particularly English ones, they cost a lot of money. That's because the best strikers are already at the best clubs and it's very difficult to get them. You saw that with the money paid for Alan Shearer by Newcastle and while you like to have these players, it's difficult to get them. In that case, what can you do but go abroad? You have to go somewhere. Sometimes that works, sometimes it doesn't, although I think all the ones we've brought in have made a contribution to the Premiership.'

Gullit accepted Liverpool were deservedly top of the Premiership pile. 'Liverpool are the best team I've seen this season. They look very solid and in the difficult games they seem to have the luck on their side. The Southampton game was an example of that. But I remember when I started my career at Ajax. We won everything, and the rival fans used to jeer at us and say "Lucky Ajax". That was because we could wait for the one mistake, score from it, and then close the game up for a 1–0 win. That's what happens with the best teams; it's not luck, but what they work for. Robbie Fowler is very clever, but it's not about how they play. In any event, it's good to play a team like this, easy to raise yourself.'

Chelsea's unbeaten record was smashed to smithereens by a Berger double at Anfield, but Gullit insisted: 'If you ask anybody, that wasn't a 5–1 game.' However, it illustrated where they had to improve. Zola, five goals in five games, was one such major improvement. Zola expected close attention. 'Football is a game for men and it is not a problem when teams try to stop me. In Italy I was closely marked all the time, sometimes too closely. I have played against Gentile, Costacurta, Vierchowod and Ferrera so there is nothing defenders can do to me here that is any worse than I've already had. The biggest difference is that in Italy the referees whistle more fouls. That makes it difficult for me here but I prefer it that way. I am not a child. I know how to cope with this sort of thing. Defenders in England don't give me any presents and sometimes they say things to me and try to be rude. I don't know if they're being rude to me over here, because I can't always understand them, as I don't speak very good English, so it doesn't worry me. And when I have a problem I just call "Marco" and Mark Hughes comes over and sorts everything out, then it's no problem!' Zola anticipated his toughest assignment. 'Life will get harder for me because teams are more aware of me now. Liverpool are maybe the best team in the country this year and Di Matteo has told me they are very organised. So it is going to be difficult for us.'

Barnes returned for Liverpool after recovering from a hamstring injury. He had no doubts about the danger man. 'Zola is an exceptional talent and I really don't think we've ever seen anyone like him in England before. He has given Chelsea a new dimension and made them a real threat. He is his country's best talent.'

Liverpool's fluid play had been stifled by the likes of Sheffield Wednesday's Atherton and Southampton's Ulrich van Gobbel, keeping the tightest of reins on McManaman. Roy Evans conceded that his side was restricted by the tactic. 'We've been frightened to give Steve the ball. We've got to throw him balls to his feet.' Gullit would not follow that example of man-marking. 'I want to use all eleven of my players. If one of mine is just staying with one of theirs, he's not playing and I'm down to ten.'

Minto replaced Phelan, with Myers, scorer of an own goal at Anfield, on the bench. Vialli was ruled out with flu, sent home from training.

Trevor Brooking provided his Chelsea end-of-year assessment in his London *Evening Standard* column: '. . . Gullit will be able to gauge the progress of his emerging team when Premiership leaders Liverpool visit Stamford Bridge for the opening fixture of 1997. The west London club are ten points behind the men from Anfield and, even with a game in hand, must collect maximum points if they are to sustain their championship hopes. But maximum points have not been easy to obtain at home, with only four victories coming from ten matches at the Bridge. Of the remaining six games they have drawn five, conceding thirteen goals in the process, and that is the main reason why they are not higher up the table, alongside Arsenal and Wimbledon. Chelsea have developed an international flavour this season with the arrival of Frank Leboeuf, Roberto Di Matteo, Gianluca Vialli, Gianfranco Zola and Frode Grodas. They have given Chelsea greater strength in depth and, with the recent arrival of Zola, more goalscoring potential in attack.

'This little man will prove a giant of an acquisition and go on to become one of the most successful foreign imports anywhere. He possesses a refreshing willingness to run at defenders and his superb balance and vision enable him to hurt the opposition by selecting the most perceptive passing option available. I think Leboeuf has been the next best arrival. In the early weeks of the season his timely interceptions and astute distribution as sweeper were a feature of Chelsea's swift counter-attacks. Unfortunately the Frenchman's form dipped and an injury caused further disruption. His return is on hold because Gullit has regained full fitness after knee surgery in the summer and has assumed the role of playmaker from the sweeper position. The Dutchman's form has been magnificent this month and he remains one of the great players of his generation. Hopefully his managerial responsibilities won't diminish his desire to carry on playing . . . Di Matteo arrived from Lazio with a massive reputation and a near-£5m price tag. Although he possesses some neat touches, he hasn't dictated the play as effectively as he should. His tussle with John Barnes and Michael Thomas will be a crucial battle for possession tomorrow and would be an ideal time for him to assert the authority expected from an Italian international. Vialli's hamstring injury hampered the chance to see whether he could build an understanding with both Zola and Mark Hughes in the same line-up. The partnership of Vialli and Hughes did not prove that potent. In his absence, Hughes and Zola have gelled much better and should start against Liverpool. Grodas is one of three goalkeepers who have struggled to provide a solid foundation at the back. Dmitri Kharine was unluckily injured, giving Kevin Hitchcock his opportunity, but a fallibility on crosses proved his undoing. Now Grodas has to convince the manager of his capabilities because he should have saved a long-range strike from Dejan Stefanovic in last weekend's draw with Sheffield Wednesday. Overall, it is Chelsea's vulnerable defence which convinces me they are unlikely to win the championship.

'They have enough talent to beat Liverpool but, even if they do, I can still see them slipping up in the sort of fixtures where they should be taking three points. Therefore, the start of this season's FA Cup campaign on Saturday offers a more realistic chance of success . . .'

JANUARY

League and Cup double over Liverpool

WEDNESDAY, JANUARY 1

Chelsea 1 Liverpool 0

Gullit again produced something out of the ordinary for a football manager. He wished everyone a Happy New Year in his programme notes the way only he could. 'I wish everyone of you good health because good health is the most important thing you can possess. Good health and, of course, freedom.'

Well, his team certainly denied Liverpool freedom of the Bridge!

And the best Yuletide record in living memory, ten points out of a possible twelve, eight goals in four games, two top-six scalps, including now the team highly fancied for the title. Good enough football to keep out the winter chill. Even the *chic*est boss in the business resorted to a humble bobble hat to keep those dreadlocks warm!

If the New Year was to herald in the champions at the Bridge, then Gullit's side denied Liverpool the chance to become the runaway leaders. Instead Chelsea inflicted the capital's first defeat on Liverpool to ensure the most open title race for many years, enhancing their own aspirations. Eight attempts by London clubs had produced only two draws. Finally, Liverpool crashed after an impressive run of only one defeat in twelve. Chelsea were among the seven clubs at the top of the Premiership separated by just seven points. Albeit still in seventh place, they were in with a shout. Newcastle led Manchester United by the same margin a year ago. Chelsea thoroughly deserved to peg back the Premiership leaders to seven points with a game in hand.

Why so open? Hughes had seen it all before. 'Teams at the top keep slipping up, its pretty obvious really!'

The game, billed as the potential champions against the pretenders, led to sweet revenge for Chelsea. The 5–1 thrashing at Anfield was finally out of Chelsea's system. Gullit said: 'I still admire them, they are a great team, but they were not four goals better than us at Anfield; we had some chances and made some terrible mistakes.' The outstanding Hughes, who forged a better attacking combination with Zola than Vialli, explained: 'We've done reasonably well against all the leading sides. We were naive at Anfield and didn't do ourselves any favours. It was nice to reverse that.'

Despite his own superb form, Gullit demonstrated his camaraderie in his quest to build team spirit – by dropping himself. Gullit sat on the bench restoring Leboeuf as sweeper and Chelsea kept their first clean sheet at the Bridge since the Coventry match in August. A defence with a reputation for leaking goals shut out Fowler and Collymore and might have inflicted a more convincing defeat on the title favourites when the brilliant Hughes rapped the bar.

Liverpool began with the airs and graces of champions-elect; sophisticated stuff, retaining possession with McManaman a central figure but often deep, in the fluent passing movements. Strangely, no cutting edge; Fowler raced to a century of Liverpool goals faster than Ian Rush, but he was twice foiled by Grodas in the thirty-second minute, when, had he been sharper, the Liverpool goal ace might have finished off Chelsea. From a corner Grodas pushed the ball away, Minto sprinting down the flank, and Di Matteo sent Zola clear. He weaved inside before bringing David James his first important save.

Evans suffered a blow when Ruddock limped off after thirty-five minutes to be replaced by Dominic Matteo. For the last ten minutes of the first half Chelsea wrestled back the ascendancy, hitting them hard and accurately on the break. A majestic ball out of defence by Leboeuf over Matteo's head was into Minto's stride, but his angled shot was just over. With five minutes to go Hughes superbly slipped the ball past Wright, collected the other side, but he was blocked by James racing smartly to the edge of his area and saving with his long outstretched leg. Petrescu brought another save from James and Hughes engineered a shooting chance on the edge of the box, agonisingly just wide, before Chelsea earned their breakthrough.

They chased, scurried and hustled Liverpool out of their standard build-up play at the back. Hughes put Matteo under intense pressure but he squeezed a pass to Thomas who made the mistake of failing to look up, and his pass intended for Wright was cleverly intercepted by Di Matteo, who sweetly wrong-footed James to slide his shot into the corner. There was even time for an outstanding Di Matteo pass, excellently controlled by Zola. His cross was knocked out to Burley whose spectacular shot was wide.

After the interval Chelsea grew in confidence, the memory of their annihilation at Anfield growing distant. A swift free kick by Burley put Petrescu clear but he misfired into the side netting. Suddenly, there was more urgency about Liverpool. They abandoned their intricate play to hit passes to Collymore longer and earlier. Barnes was most likely to find a way through but when he put Collymore clear the defence snapped at his heels to deny him any shooting chance. The Liverpool fans called for Patrik Berger. They got their wish. With Berger's first touch, Collymore was clear but again he shot wide. Gullit sent on Wise in place of Minto and he too had an instant impact. Collecting a pass from Zola he sent Hughes into a shooting position, the Welshman cracking his shot against the bar with James beaten.

McManaman did not need to be man-marked as Gullit's strategy to pack the midfield denied him space, restricting him to the occasional defence-splitting pass, once finding Berger, but from an acute angle he shot wide. To add to Liverpool's frustrations Fowler was booked a couple of minutes from the end when raising his leg in front of Grodas. Di Matteo was shown the yellow card for a trip on Berger.

Chelsea celebrated with a significant win. Zola sensed Chelsea's title aspirations had become a reality. 'On the pitch today were two teams who could win it. The championship is very unpredictable and I still think that Liverpool are the best team. I haven't changed my mind about that, but we have some chance too. Arsenal and Manchester United are also the best teams and I don't know if we can win it, it will be very hard. Liverpool play very good football and today they gave us problem but we played with intelligence, we didn't give no chances. This game was very important for a lot of reasons. We merited the win, we played better than them.' Hughes revelled in his new strike partnership with Zola. He assessed the most open championship for many years with the experience of a title with Manchester United.

The style that has helped make Gullit as much of a star off the pitch as on.

Left Still working despite injury.

Below Filming the M&Ms advert.

Above Gullit with his girlfriend Estelle, the niece of Johann Cruyff.

Above All the glamour of life
in the Premiership, part 1.

Left All the glamour of life
in the Premiership, part 2.

Right Keeping quiet on tactics.

Above At ease with one of the most high pressure jobs in the business.

Far left 'Wisey' and 'Big Nose' working hard at the training ground.

Left The fittest manager in the Premiership?

Left With Harry Harris, one of the 'lovely boys'.

Below right Latecomers to Steve Clarke's testimonial dinner at the House of Commons are forced to perform the YMCA forfeit. Left to right; unknown, Vialli, Mike Banks, Mrs Mike Banks, Dennis Wise's partner, Dennis Wise.

Right Later in the evening. Vialli misses the worst of the punishment, unknown, under just one cornetto (and one suit sleeve) is not so lucky.

Bottom left Less salubrious surroundings for the Christmas party; the canteen at the Harlington training ground. Leboeuf (far right) and Gullit are watching an exclusive performance by . . .

Below The three tenors, Vialli, Di Matteo and Zola.

Left Gullit and Wise, a relationship that has been through good and bad times.

Above One of the most dedicated and effective players in the league, Mark Hughes was a key figure for Chelsea.

Above Despite all the time spent on the bench, Vialli was Chelsea's top league scorer for the season.

Left But it was a close run thing with Zola, voted Footballer of the Year in May.

Right Duberry celebrating with his player-manager. Gullit is still regularly voted as one of the fans' all time great Chelsea players

Above Throughout it all, Wise has remained his normal irrepressible self.

Left That vest. Worn by Wise, written by Steve Clarke.

Top right Another irrepressible character, Chelsea Chairman Ken Bates. He has presided over both the transformation of the team and of Stamford Bridge.

Right Roberto Di Matteo, scorer of 'that' goal.

Far right Gianfranco Zola, always the last to leave the press conferences.

Saying thankyou to the fans.

'It will be very open and it's going to be exciting, with teams at the top taking points off each other.' Can Chelsea have a shot at the title? Hughes said: 'That's a difficult one but if we keep surprising ourselves and perform the way we did today then we must have a chance. I know it's boring but it's too early to say who will win the championship, we're just pleased we've had a great Christmas.'

Sparky thought he would be ousted by the arrival of Vialli and Zola. Instead, there was no guarantee that Vialli would win back his place, even though he was the most respected and revered of all the Italians to depart Serie A. Gullit said of Hughes: 'You can see it on his face, he is happy here, he is fit and is helping as one of the leaders of the team. The crowd are cheering him. He is having one of his best seasons ever. I have asked people who have followed his career, and that's their view.'

Zola might be better served by the subtle skills of Vialli rather than the sledge-hammer of Hughes. But Zola was won over by the player he called Hugheses! 'I play very well with Hugheses; a player who allows a player like me to do well. My best position is not the first striker, but the second.' Hughes was enjoying a renaissance under Gullit, proving that the British-based players could still excel. Hughes praised Zola: 'We all enjoy the way he's played; great skill, great awareness. He makes it easy for everybody in the team. There would be something missing if you couldn't gel with Zola, it would be a bad reflection on yourself.'

Evans criticised Thomas for the misplaced pass that gave Di Matteo his winner. 'It was a sloppy goal, but we've got to have courage about our convictions and we won't change our philosophy of our passing game. Mickey played a bad ball and he'll be the first to admit it, sometimes that's the peril of the way we play. When we face a side of the calibre of Chelsea and have one or two chances, we have to take them.'

One of Gullit's most notable successes in English football, but his admiration for Liverpool was undiminished. 'Liverpool are a quality team, but Chelsea were very well organised also. Over the whole Premiership, the whole year, they will do well, but we were well prepared, we knew exactly where their weaknesses were. It's been a long time since we kept a clean sheet at home but I liked the way the team responded to the tactics. I knew the game depended on small details, small mistakes. It was down to who would make less mistakes. The team did exactly what I asked them to do, especially in midfield.' When Berger came on Gullit brought on Wise to counterbalance the midfield. 'That gave them one more man in midfield; when we changed it, we were in control again.'

Gullit had previously dropped his most expensive purchase Di Matteo, but now restored him to the side. Gullit said: 'That was one of his best games since he came here and I was pleased for him. You saw how he scored that goal, he anticipated the ball before the pass was there and he knew what he had to do and finished very coolly. I paid a real compliment to him and our midfield of Newton and Burley, that was their best game as a unit. They were nicking balls in midfield. I spoke to him a few weeks ago and told him that I hadn't seen what I'd expected from him in some games. Perhaps it was a reaction from Euro '96 – I'm aware of that sort of thing because I've been there myself – so I gave him a couple of weeks off and he's rewarded himself and me.'

Di Matteo said: 'That was the best I've played for Chelsea. Then again, it's easy to play well when the rest of the team does, and we played very well as a team. I didn't think the goal was too bad, either! As soon as I got the ball, I knew I would score. I watched James until he made a move and then just touched it past him. I like how

Liverpool play, I think they are a great team. We pressed them, and knew they would make mistakes if we did that. It's not easy if you come to another country with another language, another mentality, but my team-mates have helped me a lot and I found some friends in London who have helped me settle down as well.'

Gullit dropped himself to recall Leboeuf. 'I played a lot of games in a short space of time and Frank Leboeuf was fit again. I had to think about the long term and my ambitions are somewhere else: as a coach you see things better from the outside, so slowly, slowly, I don't want to play as much and that's got to be the way as I'm now thirty-four and can't go for ever.'

Would the final outcome be the title? 'Potentially, we have a chance to get on top. Win it? I don't know. I don't think about that at this moment. We are a rough diamond, we have to work on it to get the shape right. What I like is that the team are aware. There are still areas in which we can improve. On paper we have a great team, but it doesn't mean anything on paper.'

Liverpool stayed top of the Premiership but Manchester United were installed as the new 2–1 favourites, replacing Liverpool whose odds lengthened from 6–4 to 9–4, then 4–1 Arsenal and Newcastle, 11–1 Villa, 12–1 Chelsea. Ferguson said: 'It looks as though it's going to be tight. We are not going to be storming off with it. It's an unusual league. Chelsea beat Liverpool, Arsenal are up there and Wimbledon, if they win their games in hand, could go top. So to say it's an exciting league is an understatement. I don't necessarily think six teams will be there in the last half a dozen games. But everyone, at the moment, is feeling that that is the case. It will be very interesting if it gets to that stage. I believe, though, that sooner or later the pattern of recent seasons will assert itself and two, possibly three clubs will break away from the pack.'

Realistically, Chelsea's best chance was the FA Cup, fifth favourites at 8–1, behind Liverpool, Arsenal, Newcastle and Manchester United. Ferguson placed Chelsea among his favourites. 'If it's not going to be ourselves this season then I have a fancy for Aston Villa or Chelsea.'

Gullit knew the thrill and expectancy generated by the competition. 'The FA Cup is totally different but it requires the same approach, the same preparation, and the motivation is the most difficult part after this. Otherwise we shall turn round and ask "What's happening here? What's going on?"' Gullit knew West Brom could not be underestimated. So, too, did his players. Zola smiled politely but had clearly never heard of West Bromwich Albion. 'No, I don't know them very well, but Leboeuf said the games in the Cup are very difficult. Everyone in the country is very interested in the Cup. It is going to be hard, but this is the target, so it is very important. We shall try to get it, the supporters want success.'

Leboeuf, interviewed in his native tongue by a reporter from *L'Equipe*, virtually drowned out the quietly spoken Zola struggling to concentrate on his English with less and less prompting from Brian Glanville, Italian journalists and his interpreter. 'I don't suppose you spoke in English, did you?' smiled Leboeuf as Zola moved toward the exit of the press room. 'Yes, I did,' responded the Italian. 'I don't think so,' said Leboeuf. 'Well, I am learning English,' said Zola and provided the Frenchman with an example ... 'f— off'.

Gullit broke another seasonal tradition. 'There were staff who wanted me to take the players to a hotel on Tuesday night, but I wanted to give them the freedom to stay at home and enjoy New Year's Eve, particularly as they spent Christmas away. But as a coach you don't want to be like a schoolteacher. The players said "We can handle it." They wanted to have the festivities and I thought I could give them the responsibility of being with their families. They rewarded us for giving them that trust and that's a good thing.' Players, renowned for being untrustworthy, said: 'It's good that he trusted us. I'm sure he sat up to see the New Year in, but then it would have been straight to bed.'

THURSDAY, JANUARY 2
No training, just a massage and gentle body exercises for the players after a gruelling Christmas concentration of games. Sometimes rest was just as important, if not more so, as training.

FRIDAY, JANUARY 3
Training hard at the Bridge as Harlington was frozen. Zola was 40–1 along with Ferdinand, Cantona and Solskjaer to score in every round including the final, where Shearer, inevitably, was favourite at 20–1. Sky 'expert' Andy Gray predicted a cup upset for Chelsea!

First for Gullit, reflection on the success over Liverpool. 'To compete with teams like Liverpool you have to be very, very concentrated. You can't just ping the ball forward and charge. You have to be patient. It's not really the English way, but it's what Liverpool do, so you must do it too. If you then make less mistakes than them you have a very good chance. We took ours. It was technically very good, and we played well and showed good discipline. The players wanted to work hard for each other, and we deserved to win.' Gullit then emphasised the importance of not underestimating the opponent. 'We enjoyed last year's FA Cup run and it was a very good one. We have had West Bromwich Albion scouted as much as any Premiership opposition, have studied them properly, and we have to keep tuned in to go on doing well. We've had a very good Christmas and New Year. So far. We have to continue that now. The good festival time is behind us. To continue it we have to be consistent, and that is the most difficult part of football. We can focus on different ambitions as we go into the FA Cup.'

Hughes was again on a unique Cup mission, to become the first player this century to win the grand old cup four times, having achieved the distinction three times with Manchester United. He got as far as the semifinal in his first season with Chelsea, scoring four times. 'It would be great to achieve it,' he said softly. 'We've certainly got the opportunity.'

Lee flew off to the Canary Islands for a week's break before the fierce rehabilitation work.

SATURDAY, JANUARY 4
Chelsea 3 West Bromwich Albion 0
Proficient rather than spectacular. And Gullit was delighted. Sometimes, the hall-mark of a great team is grinding out results. In the past Chelsea were renowned for flamboyant failures in the Cup. No longer. Gullit said: 'Everybody thought it would be typically Chelsea to beat Liverpool then lose to a team from a lower division.' This time, no banana skin embarrassment. If that continued, Chelsea could fulfil Gary Lineker's Football Focus forecast, and win the FA Cup.

Should they get to the final then Gullit, as the team's boss with a playing reputation of the highest order, would be forgiven for selecting himself. 'No!' Gullit would not hesitate to leave himself out of the FA Cup Final team. 'I've been in certain finals already, I would want to give that experience to others. I'm pleased to concentrate more on managing the side and it's better sometimes off the pitch. When Frank Leboeuf was injured I had to play, but it's not my ambition to play all the time. He's a younger player and he's part of Chelsea's future and I brought him back against Liverpool and I felt it was better for me not to be on the pitch. It doesn't mean I won't play again; it depends on the opposition, where we can hit them, where their weaknesses are.'

Nobody could quibble with Gullit's policy of leaving out players in the best interest of the team if the same policy applied to himself. It even applied to Vialli, who sat on the bench until ten minutes from time when he peeled off layer after layer, worn to protect him from the winter's chill; a coat, a warm suit, a sweatshirt and finally off came a white T-shirt over his blue Chelsea kit – no doubt there were a few layers of T-shirts underneath.

The Italians made their FA Cup debuts fully conversant with the reputation of the world's premier knock-out tournament. No one told them that the Cup can be played in Arctic conditions. What would they have made of the Racecourse Ground where West Ham forced a draw with Wrexham, with Harry Redknapp complaining bitterly about the snow-covered pitch? Madness!

Vialli decorated a match already won with a burst and deflected shot that struck the post to provide Zola with his sixth goal in seven games. Gullit shrugged and smiled when the Vialli 'sub' debate opened up again. Gullit insisted it was a coach's dream to choose from Zola, Hughes and Vialli. 'It's a luxury and we shall have to see if they can all play together, all I do is pick the best team on the day. Everything is OK. Everybody knows the situation. There is an attitude among the players and it's team spirit.'

Unlike the Premiership, where five subs were introduced, there are only three in the FA Cup. While Albion gambled without a second keeper, Gullit had Hitchcock on the bench with Burley and Vialli. He explained: 'You need players for different places on the pitch, you can't always take a risk with only two. I thought I took the right one, one came on and did the job.' Namely Burley, scoring the killer second. Can't argue with that!

How much longer would Vialli sit on the bench? Gullit said: 'I was happy the way he came in, it was a good moment for him, it gave the team an extra boost at that moment. Hughes deserved to come off to applause but if we'd have been one up no coach in the world could make any moves, you must be sure of the result.'

Those who questioned Gullit's philosophy too vigorously were sold off. Those who accepted it were part of a vibrant new Chelsea. Gullit said: 'I was surprised when I went onto the pitch and saw we were sold out again. People are coming to see Chelsea and I'm pleased by that. People are attracted to the players not because of where they come from, but how they play; they see good football.'

Just over halfway through the season, Gullit detected a change in attitudes. 'It's a whole complex thing, it's about ideas that people have brought here. It started with Hoddle, he wanted to do something new and we have seen things happening here. I was particularly pleased with what happened against Liverpool after New Year's Eve when traditionally players go to a hotel but they were given more trust and responsibility to go home and look after their bodies. It's about their whole lives. When I first came here people just asked me "How was it in Milan, how was it in Holland?" When I told them they said "How boring." They were surprised that we did nothing yet won everything and it was because we took everything so seriously.

All of a sudden we have developed a mixture of what happened in Milan and what can happen here in England. Certainly, you must enjoy yourself off the pitch, but you must do it in the proper way, and there is more awareness about that. There is no point forcing someone to do something such as a diet, if they don't want to do it.

'We go out with each other, we don't just stay at home but we go in a group into town and that creates a very good spirit. Yes, you have to stay home at the right time, but there are other times when you can relax also.'

With his usual wicked sense of humour Gullit added: 'At the beginning it was difficult understanding the Cockneys and Scots. I ask them "Do you speak English?" Now we understand each other.' Gullit analysed his own progress. 'My next step is to concentrate on doing my job as I am now. I'm learning all the time. It is my first year working as a manager and coach and I am improving with every game, as also are the team. There is much more confidence in the team. I'm happy the way they handled this game. You have to be concentrated against so-called lower teams.'

Gullit's new regime was getting through, not just to the imports used to such professionalism, but also to the Brits. Wise, disenchanted with the squad system at first, ended up with a new contract, a recall to the team and captaincy – and the vital opening goal in the Cup. Wise said: 'As the boys have done extremely well I was just pleased to be playing and, of course, to get a goal. If you want to achieve anything it is better to have competition for places, otherwise players get complacent. I've had to be patient. As Ruud has been saying it is not about eleven, but eighteen, players, and all eighteen have to stick together. We all know it now, it's as simple as that. It's easy to call people back into the side, but that ain't gonna happen if the team is winning. Just because I'm captain doesn't mean I would play.'

Gullit was particularly delighted with Wise. 'It was good to see Dennis get that goal. He knows players have to be left out but now we have everyone being happy about the situation. You can see now that everybody is tuned in well, giving a one hundred per cent job. Belief in themselves is growing. Every game I see things that make me proud of them. They had only one header, not even a chance, that is professional against a team that made things really difficult as they had nothing to lose. We had to be as motivated as we were against Liverpool.'

The First Division team hustled to ensure a typical scrappy cup tie, the vital Wise breakthrough coming in the thirty-eighth minute. It wasn't until Burley came on for the injured Minto in the seventy-first minute that the tie was finally settled. Minto suffered a cut knee and cut forehead, needing several stitches – which took eight minutes to dress by Dr Hugh Millington – before returning with his head in a bandage, and finally went off with a hamstring injury. Four minutes later Burley coolly slid his shot into the corner after Hughes and Di Matteo created the opening. Wise added: 'It was never going to be easy and they made it hard for us in the first twenty minutes by playing man for man but eventually our qualities came through. Ruud said we had to be professional about these kind of games, stop them having chances and create a lot of chances ourselves.'

Restricting Albion to a single weak header on goal, Gullit delighted in another clean sheet. 'Yes, it was very solid, a very good performance. The crowd expect us to "spank" them but that's not reality, they were potential giant-killers. I saw us improve as a team. It's typical of Chelsea, after a result like that against Liverpool, to lose to a team from a lower division, but we played as good professionals should do. Yeah, it went exactly as I thought it would; it was important that we have to approach games in a certain way.'

Subdued Albion boss Alan Buckley couldn't find a good word to say about the Italian players! 'I was too busy looking at my team. We haven't done ourselves justice, we are a good footballing side, believe it or not.'

SUNDAY, JANUARY 5

Gullit sensed 1997 would be Chelsea's year. 'This is a new year and we have changed our mentality; throwing games away is in the past. West Brom in the FA Cup, that would have been a classic Cup match for Chelsea to lose in the past but we won 3–0. It says a lot about the team.'

Immediately after holders Manchester United's 2–0 win over a desperately depleted Spurs, the FA Cup draw live on BBC 1 threw up the tie of the fourth round … Chelsea v Liverpool. You could hear Chelsea fans groan. Would it still be Chelsea's year now? Liverpool had the chance for quickfire revenge when last year's losing Cup finalists were defeated by a Di Matteo goal in the Premiership. But Gullit was not perturbed. 'Liverpool in the fourth round! It's okay. I'm quite happy. After the match with West Bromwich Albion I said now we should have a good team, and they handed us one. Motivation is easy against a good team. You see that when you play away from home, against not so good teams, then you get such strange surprises. I asked for a good team, and now we've got one!'

It was easily the glamour match of a draw which produced only three cut and dried ties because the weekend weather decimated the third-round programme. Liverpool managed only a Stan Collymore goal in disposing of Burnley at Anfield. The tie-of-the-round was inevitably picked as the BBC's live match.

MONDAY, JANUARY 6

At last, a day off. Wise turned up to do some basic exercises and strength work in the gym, Minto was in for treatment.

Johnsen rejected a £500,000 move to Manchester City, preferring to see out the final season of his contract. He planned to move back to Norway.

TUESDAY, JANUARY 7

Gullit wanted the world's number one left-back Paolo Maldini. Hutchinson scorned suggestions of a £17m bid, but confirmed the approach for the twenty-eight-year-old international, son of the new national coach. 'I asked them about Maldini and they came back to me and said he was not for sale. As far as I am concerned, that is the end of it. They were not even prepared to negotiate, although I must say that for £17m I would have wanted the whole of AC Milan.' He added that the world-record figure of £17m was the product of vivid press imaginations. 'No fee was ever mentioned, as it didn't get that far. It seems the silly season has come early this year. It is very well known Arrigo Sacchi is looking to change the team around, but it's not surprising they don't want to sell Maldini as he is one of the best players in the world. Our interest was very much tongue in cheek.' Hutchinson added the club's policy on only discussing transfers when they were signed and sealed had not changed, and refused to be drawn on further speculation. 'We are always checking the Italian scene, as well as the domestic one, as are all clubs these days.'

WEDNESDAY, JANUARY 8
Vialli said on Italian TV: 'Ravanelli will leave Middlesbrough but not for Manchester United. I think perhaps he will go to AC Milan.'

Grodas moved out of his temporary apartment into his new house.

THURSDAY, JANUARY 9
Keegan sensationally walked out on Newcastle, stress blamed for his departure. For Gullit, the manager's job was a stress-free zone. If anything Ruud thrived on big-time tension. Dalglish, Coppell and now Keegan had all found the managerial rat-race too much. Gullit said: 'Of course there is stress. It's part of the job. Without stress it would be boring. You have to use the tension to make you perform. But I never lose my temper, even though I do get angry about stupid things. My players make mistakes. I give them space to make mistakes. Yet if you make one, you have to learn not to make it again. I don't scream and shout. I keep it in. When I get angry, I go to my room, sit down and relax. Then, when you have calmed down, you go in and talk to them and find out what happened.'

FRIDAY, JANUARY 10
A football cliche says one certainty is that a manager will get the sack. Would it ever happen to Ruud? He doesn't fear the chop. Talking generally about the pressure of modern-day management, he said: 'If the team doesn't do well the manager gets sacked – if that is the right decision. It's more difficult to sack twenty-two players than only one man. You know that, those are the rules of the game, and you have to accept it. It also happens with a whole load of good coaches. But I don't fear it, or particularly think about it, myself. You know that when you are a manager it's an occupational hazard, it's going to happen. I think it would be a strange feeling if it did happen. But already this season some managers have been sacked, some have left. You have to cope with it, it's part of the job. I've only been manager here seven months and there is so much to look forward to, so much to achieve, it's very exciting. Seven months ago I couldn't have envisaged being a manager. But the club asked me to take the challenge, I'm ambitious to do well and so are they. And there will be good times and bad times. The job does change you, you have to be harder, you have to be on top of it, but also not too much. But I find it easy to switch off when I go away. I play golf, I have my music and a lot of friends in London. Stress is always there, as a player or manager. But it doesn't affect me, sometimes you can use it like adrenalin to get you going. I never lose my temper, or shout at the players or throw tea cups around the dressing room. I'm not like that. I don't think like that. I just do something until the moment I stop enjoying it. Then you say "OK, I've had enough, I'll do something else." I'm just beginning. I know there will be bad times and difficult situations when it will take more out of me. I'm ambitious but I'm aware of my situation. I'm learning all the time.

'At the end of my career I want to be able to look back and think I've done everything I could. At the moment I'm satisfied but there's more to come. That's why I'm relaxed about being a manager.'

Zola was named Carling Player of the Month after just six weeks and six goals in ten games in English soccer. Naturally, he was a popular choice to be interviewed at the training ground. 'I'm surprised I've done so well. I have to say thank you to my friends and everyone at Chelsea – they give me all the things I need. I've started like this and I want to continue this way – it's not easy but I'll try to do it. There is more to come. People have not seen the best of me yet. I don't know how much better I can get, but there is room. My confidence is growing and that will give me more chances. I love it in London. I feel at home and relaxed at Chelsea and that makes me confident on the pitch. I couldn't have imagined it would have gone this well so soon. I always believed in my ability but I didn't think I would settle so quickly. I now feel I am in my most relaxed state of mind ever. I am producing my instinctive football because I am at peace in England. When I first came here I had a problem with the language and I didn't really know anything about the whole situation. But step by step my confidence has improved and that's helped both me and the team. I'm a different person now I'm here in England, I feel very relaxed. It's probably the most relaxed I've been in my career – and that's important because my football is instinctive.'

Zola was pleased to escape the goldfish-bowl mentality of life in Serie A. 'Football is a sport and that's what I believe in – and I think that's the best way to give of your best. In Italy football is everything, a religion, and people talk about it and think about it every day. There's no time to rest. But here I can get away from it, spend time with my family.

'People in England understand that side of it, losing is not nice but it is accepted. They don't forget sport is just a sport but in Italy they concentrate on football every day. I have told Roberto Di Matteo and my other team-mates that I am like another person in England. I am so relaxed I feel I can do whatever I want on the pitch because my football is instinctive.

'Another big difference I've found here in England is that the teams think to attack first, in Italy they want to defend first. I believe the game must be like a party, a festival, right? I love the ambience and the lifestyle in England – and I love playing here. Over here when I see people in the street they say "hello" and "congratulations", and "come back to Italy" [laughing]. But no one bothers me or disturbs me. I love it here. Ruud played in Italy, he knows what it's like over there. All he wants is to play football, and I think like that also. Ruud Gullit told me just to play and enjoy myself and not to worry about anything else.'

Gullit was ruled out after a bizarre training ground accident. He stepped on a goalpost and twisted his ankle. Gullit would only have been on the bench in any event; his side in seventh spot, he wanted to be needed less on the pitch. 'At the beginning, the board kept urging me to pick myself. Now they see the team are doing well, they don't. Ken Bates gives me some stick, but mostly he leaves it alone. I might not put myself in for a lot of the future games but that doesn't bother me unduly. It's all for the benefit of Chelsea.' He would walk into any Premiership side, but he was a non-playing sub for the last two matches.

With Clarke still suspended and Minto having a fitness test on a hamstring injury in the morning, he called youngsters Clement and Nicholls into the squad. Sinclair took over from Clarke in the back three with Myers in for Minto on the left side. Johnsen was on the bench.

Wise dropped again, and Vialli still on the bench along with Hitchcock. No more Mr Nice Guy, but there was no other way. Gullit explained: 'If you have something in your mind you have to stick with it because you have the responsibility. To be nice, to be kind to the players, is very difficult also. You want that of course, but that's not possible for all twenty-two – you know that. So you have to stick to what you have in your mind. If that gives you success you have to deal with it, you have to go on with it, despite, maybe, that some players are unhappy with it.'

Gullit was still searching for consistency from a team which had peculiar mood swings, from brilliant to banal. After recent successes, players could see the merit of the squad system. Gullit added: 'Because in the end they see the results are there, they can see it for themselves. I've already had a lot of injuries, some long ones, suspensions also, and I've never moaned about that. It doesn't matter who the player is, you can't make them all happy, and a lot of them have the same problem. I have to pick the best team, I don't pick the team that maybe likes me the best. If it makes me a bit unpopular with some of the players then that is part of the job. That's the most difficult part, because you have played with them. But I have to take these decisions for the benefit of the club, not for the benefit of me.'

Confidence was up, the club transformed from title outsiders to contenders in a four-match unbeaten run. Newton said: 'We're not out of the title race by a long chalk. People keep saying it's between Liverpool, Manchester United and Newcastle but there are others as well. Everyone here believes we have got what it takes to win the title. But we don't want to shout about it. The old Chelsea, who beat big teams and lost to small ones, is in the past.'

Forest caretaker boss Stuart Pearce, beaten only once in five games, was without striker Kevin Campbell, who had an ankle knock. But Chris Bart-Williams was fit again after twelve games out with a groin injury.

SATURDAY, JANUARY 11

Nottingham Forest 2 Chelsea 0

'I ordered my players to go up one gear. I should have said *two* gears,' said Gullit.

Much was made of the way Zola was man-marked out of the game. Gullit said: 'With more top players coming over the Premier League could get like Serie A for man-marking. In Italy I was marked all the time. I would go to the loo and they would be waiting for me. I would say "While you are there, hold this, would you?"' Gullit treated such tactics with disdain, and wanted Zola to do the same.

After a chat with his former Forest pal Des Walker, following Sheffield Wednesday's draw at Stamford Bridge, Pearce set full-back Des Lyttle to man-mark Zola. Never seeming fazed by this tactic in the past, it worried him this time. Zola hardly got a kick, and probably wouldn't have been surprised if Lyttle had followed him into the Chelsea dressing room at half-time! 'I was aware that Zola could have ripped us apart. Des was magnificent,' praised Pearce. In the end, Zola's temper snapped. He petulantly pushed Lyttle's chest, a gesture which summed up all the frustration felt by Chelsea. Gullit claimed: 'I don't quite understand how we lost. We had lots of possession and opportunities but didn't produce. We never enjoy the luck which is so important in football. What I would give for one fixture full of bad football when we actually emerge as the winners.' As for the attention Zola is attracting from opponents, he said: 'It does not worry me if teams decide to man-mark Zola, it will mean there will be more space and opportunities for other players.' There were worrying signs that with Zola contained, the team had less of an effective cutting edge. Gullit said: 'We have to produce one hundred per cent every game to get anything.'

Luck certainly deserted Chelsea when Leboeuf conceded a thirty-eighth-minute free kick on the edge of the penalty area for his challenge on Alf Inge Haaland. The eight-man wall proved no defence as Pearce stepped forward to fire past the unsighted Grodas. Poor Grodas was left flat-footed again in the fifty-third minute when Bart-Williams scored his first for Forest with a screaming left-foot volley from twenty-two yards.

As Gullit said, 'nothing happened' for long spells. With Zola ineffectual, Chelsea were a shadow of the side which beat Liverpool. Gullit despaired of the banality of their final ball – often lofted towards the diminutive Zola as if he were Duncan Ferguson. They ended in disarray with Sinclair up front and Vialli in midfield. Chelsea had their moments. Haaland's spectacular full-length dive to block Di Matteo's goal-bound volley was about the best of them. Di Matteo and Burley shot over, while Zola headed straight at the keeper.

'For me it was a boring game. We had a lot of possession and created nothing, they had two shots and scored two goals.' Gullit was pretty unimpressed with the match.

Zola still felt there was a chance of the title – with none of the sides above them winning either. 'We are still in the race. Obviously this defeat is a setback, but we have shown we have the consistency to make a challenge. We have to learn from our mistakes and we are doing that. As a team we are improving all the time. At this stage the title is not beyond us.'

Another blemish was the distasteful taunts against Harding. One Forest fan was arrested as a small section taunted the away supporters over the death of their former vice-chairman with insulting gestures and appalling chants. Nottingham Police Assistant Chief Constable Robin Searle spoke out on BBC Radio 5 Live's 606 programme. 'It's not conduct we would tolerate. It's entirely the conduct likely to cause a breach of the peace. People can be prosecuted and that is what we will be looking at. We will look at the film, as we do after every match, to see who we can pick up doing whatever and we will take action after the event.'

Hughes captained the side for the first time. 'I was very proud. I haven't been captain many times during my career. The lads know their jobs and I'm not going to start ranting and raving because that's not how I am. Bryan Robson was one of the few players who could grab a team by the scruff of the neck during a game. There's a lot of captains who rant and shout during and before a game, but not many change the game doing it. He could do it with his talking, but also as a player by his deeds, and so he had the respect of everyone. You've got to have respect and lead by example to be a good captain.'

WEDNESDAY, JANUARY 15

Vialli joined Ravanelli in expressing his frustration at life in the Premiership. Vialli struggled to return to the starting line-up after injury and illness. He stated his case in no uncertain fashion during an Italian TV sports programme. 'It is not a particularly happy period for me. Ruud Gullit has used me very little and I am not satisfied about this. I think if the manager keeps the captain of the side that won the European Cup six months ago on the bench, it would mean his team are top of the league. But this is not the case at Chelsea. So it must mean either the manager is not doing an exceptional job or there is something wrong. I feel there is something wrong. I wait with patience. I continue to train and I just grit my teeth. I did not come here on holiday or to enjoy myself. I came here to play and become a legend in London with Chelsea. Staying on the bench is frustrating for me and I hope things change in the future. Certainly I am not happy and not prepared to bear this situation for much longer.'

Sidelined with a hamstring, then flu, the partnership of Hughes and Zola blossomed in his absence. Williams said: 'When Gianluca is on form he will return to the side. I have spoken to him and he was happy.' Vialli could expect no special treatment from Gullit; he was told to fight to get his place back and to keep it. If he deserved to play, he will be picked. Otherwise he stayed on the bench. Gullit operated a 'no favouritism' regime. Williams added: 'Luca has spoken to Ruud about this. We understand his frustrations. The team will be picked at 1.20 on Saturday afternoon. Then we shall all know who plays.' Williams insisted Vialli's future was not in doubt. 'We understand how he feels, but he appreciates the situation. He accepts it. We didn't want him injured, he was outstanding against Everton scoring a great goal. Then he damaged his hamstring. A team needs a large squad, to cope with injuries and suspensions.'

Ravanelli couldn't understand why Juventus sold him to Middlesbrough after winning the European Cup and he dreamed of returning to Serie A. In an interview with Rome daily newspaper *La Repubblica* he sympathised with Vialli. 'I have no answer,' the prolific striker said when asked why the Italian league leaders had sold him. Boro were bottom of the table. 'Rav' had spoken to Vialli and they could hardly believe what had happened to two of the key players who helped Juventus to win the European Cup. Ravanelli said: 'He is worse off than me. He told me about his knee, about Gullit who never plays him. Incredible. If I close my eyes, I see myself with Luca at the Olympic Stadium while we are kissing the cup. And now we are here. The England that I was expecting was not a bottom of the league place. Even a child could understand that.' Middlesbrough were also docked three points for failing to play a match against Blackburn on December 21 after Robson reported twenty-three of his players were either ill with influenza or injured.

Di Matteo had had a philosophical approach to developments under Gullit, having been dropped himself. 'Every player who sits on the bench is unhappy, because naturally everybody wants to play. But you have to wait your time, work hard and then you get back into the team.' Rix said: 'He just has to bide his time. He has to keep himself fit so that he's ready to come back in, as he surely will.'

FRIDAY, JANUARY 17
Duberry out for the rest of the season, undergoing an operation after snapping an Achilles tendon in training. Losing the England under-21 captain was a massive blow. Gullit said: 'This is a big loss, as Duberry had been playing well. The loss of Doobs is so bad. He was doing well for us and for himself. But this is the lesson of life; one day you are up, next day you are out. He will learn and come back stronger. You realise you can't waste your time. Every day you must be happy with what you are doing. Doobs will come back very healthy. In the meantime, we must do anything we can for him. I have no plans to buy new cover as I think the squad can cope with this position. He did it in training yesterday; he just slipped over and injured himself but it is a bad injury and he is undergoing an operation today.' The freak injury, on the ice-bound training pitch, wrecked his hopes of making England's World Cup squad. Hoddle gave the centre-half his Premiership debut and had kept close tabs on him since.

Duberry promised to beat the same injury that sidelined Barnes for eighteen months. 'It's hard to believe something so innocuous as a training run can have such dire consequences. I'll be back for the start of next season and I'll be raring to go. I chested the ball down, and as I was about to kick it with my right foot my left completely gave way. It felt like someone had booted my leg. It was only when I fell to the ground in agony that I realised nobody was near me.

'I knew straight away it was serious. First on the scene was Roberto Di Matteo, shouting "Achilles, Achilles." I remember thinking "What, he's a bloody doctor now?" But you can trust Wisey to make a laugh out of it all. He started smacking me round the face, going "Get up Doobs, stop messing about." At first all I could think about was the big games I'd miss. But at the hospital it became clear I'd be lucky to kick a ball at the start of next season – and that was soul-destroying. I'm OK when my girlfriend's around, but when I'm alone I get very down. But I'm sure I will be a much stronger person for all this, even though it doesn't seem like it now.'

Duberry's spirits were lifted by a call from Arsenal and England striker Ian Wright. 'I had surgery the morning after the accident. As I lay there, not fully conscious, a nurse came in and said Ian Wright was on the phone. I thought it was one of the lads winding me up because Wrighty is a big hero of mine, but sure enough it was him. He was so positive. He said: "You've got a great future in the game and you're going to be back, so keep your chin up." That was really nice of him. I maintain a positive frame of mind. I know I will beat this.'

He went under the surgeon's knife for two hours at an Essex hospital. Wise said: 'We're all ever so disappointed for Micky Doobs. But he's a top man, he'll handle it well and come back fine.' Physio Mike Banks explained: 'He jumped to control the ball on his chest and felt a sharp pain in the back of his leg. We stretchered him off and examined the injury. It seemed clear what had happened, and we got a surgeon to confirm it that afternoon and surgical repair was carried out the following morning. His leg will be in plaster for six weeks. Rehabilitation is the most important thing with this type of injury.'

Gullit's other major problem remained Vialli. 'I would hope anybody would be unhappy when they're not playing. It means they are prepared to do the business when they come in. But I don't speak about things in the paper with players – if they have something they want to say to me they should come and see me.' Gullit reiterated that he didn't want his players publicly moaning. 'Supporters do not want players who moan, they will not tolerate it. They want them one hundred per cent ready to do the business for the team. They will listen to it for so long. If it carries on, there is a danger the crowd could turn against those who only think of themselves. Supporters like what they see here. But, despite this, every month there is a player unhappy. I've had it from John Spencer, Gavin Peacock, Terry Phelan and Dennis Wise. They did not want to be part of it and if someone can't cope with the new situation there's only one solution.

'If you can't stand the heat get out of the kitchen. I have explained the situation to everyone this season. It's not my solution, they reach that conclusion themselves. I could see this situation arising with Vialli as no one likes being left out. If he was happy being out, I wouldn't be happy with him. There is no star status here. Vialli is a friend but I can't let that interfere with running the team. I have to be honest in these situations. If you make concessions, give one player the benefit, then others will moan. I have a responsibility as head coach to pick the best team. I am not doing my job properly if I am affected by my personal relationships with some of the players. I have to separate my feelings from the players in the team because of my job. I have to stand on the outside.'

Gullit indulged in a couple of gentle digs. 'When he was in Italy last season, Vialli refused to talk to the press. Yet here he went on Italian TV to air his grievances. I remember when Vialli didn't say anything to anyone but it is convenient for him to come out and say things now. I am comfortable with the way I run things at Stamford Bridge.'

Had they discussed his TV comments? 'He has said nothing to me. I said to him: "How was your trip? How was the weather? Your car?" He says nothing. That is up to him.'

Ruud really wasn't that perturbed. He had bought Zola to play behind Vialli and Hughes, but the Zola–Hughes pairing was thrown together when Vialli was injured – and it had worked. Gullit said: 'I can sleep easy at night. My conscience is clear because I am doing what I believe is best for Chelsea. Zola and Hughes are doing well. I admit I did not believe they would, but they are. It is as simple as that. If anyone wants to replace them then it is down to them. Work harder, I say.'

Gullit had no plans to sell Vialli. In fact, Gullit said: 'Vialli can still be the shining star here, I don't want him to go.'

Zola joked: 'I'm surprised Vialli is not playing . . . if it was me I'd murder someone to get back in the side.'

With Duberry out and Gullit still injured, Chelsea added teenager Paul Hughes, a local-born midfielder and no relation to Mark, to the squad. The youngster's inclusion forced Williams to dash to the club shop to prepare a number twenty-seven shirt.

Derby manager Jim Smith decided not to put a minder on Zola. Smith said: 'I've never been a fan of man-to-man marking. You might stop their guy playing but you lose a player yourself. It's everybody's job.' Derby had not won since late November, and Petrescu wanted to know the answer to the question on everybody's lips – why do Chelsea beat good teams and lose to less strong ones? Petrescu said: 'We keep losing against sides who are not as good. Yet we need to close the gap on teams above us. We need to find out why fast because we are playing Derby and they also are not as big as Chelsea. But they are unbeaten against London sides.'

Gullit arranged a friendly with AC Milan at the San Siro. 'The point in going to play Milan is not to show how good we are, but to give my players the experience of playing against a side like Milan. We were on the list with Bayern Munich and Ajax to be chosen and it's a big compliment for Chelsea to be invited to play a club like Milan. It will be a great experience for our youngsters to play in the San Siro Stadium.' Many tipped Gullit to return to Milan one day as manager, others saw him as the natural successor at Ajax. But he insisted: 'I'm not interested. I'm staying with Chelsea, my ambitions are here. You have to begin with the beginning and I want to do well here. Then we'll see what happens.'

While arranging the game, the club made another inquiry for Maldini. 'I heard the rumours that Milan were ready to sell a lot of players and I wouldn't be doing my job if I didn't ask for Maldini. I can't imagine Milan would sell him, but I had to ask. As a coach you'd be crazy not to be interested but I don't think I'm going to get him because they are asking for something ridiculous. If I could get Maldini for a good price I would snap him up.'

Chelsea had become recognised as a force on the continent. Hutchinson said: 'Scouring Europe for a box office attraction to play a prestige friendly in the San Siro, AC Milan short-listed four clubs: Real Madrid (coached by top Italian Fabio Capello); Barcelona (a big draw with Ronaldo in the line-up); Bayern Munich (another highly rated Italian coach Giovanni Trapattoni); and Chelsea. Yes, Chelsea! Unbelievable really. Less than three years ago the Blues would not have featured in a top 200 list! Such is their profile and pulling power these days that Milan plumped for Chelsea for the San Siro game – to be televised live throughout Italy. The Milan giants were so keen to get the Blues that they provided a private jet so that the team can return to England straight after the match to allow two days' preparation for the visit of Manchester United. AC Milan knew an Italian date for Ruud Gullit, Roberto Di Matteo, Gianluca Vialli and Gianfranco Zola would guarantee a big TV audience. Juventus, Lazio and Parma also want to set Italian dates for Chelsea. Changed times indeed!'

A surprise face among the media at training was Jakob Kjeldbjerg. An analyst for Danish TV since he was forced to retire he made his debut as an interviewer performing a profile on the changing face of Chelsea.

SATURDAY, JANUARY 18
Chelsea 3 Derby County 1

Vialli squirmed, unemployed on the bench as Gullit sent out new kid on the block Paul Hughes to re-ignite Chelsea's championship challenge. Ruud's rules are hard for Vialli to take – medals, reputations and international pedigree earned no favouritism. Young Hughes overcame a succession of crippling injuries to make a stunning debut while Vialli failed to move Gullit with his outburst.

Wise mischievously ran to the dug-out to lift his shirt over his head in a copy cat of Ian Wright's messages scribbled on his T-shirt. Wise scrawled 'Cheer Up Luca, we love you xx' on his T-shirt. At least that brought a rare smile from Vialli. I asked Gullit what the Italian thought of that. 'I don't know, you'll have to ask him, he was sitting behind me. I was particularly pleased with the performances of Frank Sinclair and Frank Leboeuf.' Gullit was bored discussing Vialli. 'I don't want to spend too much of my energy on this issue, everybody knows my ideas and Dennis Wise showed the spirit in this team. I'd rather speak about how good the game was if you don't mind.'

Gullit was ecstatic with the way the impish Wise had sent out his own particular message to Vialli. 'It was great, it shows how big the team spirit is. Wisey has been in a similar situation and has worked hard and given everything. He was clearly saying "OK, come on, cheer up" and we go on with our squad system. What Wise did is a great sign, not just within this club but to everybody outside Chelsea. It was all a matter of how the team responded in the last couple of games and I didn't have to do nothing, the team spirit here is extremely high. Everybody has to be tuned in with our philosophy, everybody has to deal with that. It is not black and white. It's a difficult situation but he has to cheer up because it's a team thing. I don't mind who's playing, or where they come from. It doesn't matter, everybody's given a fair chance. I am fair to everybody, I have even excluded myself out of the team. I don't think selfishly, and the players have to think like that also, not for themselves but for the team.' Wise relived that moment. 'I enjoyed my goal. A tap in. Every time I get left out I seem to come back and score. I just hope I don't get left out too often because of that! I hope everyone enjoyed the T-shirt celebration. Just a little thing to Luca to show him we all love him. And we do. I was in the same position. He got a hamstring injury, I got a two-match suspension. The lads did well over Christmas, three wins in four, so Luca and I had to be patient. I've been fortunate enough to come back before him, but I know how he feels. Sometimes you do need cheering up. Afterwards he shook my hand and gave me a big kiss. He knows how much we love him and love having him here. I'm not planning any more messages, by the way. That was my only one.'

The words were written by Clarke in the kit room behind the dressing room. Dennis quietly took Steve in there ten minutes before kick off and Steve wrote it on while Dennis was wearing his ordinary M&S vest, puffing his chest out and muttering 'I'm going to have to run my **** off today, I gotta score, I gotta score.' Clarke said: 'He knew he was gonnae score.' Only those two and kit man Bob Osborn knew about it. There is another, more mischievous, reason for Wise asking Clarke to inscribe his T-shirt – Dennis couldn't spell 'Luca'.

For all those critics suggesting Gullit's foreign acquisitions stunted the growth of home-produced talent, Hughes junior made an instant impact when he took over from the injured Wise for the entire second half, executing a double one-two with Di Matteo before finishing off dogged Derby with the third goal just five minutes from the end.

The twenty-year-old from Greenford in west London was out for the best part of a year with a pelvic injury. Rather, as Gullit put it, 'No, it's not the groin, it's higher up, between the two dinger dings, how do you call it, the bells.'

Another Gullit innovation was specialist orthopaedic physio Ted Troost as part of his backroom team who played a vital role in Hughes's remarkable recovery. Gullit explained: 'I've known Ted for sixteen years, he treated me when I went to Milan and for the past two months he has been at the club every Tuesday. Paul has had problems with his spine and the way he walked was very tight. Ted thought the problem might be related to the jaw area. The jaw was in the wrong position, and he had to put it back. All of a sudden it cleared the pain. He just clicked the jaw back. If it hadn't been for his injuries he could have been more involved, but we knew what his capabilities were.'

Hughes relived the extraordinary circumstance of his recovery. 'I had a problem with shin splints when I was seventeen but it didn't need an operation. I managed nine games before an ankle ligament injury and then another nine games before a problem with my pelvis. I've been out for up to a year with an unstable pelvis and I went to see practically every surgeon in England until Dan Petrescu, who had a similar problem, recommended a doctor in Naples. He suggested a series of stretching exercises for thirty-five minutes every day and since then the problem has gone. The Dutch physio thought my jaw was out of place and that affected my whole posture. It hurt like hell when he put my jaw back in. It's not the main reason, but one of the reasons why I had no more pain.'

Hughes was told by Gullit on Friday after training he'd be making his debut, and he said: 'Playing with so many good players is just great particularly as they trust me and give me the ball.' When the kid scored even the superstars like Di Matteo paid homage by going on their knees. 'That was a great moment, brilliant,' said Hughes.

An incredible forty-yard free kick from Aljosa Asanovic embarrassed Hitchcock, back after a run of eleven games. Chelsea recovered from that twenty-fifth-minute shock by equalising in the thirty-seventh minute when Mark Hughes made an important contribution with a pass to Zola, whose shot struck a post, and Wise followed up.

Zola was again in scintillating form after collecting his Carling Player of the Month award for December from Richard North, financial director of Bass, on the pitch shortly before the kick off. It was Zola's cross in the forty-third minute from which referee Graham Poll adjudged that Hughes had been pushed in the back by

Matt Carbon. Leboeuf converted his fourth penalty, sending Russell Hoult the wrong way, for his sixth goal.

Myers switched to centre-back in Duberry's absence, given a torrid time by live wire Dean Sturridge. Even when substitute Christian Dailly was sent off for his second bookable offence six minutes from the end Chelsea could never relax until young Hughes delivered the decisive strike, just a minute after Derby were reduced to ten men. Smith was livid. 'When I saw the ref's name I expected the sending off! The penalty was very harsh and the sending off was a joke.'

Smith paid tribute to Chelsea. 'Some of their forward play was excellent. They had good passing and good movement. They are a bright side.' This was Smith's first taste of defeat in the capital after holding both Arsenal and Wimbledon to draws. 'Arsenal are a good side but there's not much to choose between them and Chelsea.'

Leboeuf was again my Man of the Match. Clattered so often, he thought he was in a boxing match. How the fans love him. He edged Zola as Gullit's best player. 'We kept hitting Derby where they were weakest,' said Gullit. 'We gave them no chances and they were dangerous only at free kicks and corners.'

SUNDAY, JANUARY 19

Vialli pledged he won't walk out. He left the Bridge without a word after languishing on the bench again. 'There's no question that I'm considering leaving Chelsea. I trained hard today and I'm biding my time. I said something a week ago without any intent, but it has been blown out of all proportion.' Sounded like Ravanelli! Vialli added: 'I believe it is best to remain ... seated. As the Chinese proverb says "Seated on the banks of the river, waiting for things to change."' As for the Wise message on a T-shirt, Vialli thoroughly enjoyed it. 'What Dennis did was fantastic. It was his way of trying to calm things down and take the heat out of the situation. And, in many ways, it worked. Next time I score – if I play, of course – I will write on my vest "Dennis, do you want to marry me, my darling?"'

But Vialli was clearly unhappy stuck on the bench. 'I am not one of those players who don't care about sitting on the bench so long as they get their money. I want to play – for me, for the fans, for everyone.' With his English improving to give him a greater ability to express himself, he added: 'Believe me, I love Chelsea. Perhaps it is something to do with the fact they have struggled to live up to their big past. The fact that it has been up and down for so many years. I know that Zola, Di Matteo, Leboeuf and myself can bring back the good times. If I leave before Chelsea have won something, it will be the biggest regret of my career. I am still very happy at Chelsea. But it is the first time in my career I am not playing when I am fit. It is a new experience that I am trying to come to terms with.'

MONDAY, JANUARY 20

Clarke's two-match ban was over. He was an ever-present until he topped twenty-one disciplinary points. The longest serving player felt this was the most exciting side he had played in. 'The boss is always telling us, if someone comes in, and does well, they stay in. I've been at Stamford Bridge for ten years, and yet now, it's like being at a different club. Everything about Chelsea has changed so much. The atmosphere is what you notice most. When I first came down from Scotland in 1986, I didn't always play in front of a sell-out crowd. Now you cannot get a ticket for love nor money. The effect on me has been that I look forward to going in every day for training, relish being in the team and am happy to be part of something so exciting. You know when I first came to the club, we'd have a press conference and maybe one man and a dog would turn up.' Now it was not unusual for a mass turn-out, more than a dozen TV crews from around the world. 'That's a measure of the success we're having now, the publicity we're getting. I honestly don't know how Ruudi handles it. But he does, brilliantly and uniquely. Now, everybody wants a piece of Chelsea. The best feeling in the world is to pull on the Chelsea shirt and look around the dressing room at some of the greatest names in the game. Real class. Then you clatter off down the tunnel together. There's no sensation quite like it.'

Gullit says of Clarke: 'He is as important to the team as Zola or Leboeuf or any of those type of players. Sometimes, players like Steve can be of more importance than the real stars. He has been outstanding for me, and also become a leader. You can see how he's worked at his game and he's given me his maximum, a quiet player who doesn't grab the headlines but the type you can always rely on. He tells players what to do, talks to them in a nice way and gets respect without having to shout and scream.'

Clarke goes on: 'When I saw the signings that were being brought into the club, it could have worked one of two ways. You either tell yourself "I'm going to try even harder, work harder, play harder and fight to stay in the side," or you look at what is around you and fall by the wayside. I never stop learning, and when you are in a team of Chelsea's quality you cannot fail to graft the good things onto your game. I'm happier here than ever before. The football is great, it's a pleasure to be involved.'

Enjoying one of his best seasons, Clarke was indicative of how some of the British players were benefiting. No one could deny the foreign stars had captured the imagination of a new generation of fans. Just ask Steve's children who are their favourite players.

'Vialli,' said five-year-old Joe Clarke.

'Zola,' said eight-year-old John.

The anticipation of the Liverpool cup tie was building up. Clarke said: 'We've beaten them once and can do it again. It's they who will be more worried than us, because Chelsea can only get better the longer the team are together. Right now I'd say we are operating at seventy-five per cent of our effectiveness. But there is no reason why we can't find that consistency. We began to when Glenn Hoddle came. That's when things started to change. And Ruud Gullit has continued in the same way. When I look around at all the talent we have, it just makes me feel so stimulated. Nobody is in awe of these new guys. They get their fair share of stick from the rest of us. But it is all good natured. How could it be anything else? They give their fair share back, and that's how it should be. But there are no cliques in the club like I understand there are at others who have a foreign contingent. We do everything together and lads like Luca Vialli are especially ready to join in. That breeds the right kind of team spirit. That's important at any level in any club. Only Ruud has distanced himself, but then going from player to manager, he's had to.'

Clarke added: 'It's the first time in ten years that I've accumulated twenty-one points. None of my bookings were for dissent. Just for fouls. But I'm not a dirty player, my record shows that. It does, I believe, give an indication of my commitment to the cause. As you get older, obviously you cannot run so much. So the switch inside for me was ideal. I like to think I've had a good season, but in some games we've struggled. Wimbledon, Leeds and Sunderland have given us the hardest times.

Wimbledon because they are genuinely a very good side, and the other two because we were still trying to get the best system bedded down. That's what we are working on. The right tactics for the right match.'

TUESDAY, JANUARY 21

The Italians met up in Rome before making their way to the warm sunshine of Palermo in preparation for international duty for the first time under the new coach. Zola said: 'One of our first objectives is to get the supporters closer to the national team. There has not been a peaceful climate between us and the players have felt it. First of all we must play for them, then for ourselves. We must make the people love the Italian side.'

WEDNESDAY, JANUARY 22

Hoddle left Sicily knowing that Zola posed a major threat to his World Cup ambitions. Zola's eleventh strike in twenty-nine internationals came just eight minutes into the reign of Cesare Maldini against a makeshift Northern Ireland side. The smoke had hardly cleared over the La Favorita Stadium after the firework display that greeted a new Italian era when Zola opened the scoring with one of his specialist strikes. As Pierluigi Casiraghi was buffeted by Taggart, Zola stole in behind the challenge, gaining possession. And although he looked to be driven too wide, his little feet were powerpacked. There was no smokescreen as the Italians laid bare their tactical formation for Hoddle to see. Zola operated very much in the Cantona role as a second striker, difficult to pick up and lethal once he gets into the penalty area. Premiership managers wrestled with the decision whether to man-mark Zola. When the little maestro was shadowed relentlessly he proved less effective. Would Hoddle assign a specialist man-marker for Zola at Wembley? 'No' would be the answer.

Zola went off on the hour to a hero's ovation and a hug from his new coach. Di Matteo also came off as the second half took on a little more significance than the chance to give virtually everyone a game. Zola and Di Matteo would have been on their mobile phones immediately to report back to Gullit that they came through injury-free for the Liverpool tie.

Hoddle said: 'I've always thought that technically Zola is up there with the best in Europe. I also think he's very clever, very astute. We all know about international defenders who can read the game when the other side have the ball. Zola is an attacker who reads the game extremely well when his own team have the ball. If you give him space, he'll use it. I've always admired him, which is why I tried to buy him for Chelsea. He's a lovely footballer.'

THURSDAY, JANUARY 23

Relaxed in a leather jacket and open neck shirt, Ruud teamed up with Bob Geldof to unveil Chelsea Radio, a station devoted to the club and its matches, to be launched for the Manchester United league game. The station, which carries advertising, followed similar moves by Newcastle, who run Magpie Radio, and Manchester United. It broadcasts twenty-eight times a year under a special licence from the Radio Authority and coverage is restricted to home games. 'We are not in this for the money, we are in this for the love of football,' said Alex Connock, managing director of Geldof's production company Planet 24 Radio. 'We want to completely indulge the fans of Chelsea with what they love best – all the details of the players, the staff,' he added. Each home match day the station broadcasts from 8am to midnight with phone-ins, competitions and Chelsea news building up to the afternoon or evening kick-off. Fans will be wired up with microphones for spontaneous opinions to action on the pitch and there were plans for regular music slots like Vialli's top ten hits. Celebrity Chelsea fans, including MP David Mellor, presenter of Six-O-Six on Radio 5 Live, Sebastian Coe and Damon Hill, were approached to act as presenters. 'We want to get as many of them as we can on to the shows and we know they'll be interested,' said Connock.

Chelsea special projects manager Chris Manson said: 'One of the things fans find lacking throughout Premiership clubs is pre-match and half-time entertainment. We want to alter that. We are very conscious of the fact this is a community devoted to Chelsea and we want to contribute to that sense of community.'

Wise swapped his boots for a bowler as he set out to make a killing with Chelsea shares. Wise and a pal bought a block of shares for £150,000 at just over £1 each. With Ruud's Revolution taking off in conjunction with a major ground development those shares might soar close to £5. Bates said: 'Wisey rang me on Thursday out of the blue and said "Can I see you for somfing Batesie?" He was banging on my door again on Friday to complete the deal. When was the last time a player put money into football? But he can see what's going on here from the inside. It must be very encouraging to our supporters that he has committed himself to a new contract, shown his loyalty to Ruud, and now bought shares in the club. It's a terrific gesture and just goes to show what can happen when players really believe in the future of their club.'

Leboeuf's birthday was celebrated only the way the crazy Chelsea players can. In French football the players are respectful, polite, and sophisticated. Leboeuf was shocked to discover the dressing room banter and antics. 'My birthday is on the twenty-second but it was a day off – I am very happy about that. But when I arrive on the twenty-third, everybody in the team knows it is my birthday. My team-mates have funny ways of celebrating. In France, when it's your birthday, the players buy you champagne and cake. They found out about my birthday, Ade chased me around the training ground until he caught me, Erland jumped on my back and they pour orange juice over my head and shoved my face in the mud. Very strange. Okay, but it's funny, too.' Frank's English has dramatically improved in six months. When he first arrived his bald head and thick French accent attracted the dressing room mickey takers. 'I am much better now than I was so the English players can't make jokes about me as much now. They all said that I sounded like Inspector Clouseau when I first arrived. I love Londoners. I think they are extremely funny.'

FRIDAY, JANUARY 24

Leboeuf watched compatriot Cantona lift the FA Cup on French TV. Leboeuf aimed to become the second Frenchman to scupper Liverpool's Cup dream in as many seasons. In fact he didn't rule out completing the 'Double'! 'It is one of my ambitions to play in a Wembley Cup final and we are certainly good enough to get there this year. We beat Liverpool earlier this month and we can beat them again. We are no worse than them. And I also think we can still steal the championship. I played in a French Cup final for Strasbourg at the Parc des Princes, but we lost to Paris St Germain and that was a very bad experience for me. When I arrived I knew that I had much to learn, I didn't want to come in like a big star. And Ruud Gullit, a legend as a player, has been a great influence. Now we just want to be there on Cup final day in May ... and to win.'

Leboeuf did not expect Gullit to man-mark. 'McManaman is the best player in England and it's just not possible to follow him all the time. Even if you asked the best defender in Europe, Paolo Maldini, to mark him I don't think he would be able to follow McManaman for ninety minutes. I think I will be staying in my central defensive position and we will try to deny Liverpool space on the ball as a team, like we did on New Year's Day. You could follow McManaman a long way, run all day and not see much of the ball. For me he is the best English player in the Premier League. He's clever, technically very strong, fast and an opportunist.'

The cognoscenti of the game appreciate that Leboeuf is as big a personality as Cantona and Ginola, rather than just the third Frenchman in the Premiership. Chelsea applied a patient game to beat Liverpool in the league. Would it be the same strategy in the Cup? Leboeuf said: 'We waited for that mistake. I think you will see us apply the same tactics again. It will be more a game of continental football than the usual English kind.' Zola as a free spirit would be of great importance again. 'If you mark Gianfranco man to man, you must be very strong mentally,' said Leboeuf. 'He is very intelligent. He can leave a lot of space for other players, that is why the decision to man-mark him is so difficult for other coaches.'

Zola dominated Hoddle's weekend. He planned to be at Stamford Bridge when the tiny Italian changed to a Chelsea shirt. Hoddle wanted to know whether McManaman could produce the sort of blistering running and goal-scoring form that might prove an antidote to Zola in the Wembley World Cup showdown.

Zola talked about his love affair with the supporters. 'My relationship with the fans is one of the most pleasing things in my English experience.' Zola was described as a 'box of tricks' in Italy after his goal-scoring performance against Northern Ireland watched by Hoddle and his assistant John Gorman. Zola knew the English fans would not be cheering him at Wembley! 'It is not a good thing for us to play England because they are very good. I think English football is going to get better and better.'

Barnes, who returned from injury, named Zola as the best foreign player to arrive in the Premiership this season. 'Zola's been one of my favourite players for years and I think he has given Chelsea a new dimension. He would be the first name on any nation's teamsheet in my opinion. His movement, his sharpness, his brain and his awareness are all exceptional. I am not surprised how quickly he's settled in England. People said he was too small but if you play the ball to his feet, well ... We are not used to his type of player in this country and neither are Italy.' Barnes first spotted a young Zola when the striker turned out for a local side in a World Cup warm-up against England in Cagliari for Italia '90. He was impressed even then. 'We heard that Diego Maradona's understudy at Napoli was going to play. They lost 7–0 but he still showed a few good touches.'

While Barnes is full of admiration for Zola, Evans was equally impressed with rookie manager Gullit. 'He speaks openly and honestly and he says things that experienced managers might have thought but not said.'

Dominic Matteo had a special reason to look forward to facing Zola – his dad's favourite player! Matteo knew stopping Zola would considerably boost Liverpool's hopes of keeping alive dreams of a league and Cup double. It might also help his own chances of earning a place in Hoddle's England squad. 'My dad Alberto watches Italian football and he really admires Zola. He was always talking about him when he was at Parma, scoring free kicks and other wonder goals. You can't help but rate him, because he is a great player. I've worked in training this week on how Zola might play, but it is on the day that counts. I'd be lying if I said I didn't relish this sort of challenge.'

Liverpool aimed to avenge the 1–0 league defeat, but they were unlikely to repeat the scoreline from their meeting at Anfield. Matteo said: 'That was one of our best performances of the season in beating them 5–1, but they did a professional job on us at Stamford Bridge. Everyone admires Ruud Gullit as a footballer and he has taken that ability into management. He knows what he wants and he seems to be getting it from his players.'

Vialli was still sweating on a recall, but Zola was guaranteed centre stage. Zola was asked whether this side had a chance of ending twenty-six years without a major trophy. 'I don't know what the sides were like before me, so I cannot talk of them. But this is a good team. I definitely think we can win the Cup this year. It's so important to everybody at the club that we win a trophy, but we will have to be very careful about the way we approach the Liverpool game.' Zola sympathised again with Vialli's plight. 'There is not a stormy relationship between Luca and Ruud Gullit. I have never seen them argue. Certainly Luca is not happy on the bench, but no player in his position would be.'

Would Vialli play, or wouldn't he? Gullit said: 'Luca has trained hard and if his attitude is good in these situations he is still setting a good example to the younger players.' Paramount for Gullit was to select the team that he believed would win – irrespective of reputations. 'Everyone had their opinion of how I would do and where I might go but the job is here and is one I feel I can complete successfully. For now, it is time still to be patient – slowly, slowly. Chelsea is not where I want it to be yet but that takes time. The fans have less patience than I have because the coach needs patience.

'You have to put away your personal relationship with the players and that has been the most difficult part of management for me. My decisions are done for the benefit of Chelsea, not for me. I knew there would be conflict. I don't hurt players on purpose. What would be the point of that? My solution has to be what I believe suits the players, so they can play at their best. That is the point.

'The hardest decision this season was to leave out Dennis Wise. It was the first one, the big one for me and for Dennis. I know him well, I have gone out with him, we've played golf together. That made it difficult but he wasn't playing well. I needed some power in the middle.'

Of all the players at the club, Gullit noticed most change in Wise. Hoddle gave Wise the captaincy and would not be swayed over a controversial incident involving a London taxi driver that landed the player in court and almost ended in a prison sentence. Gullit said: 'Dennis is not the same Dennis any more. He has improved incredibly as a player on the pitch but he doesn't swear all the time off the pitch as well. He's much quieter. I don't think it's me. He changed himself. There is improvement in others, too. Eddie Newton is much better than he was, Steve Clarke has come on so much, Frank Sinclair is so much more disciplined. They have good examples in the likes of Leboeuf, Vialli, Di Matteo and now Gianfranco Zola.'

Gullit believed the team's relationship with the supporters was reciprocal. 'I am proud of the crowd. They have been patient for a long time. They come along to other stadiums and I know what their support means to all of us. I want Stamford Bridge to be hell for other sides. They must be thinking: "It's trouble we're going to have there." I am also proud that the fans have given me something back. They realise how I am thinking, they realise we can't always get the ball into the box. Sometimes we need to draw other sides out to achieve the space we need to work in. They see what I'm trying to do. I have experienced many bad situations in my time and from bad times you learn more, I think. I am happy but I'm not satisfied. I have the right opportunity at Chelsea. I do my job and I do it well.'

The new mood in the camp was highlighted by Clarke, anxious to get back after a two-match ban. 'I won't be complaining to the manager if he leaves me out. I know what Ruud is trying to achieve. If someone comes in for you and plays well they have a right to stay in. We are getting close to having a great squad of twenty players of equal ability and that's what we need to be successful.' Football's rumour machine insisted there was massive internal dissent within the Gullit dressing room. Clarke knocked it all down in technicolour. 'I have been here longer than anyone else at the club and believe me I have seen poor team spirit at the club before. That doesn't apply now. In fact, the spirit is one of the best I have known in my time here. Every now and then someone will say how unhappy they are at not being in the team. That happens everywhere. Gianluca Vialli was reported as saying how unhappy he was recently. He got plenty of good-natured stick. He accepted it and in many ways it helped the situation. All season we have only lost six games. You don't get a record like that if there is no team spirit.'

Clarke knew this was a huge test for Gullit's emerging team. 'Everyone keeps saying that because we beat Liverpool in the league here, we have the upper hand for the Cup game. But you can't compare the two games, they are completely different. We got to the final in 1994 and we have to believe we can do it again. We also got to the semifinals last season and it's been a good competition for us. Liverpool are top of the table, and therefore currently the best team in the land. But we are confident we can beat them if we play well.'

Gullit's programme notes gave little clue to a decision he kept from the players until an hour and a half from kick off. 'There is a good spirit in our Chelsea. It takes time for everybody to be aware of what we are doing. Now I see players sticking together as one all through the camp. They understand the squad thing. If one is not playing and the team wins, then he knows we all win. Someone is always going to be disappointed at not playing. That is good. As long as he is aware that when the team wins we all win. So I want to say this: Vialli is doing very well. He is showing good spirit in his training. The other players are supporting him. His attitude is very good in a difficult time. He is ready, always tuned in, he's been a great example to our youngsters.' As for Liverpool, he was confident it was 'the easiest kind of game for me'. He went on: 'I don't have to get the players tuned in. They already are.'

SATURDAY, JANUARY 25

Spencer was a huge scoring success with QPR; no regrets quitting Chelsea. 'I am not on an ego trip but I know I had a very good season last term. In fact Gullit didn't do any better than me on the park. Everything was fine between us when he was a player. But when he became manager it became very obvious that British players were just not good enough for him. All that interested him were foreigners. And to his credit the ones he has brought in are world-class. But at the end of the day I was bought by Chelsea for £400,000. No one expected much of me yet I became a Scottish international worth £2m. I must have done something right. Gullit knew I was good enough but he didn't want to know. My move to Queens Park Rangers has been brilliant. I know I'll keep my place if I do the business, which was not the case at Chelsea. I've scored eight goals in nine games.'

Newton's view of life under Gullit contrasted sharply. No prima donna attitude, just gratitude after fearing a broken leg would end his career. 'Chelsea have been so good to me – it was really something to offer me a new deal when they did. I've also had great support from good people around me, like my family. You wonder how your career will turn out, so it's great to be a part of all this. Sometimes you can't believe all the famous players who are here. And who wouldn't learn in company like this? Also, it's turned out just as Ruud said it would at the start of the season. He called us together and said he didn't care who were the big stars and who weren't. Everyone would get their chance on merit. That's how it's turned out for me and I feel good again. It also meant that Chelsea are no longer walkovers. The club hasn't achieved its promise in the past. But that's changed and a lot of it must be due to the intense competition for places. If you don't perform, you'll be out, it's as simple as that. But, if you do, well, it's great to be able to impress one of the all-time top players like Ruud Gullit.'

Woking caused the Cup shock of the round, with extrovert keeper Laurence Batty interviewed on *Match of the Day*. Holding up his ticket for the Matthew Harding Stand, he told the nation his thoughts were with Chelsea even more than Woking after their draw at Coventry.

SUNDAY, JANUARY 26
Chelsea 4 Liverpool 2

Vialli unleashed all his pent-up frustrations to lead Chelsea to one of their greatest FA Cup adventures ever. Verbally assaulted by the mocking Anfield coaching staff when Chelsea were humbled 5–1, Vialli had to be restrained at the end of one of his most humiliating experiences in his illustrious career. When Gullit ended Vialli's exile on the bench, Liverpool suffered one of the greatest cup shocks of their existence.

Stamford Bridge had seen nothing like it since Liverpool, as European champions in 1978, were stunned by a Clive Walker double that produced a 4–2 scoreline. Not even when Chelsea won the Cup twenty-six years ago did they come back from such a position. No one would have put a penny on their chances when they trailed hopelessly 2–0 at half-time and might have gone into the dressing room three or four goals behind.

Gullit was relentlessly taunted by Liverpool fans after his side trailed by two just twenty-two minutes into the game. Finally, Gullit turned round and gave them the answer. 0–2. He provoked fits of laughter during his after match press conference when he explained: 'They asked me what the score was and I told them; it was 2–0.' There can't be another manager in the game who would have responded to the jibes of the opposition fans in that way.

Gullit gambled after the interval by sending on an all-out attacking formation – Vialli, Hughes and Zola operating in a single forward line. It produced a scintillating four-goal burst. Every one of the 27,950 crowd were on the edge of their seats and the millions watching this BBC extravaganza witnessed an epic tie.

In front of Hoddle, Chelsea's Italian contingent mastered the Premiership leaders, with Zola issuing another grim warning before the England clash.

It was the most unlikely outcome as Liverpool, on cruise control, were in total command from Fowler's tenth-minute opener. The Chelsea defence was a shambles as Liverpool engineered a prolonged movement from one flank to the other; McManaman's cross caused panic as it flashed past everyone to be rescued by McAteer whose cross was completely missed by Sinclair. It finally fell to Bjornebye whose low cross was turned in, inevitably, by Fowler. When Zola was hassled in possession by Mark Wright, his hurried pass was miscontrolled by Newton. Collymore romped forward gleefully, sliding his shot under the body of Hitchcock.

Vialli squandered his first chance in the thirty-first minute, latching onto Zola's attempt to control a long ball, body-swerving to give himself space, but lofted his shot over the bar ... stomping on a *Mirror* sausage – the latest inflatable craze – in disgust with himself! A minute later McManaman weaved some more magic, Bjornebye crossed, but Fowler headed over. Then McManaman eluded Leboeuf to break clear, but his weak shot was straight at Hitchcock. In truth that should have finished off Chelsea.

Gullit sent on Hughes for Minto in an all-out attacking formation for the second half. After just six minutes, Clarke's pass to Hughes, a sharp turn and shot into the corner, Chelsea were back in it and everyone wondered why Hughes hadn't been on from the start.

Hughes was surprisingly benched at the expense of Vialli's return. But Hughes changed the course of events. Gullit admitted: 'When we got that goal Liverpool were afraid. I could hear them talking about it from where I sat on my bench. When a team feels like that you just have to take advantage of it.'

As crucial as the Hughes substitution was Gullit's tactical switch after Barnes became the focal point of Liverpool's domination of the first half, always available for the ball, playing it simply but effectively. After the interval Gullit delegated Di Matteo to force Barnes to operate deeper. Gullit said: 'The first-half goals were a present, we gave them away. We had no concentration and they played it simple. But in the second half we adapted our tactics and the players did exactly what I asked them to do. They were great. I was surprised also, but they really did the business. We put Di Matteo on Barnes and that was the most significant thing. But this was an easy game, in a way, because you are motivated, it's a great club and you have the crowd behind you.' Newton gave the dressing room insight into the tactical switch. 'Ruud said to give it all we had in the first fifteen minutes of the second half to try to get a goal as soon as possible. Fortunately we did.'

Gullit felt real anger for the first time. 'I was angry at half-time, because we had given away two goals that made it easy for Liverpool and in the second half I knew we had to do something drastic. All the time this team are doing things that show me they are improving. Each week they please me even more. But we can't keep making the mistakes that in big matches can be so vital.'

Of his decision to leave out Hughes, Gullit said: 'It came out right. It was difficult not to have Vialli playing and I don't think the decision affected us in the first half because we gave away two sloppy goals. Mark made an important contribution because when he scored I could sense that there was fear in the Liverpool side and we responded to that.'

Another turning point was a decision by the referee to award Chelsea a throw in the fifty-eighth minute when it was a Liverpool ball. Zola gained possession after a Hughes challenge and whipped a shot into the top corner. Breathtaking! Zola's seventh goal was his most valuable as the equaliser left Liverpool vulnerable. And so it proved when within six minutes Vialli latched onto a Petrescu pass and coolly beat James – this sixty-fourth-minute goal put Chelsea ahead for the first time.

In the first half it was a question of counting the Liverpool goals, now it was Chelsea's turn to take command. James darted out to rob Hughes on the edge of the box … a poor clearance by the keeper and Hughes almost caught him out … a Di Matteo shot clawed round the post … and a Di Matteo volley saved by James. It was all Chelsea.

When Vialli confidently tried a curler caught by James, Chelsea played the best football under Gullit's reign: imaginative, electrifying in its pace and accuracy, and rarely had Liverpool looked so shaky and lost.

Finally Evans threw on Berger for Bjornebye but it made little difference. Vialli was held back in the seventy-fifth minute, Zola zipped in one of his specialist free kicks and Vialli read his Italian compatriot's pass, meeting it at the near post with a fierce header.

'Vialli did touch this one?' An Italian journalist recalled how Vialli had claimed Zola's free kick, Zola giving him the benefit of a huge doubt. 'Yes, I think so,' said Zola with a huge grin.

No one could recall the last time Liverpool had conceded four, particularly all in the second half. The stats experts put it at thirty-three years. A few Chelsea fans stripped off their shirts and, bare-chested, celebrated in the Matthew Harding Stand.

When Hitchcock clawed away a diving header by Fowler, from McAteer's cross, in the ninetieth minute, the effort was irrelevant. Chelsea were in the bag for the fifth-round draw and Gullit was acclaimed for plotting the downfall of Liverpool in such spectacular fashion.

The capital was alive with the exploits of the three Chelsea Italian stars. Hughes and Zola strolled into the press room, spotting just one chair. I suggested that Zola should sit on Hughes's lap. Hughes smiled and Zola fetched a second chair. Hughes made no secret of his shock at being left out at the start, but illustrated the new bonding of the team by accepting Gullit's decision without question. With typical understatement he said: 'Yes, I was a little disappointed to be left out, and also a bit surprised. I wasn't expecting it. But I'm not making anything about it as Ruud explained it, and I accepted that. Ruudi felt we could cause them a different problem and I am not making any bones about it, he just wanted to try something else.' Hughes had made his point on the pitch, and discussed the dressing room switch at half-time. 'He changed the way we lined up, pushing three up, and it took them a while to sort out our new formation. By then it was too late. It was a great performance in the second half. But I wouldn't want to be two down every week,' Hughes joked: 'When we get two halves the same we'll be really dangerous.'

Not surprisingly 'name on the cup' talk started. Hughes was having none of it. Looking at the massed ranks of media, he smiled: 'We shall have to be careful what we say about things, or you lot will install us as favourites. That will be the kiss of death.'

Zola's English tuition had been so successful, he was confident to be interviewed without his interpreter. 'In the first half the way Luca and I played was a bit limited, a bit stagnant, but when Mark came on the three of us played with intelligence and gave Liverpool some surprises they couldn't deal with.'

Asked about the next league match with Spurs, he said: 'It's another kind of game, we will need more organisation, more application, more concentration.' (He meant more of the same, rather than an extra amount.) Hughes admired his command of the language. 'Very impressive,' he said to Zola. 'I'll have to change my cassette!'

joked the little guy. The humour level in the dressing room was clearly upwardly mobile.

Zola was still struggling with the colloquialisms, though. 'We must stay with our feet on the floor, that is very important, this has been a great performance.' He praised Luca: 'Today the game was not easy for him because he had a lot of pressure on him, so it is always difficult to play well. He had a lot of reasons to play well. When a player is like him, big personality, they can do big things like today.'

'What, rise to the occasion?' said the reporter from the *Express*, with cigarette dangling limp on his ageing lips. 'What does that mean?' said Zola. Hughes promised to translate later. To emphasise the team spirit, Zola added: 'Today Vialli scored two goals because the team helped him.'

Gullit had so many mikes under his nose, he could hardly move. 'In the whole of my career I cannot remember a match quite like that. At half-time I told my team that if they could score in the first fifteen minutes they could win the tie. But I never believed it would be like that. Of course, I have immense pride in them. You can say that Vialli was surprised to be in the side. And he rewarded me with two magnificent goals. I don't think he had anything to prove. I made changes for tactical reasons and he played his part so well. After all he has been the captain of a team that has won the cup with the big ears ... [European Cup].'

Gullit and Rix embraced at the final whistle, then there was a hug between the rival managers full of mutual respect. Not since Roy Evans's second game in charge, at Southampton back in 1994, had one of his sides leaked four goals and it hurt the Liverpool boss. 'I just told them to go out and do the same again. But the difference in the second half was unbelievable. They started to drop off nearly thirty yards, and when you give space to players of this quality they will punish you. Hughes made the difference, suddenly we were defending on the edge of our box. You try to get people to push up but it's not that simple, not when you've just lost a couple of goals and they are pouring through onto you. We simply didn't have the courage of our convictions. I'm disappointed not just that we lost when two goals ahead, but with the manner of the way we threw it away. Could I believe what I saw? I had to. It's hard to take because we could have gone in at half-time three or four goals ahead. Steve McManaman, in particular, had a good chance to sew it all up. But Chelsea forced us back and made us defend at the edge of the box. What did I say at full-time? There's not enough tape in your recorder to tell you. But simply we didn't have the courage of our convictions. Chelsea had quality all over the field, and I was so disappointed we gave them the space in which to show it off.'

The players sat in the dressing room watching TV replays of the goals. When Zola's appeared, he leapt onto the bench and took a small bow. Spontaneous applause. The players had taken Zola to their hearts.

The draw live on BBC: Arsenal or Leeds v Portsmouth; Birmingham v Peterborough or Wrexham; Bolton or Chesterfield v Notts Forest; Bradford v Sheff Wed; Derby v Blackburn or Coventry or Woking; Leicester v Chelsea; Man City or Watford v Middlesbrough; Man Utd or Wimbledon v QPR.

Mixed feelings for Gullit about picking Leicester. His players were able to motivate themselves better against a side with a reputation than one just prepared to scrap for a result.

Chelsea were the new 4–1 favourites, 5–1 Arsenal and Manchester United, 8–1

Sheffield Wednesday, 11–1 Leeds, 14–1 Forest and Middlesbrough, 16–1 Blackburn, Derby and Wimbledon, 25–1 Bolton and Leicester, 28–1 Bradford and Portsmouth, 200–1 Watford, 250–1 Chesterfield and Wrexham, 300–1 Peterborough, 2000–1 Woking.

Chelsea fan Tony Banks MP was already counting his winnings after the unlikely margin of victory over Liverpool. Bates said: 'He put a fiver on a 4–2 win at 66–1. I told him "With your luck your lot will win the next election."' Bates could hardly contain his delight. 'A team of stars without the star syndrome; players left out accept it. We've had a lot of hard times, all this is long overdue.' A jubilant Banks said: 'You know I had a dream; a real dream. I thought Duberry had scored two, but it was Vialli. Look, it's true, I even wrote about it in the match day programme. I bunged a chunk of the cash to John Dempsey for his charity, spent a bundle on champagne, and still came home with £50. I don't usually bet, but I cleaned up.'

Banks wanted to meet the great man. 'The closest I've been to him was at Matthew Harding's funeral and that was hardly an appropriate place to start a conversation.' There was no such hysteria from a happy but calm Gullit. Just a shrug when asked whether he had a feeling this would be Chelsea's year. 'This is just one game. The next one might be totally different. You just have to enjoy the moment. I'm happy with the way we're playing at the moment. We show a little improvement with each game and that is encouraging.'

Zola made a valid point: 'We're a strange team. We can make some banal mistakes and both the goals on Sunday were due to those sort of errors. In the second half the whole team played very well and everybody playing like that made it possible for us to come back. But it would be hard to have to repeat that every match. We have to play more like this, with intelligence. Otherwise we can win against Liverpool, and lose against Nottingham Forest; we can surprise!'

Wise stood in the corridor adjacent to the players' room, wearing a smart suit and broad grin, discussing the virtues of Zola. On the question of the impending clash with Italy, he said: 'I expect Glenn will consider man-marking him because Zola is the sort of player you can't afford to give any space. Even then, he has the ability to hurt the opposition. Perhaps man-marking could help. Nottingham Forest put Des Lyttle on him and he did okay, but I'd still blame the team not playing well for us getting beat that day. It wasn't down to Franco.

'There's only one word to describe him: class. Frightening sometimes. I saw his goal against Northern Ireland last week and when he scores like that it scares you. When he's left in a one-on-one situation he's deadly. He just says: "See you later." As he showed against Liverpool, he is as lethal with his right foot as with his left. He's a natural. He scored against Liverpool with his left when I think he's right-footed. Actually, I don't know what foot he is because he hits the ball so well with both.' Wise added: 'I can say with confidence he's the best player I've worked with and when you consider the only player who ever kept him out of a team was Maradona, it says a lot. I can't think of another foreign player who has made such an impact on our game.'

Hughes played a major part in the evolution of Manchester United, now he felt Chelsea were capable of following a similar path. 'There is definitely a sense that this club can go places. When a club haven't won anything for a long while it's breaking that cycle that is the difficult part. At Manchester United there had been a dreadfully long wait to win the league but, once we did it, it made it easier. What's happened here in the last couple of years is unbelievable and this season we've improved tenfold. You want to see the club go places and I think we're at the beginning of something special. I want to be part of it. Once we overcome that feeling of not quite doing it, once we win that first trophy, I'm sure more will follow. There are similarities with United in that respect. When I rejoined them from abroad they were at a similar stage to Chelsea now. Then Alex Ferguson went out and bought some quality players, as we have done here, but it took two or three seasons before the team gelled. It's incredible what's happening here. Who knows how far we can go?'

Hughes sensed the development of something too big to indulge in personal grievances. 'The fact is that we've got three strikers in myself, Luca and Gianfranco, and that's proof of the progress we've made here. The ambition there is in this club is very important, and that's got to come ahead of my personal ambition. You want to see the club go places and I think we're really at the beginning of something special. I want to be part of it. Everybody wants to play but if I can't play week in, week out I'm quite prepared to bide my time, just like Luca and Dennis Wise had to.'

MONDAY, JANUARY 27

Zola's mother Giovanna revealed that only days before, he heard his father, Ignazio, had been partially blinded by a burst blood vessel in one eye. 'Gianfranco has been phoning every day to find out how his father is,' said Giovanna from the remote Sardinian village of Oliena. 'I had to reassure him that we are okay and told him to concentrate on his job. A friend of the family called from London to tell us that my son has equalised after Liverpool had been two goals ahead. I screamed with joy. Then he called again to say Gianfranco had been involved when Gianluca Vialli had put Chelsea ahead. Minutes later, the phone rang yet again and it was this same Sardinian man, named Mario, to tell us that our son's free kick had set up Vialli for the fourth. The last call came on the final whistle and by then I was in tears. I am so pleased for Chelsea and the fans in England. I'm delighted for Ruud Gullit too. When Gullit was at AC Milan I was one of his biggest fans.'

David Mellor launched a stinging attack on English managers, telling them to develop a 'thick skin, like politicians have to'. Mellor believed some English managers were falling short of the standards set by foreign coaches coming to the Premiership, such as Gullit and Wenger. 'The thing I like about Ruud Gullit is that he will tell Vialli what he can do with himself. Managers have got to get off their knees to these foreign stars. You only get the best out of these foreign stars by kicking their arses and that's what Ruud has done. Some English managers are not as well prepared as continental managers. Arsène Wenger has done the business at Arsenal, he's loosened them up. I just think some players have moved from playing to managing in Britain without thinking.

TUESDAY, JANUARY 28

Vialli declared a complete truce with Gullit. 'I'm so euphoric that it will be okay if he leaves me on the bench for the rest of my days. Two goals against Liverpool have wiped out any ill feelings and I've found total happiness.' The euphoria had gone to his bald head! He gleefully relived the high drama that he believed had changed his fortunes in English football. 'In sixteen years of my football career I've never experienced such an overwhelming adventure like the win over Liverpool. Just imagine, I arrive at the ground thinking I would have to sit on the bench as for so many games before. Then, just one hour before the kick off, Gullit told me I would start in place of Hughes. But it didn't go well, Liverpool were at full revs. We are not able to settle and concede two silly goals, but in the second half Hughes comes into the attack and Ruud asks Di Matteo to control Barnes – and it works. After Hughes's goal we realise that Liverpool have shaky knees. Zola equalised with a masterpiece of his own, then Petrescu puts the ball onto my right foot for me to make the score 3–2. Then Zola places his free kick onto my forehead and it's 4–2. We were already with one foot in the grave but it turns out to be a triumph. We've taken a lap of honour at the end and I could have stayed on for ever. I'll remember this match for a long, long time.'

Vialli felt the foreign stars were changing perceptions. 'In England they're not so fond of foreigners as we are in Italy. That's why over here the foreigners are always under scrutiny. The English are a proud race but we Italians should be proud too, particularly after wins like this over Liverpool.'

To balance that view Johnny Giles made a point in his *Express* column: 'Gullit is learning fast as a manager and the lesson of how valuable a player of Hughes's stature is to Chelsea is not one he will have missed ... Gullit has already left Vialli out and is certainly not afraid of hard selection decisions, however difficult they are, or what problems they cause. The Dutchman can handle that fuss better than some native managers. He understands the complaining culture prevalent on the continent. If he needs to, Gullit will put Vialli down, no trouble. He will pay no heed to critical comments from Italy. Unlike Bryan Robson at Middlesbrough, he has enough players not to worry about individual discontent.'

WEDNESDAY, JANUARY 29
As Hoddle prepared to announce his England squad, Zola picked out McManaman as the danger. Brilliant on the ball, a wonderful dribbler, virtually unstoppable, but what a woeful finish as demonstrated in the FA Cup watched by Hoddle. Zola said: 'England have a lot of talented players, Shearer, Ferdinand, McManaman, Ince, that's why it will be a difficult match. England are full of international-class players. McManaman is excellent, he can turn a game round when it's "stalled".' Zola's English was rapidly improving, but he meant 'deadlocked'. The Italians feared the Liverpool star far more than Gazza. Zola said: 'We shall have to watch McManaman at Wembley.' With his newly-acquired English sense of humour he added: 'From what I read in the press they think they will have to watch me!'

Wise and his unlikely pal Vialli had tickets for the big game. Wise: 'I'll be slapping him across his bald head if England score. But I'll be getting the slap if it's Italy.'

David Platt was glad for England that two of his former team-mates at Sampdoria – Mancini and Vialli – did not make Maldini's squad. 'To be perfectly frank, as an Englishman, I'm glad Roberto and Luca will not be in the team. I know how good they are and it's better not to have them against us. England have to win at all costs because second place in the group is no guarantee of qualifying for the finals in France in 1998. But, as a friend of both Vialli and Mancini, I'm sorry for them because I know how much they'd like to play for the national side again.'

THURSDAY, JANUARY 30
Chelsea soared in value by a remarkable £52m in just days since knocking Liverpool out. It was certainly a wise investment for Wise! Before the weekend Chelsea Village shares were 118.5p, capitalising the company at £178m. The shares rose by another

17p in one day, the company's value soaring to £230m. The big winners were Bates and the Harding Estate.

At the announcement of the England squad, Hoddle was asked if he thought the Italy tie would be like the Chelsea v Liverpool cup clash. 'I hope we're Chelsea as far as the result goes!' He said: 'It will probably be the complete opposite. We'll have to be very patient, I know they will be. But it's one that I think the whole country will be up for.'

Gullit travelled to Dublin for the launch of a Telecom Eireann alliance with Dutch and Swedish firms. Fans mobbed *Gladiators* host Ulrika Jonsson and her star companions Gullit and *Star Trek* actor Colm Meaney, bringing traffic to a virtual standstill. As female admirers tried to get his autograph, Gullit admitted he found his heart-throb status embarrassing. 'What you have inside is what's really important,' he said.

FRIDAY, JANUARY 31

Gullit suggested his willingness to incorporate his players' opinions into his final assessment on tactics had put Hughes and Vialli's places in the hands of dressing-room democracy. 'This week I've been trying various exercises in training to try and get the best out of them and see how they adapt. Now they realise they are more comfortable in a particular system and at Tottenham we will see the method Chelsea players are most comfortable with by their own admission. Who says I will continue with three up front just because it worked last week against Liverpool? It would be unrealistic to think we could play like that every match. That's why I gave the players some responsibility and input this week, because I like players who think about the game.'

The best way to run any team, Gullit surmised, was the one that made the players comfortable and gave them responsibility. 'On the training field the squad played in sequences of fifteen minutes. After the first they go into a huddle and the players say what is wrong. Then you play the second fifteen minutes. Then you see again. If still they are not happy, you try again. And they say, "This is how we have to play." I like to give them responsibility. If you have responsibilities you are aware more of what you can do. Like in a factory. If you give people no responsibilities they may steal from you in the end. You say "OK you can have responsibility" and they are more aware of what is happening.'

This was not, Gullit insisted, the way of Rinus Michels or of Sacchi, his mentors with Holland and Milan, nor was it Gullit's way. 'It is logic.' Gullit favours players who think about the game. 'I don't like players who come here for training, take a shower and go home. I like players who discuss what has happened. It's your job.'

Gullit's only injury casualty was Burley's failure to recover from damaged ankle ligaments. Spurs had not beaten Chelsea in sixteen games going back to 1990, and Francis had ten senior players out injured or banned.

With fifty requests for interviews with the Italians and Gullit prior to the England–Italy match, a special 'second' conference was conducted at the training ground. On one side of the giant Gullit sat the diminutive Zola with his old-fashioned features; on the other Di Matteo, a slight, elegant figure. They were introduced as 'the boss and his sons'. 'He is my grandfather,' Zola quipped.

Gullit was called on to help with translation, emphasise an answer, or encourage Zola not to commit himself about Maldini returning the Italians to their old style.

Zola said the man-marking in the Premiership had given him problems, but he would not mind if England put a man on him. It is something he was used to, he said. 'I expect man-marking every game. This is no hard news. It's my job, I have to sort it out.' Gullit, interestingly, said that Zola had told him that he actually hoped they would man-mark him. 'They can mark me,' Zola said later, 'but there are other players on the pitch.' When asked who had marked him best in the Premiership, Zola grinned and would not be drawn. 'I don't remember the team,' he said, prompted by Di Matteo and Gullit. Wise said that he found man-marking Zola in training a tough task. He had 'happy feet', Wise said. 'He jinks one way and then the other and then it's "see you", isn't it?'

Few were in more authoritative a position to compare English and Italian football than Gullit, a star as a player with Milan and Sampdoria, now transforming the English game as an open-minded manager. 'The Italians are very, very serious in their approach to football. For the Dutch or English or Germans sometimes it is too much. But in that approach there's a lot of professionalism, also. They know there's a lot of pressure on them because the whole of Italy is a coach, every journalist, every man on the street is a coach. The team is for everyone, everyone has an opinion about the game, they tell you how you have to play. The English are more relaxed in their approach. There is also a lot of pressure from the press, of course, because they want them to win. But it's a different approach, there is perhaps more to life than just football.'

Brought to the Bridge by Hoddle, he was wary of being drawn into the increasingly hyped build-up to Wembley. 'I don't want to give him any advice, I don't want to get involved in this!' he said, throwing up his hands. He suggested that Italian experience in the Premiership may give them an edge, even though England did much better than them in Euro '96. 'Everyone was surprised at Italy's exit, but they were unlucky in the last game and they were in the hardest group. And they lost to the team that won in the final, just as England did. One advantage England have, maybe, is that they play already together in a certain system while Italy have only had one opportunity to try out the new way Maldini wants to play. But the Italians have a lot of experience, especially on this platform, so that gives them an enormous advantage. I think it will be a very tight game, a very tactical game and you must be concentrated for ninety minutes. I hope for the game that someone will score a goal very early because then it will be a very good game. But the longer it takes to score a goal the more difficult it will be.'

FEBRUARY

Vialli moves into a home at last, Zola scores for Italy against England in World Cup

Spurs 1 Chelsea 2

Vialli packed his golf clubs that evening for the team's Cyprus sunshine break, and not for a return to Italy. Vialli was determined that life at Chelsea wasn't a drag! He was spotted puffing away after sitting apart from Gullit and the rest of the substitutes during the game. Dropped despite his brilliant match-winning display against Liverpool, he never kicked the ball in the latest win that lifted Chelsea into fifth place in the Premiership.

Could anyone really argue with Gullit while his team selections kept paying off? Well, yes!

'Good evening, everybody,' said a smiling Ruud as he entered the tiny, smoke-filled Spurs press room after a hard-fought win. Immediately he sat down *Gazzetta dello Sport* correspondent Galavotti began his inquisition of Gullit about Vialli's absence.

'Why was Vialli standing all the time and not sitting with everybody else on the bench?'

Gullit: 'He couldn't see nothing...'

Galavotti was not put off the scent, but Gullit leaned forward and beamed: 'You are searching for a ... needle in a haystack!'

Persistence is Galavotti's strong suit. Gullit was a little annoyed: 'We showed today why we have to play like this. You can't argue all the time "he's not playing". If I do pick Vialli I get every journalist in Wales asking why Mark Hughes is not in the side. I have three strikers, only two can play. I want to talk about the game. Is it not worth talking about this game?'

Gullit launched into a long and complex explanation about the reasons behind the players' input into tactics, but at every opportunity he was quizzed about Vialli. Finally, he said: 'It's time to talk about other things. This is not relevant.' When the subject switched a little later back to Vialli, there was an abrupt halt to the subject. 'I do not want to talk about it.'

Vialli sat alone at the entrance of the tunnel for part of the game looking inconsolable. He then showed his contempt by smoking a cigarette as the manager held a TV interview. Former Spurs striker Garth Crooks said: 'Vialli looked like a bear with a sore head – he is not a happy man.' You wondered whether, if Wise had scored, he would have another message on his shirt to cheer Luca up! There was some debate over Vialli, smoking a cigarette as he contemplated life as one of the world's highest-paid substitutes. But as for a rift with Ruud, Vialli said: 'Better times will come for me and I'm looking forward to my trip to Cyprus.'

Gullit insisted Vialli would still have a key role to play in Chelsea's quest for success, but would it last beyond one season? A leading Italian journalist who had followed Vialli's career was adamant: 'He has never been treated like this before and his decision to sit in the tunnel was a definite protest – whatever Gullit may think.'

Inside the Bridge, they played down Vialli's predicament. Williams said: 'Yes, Luca had a fag, but it was after the game while he was waiting with Zola, who caught his taxi at 5.30 from the ground to catch the 8.00pm flight back to Italy. Roberto caught the 8.00am flight back to prepare for the England match while Luca was coming with us to Cyprus. In fact, the only reason I've got my mobile phone still switched on is I'm expecting a call from Luca, he wants to borrow my golf bag to put his clubs in and I'll be playing golf with him as soon as we get to Cyprus. Luca likes a fag and he's entitled to have one if he wants it. It's nonsense that he stormed out of our dressing room before the kick off once he heard the team. The team was announced at our hotel during a team meeting before we even got to the ground!'

Gullit had come to terms with the harsh realities of management; he was ruthless in selecting his team. 'At the beginning it was very difficult for me, I must admit it. Now I know I must make decisions for the benefit of Chelsea, I don't do it for myself. Even though you know the player well, there are times when you have to take a decision that is difficult for you as a person. But if you can't take the decision then you are not a good coach. With Vialli I can swap it around, I have so many options. I hope to never swap during the games, because that means we are not doing well, like the matches against Liverpool and Leicester. We're now off for three days of golf, except the Italians who are going back home, and I'm looking forward to a good holiday – I need it.'

The other major talking-point was whether England should man-mark Zola. Gullit did not recommend it to Hoddle, after Francis was the latest Premiership boss to attempt a 'stop Zola' strategy with Dean Austin assigned the thankless task. Zola was contained to a degree, but still wriggled free to play havoc with Tottenham's defence. Gullit said: 'Everybody saw what happened, saw what he did today and he was still marked. One moment he produced a very good first touch, and it was nearly possible that Mark Hughes could score a goal, and also in the first half there was a cross when Mark Hughes was not alert enough. He did all these things when he was man-marked. It's not important to me for a player to be all the time busy, I want him to be sharp for only two moments in the game. For example, Vialli, you might have thought, was not so good against Liverpool, but then in the second half he produced two moments and two goals. It's not important for a player to be working, crossing, busy all the time and it may be he's not in the game for twenty minutes at a time, then he strikes, that's what's important. If you man-mark Zola then you have one player less. We played against ten men today and the only thing they could do was boot it. He played very well, all the time available, and could have scored. He was not disturbed, he is used to playing that way in Italy, and he doesn't mind.'

Gullit's description of Tottenham's tactics will not please their fans, but it gave a clue to why there was so much emphasis on Spurs' tactical deployment of Austin. Without so many star players, Spurs often resorted to the long ball, particularly in the latter stages. Zola, despite Austin, again emphasised why he will be such a threat to England. Austin said: 'He is a great player, one of the best in Europe. It takes a great deal of concentration to mark him and I felt in the first half I made him play with his back to goal. I went everywhere with him but I thought it hurt us more than Chelsea. Glenn Hoddle will have his own ideas, but if England play three at the back I think you can get away without man-marking him, leaving him to the nearest player. What they don't want is one of the three sticking to Zola. There were times when I had to go into tackles against other players and I was left desperately looking for him. It was very hard because I wasn't in the game. Chaperoning such a player you only have to leave him for a split-second and you're dead. Suddenly the ball is in the net. Either he has put it there or laid it on for someone else. His movement off the ball is superb and his runs are devastating.' Austin left Zola at one point to tackle Hughes and no other Spurs defender reacted. If Zola hadn't slightly overrun the ball, he would have scored.

While Zola was the focal point of attention, Di Matteo produced the scintillating finish with a blockbuster thirty-yard shot into the top corner seven minutes after the break. Di Matteo capped a brilliant performance with a wonder strike with his supposedly weaker left foot. 'I knew it was a goal as soon as I hit it. But there was an element of luck.'

Gullit described Di Matteo's strike as 'marvellous'. He said: 'Often in midfield you can't be in the spotlight, you're often in the shadows, but Di Matteo was outstanding in the second half against Liverpool and now he's had two games where he's really worked well. Then again Frank Sinclair did a hell of a job and it doesn't matter to me whether they're English, Dutch or Italian provided they're doing their jobs.'

Di Matteo became more influential, an essential part of a vibrant Chelsea team. He had back problems in his first couple of months, his girlfriend studying law in Rome, concerns about his blind sister, and a cold new flat; it took him longer than the rest of the foreign imports to settle down. Now, he looked more in control and thoroughly enjoyed his goal, repeating the Roman pose, one of the most original goal celebrations in the Premiership. Chelsea took the lead after just fifty seconds when Nethercott fouled Hughes and Zola lined up for what the Spurs defence expected to be one of his specialist free kicks. Instead, he floated the ball across to the far post where Newton headed down; Hughes's shot was saved by Walker's feet and it bounced in off Campbell. But Di Matteo's strike was sheer quality.

Spurs mounted a late revival inspired by a cracking twenty-five-yarder from Sinton, pushed around the post by Hitchcock. Less than a minute later substitute Anderton curled a cross for Howells to thunder his header past the keeper.

Gullit took off Zola two minutes from the end to send on an extra central defender, Johnsen. Three minutes over time, Minto hooked off the line as Francis said: 'On another day we might have snatched something. All our plans went out of the window and it was a big disappointment to concede a goal after less than a minute. Zola has had quite a lot of success with those free kicks, so Stuart was caught when he disguised it well to the back post.' Francis stressed that half his team was missing. 'You need a strong squad, and Ruud has created that. We've got a strong squad, but eighty per cent of it wasn't out there and we needed them to match the likes of Liverpool and Chelsea.'

Spurs, once the game's glamour club, were so short of stars they found it ironic that Chelsea could afford to have Vialli on the bench. Chelsea fans mocked 'Tottenham's had a shot' when Iversen finally managed one after sixty-six minutes. Gullit asked Rix what the Chelsea fans were chanting and found it very amusing when he was given the explanation. Gullit said: 'Overall this was one of the best games we have played, despite the last ten minutes, and so I have no complaints.

They didn't have a shot on goal and that was a compliment to us. I was particularly pleased with the way we played, I was pleased with everyone.'

Gullit kept his team in the hunt for a place in Europe, with even an outside chance of the title. 'I play for a result, even if that means keeping the ball in the corner to waste time. In the last minutes they boot the ball into the eighteen-yard box where anything can happen, and we have to be alert. I put one extra defender in and hope everything goes well. It happens so many times . . . a last-minute goal. Then you ask "How is it possible?" But also that is the good thing about football.

'The fans will be happy, I think what they want is a victory. I, as the coach, have a responsibility to the team; it's about the team, not individuals. I do what is best for Chelsea and best for the team and you see how they played. Chelsea played some outstanding football.' In fact Ruud felt more at ease with the outcome than perhaps any other game. 'In the end they scored a goal from a corner kick which had been cleared, but as a whole our game was at its best. I can't help it! I didn't even have the feeling of the history of Chelsea doing well against Tottenham after just two years here. Everybody is feeling confident in the team. We have a good solid foundation, but we have to keep working hard to maintain it or it will all be lost.'

Next stop Manchester United in the league after Leicester in the Cup. 'That will be a nice game,' smiled Gullit, 'everybody is looking forward to that. But now away we go to Cyprus!'

TUESDAY, FEBRUARY 4

Postcard from Cyprus. The management team of Gullit, Rix, Williams, Niedzwiecki and Byrne off to the 'pub' to watch Sky TV's FA Cup replay . . . holders Manchester United crash to Wimbledon at Selhurst Park on the same night Arsenal lose at home to Graham's Leeds, in shock replay results. For the first time for twenty-two years none of football's Big Five will contest the FA Cup Final. You have to go all the way back to 1975 for the last time Wembley hosted two teams which did not include at least one from Arsenal, Everton, Liverpool, Manchester United and Tottenham. Back in 1975, the Twin Towers saw West Ham beat Fulham – Bobby Moore and all – 2–0 to take the trophy. And although smaller clubs have won the Cup since – West Ham again in 1980, Coventry in 1987 and Wimbledon the following year – it has always been against opponents from the Big Five. With the departure of all five from the tournament, the gate was wide open for a less fancied side to claim the honour.

WEDNESDAY, FEBRUARY 5

Marketing Week reported that shirt sponsors Coors planned to terminate their association with the club when their contract expired at the end of the season. Bates quickly put the record straight: 'Coors' three-year deal came to an end and they were not prepared to sign a new one on the terms we wanted. Scottish and Newcastle had taken over Courage, so while at first we came under Courage in Reading, now it was a brewery in Nottingham. They no longer had the same commitment. Before they sponsored Chelsea nobody had heard of the company. Now they are the top selling lager in the south. We had a number of interested sponsors with offers 120 per cent higher than the old one.'

FRIDAY, FEBRUARY 7

Vialli moved out of the Hyde Park Hotel – he had switched from the Cadogan for five weeks – into his £1m flat in Eaton Square, behind Harrods, on an eighteenth-month lease. That didn't exactly suggest he was in a hurry to get away. Few, if any, of the domestic stars could afford to join the Kensington set. Minto observed: 'I can't afford to live anywhere near them. It would have to be a hell of a new contract for me to go and live within a four- or five-mile radius of Luca, Robbie, or Franco.'

Zola felt very much at home. Harrods and Harvey Nichols, his wife's favourite shops, were close by, with his Italian pals as neighbours. Leboeuf settled further out in a 'very nice Victorian house' in Fulham. 'I am an Englishman now. I am very happy here. London is a busy city and it is very easy to adapt your mind and your French life in a city like this because it's very cosmopolitan. It's not a very big problem living in London when you're used to living in France.'

Would Vialli, though, be around longer than the lease? Vialli rejected overtures from Real Madrid just three months after arriving at Chelsea. Because of his Sampdoria connections with Souness, he was linked with Southampton. Director of football Lawrie McMenemy refused to rule out a move for Vialli. Souness was keen to sign a new striker to secure his club's Premiership safety. McMenemy, who plays a part in player negotiations at the Dell, admitted his club's search for a goalscorer was a priority. 'There is no doubt Luca is a good friend of Graeme Souness from the time they played together in Italy. Everyone knows we are looking for a new striker. We are desperate to strengthen our team and to stay in the Premiership, but are still limited in the amount of money we have to spend.' Just before the England–Italy World Cup tie it was suggested that Souness and Vialli had met for a working breakfast on a move. Yet, Souness was in South Africa and Vialli was playing golf with some friends over for the Italy game. Hutchinson completely dismissed any move as little more than a joke. 'Gianluca is obviously frustrated that he has been watching from the bench in recent matches. But he is under contract here until June 1999, has certainly not asked for a transfer and is not for sale.' Hutchinson's only recent contact with Southampton had been a light-hearted chat between himself and McMenemy at a recent Premier League meeting. 'Tongue in cheek, he said to me, "We will take Vialli off your hands", but this was jokey banter. I made it clear to him that the player was not for sale. We are fortunate at the moment in that we have three strikers for two places, but a week is a long time in football and Vialli could get a game and stay in the side. Hopefully now we can get on with business. Southampton have had their fifteen minutes of fame so we can get back to reality. The only time Gianluca will be going to Southampton as far as I can see is as a player with us next season.'

If anything Vialli was more at home at Chelsea. Newton explained: 'There are seven dressing rooms at the training ground and the Italians were in one because of the language barrier. But Vialli has come into my room and joined up with Dennis Wise, Mark Hughes and a few others. He said he wanted to sit, talk and listen so he could pick up more of our conversation. That shows there are no hard feelings. Ruudi made it clear at the start of the season that he didn't care who you were, a top international or a youth-team player, if you weren't doing it on the park you were not going to be in the team. Everyone has had a spell on the bench. No one likes it, obviously, but you have to button your lip and get on with it. If you can't enjoy this time at Chelsea as a player, you can't enjoy anything.'

MONDAY, FEBRUARY 10

A break for England's World Cup clash. Young Neil Clement joined the England squad with Rio Ferdinand of West Ham, to make up the numbers and gain invaluable experience.

Time for reflection from Leboeuf. 'At the moment my confidence is high and I'm pleased with my performances. I'm very ambitious and I want to win everything, that is why we can go for the league and Cup. My confidence was high from the start at Chelsea because when I signed I knew they were a good team to play for and we could do something. Now we are going well and I'm sure we will continue like this. Zola is a very good footballer. We can give him the ball over and over again and let him do things with it. The same goes for Mark Hughes. Also there is a lot of competition in the squad. That is why we must believe we can win something. At the same time it is true the team is developing. For me, the collective outfit is more important than my own performances but I was very pleased to be named in a Sky Best Foreign XI over Christmas. It's a very good English championship and very difficult to play in England. You must be fully fit if you want to play here and in total I missed four games, two through suspension and two through injury. I understand refs in England now, so I shut my mouth on the pitch after I was suspended in December. Refs in France didn't like me either, so now I am quiet. When I was out Ruud played in my position and I know if I want to stay in the team I must play well, like everyone at Chelsea. When you're out of the side it is difficult to take. When you are suspended you have to accept it and then when you are injured you have to work hard.'

Sometimes it is overlooked that Petrescu came from Italy, via Romania and Sheffield Wednesday. The Fox Mulder lookalike was in outstanding form. 'Now my confidence is very high, I'm very happy in London, and so are my wife and family. My wife is just finishing studying law in Bucharest and then returns permanently to London. It is fantastic, I am very happy here. I am playing more in attack but that is because Ruud asks me to play that way. I was right up front against Liverpool because we had nothing to lose. We needed a bit of luck and then we got the first goal, but you can't play like this all the time. At 2–0 down in a Cup tie you have to risk everything. I concentrated on going forward and only when we were up did I track back and defend. Otherwise I am just like a midfielder. I hope we can win the Cup or league. I'm not sure about our chances for the championship, but second place puts you in the Champions League next season and that would be good. And the Cup is very difficult because someone can always beat you in a one-off game. We have to improve on some of our home form in the rest of the season. We have given away some unbelievable points in the last minute of the game, against Sheffield Wednesday and Nottingham Forest. We have to win those sort of games to be up in the top two or three.' While Dan succeeded at the Bridge, fellow Romanians Raduciou and Dumitrescu failed at West Ham and Popescu quit Spurs for Barcelona.

Minto, playing for his future, said: 'Some players here decided to look elsewhere to get first-team football, but I never considered it. I was determined to see out my contract with Chelsea so I could at least look back knowing I had tried my best even if it didn't work out. No way was I going to chuck it all away without a real fight. After all the injuries, I'm now doing reasonably well, though I know there is plenty more to come. It takes a long time to get full fitness back when you've missed almost two years. My aim is to stay in the first team from now until the end of the season but, of course, there are a lot of people on the sidelines.'

Minto was among the handful of Brits with a regular place. 'I look at Ruud on the bench and think to myself he should be the first name on the team sheet. Then I see Gianluca also sitting there. It's frightening, really. Yet everyone has come to understand it is a squad game here at Chelsea under Ruud and that he has tactical reasons for making his switches.'

'Make sure you feed Zola stodge all week,' was the message from Hoddle to the Trimmings training ground cook, Sian Bowles.

TUESDAY, FEBRUARY 11

Gullit picked out Ince as England's biggest threat to Italy; a couple of days later he was linked with trying to sign him! In the *Corriere della Sera*, Gullit said: 'Ince has grown a lot since he moved to Serie A. He is now one of Europe's top players. Most spectators follow those who do something special, but the most important players stay in the shadows and allow the others to shine. If Gianfranco Zola did not have such players around him nobody would have heard of him.'

Di Matteo wanted Gazza's England shirt. But would Gazza play? He had competition; Pierluigi Casiraghi, another former Lazio team-mate of Gazza, said: 'Most of my memories of Gazza are unrepeatable but he was very useful to us … in the dressing room. If he plays, send him this message. I hope he does not play too well.' Casiraghi added: 'But I want Gascoigne's shirt after the game.' Di Matteo insisted: 'No, I will be the one to swap shirts with Gazza. I have promised my sister Concetta his England jersey.' Di Matteo summarised Italy's feelings. 'The team with the best spirit will win this one. And we are ready.' Casiraghi was livid when Lazio sold Di Matteo to Chelsea. It was Di Matteo who supplied the ammunition for Casiraghi's deadly shooting in front of goal. Without him Lazio have had such a tough time that coach Zdenek Zeman had just been sacked. Casiraghi said, 'You have robbed Italy of some of our best players. Only that way have you now got a domestic championship to match ours. Despite what people have said, I won't be coming to England and continuing this trend. Quite the contrary. In fact, I reckon it is time we poached your best talent to leave things back where they were.'

Zola, Italy's second-top scorer among the current players with eight goals, said: 'It will be a hard game for us – but for England also. I know there are many Italian people in London who will come along and support us but most of the big crowd will be on England's side and that is something extra for us to fight against. We respect England and I have found much to admire in the game here but we are confident in our football and we can win tomorrow if we perform at our best.'

WEDNESDAY, FEBRUARY 12

England 0 Italy 1

Bates was in the corridors of Wembley's Banqueting Hall, as befitted an FA councillor, when he caught sight of Di Matteo. A hug from chairman to player. Had Bates been responsible for the downfall of English football and Hoddle? Zola clinched victory with a memorable goal to become the first Chelsea player to score against England. In fact the first Chelsea player to score in an international at Wembley since Greaves's hat-trick against Scotland in 1961.

Di Matteo said: 'Only great players can score a goal like that and Gianfranco is a great player. Players like him can make the difference in a game and he did just that.' Perhaps they would be back at Wembley for the Cup final? Di Matteo: 'I would love to play at Wembley again and also have the same success.'

Not for the first time Bates reserved a barbed one-liner for the manager who launched the Blues' revival then quit for England. Asked whether Zola would be given a hard time back at Chelsea's training ground, he replied: 'Of course not – why should he get one? He was the best player on the pitch, and it's not his fault England played kick and rush.'

Zola's winner left English football deflated. 'It was my dream goal. The control of the ball was everything. It put me in a position to shoot and it was a wonderful moment. I was too much on one side when I stopped the ball, I put it too much wide. I could only shoot at first sight, sometimes you have not time to think, you have to just shoot. It is instinct. To score a goal like this, especially against England at Wembley, is a dream for me. It is what I dreamed about as a small boy, scoring this kind of goal on this kind of occasion. I don't know if we will qualify, because England are a team we still respect and it will be another difficult game when we play them in Italy.

'I hope the Chelsea fans will understand why I feel so happy after scoring for my country. They have given me such a warm welcome in England and I hope they will not put this goal against me. Surely they know I had to do this important thing for my country. Until the next World Cup game my efforts are concentrated on Chelsea.'

Goalkeepers usually hang their heads in shame when beaten on their near post, but Walker insisted that he had no chance with the decisive nineteenth-minute strike. 'It was brilliant work by Zola, but I had his shot covered until it took a deflection off Sol Campbell's studs.'

Gullit was on his usual BBC commentary duty, with another hilarious cross-talk with Hansen, this time arguing about the Chelsea–Liverpool cup tie. Hansen picked up Gullit on his preview suggestion that he only sought two major contributions from each of his players and that would be enough to win a game. Hansen asked him what was Minto's second contribution, as his first was to be taken off! Jimmy Hill interceded with a comment about the stress of soccer management, and said that Ruud looked younger! 'Thank you very much,' said Ruud, 'it's down to my girlfriend really, she ...' Lynam had the final word: 'I don't think we need to know any more about that...'

The BBC ripped up their own rulebook to let Gullit wear a polo shirt mono-grammed with the letters RUUD. Accountants were trying to work out how much money Gullit's new fashion line saved in free advertising! Jon Smith told me: 'The BBC lines were red hot and we spent hours with people interested in his new fashion lines.' His brother Phil said: 'It's going to make millions in royalties.'

Vialli was at the game commenting for TeleMonteCarlo. Vialli interviewed Zola immediately after the match. Vialli: 'You must be very tired now, Gianfranco?' (Clearly, angling to take his place in the FA Cup!!) Zola: 'I knew it, I knew it. Yes, I'm tired but very happy. I'm ready to dive back into English football but I hope you can come back into the team as soon as possible at Chelsea. We need you.'

A celebratory meal out for Zola and Di Matteo with their families, and the wives of Albertini and Costacurta plus Williams and Byrne.

THURSDAY, FEBRUARY 13
Zola and Di Matteo cheekily turned up for training wearing their victorious Italian shirts!

The exhausted Zola was much in demand and a press conference was held for the Italian media at the Royal Lancaster Hotel in the afternoon, with the English press turning up as well. Zola might be excused for picking out his goal against England as his most memorable in recent weeks. Not so. 'No, I pick the goal that gave me my main satisfaction, it has been the goal that Vialli scored against Liverpool, our third goal.' I wonder whether that was really the case, or Zola being diplomatic for English consumption?

Gullit put cup aspirations and the win over Liverpool into perspective as he concentrated on the match at Leicester. 'I went back to work with the players straight after that match, and I wanted them to forget the Liverpool game. I had to bring them back down to earth. The Liverpool game was a good battle, but we still haven't won the war. Becoming the first team to overturn a 2–0 deficit against Liverpool for thirty-odd years is nice for the record books, but it won't mean a thing if we get knocked out at Leicester in the next round. That's why nobody has yet mentioned winning anything to me.

'I think people at the club are beginning to understand the real meaning of progress now. When you see the building of Chelsea Village behind the goal, every home game sold out and Chelsea attracting big crowds wherever we play – that's progress. The truth is, I don't know if we are good enough to win the Cup this year. If you start talking about winning some silverware, you put pressure on yourself, and that doesn't help win football matches. I would say we are now much better equipped as a team than we were last year. We have looked more comfortable against the likes of Arsenal and Liverpool. But there is always danger when you are in too much of a hurry. You must always be aware of your limitations and try not to look two steps ahead. I don't set targets or say "I want to have this and I want to have that." The bottom line is that we are heading in the right direction, but we are still not where I want us to be. You can't go out and buy success at a corner shop. It takes time, and Chelsea fans have less patience than me. All our supporters would like to win something after all these years, and when the team is playing well their hopes turn to expectation. But if my players make mistakes, I have to give them the time to learn from them.

'How we played against Liverpool, we can't play like that every week. We had to change our game during that match to hurt them. That was the solution but it can't always be like that because each new opposing team is different. It was not my standard approach against Liverpool. I made changes against Liverpool and you hope the players can respond the way you want them to. But that game has now gone and there is the next one to think about.'

Gullit was concerned that his style and strategy was becoming known to opponents. 'People know Chelsea now so their approach to us is different.' Gullit started having a talk-in with his players. 'I want to know if the players are happy and comfortable. We make mistakes, so we have to change, but I talk to them and that has led to a unanimous solution and decision. My experience with Milan and Holland was that players talk and adapt to the situation. I have a certain group of players here and must work with them. I could not come here and decide to impose a particular system, such as Ajax's style of football, if that was not right for the players; that would be stubborn. I have been pleased with the players' response since the Liverpool game. We beat Tottenham 2–1 and they have been excited. I don't like players who just come to the training ground and do their bit and then go again. I want to discuss everything with them and give them responsibility. It is the same in a factory. If you don't give the workers more responsibility they will steal. At least that is my philosophy.

'We train for fifteen minutes at a time, and talk about how it has gone. Then we change things round and do it all over again. That way we have come across the style we prefer.'

FRIDAY, FEBRUARY 14

Valentine's Day, and Gullit was still in love with the thought of recruiting Maldini, if the price came down to a transferable level. Encouraged that Milan went into the transfer market themselves, signing Dutch aces Patrick Kluivert and, more significantly, defender Winston Bogarde from Ajax, he would use the friendly in Milan after the Leicester cup tie to sound out the latest Maldini situation. 'I heard a rumour all the older players have to leave Milan because they want to build up a new side. They've now bought Bogarde and Kluivert, and Bogarde is also a left-footed player. So, if I hear that, it's my job to say "Can I have Maldini, then?" I think it'd be crazy not to ask. I wouldn't be doing my job well. If it wasn't such a ridiculous figure, I'd still be interested. You just wait for the right moment.' A world record of £17m had been suggested. 'If that's the money they're still talking about, it's out of the question,' said Gullit. Chelsea will play AC Milan in a prestige San Siro friendly. 'Of course I will be looking at him because he's in their team, but that doesn't mean I'm going there on a mission.'

Maldini acknowledged that Gullit and Milan's acting president Adriano Galliani were in regular contact. Maldini said: 'Gullit and Galliani ring one another regularly but as far as I know there has never been an official or serious offer from any club. My contract runs out in the year 2001 and I intend to stay at Milan, but of course it takes two parties to settle these matters.'

Kluivert's agent Sigi Lens announced on Dutch TV that had the striker chosen the Premiership it would have been with Gullit rather than Arsenal. Lens suggested that Kluivert was flattered by Gullit's interest and that Chelsea would have matched any financial package presented by AC Milan.

Gullit admitted that he wanted Kluivert, but the twenty-year-old striker chose AC Milan on a four-year deal worth an annual post-tax salary of £1.2m. 'I wanted Kluivert but I couldn't get him. He made his own decision and he wanted to try things in Italy. Of course I made an attempt. I watched him at home, I did everything. Nobody knows, but I go to Holland often and I do my job. But if the player wants to make the same adventure as I did in Italy, that's OK.' Gullit has not given up: 'I've said to him maybe I will wait a year and if it does not go well then I will be back. At this moment I do not expect to make any signings before the deadline. But I am making preparations for next season and anyone can see that we are short of bodies. But we don't need just players, we need good players.'

Almost every top English club was linked with a homecoming for Ince from Inter but Gullit was not joining the bidding, and he criticised Hoddle for pairing Ince with Batty in midfield against Italy. 'I have no interest in Paul Ince. We have a similar player in Eddie Newton and having two players like that you will get the same thing that happened for England against Italy. I'm very happy with Eddie, he's doing very well, and I don't need him and Paul Ince in the same area.'

In his own inimitable style Gullit dismissed newspaper speculation he had tied up a deal for Ince. 'First Maldini, now Ince! Every time people get connected to us, it is maybe because players want to come. That's very good because it means we play good football and we're quite proud of that. But Paul Ince didn't come to us and I think someone is just trying to get a rumour going.'

More immediate considerations were the big cup tie. Would Zola do it again?

Hughes likened him in influence to Cantona. The former United legend and Cantona's ex-Old Trafford team-mate reckoned the Frenchman and Italy's midweek match-winner are in a class of their own. 'They have the same influence on games because of their sheer quality. To have achieved what Zola has done in such a short space of time is great credit to him. Zola can influence a game just like Cantona; he's a tremendous player with real quality. We thought he might need some time to settle in, but after the first training session, we knew it was no problem. Chelsea can achieve anything. We just need one trophy to get going. It's the place to be and we're all very excited by what's happening. As soon as United won the championship, everyone at the club really believed in themselves.' Gullit agreed: 'When I signed Zola, I knew I was buying class. Like Cantona, he can change things round in a second. World-class players need only a few moments to make a difference. When the chance comes to kill the game Zola is at his best.'

SATURDAY, FEBRUARY 15
Liverpool's Jason McAteer believed Gullit would become the first foreign manager to lead his team out at Wembley in an FA Cup Final. 'After their result against us in the last round, Chelsea must feel they can do anything. I'm not only backing them to win this game but to go on and lift the Cup itself. They look a classic Cup-winning side in the Chelsea tradition. Colourful and cosmopolitan, they must use sign language to understand each other. But they have players who can turn a game in a split-second with a bit of magic. They are not consistent enough to sustain a true title challenge but can beat anyone on their day. Martin O'Neill's Leicester have shown often enough this season they are no mugs. They held us at Anfield on Boxing Day and were good value for their 3–1 lead at Newcastle until a certain someone called Shearer stuck his nose in. But they've got a number of key men missing, especially Emile Heskey and Neil Lennon – and that will tell against them in the end. Chelsea key man: no, not Zola, despite his Wembley wonder show, but Mark Hughes, the man who caused us so much grief; holds the ball up so well and makes players around him play well.' O'Neill's cup battlers were not running scared despite their stretched resources. O'Neill wrote in the match day programme: 'The nearest we get to a Latin influence is when the lads go down to the local restaurant on a Friday lunchtime before a home game.' Still not fully fit after surgery, his thirteenth operation, Steve Walsh relished the job of shackling Zola. 'Naturally, he is a world-class footballer and it is up to us to try to cut off his supply. If we can do that, then hopefully he will become less effective.' O'Neill added: 'We know that Zola is one of the top players in Europe at the moment and obviously he is going to be a real handful. But I am not considering a man-marking job on him because we have no one available to do it. He scored a brilliant goal at Wembley. When he came off near the end, I was hoping that he would be hobbling, but unfortunately that was not the case, but we do respect him. If we can stifle his talent then we must have a good chance of going through.'

SUNDAY, FEBRUARY 16
Leicester City 2 Chelsea 2
Filbert Street proved a far more intimidating venue than Wembley for Zola. Zola suffered shocking insults when he stepped off the team coach. He was shaken by a group of aggressive fans screaming 'stronzo'. There can be few more offensive Italian words: literally translated 'stronzo' means 'turd'.

Zola was targeted because of his match-winning World Cup goal. He was booed by Leicester fans from the moment he touched the ball until he was substituted in the sixty-seventh minute to taunts of 'England, England' after one of his least effective matches in English football. Zola said: 'I heard the boos and jeers. I was not bothered. It was Italy who won at Wembley.' At least the Chelsea fans gave English football's latest public enemy number one their moral support. A banner fluttered in the wind: 'We still love you Zola'. Zola struck a blow against English football in the World Cup, but he found English hearts made of sterner stuff in the FA Cup.

Surely, this was a Premiership mis-match. The writing was on the programme for Leicester even before the kick off. When the team was announced, a collection of teenagers, transfer-listed misfits and recuperating injury victims were scribbled over Leicester's quartet of suspended stalwarts. Chelsea were unchanged, midweek Azzurri and all. Then Leicester's press officer announced the respective substitutes: 'Stuart Wilson, a first year professional, Jamie Lawrence, he's played half a game this year, and Sam McMahon, he was recalled from a loan to Kettering this week; Chelsea – Ruud Gullit, Gianluca Vialli . . .' The point was made.

It seemed to be a stroll for the Italians again as Chelsea raced into a two-goal lead, the first an exquisite strike from Di Matteo. When Hughes added the second Chelsea's passage to the quarterfinals seemed a formality.

During the half-time 'entertainment' Alan Birchenall suggested Leicester could emulate Chelsea's performance against Liverpool in the previous round and recover their two-goal deficit. It was not only the Chelsea supporters who tittered. The home fans reacted similarly. Even the former Leicester and Chelsea midfielder, now City's half-time MC, did not sound as if he believed himself, so completely had Chelsea dominated the first period. But Leicester did, indeed, stage a magnificent comeback, their cause ignited by stalwart Steve Walsh, with a thunderous header just seven minutes after the break. Defending is hardly Chelsea's strong suit and they suffered a shaky second-half experience. Hitchcock had already come off his line to be beaten by the Walsh header, then an equaliser just three minutes from time was a calamitous mix up.

Always susceptible in dead-ball situations, Chelsea were stunned by a Garry Parker curling free kick which earned Leicester's first goal, and it was another of his specialist free kicks that tempted Newton and Hitchcock to go for the same near-post ball without a Leicester striker in sight. Newton deflected it into his own goal.

Such is the strength of Gullit's squad that he sent on two world-class stars. First Vialli replaced Zola and then the player-manager himself came on for the last four minutes in place of a tiring Di Matteo.

The effort of guiding Italy to victory at Wembley had taken its toll on both Zola and Di Matteo. However, there was no denying the sheer class of Di Matteo's opening goal after fifteen minutes. He cut inside to crack an angled drive that curled in the air into the corner for his sixth goal of the season.

Fighting broke out behind Casey Keller's goal and threatened to spill over onto the pitch. Fortunately, the local outbreak of violence was subdued after about five minutes, but not before the referee had to consult with officials by the touchline. Ten fans were arrested, and dozens were ejected from the ground. Chelsea supporters mingled with Leicester fans behind the Kop end. Police and stewards intervened as fans spilled on to the pitch forcing the referee to halt the game for a minute. A police spokesman said: 'Eight people were arrested for public order offences. Another will be charged with criminal damage and another has been charged with ticket touting. We had to eject forty Chelsea supporters from the ground.'

Eyes were soon diverted away from the mayhem in the stands to the action on the pitch, where Leicester were full of commitment, despite being shorn of some of their most influential players and the prospect of taking on Wimbledon in the Coca-Cola Cup semifinal first-leg forty-eight hours later. Their resolve was tested to the full when Chelsea added a second after thirty-five minutes with a slick counterattack orchestrated by Newton and Petrescu, superbly finished by Hughes with a shot into the corner.

But Leicester fans roared on Parker's free kick in the fifty-second minute and they were brought to life by the sight of their giant Leicester captain, back after yet another operation to rekindle hopes of a Cup comeback. Walsh then cracked a twenty-five yarder just wide and Chelsea were holding on. Gullit, back from injury, made a rare appearance, but not even his formidable presence could quell the one-way tide of Leicester attacks. A replay was the least that Leicester's bravehearts deserved. There was still time for a Hughes diving header from a Petrescu cross, and a touch of French farce; Leboeuf fell to his knees, offering thanks to the linesman for finally raising his flag as players wandered back from offside positions. Referee Mike Reed lacked a sense of humour as he showed the Frenchman a yellow card.

If Chelsea thought it would be an easy passage to the FA Cup Final on the back of their magnificent win over Liverpool and all the other big names falling in the early rounds, then they hadn't counted for the spirit of a Leicester team with an American goalkeeper as the only foreign star. And Zola's exhausting schedule had caught up with him. 'I was very, very tired. I just could not play at my best.' Chelsea wilted, but not to the point of falling apart completely. Hughes said: 'Possibly in the past, we might have folded under the kind of pressure that Leicester exerted in the second half. But we are made of better stuff now and we have the home game to come. We are still very much in the FA Cup and that's the important thing. We are naturally disappointed that they got back into the game with two free kicks and we weren't happy about the second one. I didn't see anything wrong with the tackle Steve Clarke made which gave away the free kick. I thought he won the ball cleanly and there was no offence in the first place. But give Leicester credit; they never gave up and threw everything at us.'

Gullit dismissed comparisons with how Liverpool must have felt down at the Bridge three weeks ago. 'The difference is that we're still in the Cup – and we deserved to win. It would be different if we had wasted this game at home but we now go back to Stamford Bridge and we feel very comfortable playing at home. I feel confident that we can beat Leicester. Then we will think about going to Portsmouth in the quarter finals. I'm just waiting for our luck to change. It seems we have to be on top one hundred per cent to get a good result. That little thing called luck has not been with us all season but it will come. I was not angry at the end, there was nothing we could do about being caught by an own goal three minutes from time.' Asked what turned the game, he said: 'Two free kicks. They had two free kicks and scored from both of them. Apart from that they didn't create anything. I think they were lucky.'

When it was later put, provocatively, to O'Neill that 'Ruud Gullit said you were lucky', he bit. O'Neill poured scorn on Gullit's 'lucky' tag. The Foxes were without seven first-choice players; banned Lennon, Heskey, Izzet and Elliott, together with the injured Kaamark, Whitlow, Hill and Rolling. 'We'll try and bring our *first* team down for the replay,' quipped O'Neill. 'He's being a bit uncomplimentary considering the side we had out. We're still there, we're still in the competition and we'll try and give them a better game down at Stamford Bridge. They were not entitled to beat us today, regardless of us being at home or not. The two substitutes they brought on were Vialli and Gullit. We brought on Jimmy Lawrence and Stuart Wilson. I rest my case. Wilson will be a good player – in fifteen years' time!' Yet, the baby-faced sub played his part in Leicester's fightback. 'I'm obviously delighted we got something out of the game. I said to the lads at half-time I just didn't want to go out of the Cup so meekly. We didn't get in amongst it in the first half and that's nothing to do with the team we had out. In the second half we competed and kept going. I don't care what anyone says, we deserved the equaliser. Mind you, before the game I would have settled for something like this out of the match, but at half-time I would have settled for us just getting a corner.'

Newton was inconsolable in the dressing room over his own goal. 'My first thought when it happened was "Oh no". As I went to clear the ball it hit the bottom of my studs and went in. There was nothing I could do. Kevin Hitchcock told me he'd called for it, but I just didn't hear him at all because of the massive roar. Now I want to put it behind me by getting us through.' Sinclair revealed: 'We had to have a little joke about it in the dressing room. I told him he was spoiling the share price!'

Gullit summed it up succinctly: 'We were too polite.'

The draw for the sixth round – Sheffield Wednesday v Wimbledon; Portsmouth v Leicester City or Chelsea; Derby County or Coventry City v Middlesbrough; Chesterfield v Wrexham.

Chelsea were 2–1 favourites with William Hill, 7–2 Wimbledon, 5–1 Sheffield Wednesday, 11–2 Middlesbrough, 10–1 Derby, 11–1 Coventry, 20–1 Leicester and Portsmouth, 25–1 Chesterfield, 33–1 Wrexham.

MONDAY, FEBRUARY 17

Vialli took a knock late on at Leicester, needed treatment and looked doubtful for the match in San Siro.

TUESDAY, FEBRUARY 18

Ferguson planned to wipe the smiles off the faces of Chelsea and Arsenal, two of his biggest title rivals, over the next week, as they delighted in the absence of suspended Cantona. 'It's not a question of living without Eric. We have shown we have made progress already in dealing with this situation. I don't think anyone can accuse us of being a one-man team. Our results show that the rest of the team can produce and perform without Eric. Cantona is going with us to London. These are two of the most important games of the season. It's vital we pick up the points.'

Gullit's twenty-man squad departed from Gatwick, arriving at their Milan hotel at 5.30pm. Bates joked to Zola. 'You are the smallest person around here, you push the President's baggage trolley to the check-in desk.' Zola: 'Yes, El Presidente.' Bates tipped him with a ten-pound note. And he took it!

Zola was mobbed by fans and press on arrival at Milan Airport as Italy continued to celebrate his winning goal against England. Zola: 'It is a big thing to be coming back to Italy. But it is very strange coming here with an English club. I have great memories of the last time I played at the San Siro because it was when Parma beat

Milan to win the European Super Cup against all the odds. That still ranks as my greatest memory in football.'

Bates: 'I have a love-hate relationship with Ruud. He recommended the best shopping street (Via Monte Napoleone) and the best restaurant (Al Girorosto) on Corse Venetia. Unfortunately we went shopping first, so I was lucky to have enough money to pay for lunch.' Bates returned from his expedition armed with a photo of Ruud when he sported a moustache playing for Milan, for the March issue of *Onside*.

Gullit was linked with striker Marco Simone and goalkeeper Sebastiano Rossi, plus swapping Di Matteo for Maldini, as the rumour factory swung into overdrive, but his only interest was returning to the scene of some of his greatest triumphs and letting his Chelsea youngsters experience the atmosphere of one of the world's finest stadia.

Half an hour after getting to the hotel they were off in the rush hour traffic to a training ground near the San Siro, attracting 200 fans to see Gullit and his team. Aron Winter popped in, Vialli and Gullit were mobbed; Zola warmly applauded. Ruud said: 'I'm looking forward to seeing the San Siro again, I played some good matches here. It is something else now, a different adventure.'

But Hughes wondered about the timing at such a vital stage in an exhausting season. Gullit added: 'It will be a great opportunity for us and all the youngsters also; a different environment, Kingstonians [the reserves' pitch] to the San Siro.'

At least the weather was better. Or was it? 'It may be Italy, but its flippin' cold,' said Rix. 'It's the same temperature as in England, only not windy,' said Gullit.

Wise said: 'We didn't get a chance to do any proper sightseeing but there were some lovely shops out there. Roberto took us shopping and got us thirty per cent discount off everything. We bought some clothes but his taste is a little different from mine. What taste? I don't think he's got any taste, and Frank Leboeuf's is even worse!'

Zola went to the cinema ... to watch *Arise* starring Arnold Schwarzenegger – in English. In the hotel foyer, he was persuaded to play some Elton John at the piano. 'I was able to play the piano but now I lost a lot because I don't play for a long time. I played just a little bit, but I forgot the ... I'm not sure how you call it, the scales. I had lessons when I was in Naples for three years, but when I went to Parma I stopped having lessons. I didn't have a lot of time to do it. I haven't played a piano at home in London yet. I will have to buy one. Sometimes I like to play because I find it very relaxing. I love classical music, it is very nice. And pop music I try hard to play but I have not been able to. I like Elton John, he's a great singer. I'd like to be able to play all his songs, but it's not possible. It is just a dream.'

WEDNESDAY, FEBRUARY 19
AC Milan 2 Chelsea 0

Gullit received a rousing reception as a second-half sub in the match shown live on Italian pay-per-view TV. By then Milan were two goals up. French international Christophe Dugarry scored a goal in each half. Gullit used eight substitutes after the interval, including himself, to blood youngsters, giving them a taste of the big time, and to leave his first-choice stars fresh for the confrontation with Manchester United. Zola's brilliant free kick was spectacularly saved by Rossi, and young Paul Hughes headed against the post as well as shooting over. Ruud almost snatched a goal in the closing minutes with a shot that flew just over. Milan coach Arrigo Sacchi said: 'Ruud has been a great player, and I'm sure he will become a great coach.'

Gullit said: 'It's a great honour for Chelsea to be invited here. It used to be teams such as Bayern Munich and Real Madrid, and now Chelsea are in that bracket. This is good preparation and experience for the players when they have to face European competition. It is also interesting for me, now I am a manager, to see what it's like with all the pressure in Italy. It was a great feeling to be back here and I was very happy with the team's performance.' Vialli, Albertini and Baresi were all missing through injury.

Di Matteo's fine display at Wembley ignited interest from AC Milan but Gullit said: 'Of course we don't want to let him go. Milan did not ask about him because this was not the occasion and we were not here to negotiate. The same goes for myself and Milan players. I have not mentioned any names to them.' Albertini was also linked to Chelsea. Albertini spoke at length to Di Matteo and said: 'I don't want to leave Italy now so that's that. But Roberto has told me he is very happy at Chelsea and is not joining us.' It had been suggested that Di Matteo told former Lazio team-mate Giuseppe Signori that he wanted to return to Italy as he was unsettled in London. Di Matteo's agent Vinicio Fioranelli said: 'Roberto is fine at Chelsea.' Gullit confirmed that Milan had told him Maldini was not for sale.

Later in the month, the club issued opening page denials, first from Vialli in the Manchester United issue, then Di Matteo for the cup replay with Leicester. Di Matteo said: 'I feel good. I feel my team-mates and the club expect something special from me. I will try to do my best, and it's a good time for me. I feel very good and the team is playing well. It makes everything much easier for me. I don't want to leave, and that's for sure.' Despite explaining the situation, the rumours persisted. Gullit said: 'But I don't mind. Really, it's great that newspapers keep linking Chelsea with big players from big clubs. Would that have happened two years ago? I don't think so. But now it's just a part of the business.'

Di Matteo admitted: 'Of course I miss my country a little and was sorry to see my international team-mates go back to Italy after our game at Wembley. But I love it at Chelsea and that is the important thing. London is a great place to live and I'm enjoying myself. It was a very close game at Wembley and it was great to play there. We were delighted to win. There is still a long way to go but we have taken a big step towards the finals. I think Serie A is the best league in the world but the Premiership is catching up. So many of the best players want to come over here and that is a good sign. Also, there are no easy games which shows how strong the standard is throughout the league. I play the same way for Chelsea as I do for Italy and that obviously suits me. Now we have to continue working hard for the rest of the season and make sure we give ourselves the best chance possible to win something. We know what the supporters want and we are trying our best to give them something to sing about.'

Hughes came through the first half before making way for Mark Nicholls, as Manchester United won a tough encounter with Arsenal at Highbury 2–1. Hughes said: 'United are still the top club in the country. They have got all the prestige and glamour which they've built up over the last thirty years. The thing I would say about Chelsea is that they've got the right set-up to emulate what United have done. The ground, players and whole feel about Chelsea makes you think they are serious about attempting to be the number one club in the south.'

THURSDAY, FEBRUARY 20

The team left straight after the match for the airport. With a short delay due to bad weather back in England, they arrived back at Gatwick just after 2am, and were home around four in the morning. Wise said: 'It was a tiring journey home. We got back about four in the morning, then we were in at twelve for training. Had a warm down and went home.'

Radio Chelsea 1494AM and a dedicated Chelsea Internet site – www.chelseafc.co.uk – were launched. One record sure to get plenty of air time – 'Matthew's Dream' by the True Blue Crew. The charity pop song was by Chelsea fan Steve Lima, founder member of seventies punk band The Members, and Chelsea Independent Supporters Association chairman Ross Fraser. Ruud pays his own emotional tribute to Matthew at the end of the record. 'We have Matthew Harding always in our hearts and he will be with us for ever.' A crowd of Chelsea fans teamed up to record the track at London's Red Bus Studio.

FRIDAY, FEBRUARY 21

Ruud laughs off racist taunts, making his point with supreme skill. Asked his views about Ian Wright's allegations that Schmeichel taunted him with racist abuse, the dreadlocked star said: 'No, I've not really been the victim of racism in football. But, if someone called me a black b***** I wouldn't take it as a racist thing – because I *am* black.' Ruud laughed and pointed out that he'd be more insulted if someone questioned his legitimacy!

Schmeichel faced Chelsea following the furore over the clash in the tunnel at Highbury after United's 2–1 win took them closer to retaining the title. Gullit added: 'The key is that in a game there are emotions. If somebody is red, you'll call them a red whatever. So it depends on how somebody approaches you and what they say. And I'm so busy in the game I don't care. I think that the best thing always, for every player, wherever he comes from or whatever, is that he just tries to play well. Just play well and play your own game and all these things will vanish. Then people will realise that you may also be a good player instead of a [laughing] red herring.' Gullit added: 'I don't know Schmeichel and I wasn't present in midweek. I don't know what happened, I don't know what they said so I can't give an answer to that.'

On a general level, Gullit doesn't believe racism is prevalent among domestic players although it can still occasionally occur in the stands. 'I don't think it's a problem in our game. People work very hard, they may have a boss who breaks their balls all week and they have to get rid of their own frustrations. In that ninety minutes there is tension for everyone and sometimes they call things. I just see it in that way. But whatever they shout is not personal for me. And at the end of the game when they appreciate what you have done they also applaud you – that's the strange thing. So, in that ninety minutes it's tension for everyone.' And abuse from players? He replied: 'For me it's never been a problem. If people are swearing at me or whatever I just turn around, it means they're afraid of me, so that gives me a sort of superiority.'

Gullit is firmly opposed to any organised racism, as he recalled: 'Ajax played in a match in Hungary and whenever a black player touched the ball, the home crowd made some jungle sounds. Now that's abusive, it's not funny any more, it's got nothing to do any more with emotions. So Ajax complained to UEFA and the Hungarian club got fined and that's exactly right. Because that had nothing to do with the game, that was just to abuse them.'

Gullit remained a huge admirer of Schmeichel: 'He is their key figure and the man who won the championship for them last year. It's just his presence. The opposition get a lot of chances which means United's defence is not as good as it seems but he so often makes the vital save.'

Hughes knew it was win or bust against his old club; Chelsea were twelve points behind with two games in hand. 'If we don't get any kind of result tomorrow it will be difficult for us to make a challenge,' conceded Hughes, who won three championships and five cups during his thirteen Old Trafford years. 'I'm not saying it would be the end for us, but it would make them very difficult to catch.' Wise insisted: 'We always seem to do well against them and now everyone is praying that we beat them again and open it up and give everyone else a chance. It's a real six-pointer, a big game for us. We have a plan, which we'll stick to. We know we're capable of achieving a place in Europe, now we will find out if we can go on to something more.' United were unbeaten in fourteen Premiership games, winning the last five. They had won 4–1 at the Bridge last year and 3–2 the season before. They last lost a Premiership match in London at Spurs fourteen months previously. 'The difference is we do well in the big games but not always so well against the smaller clubs, while United always plug a result out,' added Wise.

'United have been setting the standards for the last five or six years,' said Hughes. 'Week in, week out they turn round results. That's what we have to find. They know everyone's waiting to pounce on them if they lose, and they'll take a lot of stick, so they do their best not to give their critics any ammunition. They never panic, they always keep their shape and do what they believe in because they know it works. That's why they win so many games in the last ten minutes. We've got to get onto that level. What helps United is winning things for years, that breeds confidence. Until we win something we'll be behind them.'

Inevitably there would be comparisons. Gullit said: 'I don't think you measure yourself against other teams. You measure your progress over the season and I think we've made some big steps during this championship. United have always been favourites because they won the title last season, but they're looking different at Chelsea now, that's for sure.'

Cole, whose £7m signing signalled a premature departure for Hughes, led the attack again after the success of his partnership with Solskjaer at Highbury, where both scored. 'I think that they were a real goal threat all the time on Wednesday and their incisiveness and quickness was really a great advantage for us,' said Ferguson. 'Our record at Chelsea is unbelievable. We have a marvellous record there. It is a funny thing. They always seem to beat us at Old Trafford and we win down there, so we will be quite happy to keep that format going.'

Ferguson, Schmeichel and the rest of the players kept a low profile as they prepared at their Burnham Beeches hideaway. Ferguson said: 'They are handling the whole thing in the right way. They are not going to be derailed. They know what we are after. We have to keep our concentration. These players know they have to keep focused and not think of any side issues. We're after another good performance. The players are really looking forward to it. I know it's going to be difficult at Stamford Bridge, but the lads are looking really hungry. They all want to play at the moment and that can only be good for us.'

Burley failed to recover from his ankle injury in time, but Gullit hoped he would be available for the FA Cup replay. Chelsea, the last team to beat United at Old Trafford back in November, returned from their midweek friendly in Milan with no injury problems, and Vialli had recovered from a leg injury. Minto conceded a home win was essential if United were to be stopped from lifting a fourth title in five years. 'I believe if anyone finishes above United, they will be champs. But Chelsea are not out of it by any means, although beating United for the second time this season is probably vital to remain in the hunt.'

It was another high turn out at Harlington. Ruud, sporting a blue woolly hat covering his dreadlocks, signed every single autograph. Richard Williams of the *Guardian* observed: 'The manager strolls over. Quietly, carefully, firmly, he shepherds the children back behind the barrier, touching them gently on the shoulder, encouraging them to observe the etiquette, to respond to his good manners with their own. Then he stands there himself for twenty minutes, wielding a pen until every request has been satisfied. Ruud Gullit is presiding over the first Chelsea side since the days of Osgood and Hudson to command the affection of enlightened neutrals, and the atmosphere created by the civilised behaviour of the manager and his staff is not the least of the reasons.'

The team building will go on; if not immediately. Gullit had already started planning for next season. But he denied he had been on a shopping trip to Milan. 'Shopping with my girlfriend, yes. Shopping for players, no.'

SATURDAY, FEBRUARY 22
Chelsea 1 Manchester United 1
The unveiling of Chelsea Radio ... The Spice Girls ... Tony Blair and United fan Angus Deayton. The Bridge once more the place to be seen. The big game of the weekend was a vote catcher. Not just for the leader of the opposition but also for the two main protagonists for the major individual award of the season.

Would the Footballer of the Year be one of England's budding young talents or the pick of the recruits from Serie A ... Zola or Beckham? Each scored another spectacular goal; Beckham's brilliant volley and Zola's trickery illuminated a contest Manchester United couldn't afford to lose and Chelsea had to win. Gullit said: 'The Premiership now has world-class players and that is well known now in England and Europe. Both Zola and Beckham's goals also illustrated the kind of players who could offer something extra. England can be proud of its Premier League. I've played abroad and I know that the Premier League is now an example for the rest of Europe, notably in its organisation. When we were in Milan last week the directors asked me more about the Premiership, about how it's organised, how it divides the money. And on the field is getting better and better all the time, not just because of the foreigners.' So, would Beckham be Ruud's player of the year? 'So many good players who have done well...'

Gullit added: 'Neither team deserved to lose. United had to take risks and pressure us and they achieved just that. The good thing is a few months ago we would have lost a game like this.' There were tactical changes throughout the game, with Ferguson and Kidd bellowing instructions from the touchline. Not so Ruud. 'I don't want to be on the border of the pitch all the time, the players are the bosses on the pitch. I admire Ferguson and I heard him and he showed some good stuff chasing his team around.' Gullit gets his message across at half-time for major tactical alterations but the players are equipped to make adjustments for themselves as the game progresses.

Gullit's nostalgic excursion to his 'home' club Milan took its toll, a second-half collapse, after Chelsea produced the sort of dynamic football that destroyed Liverpool in the Cup in the opening half. Zola said: 'I knew in the second half we would suffer. During the week we couldn't train a lot, because of the friendly game in Milan, and we were very, very tired in the second half. We had to score again in the first half, that was the only way to win.' Was it a mistake going to Milan? 'I don't know, it is not my job. We looked very tired in the second half. We had to play in Milan, because the game was already organised.'

'Organised' was a word supplied by the ever attentive translator Gary Stalker, a member of the club's staff fluent in Italian, who carried a giant dictionary. (Zola nominated Gary as his 'unsung hero at Chelsea' in the match day programme: 'He is a good person, poor Gary will have a fit, he helps me a lot. And Dennis helps me out a lot too. It's important to have people like that when you are new in a country.')

Wise added: 'It's not an excuse, but getting back at 4am did not help.' Zola was unable to make a judgement on whether Manchester United or Liverpool were the better side. 'It is not easy to compare, because we were not in the same condition. Today they made a great step, because Chelsea are one of the most difficult games for them. They obtained a good result.' Zola and Di Matteo were playing their fourth game in eleven days and it showed. The pair ran the first half but, as at Leicester, tired in the second.

When Zola and Beckham met at Wembley Zola's opening strike proved to be decisive. Shame, that Beckham didn't score against Italy! When that was put to Zola, he smiled: 'Why? It's okay.' Significantly, Zola added: 'Today he played very well, but not at Wembley, because we marked and didn't give him a lot of opportunities, that's the key. I knew he could be a big problem for us and he did give us a lot of problems today, he played a very big game, a great game and he scored a beautiful goal, a fantastic goal.'

So too did Zola. After two minutes, Zola outfoxed Irwin as the full-back slid along the ground expecting the cross. Zola kept possession, took him out and then weaved past Pallister before shooting inside the near post leaving Schmeichel standing.

Newton handled to begin a move as Zola broke leaving United stretched two against two; the Italian dazzled their defence and left Hughes unmarked, but his side-foot attempt was saved. 'I'm glad he tried to place it. It could have been different if he had blasted it,' said Ferguson of his former striker. A second goal would have given Chelsea a cushion for a second-half onslaught by United once Beckham's volley put them level on sixty-eight minutes. As Ferguson put it: 'The chances we had, yet we scored from the most unlikely opportunity. It was a fantastic hit.'

Ferguson added: 'Of all the teams we have played this season, Chelsea had the best imagination in the last third of the field and we had to cope with that. I am glad they didn't win this match because they could go very close. Ruud Gullit tried to change it, Di Matteo was pushed further forward, but the momentum was with us and it was difficult for Chelsea to do anything about it.' As for Zola, Ferguson said: 'We watched him in the last three games and saw him against England. We pushed Roy Keane into his space, but he was clever enough to go wide and still cause us problems. He's a clever little bugger. Zola has got a very good head on him. He sorted out how we were playing very early and was clever enough to hurt us. He is a better player than I thought.'

Zola explained: 'You can find space when you play in the right position and make the right movement, you can find space in every game. There's not a game where it's impossible to find space. I do my job when I try and find space.'

Chelsea might have had two games in hand, but twelve points was a colossal gap to bridge. Zola felt that Liverpool were most likely to still challenge United for the title, or as he put it, 'the season'. Zola said: 'Both teams can win the season, I can't judge which one. It was not easy for us to upset Manchester United. A win would have made me more happy, but I have to think we played against the Manchester United who will be first in the season. So I have to be happy with that.'

A successful short stay in the capital for Ferguson; victory at Highbury and the draw at the Bridge. He said: 'We won the right one and drew the right one.' As Cantona and the entourage on the bench leapt up at every chance of a winner, the significance of this game for United was not lost. During the heat of battle, Ferguson went over to Gullit on the bench to complain about Keane's booking. Gullit explained what Ferguson had said: 'He said Keane got booked after two tackles, and we have nobody booked. Everybody reacts differently to a game; he does it his way, I do it my way.' Somebody suggested that Gullit went on as a second-half substitute to get away from Ferguson! 'That's a good one,' laughed Gullit. Ferguson was furious with referee Gerald Ashby for booking Keane; he called it 'an absolutely disgraceful decision'. He added: 'Hughes had nine fouls and nobody bothered. Roy had just two in the match.'

Ferguson patrolled the touchline, bellowing, complaining, his facial expression changing as much as the deepness of its colour – red, naturally. In stark contrast, Gullit was a picture of serenity. 'I get rid of my nerves by not watching the game as a supporter. I watch how our players behave during the game. I'm watching the moods and behaviour of my players. I do not follow the ball. I follow their movements. I look to see if the team is in the right shape.

'Sure, I get tense sometimes, but I am used to living with pressure. It's more of a problem for other people than for me. Maybe if we weren't doing well people would look at me and say, "He doesn't care enough." But I work the way I do.'

The press box was packed. Those arriving a few minutes late discovered no seats available, ending up in an uncomfortable overflow with the fans. Ruud had become well acquainted with the quaintness of the media's requirements. TV, radio, the main interview, then a special for Dutch TV, and the national newspapers' Monday sector. 'Ah,' said Ruud with a broad smile, 'the lovely boys corner' of the press room.

Pinned with his back to the wall and tiny recorders under his nose, Ruud spoke passionately about his vision of the future for Chelsea. 'I'm very happy, they had to take risks in the second half to get a result and had to work very hard for it. The supporters have another vision, they can see us growing as a team, we are growing as a club. I am inside, so I am not as aware of it as you. I am not aware of that ambience. I am just aware that my players are playing better football every week. The chairman is very happy, he gives me full responsibility with the team and it works very well. We are all working very hard for the future, he deals with the organisation of the club and I just do my job.'

Talks about a new contract? 'No. Not yet. This club is the best, one of the best. Overall, we are on the same level as Manchester United in everything but history. The difference is that they have history behind them, and that gives them something extra.' Chelsea need a trophy to start a new era in their history and build on that.

'I can feel the demands growing from our supporters but I can handle it. It is good for the players to have that pressure, I've had that all my life, that is the motivation. To wake up every morning ready for the challenge, ready to succeed. Everything about it is getting better, better, better. It keeps you awake!' Gullit understood the need for a combative figure like Keane in his side. 'I'd have a Roy Keane, he's a team player. Same as Mark Hughes, and they are favourites of the coach because they never let you down.'

Vialli was again stuck on the bench without coming on even though Hughes took an early knock and there were several changes in the second half. But he was not giving an inch to any questions about Vialli. 'I don't have to discuss my tactical reasons. Think about it. Vialli! Yes, he's okay.'

In the Football Focus pre-match chat, Ray Wilkins told Gary Lineker: 'I'd like to see Ruud play a bit more, I still think he's their best player ... He's so laid back that even when he strips off he doesn't look as though he really wants to come on, but when he does he can do precisely what he wants them to do.' Lineker: 'You've been a player-manager, is it difficult?' Wilkins: 'The hardest part is that when you're playing you're a team-mate, then when the game is finished you're the manager and have to detach yourself.'

Gullit came on as a late substitute, but made little impact; the impetus was impossible to win back from a rampant Manchester United.

Chelsea announced their new season ticket prices in the programme, the best seats jumping from £650 to £887 – the price for the new superstars at the Bridge. Hutchinson said: 'Everything has its price and at Chelsea we are trying to bring the best players to the club. A majority of the seats have gone up by around six per cent. The biggest increase is in the upper tier of the main stand. Those seats will have their own bar and club room. They will be right up there in quality with the Executive Club. Our target is to have the best team and club in Europe. If a top artist was appearing in concert in London, people would expect to pay top prices to see him or her. We are also in the entertainment business and providing value for money.'

SUNDAY, FEBRUARY 23

Ruud refused to answer calls from journalists about his private life. It was reported that estranged wife Christina Pensa was 'obstructing' him from seeing their five-year-old boy Quincey and three-year-old daughter Cheyenne. The couple reportedly fell out when Quincey wanted to spend an extra day with his dad. Gullit took legal advice and was due to go to court in a bid to see the children again. A hearing was set in Milan's family court where Gullit claimed the Italian ex-model had broken a separation agreement allowing him regular access to the youngsters in Italy and Britain. Gullit left that to his lawyers and would still be on duty with Chelsea for the Blackburn game.

His first marriage to childhood sweetheart Yvonne de Vries, on August 30 1984 produced two daughters, Felicity and Sharmayne. It ended in 1990 after the then AC Milan star was linked to a pretty reporter. Yvonne received a settlement reputedly worth £1.5m. Then Ruud married Christina five years previously, but split in 1995. Gullit is reputed to be paying Christina £3,000 a month. Gullit's lawyer said the separation pact allowed him to see the children when he is in Milan. But Christina insisted that if he wants to spend time with his girlfriend Estelle in London, he must fly to Milan to collect them then return them in person, the lawyer said. Gullit maintained that was unworkable because of his football commitments. Christina claimed Ruud had not seen his kids for ten months.

Gullit might even have been contemplating marriage for a third time. He was living with the tall blonde student Estelle, a regular at home games. But Ruud took his role as a father seriously, and he was annoyed at the intrusion into his public life. Gwyn Williams said: 'He's a private man and does not comment about his private life.'

In addition, Gullit suffered more intrusion into his privacy – he was seeing a psychic hypnotist, according to a Sunday paper front-page. Owen Potts, specialising in helping people with sexual and emotional problems, was quoted as saying: 'I have been helping Ruud therapeutically. I am a friend of his. I am a clairvoyant and I treat tension and stress.' Phil Smith said: 'I spoke to Ruud about it. He thought the whole thing was stupid. Owen is a faith healer and he helps people through bereavements. Just look at the girl with Ruud – does he need sex therapy? And, he's hardly under stress, is he? Ruud was hardly going to react to something as laughable as that.'

Restaurant manager Silvan Grandi, who runs a restaurant on the floor beneath Potts's clinic, said: 'Mr Gullit has been here many times. He was here again last week with his blonde girlfriend.' Gullit happily posed for a photograph with Silvan and promised to bring Zola and Vialli to his restaurant if they win the league. Silvan added: 'He is always serious when he comes but always polite. He is a real gentleman. He likes the peace and quiet here. Most times he comes alone, but sometimes it is with his girlfriend or another male friend.' Silvan's partner Walter said: 'You can imagine our surprise when Mr Gullit first walked in to our restaurant four months ago. We don't ask him questions. Everybody in the building knows why he comes here and who he is. He is a big star. I say good luck to him.'

Ruud was out when Sunday newspaper journalists arrived at the mansion block off trendy Sloane Square where he lives. Estelle's father Hennie, Johan Cruyff's elder brother, who runs a sports shop in her home town of Amsterdam, said: 'They have lived together since August. I have known Ruud since he was a kid. I sold him his first pair of football boots. I know he is a good guy. He and Estelle are very happy, and both our families are happy. I come to London often to watch the games and stay with them. I have a good feeling about everything. They share a love of football. How could Estelle not be a football fan after being born a Cruyff?'

Former Spurs star Garth Crooks interviewed Ruud about his personal and private life for the *New Nation* weekly newspaper. Ruud told the likeable Crooks, footballer turned radio and TV journalist: 'People tended to go out with me in the past because it's Ruudi. It's very difficult for me, because of who I am. Suddenly you open your eyes and ask yourself "What's going on here?" – so I change. I decide she can't do that any more, and I wait to see their reactions. From there I can assess their motives.' He disclosed his feelings about his impending divorce from second wife Christina. 'I'm not a romantic. I've been married twice and I'm about to go through a second divorce. You're always looking for the one love dedicated to yourself, but I've had some really bad experiences. The two divorces really hurt me but I'm not bitter because I've made mistakes too.'

Gullit was being hailed as the man to revolutionise traditionalist English thinking on the game; he owned up about mistakes he makes in football, too. 'I don't know what impact I've made here; it's perhaps a good thing that I don't know. But I do demand the best. The best food, training facilities and so on. When I arrived here at Chelsea I never dreamed I'd be manager. I thought I might coach the kids, maybe.' He has taken to coaching like a natural. 'I've always given people an opportunity to make mistakes. I've spent most of my life trying to take pressure off people. I make mistakes but I learn from them.' He isn't a sergeant major type of boss, rather one who likes to educate. He doesn't demand extra training, for example, but, as he puts it, they know he 'appreciates' it.

MONDAY, FEBRUARY 24

A full ninety-minute work out in the reserves' 2–1 defeat by Portsmouth that night. The effort required an hour with the masseur the next morning! 'I played in the reserves for the first time this season in strong rain and a great gale. We wore blue socks! It felt strange, Chelsea playing in blue socks. Chelsea are white socks.' Ruud has a thing about the colours of the kit. Red sends out vibes of vibrancy, aggression, winners. Blue is cool, not as dynamic. 'But it was good, with games coming Saturday and Wednesday, it is very difficult to do hard training. I needed the game. I left my backside on the pitch a few times, but at least Kingstonian is a better pitch than the San Siro. It really is.' Danny Potter, seventeen-year-old second-year trainee goalkeeper, hoping for a professional contract, was playing only his second ever reserve game with *the boss* in front of him as sweeper. In the first few minutes the player-manager badly underhit a back pass that required a last gasp dash off his line to block the oncoming forward. It deserved a rollicking. But Potter telling off Gullit? Sources close to the incident say that young Danny said: 'Oi, Ruudi!' And Gullit gestured a sort of apology or acknowledgement of his mistake.

Team: Harrison, Gullit, Clement (Quinn), Demetrious, P. Hughes, Morris, McCann, Myers, Nicholls, Aleksidze (Sakhvadze). Scorer: Nicholls. Reserve coach Mick McGiven said: 'He thought he might only play some of it, but we couldn't get him off. We took a 1–0 lead, good play at the back by Ruud, he found Paul Hughes in the centre circle and a good pass fed Mark Nicholls who took his opportunity well.' Shane Demetrious played right wing-back, a schoolboy in the same side as Gullit!

TUESDAY, FEBRUARY 25

Holding court at Harlington, Gullit discussed virtually every subject from Dennis Bergkamp's fear of flying to the way he deals with stress, and, of course, the vital Cup replay. His own peace of mind in the job was no guarantee of success. 'I do not think about the end of the season and about what we might have won or what we might not have won. I do not live that particular way. I have both feet on the ground and I want to keep them on the ground.' Gullit was concerned about keeping a lid on the soaring expectations, with his side favourites to win the Cup and end their twenty-six-year wait for a major trophy. 'I have never in my life stopped to sit down at home and think about all the trophies I've won. I never feel satisfied. I have won trophies wherever I've been but that was because I worked very hard and have got used to people always putting pressure on me for more. My philosophy is to think of the next match and put out a team which plays good football and which wins. Trophies can come if you do that.

'But I've got to be realistic and I don't know if I can do it for ever. I work hard, give my very best and can't do any more. It's difficult to be both player and coach. A time will come when I can only do one job. Chelsea wanted me to do this job. It took me a while to think about it but it was an opportunity. Now, after just a few months, you are saying I have to win trophies. I am very happy with our progress but I am not finished here by a long way. I am not satisfied yet with what I have done at Chelsea. I want to get better and better and what the result of that will be I do not know. I just want to keep doing things in my own way, in the way I have been doing them throughout my career.

'I am proud of my players. There was so much more inside them than they had showed before and now they are turning it round. They are doing things now that they did not know they had in them. People here don't realise there is so much interest in Chelsea throughout Europe. The interest in our team when we go away speaks for itself, the stadiums are always crowded, people come to see Chelsea because something always happens at our games now and this is a good feeling. It is having a snowball effect, too. They talk about us all the time and how we're developing. I see television programmes from all over the continent and they talk a lot about Chelsea. It means that the players are doing something that impresses people. It is the players, too, not me.'

Gullit laughed off suggestions he had fired up Leicester by branding them 'lucky', but O'Neill was furious and skipper Steve Walsh carried on that attack: 'I could understand their disappointment at not winning, but there was no reason at all for their manager to have a go at us for the way we played. Maybe he didn't realise we had been going through with injuries and suspensions. We had to put up a battling type of display to stay in the competition. We had a makeshift side then and we'd like to show them something and put them out with a stylish, passing game.' But such complaints brought no backtracking from Gullit. 'I don't worry about what I said, because I didn't lie. What I said wasn't designed to upset them. I just said what happened. It was a fact, and I don't know why they have to be upset about it. If a coach says what happened, then that isn't an insult, it's reality. I watched Fiorentina versus Juventus on TV on Sunday and Fiorentina had just one chance and scored from it. For the Juventus coach to say that was not damning Fiorentina. It was reality. I didn't say it to embarrass Leicester it was just a fact.'

Gullit had injury worries this time: Hitchcock was out with a shoulder injury, so he would not have a spare keeper on the bench, and Petrescu was carrying a calf strain. O'Neill welcomed back suspended quartet Lennon, Heskey, Izzet and Elliott. Gullit said: 'It's different when you have to go away next time after being 2–0 up, but we're at home now, and everybody knows the good football we're playing at Stamford Bridge. Our fans make it really hard for the opposition and I feel very confident about the game. It's fair to say that we helped them to get another game, but while I wasn't happy that we have to do it all over again I was pleased with the way we'd played overall. Of course they scored two goals from set pieces, and we've worked on them, we've trained about kicking the ball away instead of into our own net! We know that they might have a stronger team this time. But they had a full-strength team when we played there in the league and we won 3–1. We've nothing to worry about there.'

The players were in no mood to sit back and wait for the trophy to come to them, especially after their Filbert Street fright. 'I think there was a bit of complacency because of the team they put out that time,' confessed Sinclair. 'But even though we know they'll be stronger this time we still really fancy ourselves against them and we won't be getting distracted by Wembley yet either. We've been close in the past, and we want it badly. Ruud wants success, so do we, and that's what it boils down to. And we can promise one thing this time: if we're 2–0 up again they won't be coming back.' Newton was determined to make amends for his Filbert Street howler. 'Leicester won't be a walkover and they won't lie down for us.' The midfielder's impressive displays since returning to action in October led to Gullit suggesting he already had his own 'Paul Ince' and did not need to bid for the original. Newton, whose last senior goal was against Bolton back in November 1995, admitted there would be no better time to end his drought, but added he was fiercely intent on a Wembley victory parade in May. 'When we lost 4–0 to Manchester United in the 1994 final it was hard for me to swallow. As far as I'm concerned, and I'm sure it's the same for the rest of us who were there, I want to rectify what happened that day. I think we really feel we can go all the way this time and that we can win the Cup. We must get past Leicester first, and even then not get carried away. But after what happened up there I'd love to score.'

Hughes, veteran of four Wembley finals for Manchester United between 1985 and 1995, observed: 'Cup competitions don't usually have the same importance abroad but, even so, I think everyone knows our FA Cup is different. I know our Italians had a fair idea of what the Cup was like even before they came here, but now they know for sure. They've seen the crowds and sampled the atmosphere so far, and now they know just how special the FA Cup is in England. We messed it up a bit at Leicester, but the main thing is we didn't lose. I think you will find that, if we go two goals up again, we will not make the same mistake twice.'

While the bookmakers fancied Chelsea to make home advantage tell then go on to Wembley glory, Lennon was willing to risk a small investment elsewhere. 'I'm sure many people will say Chelsea are red-hot favourites, but I don't agree. I honestly think we will beat them. And with so many big clubs out, who knows how far we can go? We'll be a lot stronger now with the four of us back. We all saw what they did against Liverpool, but we're certainly not going there feeling scared. We're going to win.'

A final little pre-cup tie dig came from O'Neill. Gullit's TV campaign for M&Ms had just been launched. The whimsical Leicester boss remarked: 'I think you've arrived in this life when you are doing adverts for chocolate sweets. I haven't been offered any adverts, not even Walkers Crisps who sponsor us. I suppose after paying Gary Lineker they can't afford anybody else. Seriously, I'm sure our lads will be fired up. I think we're in with a definite chance of winning.' Extra police were on duty, 260 compared with fewer than one hundred, after the crowd trouble at Filbert Street.

Despite France hosting the World Cup, Leboeuf was happy to put his international ambitions on hold for Chelsea. France took on Holland in a prestigious friendly in Paris on the night of the replay, but Chelsea successfully negotiated his release with Aimé Jacquet. Leboeuf said: 'The French coach told me that he was very pleased with my form and said that Chelsea doing so well was very good for me. Of course I want to be involved for my country. You know I was very disappointed that I did not play during Euro '96, although I was in the squad. Each time a squad is announced, I hope that I am included. But really Chelsea comes first at the moment. The most important thing is that Chelsea win something. And it's helpful to me that Ruud uses the same formation as the French side. But if I'm not picked then so be it. Far more important is that I play well for my new club and they in turn do well.'

WEDNESDAY, FEBRUARY 26
Chelsea 1 Leicester City 0 (aet)
'I feel one year older.' Just when Ruud thought life on the bench was stress free! 'I felt it also. I was as tense as anybody. I'm not relaxed. It's just that I see the game a different way. I'm not a shouter, just want to watch and see where we can hurt the opposition the best, but the longer the game went on the more nervous I got. Even though I might not express myself in the way some other managers do, I still feel it. At the end of the match I felt as if I was a year older, not just two hours. That's what it's like. I felt real frustration.'

He couldn't watch as Leboeuf converted the 117th penalty. He sat motionless on the bench, his legs stretched out. When he was told, he raised his eyebrows. Real relief. Management had taken a grip. O'Neill, so emotional over the penalty incident that settled the tie, felt Chelsea might not get the breakthrough.

Gullit: 'He was wrong, I think!' When he was asked about O'Neill's furious reaction to the penalty decision, Gullit's reply was brief yet full of meaning. 'So!' His eyes opening wide, he added: 'I didn't see it so I can't discuss it.'

Johnsen, rather than Vialli, was the ace card played by Gullit to earn a quarter final place in the most controversial of circumstances. Vialli emerged from the bench for the start of the second half, after seventy-one minutes in the last seven games, with a flurry of fancy overhead and scissor kicks, but it was the basic tough guy Johnsen who turned the match just as it seemed this frenetic, intriguing replay was heading for a penalty shoot-out. The stocky Norwegian burst from defence and after a touch from Vialli steamed deep into the penalty area buffeting into Spencer Prior and crashing to the ground. Referee Mike Reed ordered a penalty minutes from the end of extra time; a penalty that Leicester claimed should never have been. A dozen players stood eyeball to eyeball in what threatened to be an ugly confrontation that fortunately never went any further than a few pushes in the chest. With ten yellow cards already handed out, the first red one was not far away.

Despite emotions running so high and with so much at stake Leboeuf was spot on with his execution of the penalty kick; the adrenalin was even running through Gullit. Leicester mounted a stubborn and courageous rearguard action, always troubling a fragile Chelsea defence on the break.

From the start Zola was in majestic form, so tricky he could have wriggled through the legs of giant cropped-haired centre-back Matthew Elliott. Zola set up numerous chances and Di Matteo was a constant threat around the penalty area with his accurate shooting. Nothing apart from the penalty could beat keeper Casey Keller.

Leboeuf headed off the line from an Elliott header one minute from the end of normal time, and in extra time it seemed to be Zola v Keller. Twice the American keeper saved mesmeric free kicks. A courageous display by Leicester in this season of the underdog. Leicester left feeling cheated, deserving the lottery of a penalty shoot-out. However, there was much relief within the corridors of power within the FA that the last remaining glamour club had made it to the quarter finals.

O'Neill expected to be hearing from Lancaster Gate after he blew a gasket at the referee. While O'Neill's comments were intemperate, his actions in attempting to speak to Reed at the end were wrong and his manner ill-fitting. O'Neill was a mixture of crestfallen, bewildered and downright furious, and articulated all those feelings. 'It's a disgrace, shocking and heartbreaking. Everyone will see it and agree it was nowhere near a penalty. If you're beaten fairly and by a proper goal you don't mind so much. You just accept it and get on with it. The referee was only five yards away. Johnsen just fell at Prior and I don't see how he could possibly have given it. This was a big competition, a big occasion and the players know they might never get a better chance of going to Wembley. The lads have come back in and told me he [Johnsen] was not touched, so it's a disgrace. Absolutely unbelievable. All people will remember in a few weeks is that Chelsea went through 1–0; the magnificent efforts of my players will be forgotten. We have put in a sensational display against Chelsea, who are a very talented side, but that decision means we are beaten, which is shocking. The efforts of my players were heroic and after going out like that, with that penalty, we are all heartbroken to be honest. But after that I'd honestly rather we'd been dumped out by Southend in the third round than lose like that. Penalties are a lottery and no way to settle an FA Cup tie, but I'd sooner have a lottery than lose that way. The players are down, absolutely down. I won't even try to pick them up tonight.'

Reed's decisions had infuriated the Leicester bench all night, with the visiting chant of 'How much have you paid the ref?'

'I think there were ten bookings,' said O'Neill. 'How many for us? Nine? At half-time I asked the fourth official to remind him you must apply the rules for both teams. I'd like to speak to him even though it wouldn't change matters. But I'd say he must go and genuinely study his own performance. We must criticise and praise our personnel and he must have a strong look at his performance. I'm probably in massive trouble now and I'm sure I'll get a letter from the FA. But he knows himself what he's done. I would rather that Zola or Vialli had whacked one in from thirty-five yards, or even that the keeper had let it through his fingers. I don't want to take it away from Chelsea, because they are a talented side who could well go all the way to win and it isn't sour grapes.'

Gullit said: 'I can understand that he might be unhappy but you always are when you concede a penalty and I don't want to be quoted that I agree he has a right to be unhappy. As far as I am concerned we deserved to win the game. We had all the chances and it just looked as though the ball wouldn't go in. I'm really proud of my team, really proud of the way they played and the way they worked.'

Gullit explained he didn't see the penalty incident clearly enough from his position on the bench to pass comment. 'The frustrating part was we played so well. The ball just didn't want to go in. Their goalkeeper was magnificent, he had magnets in his gloves. We hit the crossbar and the ball falls in his hands, we hit the post, and I was starting to think it was one of those days when we would do everything and get beaten by one lucky goal. We showed great fighting spirit. We dominated and kept searching for a goal all game long. I had the feeling we just had to win as it would have been so frustrating if we hadn't. If you look at the game as a whole you can't say we were lucky. We kept our shape and I was just telling the players it would come.'

Johnsen angrily denied he dived to win the crucial spot-kick. 'I was probably a bit off balance but I would definitely have scored. If Martin O'Neill says it wasn't a penalty that's his problem. All I know is that I went forward and was squeezed between two players. Whether or not it was a penalty, I can't judge. But if the referee gives it, that's it. Leicester were fortunate to stay in the game for so long, anyway. Their keeper played very well but it is very difficult when a side just sets out to defend all the time. Every week in training we play eight against eleven reserves who just get everyone behind the ball and hit long balls to the strikers. And we struggle to score in those games, too. It's something we have got to work on because it's happening more and more as we get better. A lot of teams are going to defend like that against us out of respect for how good we are becoming.'

Elliott, blamed by Reed for pushing Johnsen into Prior, said: 'I didn't make any contact and I've seen a video of the incident which backs me up. It's a terrible way to go out and I'm still feeling fed up. I'd love to say what I really feel but the manager has told us not to talk about it or we'll be in trouble.' Wise insisted it was fair. 'It looked a definite penalty to me. As far as I saw it Erland has gone through and he has been totally wiped out in the area. But there is a long way to go in this competition yet.'

Keller said: 'I don't blame Chelsea but maybe, instead of a third eye up on the grandstand for controversial incidents, there is a case for having two referees, one in each half. It was a bad decision. Call it cheating, a professional trick or whatever but Johnsen just went down in a heap and the referee bought it.'

Iceman Leboeuf, sporting his favourite ICE baseball cap, was in effusive mood as the last of the players in the press room. 'I may have looked calm and cool but I must admit I was nervous. There was a lot of arguing going on but I just ignored it all. I concentrated hard and said to myself "If you score this we are through to the quarter finals." I knew if I scored we would win and be another step closer to Wembley. There was a great deal of pressure on me as I ran up to take the kick, but I was sure I would score. I think we deserved the victory because we created a lot of chances. It is vital to win matches like this one and I am very happy we have done so. It is, how you say, the kirsch on the cake.' Surely, he meant cherry. 'I like cherries too.'

The amiable Frenchman was so popular he was favourite to pip Zola as Player of the Year. Leboeuf's spot-kick conversion endeared him to the fans even more.

The cultured sweeper admitted that he had told himself he simply had to score, or it would have spelled the end of his Wembley dream to follow Cantona.

'Keller had been outstanding for them, and I was sure that if it had gone to a shoot-out we would've been knocked out. I think it would've been impossible for us to have beaten them on penalties when he was in that sort of form. What I was also thinking was that I've said all season that I believe we will win the FA Cup. I swear that as I stood there waiting to take it I thought about that, and knew that I had the opportunity to score the goal that could mean we will win it. That made it the most important penalty I've ever taken. I've never missed one, but I knew I needed to score.'

Leicester's fury had not abated as Leboeuf stepped up, and he understood their feelings. 'I think it was impossible for the referee to see what had happened, it was all too fast for him, and I know I would've been bitterly disappointed if it had happened to us. But that's a pity for them! I don't play for Leicester and I can't care what they feel. There was a lot going on, but I had to clear all that from my mind. Big players, people like Michel Platini and Diego Maradona, have missed them before, so I had to stay concentrated on what I had to do. I just took a picture of the net in my mind, concentrated on where to shoot, and put it there. Now I think my dream of playing at Wembley will come true.' Leboeuf's dream was to emulate Cantona and become the second Frenchman to lift the FA Cup. 'I saw Eric Cantona lift the Cup three years ago – I cannot remember who the team was. But it caught my imagination. I wanted to win the Cup like him, and I will win the Cup.'

Leboeuf will be remembered for the ice cool penalty after all the hullabaloo, but he also made an astonishing goal-line clearance in the last minute of normal time. 'How did I get there? Just call me Zorro!' he grinned.

Leboeuf played in a Cup final two years ago with Strasbourg. 'We lost one-zero. We had to play at their home ground because they play at the Parc des Princes. Now I hope we play another final and we win this time. The French Cup is one leg and you play until penalties. No replays. We played five rounds to get through to the final. In the semi final against Metz it was a derby. Maybe there is a hundred miles between Strasbourg and Metz. We won one-zero in a big, big atmosphere. This was played in Strasbourg. The French Cup is normally a bigger atmosphere than during a championship game. If you are special you can continue or else you are, how do you say, eliminated. It is very special. Everybody knows that you can't make a mistake. In the championship you can play a very bad game but still win the championship. Not in the Cup. We reached the final in 1995, this was the first time we had done well. At Strasbourg we were always eliminated in the first round. In my first season there we lost to a Fourth Division team. It was 2–1 after, how do you say, extra time. Strasbourg was really bad. But a score like that is not unusual, like in England.

'I think over here it could be more difficult to beat Portsmouth than to beat Leicester. In the next round Portsmouth will play the game of their lives. We had problems at Strasbourg with small pitches and pitches that were very bad. We needed to be more concentrated.' Did he need a rest after such a hectic schedule of games? 'Of course. Maybe a couple of weeks. Maybe fifteen days in the Caribbean.'

THURSDAY, FEBRUARY 27

Mike Reed, area sales manager for insurance giants Commercial Union, insisted he got it right. 'It's my opinion that counts. I was only ten yards away from the incident, with a clear view of exactly what happened. I thought there was contact between Elliott and Johnsen. Elliott caught Johnsen with sufficient force to push him into Spencer Prior as he fell.' Reed, who handled international matches until forced to retire from FIFA's list after reaching forty-five in December, declared: 'I gave a totally honest decision based on what I saw. That is all any ref can do, because we don't have the benefit of twelve camera angles and sixteen slow-motion replays. I appreciate that Leicester's players were unhappy about the penalty. You wouldn't expect them to applaud it. Although I heard a few remarks shouted in my direction immediately afterwards as I walked down the tunnel towards the dressing rooms, I took no notice. No one from Leicester came to see me afterwards. It wouldn't have made the slightest difference if they had. My conscience is clear, completely clear. It was a full-blooded FA Cup contest, with no quarter asked. I thought my overall performance was satisfactory. I shan't be carrying any mental scars into my next few games, that's for sure. A referee must endeavour to keep a clear head at all times for the benefit of the teams involved. You can't afford to have your brain clouded by other issues. I arrived back home from London at 1.20am. I was up and out again by 7.45 to go to work. I haven't watched the Chelsea–Leicester match on television, listened to the radio or read the papers.'

TV cameras showed the susceptibility of match officials in key decisions, hastening the day when new technology and the all-seeing eye of the TV cameras are called upon to adjudicate. FA chief executive Graham Kelly said while measures were being investigated to see whether officials could be helped in assessing offsides and whether balls were in or out of play, fouls were down to personal opinion. 'Penalties are difficult. It is the referee's opinion that counts. He has to decide was it a foul, wasn't it a foul? The question of fouls is the most difficult area. The others are comparatively simple.' Asked whether technology or a 'third umpire' could be used to judge penalties, Kelly added: 'I think it's a very major step and maybe it's inevitable that football's got to look at it. We are talking about stock market flotations, a lot of money involved, but will it be used on Hackney Marshes on a Sunday afternoon and will it be football?'

PFA chief executive Gordon Taylor agreed with Kelly that video evidence could only have a limited use. 'I think it's inevitable that there will be discussions about whether technology can be used to ensure referees make the right decisions but it will be a question of degree. Technology could be used to decide whether the ball has crossed the line but, in the case of grey areas such as contact between players and handball decisions, it will surely be impossible to have anyone other than the referee making on-the-spot decisions. If it's going to take three or four minutes for a fourth official studying four or five different camera angles on a video, that would cause more problems than it solves.' Arthur Smith, general secretary of the Referees' Association, said: 'We are not averse to new technology coming into the game. We would have to look at it, but it would have to benefit the game in general. What we all have to remember is that football has always been a controversial game and a fast-flowing one. So if we have a third eye in the stand how long are the crowd and players going to be prepared to wait before a decision comes back to the referee, and how many camera angles will you need to ensure that decision is absolutely right?'

FRIDAY, FEBRUARY 28

Gullit called for two referees on the pitch rather than video technology. 'It would be a good idea to have two referees, and I actually suggested it a couple of years back. In basketball they have three referees on a very small pitch, and no offside either. In football you could have one referee in each half, and they'd be closer to the action. It's best if TV doesn't show what happens on the pitch from every angle. It only makes people angrier than they already are. They have special lenses and you can see if it "just touches his laces" or whatever, and you then get a lot of debate. If the referee can have some help, that's okay. Not on things like offside or penalties, but on something like whether the ball crossed the line or not. Otherwise you'd have to constantly stop the match, and the best thing is to let it flow. I also think it would be dangerous to remove the human element from refereeing. The important thing is to keep football as simple as possible.'

Gullit's philosophy is to grin and bear it. 'We've had things go against us at Chelsea. It's hard to accept but you can't do anything else.'

MARCH

Ruud breaks leg. Four goals at Pompey. On to semifinals on crutches

SATURDAY, MARCH 1

Derby County 3 Chelsea 2

Gullit was hounded for stories about his private life. He spent the morning in bed on the third floor of the plush Hilton International hotel near the East Midlands Airport, emerging at 11.30am for a pre-match meal of chicken, rice and fruit.

It wasn't Ruud's day. Newton strained a calf in the pre-match warm-up and had to be replaced in the starting line-up by Hughes, rival manager Jim Smith allowing the switch after the team sheets had been submitted to the referee. Zola rested. Johnsen failed a fitness test before kick off. Petrescu was ruled out with a calf strain. It was a disaster away day at the Baseball Ground as Vialli started a rare game.

'Things weren't too good before the match but are now considerably worse,' Rix said. 'We have got a busy programme ahead and, despite everybody saying that we have got a big squad, we are now down to the bare bones.'

Leboeuf's week descended into disaster. When his goal put the Blues 2–1 in front after fifty-two minutes he was entering football heaven. Then came the end of the fairy tale. Forced to handle Darryl Powell's shot on the line, Leboeuf knew he had to go. He was heading for the dressing room almost before referee Alan Wilkie reached for his top pocket.

Croat Aljosa Asanovic put Derby level from the penalty spot, leaving Chelsea almost half an hour to survive with ten men. Gullit immediately replaced Vialli to take Leboeuf's sweeper role. Fifteen minutes later the great Dutchman was gone as well, limping heavily after apparently damaging ankle ligaments. No Zola, and the lack of experience in the dwindling line-up, cost them Derby's injury-time winner by Ashley Ward.

Leboeuf, a true French philosopher, said: 'Football is like life. You think you have cracked it, then everything collapses. I had the first intimation of mortality when we changed ends at half-time. The wind was against us in the opening forty-five minutes, yet it was still blowing hard in our faces for the second period. But I scored my goal, and you hope that the match will remain in your favour. Some hope! It was my intention to head the ball off the line, until it received a slight deflection. I was thrown off balance, and it became pure instinct to stick up my hand to prevent the ball entering the net. Perhaps it would have been better for me to have let the goal happen because then I would have stayed on the pitch.'

Gullit faced being out for the rest of the season with a badly damaged ankle as fitness and suspension worries threatened to destroy the season. However, Rix insisted that Chelsea could still win the championship as Gullit was helped onto the team bus. 'It's a big enough problem dealing with a mounting injury list – now it looks like Ruud could be out for the season. He will receive a check-up at the hospital tomorrow but it looks very bad and we suspect ligament damage. A few things went wrong today but we can't have any complaints about the sending-off of Leboeuf. He handled the ball. It's been a hard, pressurised month for us and a lot of the players look jaded. But we have some big games coming up so it's important for us to sort things out. We haven't given up on the title by any means.'

MONDAY, MARCH 3

Gullit would be in plaster for a month after an X-ray at Charing Cross Hospital revealed a hairline fracture in the ankle. With his leg immobilised in plaster just below the knee, Ruud said: 'Someone fell on my ankle. I tried to see if I could carry on, but it felt like a break. It's painful! But, okay, that's how it is. My morale, even then, was not down. Maybe this is something that had to happen. I don't know why, but you can feel like that sometimes. After all, a lot of strange things happened in that game. Even nature went against us. In the first half the wind was against us, and at the start of the second half it was against us again. But I feel strong. I've been in this situation before so many times when things are going well, then strange things happen. There's a feeling around you and you have to be aware. It can be anything – an accident, the people around you, jealousy. I'm a patient and tolerant person, but now I feel like a beast is coming out. Not a violent animal, but something which gives everyone a lift – an extra force, giving me more energy. Saturday has gone. Let's all be strong for it. We still have to do well in the league.'

The season looked a write-off for Ruud with this, his third serious injury. He had made his first appearance as a player in October after a knee operation and had started only seven games, although he's regularly selected himself as a substitute. His absence deprived the Cup favourites of another valuable option as they faced a growing injury list ahead of a critical period of six games in eighteen days.

Physio Mike Banks felt Gullit faced a lengthy lay-off if a scan showed up ruptured ligaments too. Banks said: 'Ruud has a hairline crack in the fibula, which is the bone on the outside of the ankle. If there's no serious ligament damage we can expect to have him working quite hard again in about six weeks, but if he has damaged ligaments as well he would have to be out for longer than that. We will do a scan later this week. Ruud is under no illusions about how long he could be out and how hard he will have to work to get back.'

Williams explained why Zola was rested. 'It has been a long time without a break for Franco and people also have to remember he has been travelling with the Italian squad as well as coming to terms with a big move to England. He will be assessed again tomorrow before Ruud picks the team to face Blackburn.'

Ade Mafe felt the extra time in the cup took its toll. 'The emotional, mental and physical stress is immense. Especially against Leicester, with the extra time. The one thing the foreigners have said several times is that they've come here to win trophies. And the Cup is our best chance. Extra time took a lot out of them. If it had just been a ninety-minute game it would not have been so bad. But it was on the line. Perhaps they all put an extra twenty per cent into extra time and paid for it on Saturday. Both teams looked tired. We didn't have our usual fire in our bellies, and when you're tired you make sloppy errors. There were a lot of tired legs and tired bodies.' Mafe toned down training: rest was all-important. 'We're doing the minimum now to keep engines ticking over. Too much training will make them more tired, then in games there'll be nothing left.'

Tickets were sold out for the Cup quarterfinal, an instant 15,500 sell-out. The 2,000 allocated to Chelsea sold out in sixty-seven minutes, hundreds of disappointed fans being turned away. Less than 1,000 tickets went on sale at the First Division club at 9.00am, and were snapped up within two hours of the ticket office opening.

Di Matteo received the *Evening Standard* Footballer of the Month award for February from Zola at the training ground – a handsome cast bronze limited edition statuette and a magnum of Moet. 'This will look particularly nice in my drawing room.' But, pointing to the champagne, he added, 'I will look forward to drinking very much – not now, of course, but when we have something to celebrate, like reaching the FA Cup Final.'

Gullit said: 'He has played well, growing all the time, and what has been unusual for him is that he's been scoring goals. In Italy he didn't score when he had to hold all the time. I knew his qualities, I knew he would do well and it is good to see.'

Di Matteo had finally settled in after a disruptive start. 'I have only one complaint – I have a nice apartment near the Royal Albert Hall but whenever there is a concert there the parking is terrible. That apart, London is a good city in which to live. When I have spare time I like to go shopping for clothes, go to the theatre, have dinner with my friend Gianfranco. Yes, life is very good to me. At the moment though, I have no spare energy for these things. There are so many matches that when I go home I just like to rest and keep my energy for the next game. It's no problem, though. We played a lot of matches in Italy too and it is the same for everybody, I think.

'The most important thing is that the football has been so enjoyable. I like the fairness on the pitch. Here it is important to win, of course, but it is still a game. Players can still have a smile on their faces. In Italy it is too often a battle. I also enjoy the crowds here. They give their teams good support and they are very enthusiastic. For Lazio I was the third or fourth defender and, if I was lucky, I would have one opportunity to shoot in a game. Playing for Chelsea, I am able to go forward more and I enjoy that. I have already scored six goals this season and that equals the best in my career.'

Rix said: 'I couldn't be happier that Roberto has won this award. He's a credit to himself and the club. He's always on time, he never misses training and he's very conscientious. He will come and make private points about the team to both Ruud and myself and, importantly, the lads like him a lot. Gianfranco grabbed the headlines after the match against England and quite rightly – he's an exceptional player – but I thought Roberto was the best player out there that night. He's top quality. I can't put it better than that, and at £4.9m at today's prices he's one of the bargains of the season.'

Duberry returned from a two-week holiday in Florida still with his leg in plaster, but the surgery was successful and he faced a tough summer lengthening the calf muscle and tendon.

TUESDAY, MARCH 4

Reed was dropped for the rematch between Chelsea and Leicester City to be played on April 19 in the Premiership. Reed's penalty decision incensed the Leicester fans so much that his car, which also contained members of his family, was attacked at traffic lights in London on the way home, and police were concerned that his earlier appointment for the league match would create problems.

WEDNESDAY, MARCH 5
Chelsea 1 Blackburn Rovers 1

Gullit, watching the match on crutches, was told to cut his dreadlocks by acting Rovers boss Tony Parkes! Ruud offended Parkes by accusing Blackburn of playing for a point. Parkes saw his side claw their way closer to Premiership safety then laughed at suggestions that they had come to put the shutters up on the Cup quarterfinalists.

'I don't want to get into a row with Ruud because he's a proper manager and I'm only a caretaker boss. We all saw what happened out there and if he thinks that we didn't want to win then he probably needs a haircut.'

Gullit's injury-depleted side looked jaded just four days ahead of the vital Cup tie. 'The most important thing was just to come through this game with no more problems. They came there to stop us and we weren't one hundred per cent. We did what was necessary and I'm happy with my players' efforts, but there really wasn't much to get excited about.'

Gullit confirmed that he would not play again this season. 'I'm not in any pain but I don't rate myself for the rest of the season. So I'll just concentrate on my coaching and although I can't hop around any more I have a very comfortable chair.'

Gullit put a brave face on the injury worries hindering Chelsea's form in the most critical phase of the season but admitted he might go into the transfer market before the deadline at the end of the month. Newton was out for several weeks after a knee operation, Petrescu, Clarke and Johnsen struggled with minor knocks, but most worrying was that Zola was carrying a pelvic strain. Gullit said: 'It is difficult getting the type of players we want at this stage. We will see what happens in the next few days. There may be some news. We have some injuries now and would maybe like to bring somebody in.'

Zola missed two presentable chances in a dismal first half and the second period was not much better until by far the best of the action was squeezed into a single minute just after the hour mark. Per Pedersen, Blackburn's new £2.5m striker from Danish club Odense, opened his scoring account in only his second start with a brave flying header from danger-man Jason Wilcox's cross. Minto equalised with a searing twenty-five-yard blast just seconds later. 'I can't recall much else worth talking about,' admitted Gullit. 'The main thing is we came through without more damage. And we could emerge even stronger from this period because people have come in and shown they can do a good job when others are tired or injured. Under the circumstances we did pretty well. I was pleased that our most important players did a good job out there. Dennis Wise was a great example and is a great captain. Frank Leboeuf and Mark Hughes did well and Frank Sinclair is in great shape.'

The Blues had dropped to eighth in the Premiership, with just two out of a possible last nine points, leaving a Wembley triumph as their best bet to qualify for Europe.

THURSDAY, MARCH 6
No day off. Training, however, consisted of more relaxation therapy in the hotel swimming pool and sauna in addition to the regular massage sessions.

Discussion centred on the Cup. Zola was confident he'd be fine for Pompey despite his pelvic strain. 'It's such an important game for us because we need to go on in the Cup and of course we'll be giving our best to do that. I have a little problem but I hope to have recovered by the end of the week.'

Hughes was still convinced the side were close to success. 'We have done so well so far this season, but we need to go the next step now. We've got a great opportunity this year and it'd be a great shame if we didn't do it. We've all got goals here and obviously it's a shame that Ruudi's not going to be involved now but he's going to point us in the right direction and hopefully we can do it for him.'

Paul Parker signed for Chelsea, having been released by Ferguson on a free transfer last summer. He was snapped up on a free by Gullit on his return from two months in Hong Kong, where he'd played exhibition matches. Parker had returned to find a message on his answerphone from former team-mate Hughes. 'I thought Mark was just looking to get together for a pint, and when he told me Chelsea were keen to sign me until the end of the season I was gobsmacked.

'When Chelsea contacted me I didn't know where I was going or what was to become of me, even though at thirty-two I know I have at least four good seasons left. Chelsea are a club heading for the big time. When we used to play them they never expected to beat the big boys but now they do. This is a great chance for me to prove I've still got something to offer. The boss, Ruud Gullit, knows exactly what he wants. Alex Ferguson thought he was doing me a favour when he gave me a free transfer, but it has backfired, because the feeling in football was that if United got rid of me then I must be injured.'

Williams said: 'Paul is an experienced defender who was available and not Cup-tied. He'll give us valuable cover for the five games in twelve days coming up.'

Parker was not registered in time to play at Portsmouth but was available for any replay.

Another Gullit target was Beagrie. Frank Clark confirmed: 'Chelsea did contact us about taking Peter on loan but he wants to stay here and battle for his first-team place.' Chelsea wanted the tricky left winger on loan for the rest of the season with a view to a permanent deal.

Youngsters Paul Hughes and Mark Nicholls were awarded new contracts for three-year deals, reward for breaking into the first team.

FRIDAY, MARCH 7

Venables took charge of a top-secret Portsmouth training session. Tel, a Wembley hero with Tottenham in 1991, was invited to lend his tactical nous by Fenwick. New chairman Venables, who had bought control of the club for £1 the previous month, was hailed by Fenwick as Pompey's ace in the battle of wits with Gullit. 'Terry and I have studied videos and we won't be in any rush to fling ourselves at them. This is more of a marathon than a sprint and we're quite prepared to go the distance over two games if necessary – right down to penalties. Chelsea are the favourites and the fashionable side left in the Cup, but the way they play gives us a chance. If we are patient enough we will get good chances against them.'

Gullit admitted he was more worried about Venables returning to the training ground to mastermind a quarter final giant killing. 'I haven't seen Portsmouth, but I've a great admiration for what Terry Venables did with England in the summer. He will be very influential on Sunday. He's an authority on the game and knows how to make the players work with each other.'

He clarified Zola's position after rumours that Zola was mentally and physically drained after sixteen weeks in English football and had to recover at a health farm. 'He has been given treatment and massage, like several players who are feeling tired. He's played a lot of games and has spent time away with Italy but he's one hundred per cent.

'Zola and Di Matteo have played a lot of games because they were involved in Euro '96, so naturally they have been a bit tired at times. No one is a robot and no one can play on top form all the time. We have to use him carefully and save his energy. We did the same with Roberto Di Matteo and he is playing well again after a rest. Franco has had a couple of slight injuries but it is not a worry. I certainly believe in Franco, just as I did in Roberto earlier this season when we put him aside for a few matches.'

Gullit would be happy if his team pushed him into retirement as a player. 'I want to get to a position where the team are strong enough not to need me playing. I am not aiming to play again this season although, physically, it could be possible.'

SATURDAY, MARCH 8
Leboeuf shaved his head for the Cup!

'My wife Betty did it for me and I must say that it's better like this, but it is bloody cold! I just thought to myself, "You have a hole in your hair here, another here and another there. What's the point? You might as well get rid of it all." We bought a razor and hey, *voilà!*'

He added, 'We have a good chance to win the FA Cup because so many top clubs have been eliminated. Chelsea doing well, winning cups and playing in Europe, will help my international career, too. How about winning the FA Cup with Chelsea in May and the World Cup with France next year?'

SUNDAY, MARCH 9
Portsmouth 1 Chelsea 4

The coach arrived at the end of the A3 and a police motorbike appeared waving to the driver to follow him. The escort took the coach all the way to the ground, stopping near the main entrance. A steward ran over, directing the first person off the coach to the dressing room – only for the policeman to realise that it was not the team bus but a supporters coach! After a severe reprimand the police tore off to the team hotel, arriving just in time to provide the right escort.

A tracksuited Gullit hobbled onto the pitch at 12.25pm to take his first look at Fratton Park. There was no sign of pre-match nerves as Ruud jigged to the music, then raised a crutch in Bates's direction after spotting his chairman in the stand.

The edicts of TV dictated a 1.30pm kick off.

Chelsea refused to be intimidated, giving Gullit revenge on Venables for Holland's 4–1 defeat in Euro '96. Unfortunately for Venables he didn't have England's stars at his disposal and Fenwick resorted to a none too clever battery of long balls. 'Sparky' Hughes suffered most as referee Jeff Winter added six minutes of injury time at the end of the first half when Leboeuf, Sinclair and Wise also needed treatment. Incredibly, the referee allowed play to carry on with Hughes and Sinclair clobbered; when the ball went out of play Thomson received a yellow card.

Leboeuf did more than anyone to ensure Chelsea's passage to their third semifinal in four years. Roughed up by Wimbledon earlier in the season, there have been those who believed Leboeuf was Chelsea's soft centre. But Leboeuf was rock solid and on the rare occasions Pompey managed to breach a well-organised midfield Leboeuf was everywhere.

Knight made a brave flying block from Zola, who brought down Minto's cross, and the keeper hurt himself in the process in the eighteenth minute. Inevitably it was Leboeuf, initiating attacks from the back, who launched a magnificent long ball in the twenty-sixth minute, taking out two defenders. Hughes cracked it into the corner after just one bounce. He had his shirt pulled once more and Pompey paid the price with an intelligent Zola free kick in the forty-fourth minute. With Venables and Fenwick working relentlessly with dead-ball situations all week, their defence was caught flat-footed as Zola lined up for one of his specialist free kicks five yards outside the box. Instead of one of his vicious curling shots, the impish Zola chipped the ball to the far post where Clarke stole in unmarked. His header was saved but Wise finished off on the line.

Hughes was chopped down again a few minutes into the second half. Young Paul Hughes supplied Roberto Di Matteo who burst into the box, changed direction but curled his shot the wrong side of the post. That inspired Pompey to their best period, a flurry of attacks until they were really finished off by the third goal in the fifty-fifth minute. Awford fumbled the ball and then slipped, allowing Mark Hughes freedom to attack. He linked with Di Matteo, and the final pass was perfect for Zola to slide past the keeper.

Di Matteo came off for a rest, and was replaced by Burley. Pompey refused to give up and pulled back a goal seven minutes from time when Hall cut the ball back for Burton to shoot past Grodas from close range. No one really believed that would inspire a comeback and Knight pulled off a wonder save from Burley, Zola struck the post from a rebound and Knight saved again from Paul Hughes. The keeper was injured and the last thing he needed was a back pass, his clearance going straight to Wise. A slick one-two with Hughes and Wise virtually walked in the fourth four minutes from time. It could easily have been seven or eight. Chelsea had the taste for the FA Cup after slipping out of the top six in the Premiership winning only one of their last five matches prior to this tie.

Hughes had managed to keep the lid on his boiling anger, something he has failed to do in the past. 'For ten years or so I've always retaliated; got my own back. Now I've realised it has been a waste of time. I should have saved my energy.'

Leboeuf hobbled off in the seventy-sixth minute, making Vialli strip – eager to come on. But Johnsen was chosen and Vialli dressed again, furious.

New Cup favourites Middlesbrough were paired with a Second Division side in the semifinal of a major competition for the second time this season. Struggling in the Premiership but still in the cups and their luck seemed to be holding. After their 2–0 quarterfinal win at Derby, Middlesbrough drew Chesterfield in the semis. Chelsea drew the dreaded Wimbledon!

Odds were quoted at 6–4 Middlesbrough, 15–8 Chelsea, 5–2 Wimbledon and 16–1 Chesterfield.

MONDAY, MARCH 10

A noon semi-final showdown at Highbury, decreed the FA.

Joe Kinnear hoped Highbury would remain a lucky venue for Wimbledon. 'We couldn't be more pleased. We just hope our luck holds out at Highbury because we're unbeaten in the last nine matches there against Arsenal. We're up against a great team in Chelsea, who have some marvellous players, but we beat them earlier in the season at Stamford Bridge and when it comes to semifinals anything can happen.'

Middlesbrough were to kick off at 3pm against Second Division giantkillers Chesterfield at Old Trafford in the other semifinal.

Chelsea pleaded with the FA to stage their semi at Wembley. Highbury, with a capacity of 38,000, just wasn't big enough to accommodate all the Chelsea fans. Hutchinson said, 'Purely from a supporters' point of view we suggested Wembley. We faxed the FA, requesting that the match be played at Wembley. We have a database of 40,000 fans and we know they will all want tickets. We could certainly have filled Wembley, but the FA in their wisdom have opted for Highbury.' Bates, himself on the FA Council, said: 'It would have made sense to play it at Wembley and so let all our fans see the game. But tradition and the Colonel Bogeys prevailed. Stuff the supporters – tradition comes first. So Highbury it is and some 20,000 supporters won't get tickets.'

The big concern for Chelsea was the split of tickets. Hutchinson canvassed the FA for a bigger proportion than Wimbledon who had the lowest average attendance in the Premiership at 11,000. Hutchinson argued: 'Last season we received 17,000 tickets, compared to Manchester United's 19,000.' Chelsea were fairly successful awarded 19,881 by the FA, slightly more than Wimbledon's allocation of 15,058, but nowhere near enough to cater for the massive demand.

There wasn't even agreement over the strips. The result was that Chelsea were to wear their change yellow colours and Wimbledon red shirts, black shorts and red socks – no blue in sight. Hutchinson explained: 'Clubs must agree, otherwise both change. Wimbledon, classed as the home club because their name came out first, thought they should have the choice, but this is not what the rules say. In such circumstances the FA normally toss a coin. Chelsea were happy for this decider but Wimbledon declined.'

WEDNESDAY, MARCH 12
West Ham United 3 Chelsea 2

Wimbledon crashed at the last hurdle before Wembley in the Coca-Cola semifinal second leg. A 1–1 draw with Leicester at Selhurst Park gave O'Neill's side a passage to the final on the away-goals rule after a goalless draw at Filbert Street. The Dons were gunning for Chelsea. Earle said: 'Europe is very important to us. We had three opportunities to get there, now we only have two. We hoped to face Chelsea in the cup final but will be well psyched up for the game. I think we have the advantage because we have a good record against them and beat them 4–2 earlier in the season. Last night's defeat will only spur us on. We know we are a good side and we refuse to let this season peter out.'

A place in the FA Cup semifinals did not satisfy Gullit as he wanted to ensure a place in Europe via the league. The decision to rest key players Hughes and Di Matteo meant a rare start for Vialli and a return to the team for Burley. Perhaps the player missed most was influential sweeper Leboeuf, out with a calf tear and missing from Sunday's clash with Sunderland with a one-match ban. Clarke took the sweeper's mantle, with both Gullit and Lee on the long casualty list. Fourth-choice keeper Nick Colgan made his debut, and couldn't be faulted. There were four changes from Portsmouth, with Vialli making only his third start in seventeen games.

Vialli must have wondered whether his call-up was a reward for his patience or a reprimand for daring to criticise Gullit's decision to leave him on the bench. For

Vialli came face to face with Julian Dicks. In the battle of the baldies the Italian was the master in the first half and he might have easily had a hat-trick. Slick in their passing, cutting the Hammers' defence wide open, it was no surprise when Chelsea scored, albeit from an error by Bishop in the twenty-fifth minute. A poor pass intended for Breacker was easily cut out by Zola. He attacked down the flank, his square pass was perfection and Vialli was able to pick his spot for his eleventh goal of the season.

The warning signs came after thirty-three minutes when a Bilic header from a Michael Hughes corner was headed off the line by Petrescu. Zola almost increased the lead five minutes before the interval with a cross shot just touched round the post by Miklosko. Boos rang out at the end of the first half and Redknapp made his feelings known to his players in the dressing room. He sent out Hugo Porfirio and Danny Williamson in place of Bishop and Rio Ferdinand. It paid immediate dividends. Williamson's pass found the Portuguese star who began to cut inside when Sinclair challenged just inside the area. A slow-motion, delayed-action decision by referee Keith Burge infuriated Sinclair and Wise carried on the protest once the dust had settled on this amazing Hammers comeback. The fifty-third-minute penalty, perfectly executed by Dicks, was the platform for their thrilling fightback. A few minutes later Dicks cracked a shot at keeper Colgan. It spilled to Dowie two yards from goal, but somehow he contrived to strike the bar and the keeper caught the ball from the rebound. The Hammers suffered a setback when substitute Williamson had to be substituted himself through injury in the fifty-ninth minute. But Chelsea surrendered the impetus and the East Enders went ahead after sixty-eight minutes. Burley over-hit a pass intended for Zola and the counter-punch was a flick on by Dowie for Kitson to cruise into space and shoot into the corner.

Another substitution changed the course of the game again, this time Gullit sending on Hughes in place of Petrescu. Five minutes from the end saw a Zola back heel and Minto showed superb control and accuracy with a deep cross to the far post where a towering header from Hughes conjured the equaliser. The odds favoured a Chelsea win even with the last few minutes remaining but from a Hughes corner Dowie won the ball in the air and Kitson headed into the corner. The Hammers celebrated only their third Premiership win in sixteen games, deflating hopes of climbing back into the higher echelons of the Premiership.

THURSDAY, MARCH 13

Day off. Quite a few players travelled together to Cheltenham for the Gold Cup – but there were no winners. Wise said, 'Well, there was one horse everyone won on called Sparky's something. Otherwise we lost all our dough.'

It was another unique experience for the foreigners. Vialli said, 'We enjoyed ourselves having the journey, having lunch together, betting on the horses and losing, and drinking, and coming back by coach. That was a very nice, very long, very hard day, but I enjoyed it a lot because I share the team spirit with all my team-mates.'

Who ate all the pies? Wise recalled: 'We tried to introduce Luca to steak and kidney pie. I think he only ate the pastry. He couldn't believe it. The Ities eat funny food. Robbie eats rubbish, all the things we've been told not to eat. I can't believe that. I reckon he could be a right little fatty when he gets older. He's not doing bad now, though, is he?' And, of course, he was caught eating an ice cream when he went to Milan!

Evenings are a time for expensive dining out. Vialli joked, 'Every time you go out for dinner in London with Roberto and Frank Leboeuf I spend three or four hundred pounds because they never want to pay so I pay, and you can spend a lot in London. You can be ripped off if you go out in the wrong place. Every time I call Ruudi to go out he's always engaged – with Dennis.'

Frank Leboeuf likes his surroundings and his new career so much he has no reason to leave. 'I had never visited England, not even on a day trip, not even a school trip. I was looking forward to being a tourist. But I had to spend my first couple of nights in this country in a hotel at Heathrow, near the training ground. Boring! I couldn't wait to sample life in London. I wanted to settle into London life as quickly as possible so we went house-hunting as quickly as possible. We had one house to look at in Windsor and another in Fulham. We wanted to be close to everything and refused to go to Windsor. We love our Victorian house, it makes us feel very English.'

He went on, 'It's true what you hear about London taxi drivers – they really do behave as if they've known you for ever. I took a taxi home one evening recently and the driver started chatting to me about football. He said all his family were big Chelsea fans and that they would love to meet me. I couldn't believe it when he suggested I call at his house for a cup of tea on the way home. Because he also lived in Fulham he suggested we could go to his house on the way home to mine. I was very amused and didn't want to refuse him. So we parked outside his house, the cabby marched me in, asked me to wait a minute while he shouted out to his wife and four children and then brought me into the living room, shouting, "Surprise!" They couldn't believe it.' Frank illustrated their shock; he opened his mouth wide with staring, disbelieving eyes. 'One of them had a Chelsea shirt on. They all just stood there staring at me with their mouths open. I stayed with them for about half an hour before the guy drove me home. It was very funny but also very endearing. It would never have happened in France.'

His relationship with his coach has been another culture shock. 'He sometimes calls me "Frankie", then it's "lovely boy" when he wants to make fun of me. I know when he's angry with me – he calls me Leboeuf.' It was simple to follow most of the nicknames ... 'Sparky', 'Wisie', 'Clarkie'. 'I liked to call Scott Minto Hugh Grant, but since he changed his hair cut I call him Mr Bean. He wasn't too keen on his first nickname. Gwyn Williams was Slaphead 1, Luca was Slaphead 2, and I was Slaphead 3.'

FRIDAY, MARCH 14

Gullit ruled himself out of the FA Cup Final, assuming the Blues beat Wimbledon. 'Normally a break takes around six weeks to heal, and then you have to build up your muscles again. To get the power back will take time and, in any case, I'm not thinking about the final or semifinal.' But he was still thinking about carrying on as a player.

Ruud was far more concerned after just two points from their last four league games. He demanded a fresh assault on the Premiership's top six after watching his side slump to eighth. He issued a blunt ultimatum: be more ruthless, concentrated and clinical or there's a big danger of failing to make Europe. 'I told the players before the Cup tie at Portsmouth it was important to finish as high as possible in the Premier League. At the moment our league position doesn't reflect our potential. We've played some good football, but that's not enough. You have to translate that into winning, and for me the Premiership is our most important route to Europe.

That is your stage, where you do it all year. It's where you make your points week in, week out. If we were more concentrated and ruthless we would have so many points more. At least it shows what we are capable of. I don't like to look too far into the future at things like cup finals and that's what I want to transmit to the players.

'Having said that, I'm happy with the way the players reacted after the West Ham game – they did not go round pointing the finger at someone else but looked at their own contributions. I think they are coming round to the fact that we can succeed without me on the pitch. These players are better than they think they are and if they can win games without me I won't be hurt by that at all. As their coach, I will be proud of them. If you look at how much certain players have improved their game this year, it's incredible. You've got Dennis Wise playing at a really high standard every week, Scott Minto, Frank Sinclair and Eddie Newton have made great strides, Steve Clarke has had an excellent season and everyone can see how well Mark Hughes is performing. That makes me a very happy man. All that they achieve this season they will have done for themselves. And next season it will be easier because they know the system.'

Minto, one of the players singled out for praise, was sweating on a new contract as well as a place in Chelsea's march on Wembley. Signed for £775,000 by Hoddle three years ago, the former England under-21 international had finally established himself in the side after injuries disrupted his first two seasons at the club. But Gullit's daring bid for Maldini cast a shadow over Minto's long-term presence in the side. Minto said: 'There's a lot of pressure because Ruud can bring in big-name internationals at the click of his fingers – he has that pulling power. I don't just want to establish myself for the cup side but next season as well. My contract's up in the summer and I'm looking for another good one for next year. If the manager brings in a player like Maldini, who's probably the best defender in the world, there's nothing you can do about it. But all these world-class players coming into the club don't make me depressed or think I haven't a chance here. They make me work even harder. Anyone can see this club is going places. We're going to win trophies in the next couple of years, and I want to be part of that.'

Di Matteo was recalled after a one-game rest, Grodas had recovered from a groin injury, Parker was on the bench, alongside Vialli, dropped despite scoring at West Ham. Vialli made way for Hughes.

SUNDAY, MARCH 16
Chelsea 6 Sunderland 2

Seventh in the table. Seven floors of the hotel infrastructure were now visible at the Bridge. The giant screen had been in operation for several weeks. Construction of the flats and hotel complex was taking shape and so, too, was the team. Bates observed: 'You can notice the difference in the eleven days since the Blackburn game. The contractors are to be applauded for the efforts to catch up the lost week when high winds stopped work.'

The wind of change was still blowing fiercely through the Bridge. Fortunately Ruud has the perfect temperament to cope with a Chelsea team that's a nightmare in defence but a dream in attack. On a balmy afternoon in west London Italians Zola, Di Matteo and Vialli must have felt they were back in Italy. Gullit could smile as his team rattled up six goals but for Reid there were a few more grey hairs. Gullit, in contrast, sat impassively on the bench admiring the inventiveness, adventurousness and fluency of his star-studded side. But even three goals ahead their defence was still capable of throwing the game away.

The opening strike from Zola in the thirty-ninth minute was magical in its execution. Wise and Hughes combined as Petrescu's cross was met perfectly on the volley.

Zola, with so many options open to him, in the forty-third minute bamboozled the defence before he directed a precision far-post cross, picking out both Myers and Sinclair unmarked. Marginally on side, Sinclair's header bounced tantalisingly just under the bar.

In desperation Reid made two changes for the start of the second half, throwing on Paul Stewart and Alex Rae in place of Mullin and former Chelsea player Gareth Hall. Chelsea were soon three goals up when an astute Di Matteo pass, first time on the volley, found Zola running into space. His shot was brilliantly saved by French keeper Lionel Perez, only for Petrescu to follow up and whip a first-time shot past the keeper. It seemed only a question of how many goals would be scored in front of the 24,027 crowd basking in the glorious sunshine and illuminating football.

Then both Reid's substitutes scored within the space of two minutes. A deep cross by Bridges should have been claimed by Grodas but he missed and Stewart applied the final touch from close range on the hour. Another cross frightened the life out of a shaky defence, missing the suspended Leboeuf, and in the scramble Rae brought Sunderland right back into the game. In fact, the club struggling against relegation almost equalised in the sixty-fourth minute when Grodas's punch was hooked over the bar by Gray.

Just as Sunderland could smell a point, Hughes superbly anticipated a back pass from David Kelly intended for Andy Melville, raced past the last defender and beat Perez in the seventy-ninth minute.

With just five minutes left, Vialli came on in place of Zola – time enough to terrorise the defence. Perez tackled him on the edge of the box. But when Petrescu put Vialli through on the stroke of full time he unselfishly squared where both Di Matteo and Hughes were unmarked, and it was a gift for Hughes. A minute into injury time Di Matteo claimed the sixth from Petrescu's pass.

Gullit savoured the euphoria of Chelsea's biggest win of the season, the first time they'd scored six goals for seven years (6–4 at Derby) and the first time they'd rattled up six at the Bridge for nine years (6–2 v. Plymouth in the Full Members Cup). But he talked about his personal 'hurt' over Vialli. Gullit had planned to bring on Vialli after going three up, but as he was about to send him out Reid's team amazingly came back with two goals. Gullit left Vialli on the bench until the last five minutes. It was even worse at Portsmouth when he didn't come on at all. 'What is hurting me the most is that every time I want to put him in, the opposition score a goal and I have to wait to see how my team responds.'

A wonderful start and a breathtaking finish, but what a woeful period in between. Enough, though, for Chelsea to climb above semifinal opponents Wimbledon in their quest to guarantee a place in Europe next season.

There had been bookings for Hughes and Wise. Hughes was out of the clash with Arsenal, having topped twenty-one points. Gullit added: 'They were fighting for it, which is good to see, something to admire. It's never easy when you play a team that's struggling against relegation. Perhaps the best thing for me was the reaction of my players in the dressing room at the end. They knew that we'd been cruising it and then made some bad mistakes for their goals, and in the dressing room they were discussing the goals we'd conceded rather than the ones we'd scored.'

Zola strolled into the press room, first for an interview with the Italian journalists, then, without the safety net of the interpreter, for a full English conference – though Gary Stalker wasn't far away with a helpful word or two. Zola delivered an I-love-you-too message to Vialli, almost embarrassed to be keeping his friend out of the team. Zola's partnership with Hughes was the reason Vialli had started just three of the last eighteen games. Despite his eleventh goal of the season at West Ham, Vialli had been relegated to a late walk-on role. Zola said: 'I feel very sorry for Luca because he is a good player and a good man. But I imagine it isn't easy for Ruud to leave him on the bench so much either. Luca is a great player and when he has had the chance to play he has always done well, like he did at West Ham when he gave a great performance and scored. I also know that it hasn't been easy for Luca to accept that he's had to be a substitute but he respects the decision, and only a big person can do that. I respect Luca, I have to respect Mark and I have to respect the coach. The only way I know to do that is to keep playing so good.'

Vialli was guaranteed a game when Hughes was suspended against Arsenal. But Zola didn't feel he needed to rest. 'If I'm playing well I want to play in every game. If the coach wants to give me a rest that's his decision, but I want to play all the time. I'm not having a problem with my back any more, and if there isn't a problem I will play. That's how I feel. I am getting better. During the week I can now train myself. I am leaving my problem behind me. This is a very important moment for me, for Chelsea. All the players must be in good form. If you can't train you can't always play.

'There was a moment we were in difficulties and Sunderland could draw the game. It was imperative we win. In the last four games in the Premier League we did not play good football. Now we have to win on Wednesday; we can get a good place.'

Vialli's body language was unmistakable. After warming up for so long, Rix signalled that he was to come on with just minutes left. Vialli was stretching with his legs apart and his arms folded as he watched the action. When he spotted Rix he remained motionless for twenty seconds, his arms remained crossed and his face expressionless. Finally, he raced along the touchline one last time, stepped off and performed incredibly for just five minutes.

MONDAY, MARCH 17

Vialli counselled Galavotti for an article in *Gazetta*. Vialli pointedly did not criticise Gullit and again spoke of his love of living in London and playing for the club. 'The fans and the team are magnificent with me, and I couldn't ask for more. But every time I go to a match I feel a stomach ache because of the tension and because I know that I will only play if things turn a certain way. I feel myself almost wishing the opposition will score first if that means I'll get the chance to go on and play. It isn't nice at all for a player to feel pushed into these kind of thoughts. I will use the remaining months of this season to decide what I should do with my career regarding the two years I have left. I believe they are pleased with me and my attitude and do not want to sell me. Perhaps I can adjust to the stomach aches and the role of a super sub that can have its own meaning and value, even though I would like to play regularly. But I must understand whether going on like this for two seasons will cause me problems. If leaving Chelsea is the best option I will do it but it would grieve me terribly.'

TUESDAY, MARCH 18

Nelson Mandela had not forgotten how Ruud had dedicated his World and European Footballer of the Year awards to him. Now the South African leader requested Gullit and the Dutch team to play in a special match in Johannesburg. Gullit was to be approached for a last international appearance, three years after he had walked out on the eve of the 1994 World Cup Finals.

The Dutch federation agreed to play in South Africa on June 2 or 8. Gullit's departure from the Dutch national team, apparently in a dispute over tactics with then manager Dick Advocaat, had raised a storm of controversy. The Dutch federation believed it was time to mark Gullit's service to Holland.

But would he be fit to play? It looked promising. After an X-ray check on Gullit's ankle last week, physio Mike Banks said: 'It's looking very good; we won't need any further procedures.' Now he switched to a cast brace, enabling him to keep his ankle mobile while it's healing. 'That will reduce any complications after the plaster comes off.'

Leboeuf had had an ultrasound scan the day after the Portsmouth tie. Duberry started treatment and Newton was recovering from his knee surgery. There was an outside chance he might make the semifinal. Hitchcock was due to start training again. 'I'm optimistic. Everything is going well right now, though I'm not going to take any stupid risks. I don't want to run out at Highbury and let down the lads. But I'm so determined to make it.'

Gullit travelled to Milan, dined out with friends, and attended the court hearing where he won custody of his two children, but was told he can bring them to England but they couldn't stay with Estelle. Ruud had to agree to the order before an Italian court would grant him access to his children. Ruud's lawyer, Cesare Rimini, said: 'He cannot cohabit with Miss Cruyff when his children are with him, until they come to accept her.' Ruud said: 'I do not discuss family affairs.' Under the access agreement, Ruud gets the children for one week per month provided he flies to Milan to collect them and returns them home, or if Christina delivers them from Italy and comes to take them back. Christina said: 'I want the children to grow up serene. It is important they see their father but not with another woman.' But Ruud's lawyer said after the hearing: 'He got all he wanted.'

WEDNESDAY, MARCH 19

Chelsea 1 Southampton 0

Zola is presented with his award for the Goal of the Month. *Match of the Day* announced his goal against Manchester United to be number one for February, while Di Matteo's long-range strike against Spurs came second.

Hughes, known for his bulky physique and labelled Popeye in the programme, has always been noted for his muscle rather than his mind. But Zola said: 'Off the pitch Mark is a very serious man, very quiet. He reads a lot of books. It is easy to see that he is a very intelligent person, and that comes across on the pitch. Look at the goal I scored against Southampton. Yes, I was very pleased with my shot and I guess I got all the headlines. But without Mark it just wouldn't have been possible. He conceived that goal in his head long before the ball got to me. He could see the possibilities and knew exactly where he was. I stayed a short distance from him, he won the battle with his marker in the way he does so well and he delivered the ball just right in front of me to hit. He is the ideal partner for me, and I enjoy being alongside him. He allows us to keep the ball when we are in difficulty because he is so strong, and he allows me the freedom to play the way I want and work around him. Our manager, Ruud Gullit, seems very happy with the way the combination is working and so am I. We are playing well together and we both have a good feeling about the way things are going. We have already scored a lot of goals together and there is no doubt the partnership is working in the right direction.' That partnership had produced twenty goals in just eighteen games.

Gullit settled for a rare clean sheet, a scrappy victory secured by yet another wonder strike from Zola which lifted Chelsea into fifth place, leaving Southampton's eighteen-year tenure in the top flight hanging by a thread. Zola struck in the twenty-second minute while Le Tissier was a forlorn figure alongside Souness on the bench. A long clearance was chested down by Hughes and Zola cracked one of his specialist long-range shots into the top corner past Mark Taylor, the promising young German keeper who had been on trial at the Bridge earlier in the season. His eleventh goal in a mere twenty-two appearances was a lesson for Le Tissier in goal-scoring consistency. For a player supposedly exhausted, five minutes from the end Zola worked back into his own half to win the ball and run half the length of the field to take a return pass from Di Matteo, his shot bringing a full-length save.

This was not a vintage performance but it was enough to make Gullit proud. 'I don't think we played like we are used to, but we can't always play the passing game. I'm particularly proud of this victory because people say we can't fight, we can't head, we can't do nothing. But when they kicked the ball into our box we could handle it, and that means a lot to me. I'm more proud of this than when we play really good football. In games like this you also have to fight and we showed great character.'

Gullit insisted Chelsea would stay in the top five. 'From what I've seen this year, Chelsea should be in the first five for me. I'm quite happy that we're there but it's still difficult to maintain it. We have a whole lot of games against teams who are fighting against relegation and they give something extra. Southampton were fighting for everything and that makes it so hard, especially at the moment. But it's pleased me because people are always saying that we can't play this sort of game but when we do they say we didn't play well. They've always got something to moan about! They want us to win by four or three, but I'd settle for more like this, one- or two-nil.'

He was pleased with the contribution of Parker. 'I am not surprised, otherwise we would not have taken him. When you are in a side that is not playing and if you're struggling as well, it is difficult. Then you can grow in a better side.' Parker's flexibility was proving invaluable for Gullit's tactical changes.

Gullit, with a much lighter plaster and dispensing with the crutches, spoke at the tunnel entrance after the game with fellow Dutchman Ulrich van Gobbel, who cost Souness a club record £1.3m from Turkish side Galatasaray. The powerfully built defender and Ruud made arrangements to talk later. When Ruud left the dressing room he bumped into the familiar figure of Robbie Earle, who was commentating on a Chelsea game for the second time since the Cup draw. Ruud smilingly accused him of spying and Robbie had to admit he was gathering some information for Kinnear.

THURSDAY, MARCH 20

Relaxation 'training' at the hotel. Gullit said: 'It's not a clinic, just a shower, massage, bubble bath, relax. It's the second time we've been able to do it and it has worked out well. We can't do any work between games to prepare, there's not time. We played on Sunday and took one day to recover. We can't do a lot of training. This is the only thing that is hard right now. Obviously, with the more games you play the players' condition goes backward. You warm down after a game, but the rest of the time now is spent resting.'

Gullit bought a domestic player at last – Cambridge United's twenty-two-year-old Danny Granville, a top target for several Premiership clubs. The Granville deal for cash-strapped Cambridge was an immediate £300,000, with the remainder linked to appearances. Cambridge secretary Steve Greenall said: 'Danny is a hard-working left-sided defender, exceptionally quick and whole-hearted. We are sorry to see him go as a player but delighted to see him further his career in the Premiership. He's played over a hundred times for us in six years, is a product of our youth system and is our longest-serving player.'

'You have to have plenty of good young players,' said Gullit. 'We have needed extra bodies, and we have needed youth. We have so many good examples of older players who will teach youngsters like Danny Granville well. It is a good blend.'

It didn't take Wise long to comment, 'He's from London as well. Gordon Bennett! Chelsea buy a Londoner. He must be a quality lad.'

Chelsea went after numerous keepers, coming close to a deal for Welsh international Neville Southall. But it fell through days before Royle was sacked at Everton. Hutchinson said: 'Neville had a gentlemen's agreement that he could find another club and he would be released, but Joe couldn't find a replacement and it all fizzled out.' Royle blocked the move as Everton evoked the clause whereby Southall had to give twenty-eight days' notice. Just forty-eight hours after the move broke down for Southall, he was dropped by Royle. Southall would have been offered an eighteen-month deal by Chelsea had it advanced any further.

Eventually, just before the deadline, Canadian number one Craig Forrest, twenty-nine, arrived on a month's loan from Ipswich. With Hitchcock still struggling, Gullit needed cover for Grodas. Although not Cup-tied, he was ineligible for the Cup while he remained a loan player.

Gullit was also linked with Anderlecht's Nigerian defender Celestine Babayaro, who said: 'Chelsea and Inter are the most likely candidates at the moment and Chelsea say they want an answer from me soon.' The major stumbling block was Anderlecht's reluctance to sell the eighteen-year-old, under contract until 1998. Ajax were also interested in him, but Babayaro said: 'Ajax are a great club but the Dutch league is not as strong as England, Italy or Spain.' Babayaro was linked with a move to Arsenal when Rioch was in charge.

There were so many names linked with Chelsea that it was reaching epidemic proportions. Would they buy Norway centre-forward Tore Andre Flo? Or would it be Finland's Jonatan Johansson?

Johnsen turned down lucrative moves to QPR, Manchester City and Sheffield United to join home-country club Rosenborg – to play for the current Norwegian champions and use the rest of the time to cash in with a new job in finance. 'There was an approach from QPR made through an agent, and he was talking good money,' said Johnsen, 'but I need fresh goals. I am getting stale at Chelsea and I will join Rosenborg next season. I also plan to have a second career in banking. Believe it or not, it's something I've wanted to do for a long time. I don't really figure in Ruudi's plans. I get a game here and there, but although he hasn't said anything specific I know I'm not wanted at Chelsea any more.'

FRIDAY, MARCH 21

Vialli's presence on the bench was inspiring Hughes to play some of the best football of his career. 'At the moment, yes, I'm keeping him out of the side. It's very pleasing for people to say how well I'm playing – well, that's the reason. Because I've got Gianluca waiting on the bench to come in and take my place. If that doesn't inspire you to try and play your best, nothing will.'

SATURDAY, MARCH 22

Middlesbrough 1 Chelsea 0

Gullit accused his players of lacking commitment and spirit. After promising supporters that his highly acclaimed team would continue to fight for Premiership points before their semifinal, Gullit was upset by a poor performance. 'Middlesbrough showed more spirit than we did. It was disappointing that so many players played under their true standard. I expect more from a whole lot of players than that. Chelsea were not a team. There were a couple that battled but that's not enough. It upset me and it upset the team.' Gullit refused to name names, but pointed out that the forward players in particular were not involved enough.

Vialli almost made a spectacular start when he turned neatly out on the left to slip a clever ball into the area for the on-rushing Minto in the seventh minute. Minto picked out Zola in the box but, for once, his shot lacked the power to trouble keeper Mark Schwarzer.

Having rested Hughes from the starting line-up because of a slight groin strain, Gullit gave Vialli an opportunity to impress. Gullit made the point that this was 'Gianluca's chance to show everyone what he's capable of'. His ineffective performance merely underlined Gullit's astute judgement. But Vialli was not alone in failing to make much of a contribution. Zola was little better and only when Hughes was introduced in the second half did Chelsea begin to make an impact as an attacking force. Gullit said: 'I told them at half-time they should be grateful not to be down and at least we were a little bit better and got nearer to their goal in the second.'

Chelsea could not cope with Juninho, whichever formation they played in. They started with three centre-backs, but the tiny Brazilian's telling control, devastating acceleration and immaculate passing left them in tatters. At the interval they reorganised, sending on Hughes to add some bite to a toothless attack led by Vialli. Zola moved to left midfield. The reorganisation left a flat back four no less at the mercy of Juninho's wiles. In the fifty-third minute he danced between Wise and Di Matteo, slipped the ball to Mikkel Beck and then threw himself at the cross to head in the winner.

Gullit was so incensed with his side's inept showing that he couldn't bring himself to talk about their destroyer-in-chief. Asked about Juninho, he snapped: 'I'm more concerned about my players and the fact that at least six of them were not in any sort of shape.

'Mark Hughes went on for the second half and battled in a way that should have been an example to everyone. But what can you do when so many of your team fall so far below acceptable standards? International games may be coming up, but that's no excuse. Chelsea were not a team today and I expect a lot more from them. It upsets me – we have to do better than that, and not even half of them came up to the required standard. Middlesbrough fully deserved to win and we were lucky not to be two goals down at half-time. We have obviously got a lot more work to do.'

SUNDAY, MARCH 23
Zola and Di Matteo flew off to Italy to prepare for their two World Cup games. Petrescu joined up with Romania.

TUESDAY, MARCH 25
Wise was available for the semifinal. Having passed twenty-one disciplinary points, it was a two-game ban and the fixtures gave him a cup exit route. He missed the Arsenal and Coventry league games. 'I'm disappointed, obviously, missing matches but at least I'll be available for selection against Wimbledon. But I don't care if I don't play so long as we reach Wembley.' Chelsea's late lapses were threatening their European charge through a Premiership place. Wise added: 'We get ourselves in a great position by going into fifth place, then seem to mess it up.'

WEDNESDAY, MARCH 26
Zola was nominated for the Players' Player of the Year. The PFA short list for their annual awards were Zola, along with Wright, Shearer, Beckham, Keane and McManaman. The contenders for the main award, voted for by their own fellow players, were all British, plus the Premiership's number one Irish ace, Roy Keane ... apart from Zola. No Cantona, Bergkamp, Ginola, Asprilla or Ravanelli.

THURSDAY, MARCH 27
All 500 guests and celebrities left the Matthew Harding memorial service at the Queen Elizabeth conference centre in Westminster clutching a bottle of brown ale to drink his health, brewed for the occasion by the London brewery Young's and called Celebration Ale. The picture on the label was one of Matthew, raising a foaming pint.

The occasion, said the Rev. Steve Chalke, was one for tears as well as laughter. The unusual ceremony – an 'event' rather than a service, interlaced with music and videos – was a joyous celebration. Guests included Matthew's biggest hero, Peter Osgood, Southampton's Lawrie McMenemy, broadcasters Jimmy Hill and John Motson, comedian and football fan David Baddiel and injured Chelsea stars Duberry, Lee and Hitchcock. Other players were sad not to be able to make it because of training. Wise said: 'It's disappointing that I couldn't be there for him. The boss said training came first so I trained.' Labour leader Tony Blair took time out of his hectic schedule to pay tribute. Former *EastEnders* star Tom Watt spoke about their shared passion for football, although he was an Arsenal fan while Matthew showed how much he loved Chelsea. The reception afterwards in 'Football Football' in London's Haymarket was addressed by Jimmy Hill and Peter Osgood.

MONDAY, MARCH 31
For the first time there was no football over Easter, and Gullit was delighted. Certain players urgently needed a rest, notably Wise. Gullit said: 'The Easter break was what we really needed. Players like Dennis really needed it. He's played nearly every game.

But a whole lot of players didn't get it because they were away playing internationals. It is hard for them at the moment.'

Gullit dispensed with the plaster and brace. Physio Mike Banks observed, 'The brace was designed to shorten the time he spent in plaster. It helped him mobilise the ankle while stabilising it. He's now working very hard with Terry Bryne in the hydrotherapy pool and is busy trying to restore normal movement in his ankle.' Ruud was thankful to rid himself of the burden of the plaster. 'My plaster is off so I'm okay. I'm busy now trying to work again. It will take some time, but I'm happy with my progress.'

APRIL

A bad run in the League, but the Blues make it to Wembley

TUESDAY, APRIL 1

Vialli is in the reserves. A training ground friendly ends with a 2–0 win against Fulham, with goals from Joe Sheerin and Mark Nicholls. Vialli desperately needed match practice. But to be in the reserves ...

WEDNESDAY, APRIL 2

Five fire engines were called to the Bridge after smoke was seen billowing from the top floor of the hotel development. Investigators did not rule out arson at the top of a seven-storey stadium wing. The alarm was raised by security staff at the site at 11.30pm. London Fire Brigade said a small section of the top floor was affected, although there was no structural damage.

THURSDAY, APRIL 3

Ruud was about to appear wearing next to nothing on bus routes near the football club's west London stadium. His underwear-clad thirteen-foot image was to be emblazoned on buses next season in an advertising campaign for the new Ruud fashion range.

FRIDAY, APRIL 4

Ruud strolled hand in hand with his son Quincy and daughter Cheyenne at the training ground, enjoying the company of his children after all the court in-fighting. With the children over for an extended period, the next day it was a trip to Battersea Park with Ruud in dark glasses and dreadlocks hidden by a baseball cap – as if no one would recognise such an instantly identifiable figure.

As usual he was in a good mood. 'Vialli wants to stay, of course,' said Gullit. But the coach explained why he wasn't in the side. It was a touch of psychological warfare, but inevitably interpreted in huge headlines by the tabloid press. It was Gullit's way of throwing down the gauntlet, challenging Vialli to prove he can fit into the attack in the absence of suspended Hughes. The statistics can't lie, argued the boss – Chelsea had not won a Premiership match with Vialli in the starting line-up for five months. 'Every time Vialli plays we lose. If we play a certain way all the time and win, then play a different way and lose all the time it's an easy pick for the coach. I know Luca wants to show the statistics can be changed.'

Gullit purposely wanted Vialli to react, to use the big stage against Arsenal to show his value to the side. Gullit added: 'He feels two hundred per cent and wants to prove a point to the crowd. They love him and I think he will be on top form for this one. He will be on fire. That is what the staff here expect and I will be very happy if he does well and gives me a problem when I have to decide on the side for the FA Cup semifinal against Wimbledon next week. Coaches like these problems.'

But Vialli was taken aback when the next day he was labelled a jinx and branded Chelsea's bogeyman on the back pages. The man keeping him out, Hughes, was ready to extend his contract, with Gullit believing he was playing the best football of his career at the age of thirty-three. Hughes began the season fearing he might be sold off. Instead he was the reason for Vialli sitting on the bench. Hughes said: 'I'm playing in a team full of internationals and I've never been happier on the pitch. I understand the club will offer me a new deal and I would be happy to sign one.'

Because of the early kick off Gullit ordered his squad to a hotel overnight, breaking the routine for home games – something he had not done even for the New Year's Eve game. Hutchinson explained: 'The match was brought forward because of the Coca-Cola Cup Final and because it is televised. It was a choice of a 6pm kick off, or 11.15. The clubs agreed on the morning start.'

SATURDAY, APRIL 5
Chelsea 0 Arsenal 3
Ruud felt badly let down. It had been the worst performance of the season at the Bridge. What did he tell the players in the dressing room? 'You don't want to know!'

'Today I can take my conclusions by what I've seen,' was his ominous opening remark. He went on to deliver a stinging attack that left no room for doubt about his feelings. Without the suspended Hughes, Wise, Di Matteo and Sinclair, plus Leboeuf not risked, this badly depleted side had strolled in the morning sunshine as if it had been, in Ruud's words, 'an exhibition'.

You had to get up early in the morning to put one over on Wenger, but Chelsea looked as though they had forgotten to put the clocks forward. Wenger ordered his players a 7.30am wake-up call and fed them a combined breakfast and lunch. The brunch street kids looked more motivated in their quest for Europe and maybe an outside tilt at the title. Chelsea were so lethargic that they might as well have stayed in bed.

Arsenal's front line of Wright and Bergkamp were full of beans, while Vialli and Zola resembled tourists. No more 'lovely boys' for Gullit – they were bad boys. Wenger was full of pride, Gullit felt his players should be ashamed of themselves. The contrast couldn't have been more vivid as Chelsea went away with only the possibility of the FA Cup to salvage their season, but for Arsenal the day got even better as the championship opened up for them with Manchester United's shock home defeat by Derby.

Zola looked drained after two World Cup ties in four days. Vialli did little to prove Gullit wrong that his best position was on the bench. He even struck the post five minutes from the end, the rebound scraping the top of his head as he leapt for the bouncing ball. He used to be called Lucky Luca but his luck had ran out.

Only two youngsters, Morris and second-half debutante Granville, escaped the manager's wrath.

'Everybody has got to look in the mirror,' said Gullit. 'Rather than point the finger at somebody else, point it at yourselves. Everybody thought I'd come for a rest to play in England, but when I played I gave a hundred per cent; people expected it from me. When you play international football you have certain standards and you ought to see that every week. It has nothing to do with being tired – it's what's in your mind. It's too easy to blame the youngsters. Dan and Jody were let down; they needed some help and they didn't get it.

'This game was very important for us to get somewhere and they should be ashamed of themselves the way they performed. After the game they went into the middle of the pitch and said, "Oh, yes thank you". It was as if it was a friendly, a summer evening of football, and I didn't want to see my players react that way, especially after being booed by their own crowd. As a player at least I expected some passion, at least they should be angry. I saw nothing – no passion, no battling – it was embarrassing. Everybody in the stadium was astonished.'

MONDAY, APRIL 7

The Inquest. Gullit ordered his players to 'earn your money'. He told them to win all of their last six Premiership matches to guarantee a place in Europe, reminding them of their standards. He stressed he would never again accept a similar performance. Gullit's comments produced a practice match that was described as 'a bit lively'. Minto said: 'No one went out on the field prepared to give anything less than a hundred per cent, but it was just one of those days when nothing went for us. We have worked hard in training to try to put a few things right and now it is up to us to show what we can do against Coventry.'

Vialli and Gullit came face to face at a team meeting before training, but hadn't thrashed out their growing rift. Gullit and some of his players exchanged views. Inevitably, Vialli faced the axe again for the midweek game at Coventry and also for the Big One against Wimbledon. Hughes was back from a ban.

Vialli versus Gullit became a focal point of two tabloid newspapers coincidentally claiming that the manager was 'jealous' of his star player! They both made the outlandish claim that Ruud didn't like it when fans bought twenty-five Vialli shirts to every four of his. It was vindictive nonsense that Gullit would address in his own good time. But the *Daily Mail* perpetuated the attack. Holland's former national coach Thys Libregts, a man with a grudge, was allowed huge space to indulge in a character assassination. Gullit said: 'That man was quoted in a paper in Holland as saying "once in a while you have to get on Gullit's butt because you know how black people are". I couldn't have any respect for him after that. He denied saying it, but the reporter involved said he definitely did.' Ruud was unmoved by general media tittle-tattle, transfer news, even criticism, until it became personal.

TUESDAY, APRIL 8

Vialli launched a TV attack on the way he had been treated by his manager. On the *Tutto Calcio* programme Vialli could no longer contain his anger at Gullit. 'Ruud Gullit has humiliated and embarrassed me. I have become more and more surprised with the fact he continues to have a go. He has called me a loser and a jinx. That is not fair. Every manager has a duty to defend his players. I am asking him for some respect. Indeed, I would like only a little from him. I am asking from a human point of view. I believe that in the last few months I have behaved well. I have kept quiet, I have trained hard and played to the best of my ability when asked. But still there is no respect from him. It doesn't matter if he sits me on the bench or in the stand. I can go along with those decisions. What I cannot have is lack of respect from one professional to another, from a manager to a player, from one human being to another human being. These things should not be arising. But I felt I just had to say something. A great manager often takes time to get established, a lot of time. And it is not only results that are important but other things. You have to be a man in every way. You have to respect other human beings. That is what I am asking of him.

'Respect is fundamental in human relationships and should never go amiss, no matter how great a manager you are. One should first and foremost be a man. I've worked hard and well in training and I have accepted embarrassing and humiliating situations, and yet Gullit goes on picking on me. I will always give one hundred per cent – as I have done throughout my career. Let him make his decisions; it doesn't matter if he keeps me on the bench or in the grandstand. My conscience is clear.'

WEDNESDAY, APRIL 9
Coventry City 3 Chelsea 1
It was all going badly wrong, with three straight defeats.

It became a farce as Chelsea wore the home team's away outfit because they had not packed their own yellow away kit and had turned up with only their blue shirts. Referee Dermot Gallagher told Chelsea their royal blue clashed with the Sky Blues. Red-faced Chelsea officials could not persuade the referee to change his mind; under the Highfield Road lights, he felt, there was insufficient contrast with Coventry's sky blue and navy stripes. There was a stalemate in the dressing rooms. The fans thought the delayed kick off was to do with late arrivals. Chelsea's suggestion that Coventry should change their shirts was rebuffed. In the end Chelsea played in their own shorts and socks and the red and check away shirts normally worn by Coventry's reserves as they were the only ones without first-team names and squad numbers. The home club had to race off to their training ground to fetch their strip, causing a fifteen-minute delay. It might explain why Gullit's players had trouble passing to their own players!

It was a nightmare for the Blues yet just before the break Paul Hughes put Chelsea ahead, when Clarke's pass found Minto. His effort was blocked but Paul Hughes slid the ball over the line from an acute angle. Coventry's response was to score two in two minutes early in the second half through Dublin and Williams. Then Strachan played a part in goal number three from Whelan.

Gullit felt his side were saving themselves for Wimbledon. 'Maybe some of the lads were concerned about not getting injured. We didn't show the sort of passion that was required when going into the tackle. Good luck to Coventry – they took advantage. I think we have to forget it and do what we have to do against Wimbledon.'

Gullit made changes, bringing back Hughes, Di Matteo, Leboeuf, Newton, Burley and Sinclair, resting Petrescu as well as dropping Vialli. Gullit refused to respond to Vialli's comments.

He hoped his assumption that his players had their minds on that Highbury tie was accurate. This had been another shambles of a display. Gullit stood back and watched an amazing dressing-room slanging match. Clarke, skipper in the absence of suspended Wise, admitted: 'I got a bit carried away in the dressing room and said a few things, but there were a few things that had to be said. It was another second-half collapse, another poor performance. And it means we're going into a major semifinal on the back of a terrible run – and that's not good enough for the players we've got. We've got a few days to sort it out, but I don't know if that's long enough. I don't know if it helps that Wimbledon are on a bad run, but it's certainly not good enough from our point of view. With the players we've got, our performances haven't been good enough.'

Goal scorer Paul Hughes agreed. 'The boys sorted it out between themselves in the dressing room. Steve Clarke made a few points, Frank Leboeuf made a few points, and the boys and I joined in. Ruud didn't even have to say a thing. It was the best way to go about it, to have it out ourselves. Hopefully the boys will get their minds right for Sunday now. We're such a good team we should win.'

Leboeuf said: 'We seem to have a problem with our spirit at the minute and that is a big problem when you're facing Wimbledon. We have better players than them, there is no doubt about that. But if we can't match them for spirit we'll be in trouble.'

THURSDAY, APRIL 10
Ted Troost's six-foot-four presence was beginning to have a major influence in the change of direction behind the scenes. Gullit referred to him as 'my inspiration and my motivation' throughout his own glittering playing career. He explained Troost's value. 'I brought him to Chelsea to do a job. There were too many players at the club who could not cope with stress. Now they don't want to be without him. He makes a player better. He makes them relax. They want to see him before every match.' Described in Holland as a psychologist and a manual therapist, Troost mixes the physical and spiritual natures of sport. Gullit admitted: 'A lot of people here thought he was strange, a kind of magician. They didn't believe in certain methods he uses. I don't care. As long as it helps I let him do what he likes. His methods unlock the frustrations and emotions of players. One phrase he says to me all the time is "Everything is allowed". I can't explain it, you just have to feel it.'

Troost's relationship with Gullit has been personal and intense since they met when Gullit was a nineteen-year-old genius with glass knees. He has been with him ever since, following him through his early career in Holland to European Cup success with PSV Eindhoven, more European Cup and World Club Cup triumphs at AC Milan, victory for Holland in the 1988 European Nations Championships and now to Chelsea. Gullit insisted the Dutch FA called for Troost for the European Championships. Van Basten recovered with amazing speed to score a hat-trick against England, and Holland went on to lift their first major trophy. At AC Milan van Basten and Gullit wanted Troost and got him whenever they needed him. 'He is a true friend, the only person who is allowed to read my diary. Ted was with me when I hit rock bottom, in football and my private life. He has taught me how to cope with stress and with pressures. At Chelsea, now I am manager, everyone wants something of me every day. The fans, the players, the club officials, the media, they all turn to me. There is so much to be done. Ted makes sure I can cope.'

FRIDAY, APRIL 11
A closed Bridge training session. Gullit organises a vital practice match with the first team playing 4–4–2 and a midfield diamond to unleash on Wimbledon.

The press conference was the perfect platform for Ruud to put his point of view to the large media gathering. Gullit was amused that the players' honest opinions in the dressing room at Coventry should be interpreted in back-page banner headlines as 'Chelsea at War'. Gullit planned to turn it on its head in a typical backhanded fashion, trying to make it to his advantage.

He astonished the gathered media hungry for more of the same when he claimed he orchestrated the dressing room row! Gullit explained why he stood back and 'approved' of his players at each other's throats. 'Sometimes it is good to have confrontation before important matches and this is my way of doing things. I did it with the Dutch national team and so did Johan Cruyff. I do things like this from experience. When I was with the Dutch national team there was always something happening, some issue or other, but it made players play well for their pride. I don't know if my players at Chelsea all like me. It is not a concern whether I am popular or not. My only job is to get the best out of them. And when you get spanked I find that this is often what happens.

'Angry players often perform better. I know I did when I was criticised in Italy. Sometimes there were papers which said "He's not what he was". Then when I was on the pitch I performed so nobody could say it was true. After a while they said, "Ruud has knees of glass; he can't play two or three games in a row." Then I played in Sampdoria week in, week out. It's pride. If you feel attacked you react.

'Sometimes you try to look for a confrontation to get something out of a player. And I'm quite happy that the press helped me to do this by highlighting it. It was the right moment to do it and I believe it has worked because when Vialli came on as a substitute at Coventry he gave us something extra. I was very pleased with him. The good players get angry when their pride is hurt. They go out and want to show you everything they have. You use it to get a reaction from them and then you talk about it and things are fine. Vialli will still not be happy while he's not been in the team, but I've spoken to him one-on-one and he knows now what I want. I know he wants to stay and I want him to stay also.

'He's OK now – we understand each other and I've told him exactly what I want. The most important thing is that I believe in my players. I'll give them every chance and I'm honest with them. They have not been satisfied with their performances and want to put things right. Our form has been poor because we have been too much focused on this semifinal, but now that it has arrived I am seeing a different team in training. Players were talking to each other about the situation and they are really focused on this game, which gives me great confidence. They want to make up for being beaten by Manchester United in the semifinal last year and I believe in them. It's incredible how players can change when a big game comes round. We're pumped up and Wimbledon won't out-power us. I know how they play and I know how we can hurt them.'

After Gullit ended the official session Vialli went off to do some sprint training with Ade Mafe, while Petrescu did some dribbling and Zola practised volleying with Grodas. Clarke led a few players on a jog round the perimeter. Clarke said 'You see, these players come over here, earn a lot of money and are top-quality players, but they don't just train and go home. They are prepared to stay, do a little bit extra and work on something in their game. The Italians believe if you are not training you lose your conditioning. We tend to play so many matches we just have a rest then get ready for the next one. They are still prepared to do the conditioning work. That was an eye-opener. When I started playing the manager just said, "That's it, get changed and go home." It wasn't open for debate. This morning Ruud said you're finished and it was thirty to forty minutes before a lot of the players came in. Of course, it was a nice day, but if it's raining you'll still find twelve to fifteen people doing their exercises in the gym.'

Zola was thirsting for glory in English football. 'I have also never worried about the size of the match. This semifinal is big but the final is bigger. It is no good reaching the semi if you do not go all the way to Wembley. There is no such thing as tiredness when you are winning. In a short space of time I have already been caught up in the Chelsea dream. I know how much winning the FA Cup would mean to them.

'I'd far rather score for Chelsea at Wembley than be responsible for ending England's chances in the World Cup. I get some terrible stick from fans for that goal. But you have to expect it. My team-mates have had a few laughs at my expense, but the Chelsea fans have been brilliant, even though I suspect deep down they are not entirely happy that I scored against England. But I'm sure both teams will qualify for the World Cup in France, regardless of the result. It is difficult, of course it is. I regard this country as my second home and I would rather England weren't in our qualifying group for the World Cup. But, as much as I love England, I'm Italian and very proud when I play for my country.

'I adore Wembley and it would be nice to go back and score a vital goal for Chelsea in the Cup. We have had a mixed season in the league. We are learning all the time, but you cannot expect to compete with teams like Manchester United and Liverpool overnight because they have played together for a while. But now we have a good chance of winning something and qualifying for a place in Europe.

'It will be hard against Wimbledon. They are a good side and difficult to beat. But if we can play as well as we have done in the competition, we have a good chance to make the final.'

Zola was surprised by the passion of the FA Cup. 'In Italy the cup is not so big. Here it has a greater importance. When you are not involved it's hard to understand, but I appreciate it more now I'm here. I like the way the club play football, it's more European. The way Ruud wanted the team to perform was something I considered before I signed. I haven't had any problems since I came to Chelsea. My life is football. The weather and the language may be different, but you can still eat the same food, drink the same drinks and enjoy the new adventure.

'What has happened to me in England has been one of the most extraordinary times of my life. I cannot really find the words to express how I feel. Last summer I left your country disappointed. Italy had been knocked out of the European Championships and I had missed a vital penalty against Germany. But you have repaid me with this transfer to London. I now have only happiness and pleasure. That feeling has allowed me to play without inhibition. I have the confidence like never before. I live in a beautiful city and my family have settled in well so why should there be any problems? I only want to be happy and make others around me happy. I am not a clown, but I like to have a laugh with everybody.

'It has hurt me when people have said the Italians and other foreign players have come here only to rest, make money and to finish our careers. I have come here to achieve. I won one championship in Italy with Napoli and would like another. You must never say, "I do not want to do that." I have come to London to enjoy England and to play to the best of my ability. London is a fantastic city; it offers anyone everything he wishes. There is always something to discover. About life, about yourself. The same applies to football.'

Zola was brought up in the small village of Oliena in the heart of Sardinia. He describes himself as a proud, stubborn man. 'Sardinians,' he said, 'achieve with heart, body and soul. When we have our minds on something we have to achieve. In football that attitude is not uncommon.'

Music and computers are his weaknesses. For at least one hour every evening he plays on his computer. 'I can stop when I want. I have not developed a chronic phobia.' Wife Franca and children Andrea and Martina enjoy a trip to the Trocadero and Sega World in Piccadilly 'to play on the computer games and then out for a meal'. He has been determined to learn English fluently with nightly lessons from a man Chelsea recommended. 'I thought I was getting on well and then I try to listen to Dennis Wise and do not understand a word.'

The Bridge was buzzing, thanks to Chelsea's Foreign Legion. Wise said: 'I keep reading stories about problems at the club but it's all nonsense. The foreign stars are great blokes and we all get on well – although I still haven't managed to persuade Zola to start drinking.

'As for the so-called rift between Vialli and the manager, all I can say is that it isn't apparent to the rest of us and if there is a problem it's a matter for them to solve. Because of the number of good players we now have at Chelsea it's obvious someone has to be left out. We've all had to put up with it and I think we all accept it.'

But if anyone thought there was a rift within the camp wide enough to disrupt their concentration they were wrong. Hutchinson described it as little more than 'mischief-makers who tried to rock the boat with lurid and untrue stories about unrest and disharmony'. They were about to get their answer ...

SUNDAY, APRIL 13
Wimbledon 0 Chelsea 3
For Ruud it was a moment to savour, a special achievement even in his distinguished career. 'I have just been told that I am the first foreign coach to take a team to Wembley in an FA Cup Final and am very proud of that. But it is important we win. First place is the only thing that matters in any competition.'

Zola and Hughes claimed the glory goals, but Gullit proved he has a tactical brain underneath those famous dreadlocks. He rendered all the absurd pre-match criticism useless by masterminding success over the team Chelsea dreaded the most by dismantling his wing-back system in favour of a hybrid English-style back four to counter the Wimbledon bombardment that crushed Chelsea at Stamford Bridge.

Zola's genius for spectacular goals pushed him closer as Footballer of the Year, with Hughes and Juninho his closest rivals for the prestigious fiftieth anniversary award.

The 'foreigner' who did most as the standard-bearer for Chelsea's route to the final was Hughes. When he scored his second goal in injury time, his twenty-sixth FA Cup goal of his career, Gullit, who had been sitting serenely, leapt from the bench and punched the air. As for the feud with Vialli, the two men embraced three times at the end. Di Matteo threw his shirt to the crowd as the players did a lap of honour round the two sides of the stadium where a sea of Chelsea's fans were decked out in the Cup hats, scarves, flags and shirts. The crowd of less than 33,000 was more than 5,000 below capacity, and the empty seats were greeted with boos by the majority Chelsea contingent. It was a terrible waste of tickets that could have been utilised by Chelsea fans. Worse was the inability to prevent Chelsea fans buying some of Wimbledon's allocation. Around 250 Chelsea fans managed to gain tickets for an area reserved for Wimbledon supporters, and about fifty of them were thrown out to avoid the threat of trouble. The vocal support was terrific and was always going to subdue the undermanned Wimbledon fans. The players responded to the volume of support.

Fundamentally, Gullit can point to Chelsea's place in the final as vindication for his decision to play Hughes ahead of Vialli. The Italian joined the celebrations; the scene did not look like a manager envious or jealous of his star player, nor did Vialli seem to be in dispute with his coach. They were both heading for the final and in the games that remained Vialli had to convince Gullit that he was worthy of a place in the starting line-up.

Wise wore his lucky cup vest: 'Cheer up Luca, we love you.' Vialli never kicked a ball but his sheer joy at Chelsea's victory and his part in the celebrations confirmed his willingness to stay part of the set-up under Gullit's guidance. Wise said, 'I thought we showed a lot of people that when it comes to the big event we're up for it. We showed a lot of class. I think we shocked people outside Chelsea the way we played.'

Gullit had watched a video of Wimbledon's performance against Newcastle, but leaning more heavily on the bitter experience of the way Kinnear's team steam-rollered over Chelsea at the Bridge Gullit sent out a more tough-line defence of Johnsen and Sinclair alongside Leboeuf and Clarke. Petrescu's back injury was the final telling factor in Gullit's mind: it convinced him also to do without his other wing-back, Minto. Gullit explained: 'I watched Wimbledon play against Newcastle a few weeks ago and knew from that what we had to do. They tried to put the pressure on us as we knew they would, but we survived it well then played our football.'

The Crazy Gang left no one in any doubt of their intent when Ardley was booked by referee Gerald Ashby within seconds of the start after a foul on Clarke. Jones and Wise swapped some pleasantries – at least I think that's what they were doing when they came face to face to discuss such a ridiculously early yellow card.

Importantly, Grodas was not intimidated, and two early incidents proved he was up to the task. He fisted away a long throw from Jones and punched away a free kick. A Chelsea defence that had looked vulnerable when tested by such tactics was remarkably solid.

Kimble launched a high tackle on Zola after just seventeen minutes, with the little Italian taking the full brunt in the face, but the dangerous clash went unpunished. When Zola was caught offside a minute later he showed his frustrations by throwing the ball back, not away, and it seemed a harsh decision to be booked for that.

Chelsea gradually gained more space. Wise burst through from the halfway line to launch a shot that Sullivan was right behind, and again the keeper was well positioned to save from Zola after a clever turn and angled drive. Earle headed over and then an overhead kick was pulled out of the air by Grodas. They gained a touch of luck for the opening goal a couple of minutes before the interval but it began with a glorious long-range crossfield pass from Leboeuf at the back. Zola's perfect first-time control, then reverse pass to Wise, gave the midfield player the space to cross with his left foot where Burley was lurking at the far post. Kimble intercepted but the ball bounced off Hughes's chest and he couldn't miss from such close range.

The ball was hardly on the ground long enough to disturb the pitch when it came to Wimbledon's simple and direct approach. For once Chelsea's susceptible defence was not prepared to wilt and that was the key to success.

Hughes cracked a twenty-five-yarder just over the bar and Di Matteo followed suit. Kinnear threw on Holdsworth for full-back Ardley after sixty-three minutes but there was no time for the all-out attacking formation to settle down before Zola's decisive strike. His superb, swift switch of direction was enough to open up the space for one of his typical whiplash shots into the corner. His twelfth goal was another gem. Zola struck the outside of a post, was denied a second by a slight deflection and then conjured another blistering shot just over. Hughes embellished Chelsea's win in injury time when Perry mis-headed and Hughes was sent clear, lifting his shot into the roof of the net.

Afterwards, Zola sat next to his boss, smiling proudly when Gullit talked about him in glowing terms. He probably didn't catch every complimentary adjective, but he got the drift. Zola was much slower than the Dutchman in his delivery of his words. 'I like Wembley. When I left Wembley after scoring for Italy I vowed to come back and do the same with Chelsea. The atmosphere that night was unbelievable, and now I have an opportunity to put on another performance. I have a month to prepare for the Cup final and I will do all I can to give the Chelsea supporters the trophy they have waited so long for. I haven't been playing very well in recent league games and I badly wanted to give my best against Wimbledon. Now I want to join all our supporters in celebrating this success and to take it a step further by winning the Cup.

'All my family and friends have been waiting for this moment back home in Italy; they know how important the FA Cup is and how much it means. My goal was special for me personally, but it was just as special for them, too.' Two-goal Hughes led tributes to Zola. 'He wasn't bad today, was he? If he keeps playing like that he's got a chance! To be honest, I didn't get a good view of his goal because I was running about trying to make a few angles. But I will settle down with a few beers in front of the telly tonight and enjoy watching over and over again the action replays.'

Hughes has the Midas touch in this competition. He entered Wembley's Hall of FA Cup Fame, his fifth final. Gullit announced in the after-match press conference in the Highbury 'cinema studio' he had 'agreed' a one-year extension to his contract.

Hughes arrived last as Gullit and Zola gave their views, and once the manager and his prized Italian signing had left the luxury press interview room he said he would prefer at least a two-year extension, and added, 'I haven't discussed it with my wife yet. Everyone would like to stay for more than one year at my age, but I'm reasonably pleased with the deal.' Hughes's dilemma was that his family had moved back up to the north-west while he stayed in London.

Gullit said: 'You'd have to ask him about that. Mark has been very important to us all season and extending his contract is a sign of how much we believe in him. He's a character player – he's been around Europe with United, Barcelona and Bayern Munich so he knows exactly what the demands are in playing in games like this.'

Hughes was happy with a special arrangement that persuaded him to shake Gullit's hand on an extended contract. He could spend four days in the north, flying down to train at the manager's behest. He said: 'In a sense, I feel that I've come home at last, playing for Chelsea with such an exceptional bunch of lads and supporters. I still have a home near Manchester but the manager knows where I am. There's no problem with it. I'm probably happier now than I've ever been in my career.'

The hero of Chelsea's 1997 odyssey added, 'The Cup has been good to me and it would be nice to earn a place in the record books. Of course, I never thought I would get the chance to play in another final after leaving Manchester United, but you can never look too far ahead in football and it's turned out to be a great move for me. It might have raised a few eyebrows but I knew which way this club was heading and I haven't been disappointed. We haven't won a major trophy now for more than twenty-five years and the longer such a run goes on ·the more pressure builds up. But after the way we came back against Liverpool in the fourth round we've always had a sneaking feeling we could go all the way this year, that our name could be on the Cup. From a personal point of view, it would be nice if I could go from here and get that fourth medal. But I will take just as much satisfaction if I can help Chelsea win their first trophy since 1971. I know from experience with Manchester United how the pressures build up every year you go without a trophy.'

Gullit had to deal with questions over his own future sparked by a *News of the World* article that morning linking him with a swift return to his favourite Dutch club, Feyenoord. Gullit scoffed. 'I spoke on Dutch television and was asked whether I would come back one day. I said that was possible. Everyone there knows that I have strong links with Feyenoord so they then assumed I will be taking over from Arie Haan. I said no. At the moment any move there is not negotiable. I told them I am here for two more years yet and maybe more. Feyenoord is something for the far future. I haven't spoken to the Chelsea chairman in any new negotiations yet as I already have next season, but it is a question of what the club wants. At the moment that's not even negotiable. I have a lot of work to do here. I have one year of my contract left and, of course, whether I stay will depend on what the club wants. Don't forget, for me the job is new – it's an adventure – and Chelsea gave it to me; I didn't ask for it. But I'm still learning and enjoying the job – and if you enjoy it, you can transmit that through to the players.'

If it was true that Matthew's name was on the FA Cup then Gullit also wanted to dedicate the triumph to the club's long-suffering fans and sixty-five-year-old Bates, the most irascible Chelsea pensioner of all time. 'It will be a fitting tribute to Matthew Harding if we win the FA Cup, but I also want to do it for the supporters and chairman Ken Bates. A lot of people do not realise how hard Ken Bates works for the club, how much he puts into it. He also gave me the chance to be manager when I wasn't sure I wanted to do it, but now I am very grateful I was given that chance.'

Bates needed Gullit's backing at a time when he was coming under fire for another swipe at Harding's memory. Bates had been putting down the notion the Cup run was inspired by Harding. The chairman had been quoted as saying: 'No chance. That would be unfair to the 28,000 other fans who have gone to every game this season and the 500 or 600 Chelsea fans who have died this year, some of whom were richer than Matthew and some who were poorer.' Bates tells it like he sees it, but such a comment was bound to provoke an angry reaction.

Gullit's master plan went well beyond winning the FA Cup. He did not want that construed as any lack of passion, far from it. It was born from an air of realism that comes from winning his favourite cup (the 'one with the big ears' – the European Cup). He said: 'My feet are on the ground. I am not thinking of Wembley. My mind is focused on next season. We have not won anything. This is no time for celebration, this season has not yet been a success for me. Success is only about winning. In England the Cup final is a big thing and I can understand how romantic it is for everyone.' But Europe was also Gullit's goal.

The scenes in the 'away' dressing room were described by Bates. The chairman's rapport with Gullit was evident when his coach paid him a tribute on national TV. Bates strode into the dressing room and told Gullit: 'If we win the FA Cup we are going to shave your head.' Gullit replied with a smile: 'In that case, Mr Chairman, I will be bald every year.' Bates didn't need Vialli to shave his head; it gave him enormous pleasure to lay to rest another misconception about the Italian's relationship with the club. 'I saw all the players on Saturday and shook them by the hand to wish them good luck, and I spoke specifically to Vialli. He told me he was physically okay but I said to him there was nothing wrong with him. I told him, "You are an important member of our squad and you will play an important part in it, I am sure." I went into the dressing room again before the match and wished them all good luck, and then again after the game I was in the dressing room and said to him, "What did I tell you, you are loved by the Chelsea fans." He got the biggest cheer when he came on the pitch to join in the celebrations and when I told him what I thought he didn't have to reply, he just gave me a lovely Italian smile. He's a lovely fella, he really is, and he loves it here.'

Vialli smiled with deep satisfaction as he lapped up the fans' adulation. 'It means that they love me as well as I love them. They understand exactly my feeling at this moment. They know sometimes my desire to play, but I can't because Sparky and Gianfranco are playing so well. But I want to be part of the amusement, part of the party.'

Bates enjoyed a champagne celebration at his Buckinghamshire farm. His whiplash tongue made mincemeat of the Sunday paper banner headlines proclaiming that Gullit would be leaving. 'Prostitutes have more morals than people who perpetuate such garbage. Reaching the Cup final is a giant step forward for the club, and we want Ruud to be part of its future.'

Ravanelli was desperate to follow Zola and Di Matteo to Wembley, after sparking an amazing Middlesbrough fightback when his twenty-eighth goal of the season undermined Chesterfield at Old Trafford. Boro trailed 2–0 and were down to ten men, following Vladimir Kinder's first-half dismissal for two bookable offences, when Ravanelli struck. Hignett's penalty then restored parity and Ravanelli's compatriot Gianluca Festa looked to have booked a Wembley date with Chelsea. But the last-gasp equaliser by Hewitt left the Spireites to fight another day at Hillsborough and left Ravanelli still hoping of a dream Wembley confrontation with his Italian international team-mates.

'It is important to get as many Italian players as possible into the final. If Chelsea win the Cup then Italy wins because of Zola and Di Matteo, and if Middlesbrough win the Cup Italy wins because of Festa and myself. And I think we have a very good chance of reaching Wembley now as we have learned some lessons from the first game against Chesterfield. It was an incredible match as Chesterfield are not a big team. Twenty minutes into the second half, when we were 2–0 down with only ten men, I thought the match was finished. But we played very hard and, although unhappy to have allowed Chesterfield to score a late goal, I think 3–3 is an okay result for us.'

MONDAY, APRIL 14

It was a day off for Gullit and his players, but at the Bridge the building work was at frantic pace. Donning my white protective builder's hat and Bates a bright yellow one, the chairman gave me a first guided tour of the new super-stadium.

Bates oversees the rapid construction work, now elevated to the seventh floor of luxury apartments and the ninth landing of the hotel. Bates builds off the field, Gullit is in sole command of events on it. 'When I said a year ago that Chelsea would be the Manchester United of the south everybody took the piss. Now they can see it beginning to happen for themselves. A year later we have Gullit, Di

Matteo, Zola, Leboeuf, Vialli and Grodas. These are quality players who have come in and helped the existing ones to raise their game. And we are far from finished here. So we can become the Manchester United of the south in every sense of the term, in terms of income, in terms of entertainment value and hopefully in terms of success, and in that department we have made a start.'

Shares in Chelsea Village made a dramatic recovery after slipping at pace with the team in the Premiership. At one stage they were up 12.5p, but settled down at an 8p rise on the day. The club announced a mega new shirt sponsor, a four-year £5m deal with Autoglass.

Bates paid tribute to Gullit as the catalyst for Chelsea becoming 'big time', building on Hoddle's tenure as manager. 'Gullit is part of our whole new philosophy. He is a one-off. When they made him they threw away the mould. He's brought in a depth of international experience of different levels and different cultures. He's the first of a new breed of continentals. We are an international club as a result, now with an international manager and an international team, and we are playing with flair and excitement.

'I inherited John Neal and he was very good and would still be here today if it wasn't for his heart attack. Then there was Hollins, Campbell, Porterfield and Hoddle. To be fair to the majority of those previous managers, they were burdened by the uncertainty of the ground but now everyone can see what's happening. It's not a dream or vision and we are becoming one of the elite, not a feeder for the elite. Our plan is to get Chelsea Village fully developed and paid for before costs get out of hand. I envisage good profits and dividends by the end of the century.'

The lavish galleria for 445 executive seats is part of a 2,200-seat new family centre and 4,000 upper tier seats in the hotel and apartment complex that will open at the beginning of July. The club had planning permission for the £25 million new West Stand and by September the 6,900-seater stand will be taking shape. The hotel will be opened on 1 December and it won't be long before Chelsea Village will be selling the penthouse apartments for £775,000. Bates, who's claimed a penthouse, boasted: 'Our location is unique and our hotel will be earning between £2–3m a year.' In addition there will be four restaurants and bars, the Shed Sports Bar and Grill, the Fishnets restaurant and Arkels Irish bar. The asking price for one of the fifteen 'millennium' hospitality suites is £1.5m for a ten-year lease.

The site resembled a scene from Bosnia but within months it will be transformed. 'We will build the annexe to the hotel and a sports and leisure complex that will be finished by August '98.'

Back in Bates's enormous office overlooking the construction work he relaxed in a huge green leather chair and smiled and took a deep breath. 'Yes, it all fills me with a great deal of pride. I love a challenge and there is a challenge for even greater things ahead. I've always been in pursuit of excellence and I haven't changed.'

Bates no longer had a dream because the concept of the 'greatest stadium in the country' was rapidly becoming a reality. He destroyed all doubts about Gullit's future. 'As far as we're concerned, he's here till he retires. Why would Ruud want to go to AC Milan or Feyenoord when we will be as big as them? We are very happy with Ruud and come the end of the season I will be looking to sit him down and discuss the future. Getting to the Cup final is a giant step for the development of this club and we want Ruud to be part of it.' Flourishing Chelsea had £13m in the bank to finance the development of the south and lower west stands. Cash from the FA Cup Final was still to come. Season ticket sales were set to top 10,000 next season. Bates, Gullit and Hutchinson discussed the new budgets for players and sizeable sums were to be available for Gullit to make other summer purchases.

TUESDAY, APRIL 15

Relaxed after a shower in the changing rooms at Harlington before the team flew off to Newcastle, Zola reflected on his FA Cup memories. 'The atmosphere was maybe even better than Liverpool. Against Liverpool we were at home; there were more people for Chelsea at Highbury. But again the atmosphere was unbelievable. The crowd was so excited that you could feel that. So I got like them.' As for his goal – 'I knew what I was doing. I knew the defender was behind me and I had to try to pass him. I thought that way could be the right way. It was a very good goal because the goal was good to see and important at that time of the game.' Zola knew Wimbledon were outsmarted. 'They tried to play their football; we stopped their football. I know if we let them play like they wanted, it would be more difficult for us.'

Zola was baffled by the possibility of facing Chesterfield in the final. It was the first time he had heard of them. 'But I think they're a big surprise, not only for me but for everyone. Sometimes a team from the Second Division in Italy get good results and get to the final. It happened a couple of years ago, but it is very, very hard. But not a team from the Third Division, not ever.' He wasn't fussed who won the replay. 'It doesn't matter. We must think to play how we play. We can get the Cup only when playing our best football. If we play our best we must be confident. We must be sure we can do it. If we don't play our best we will lose, against Chesterfield or Middlesbrough, it doesn't matter which.'

Sinclair purred when he recalled Zola's goal. 'He's just a pleasure to watch. When he got the ball and turned it was unbelievable. There was going to be only one conclusion. It was going in the net. I didn't know how, whether he'd blast it in the roof or what, but I just knew he was going to score. It was brilliant, and it made the game comfortable for us.'

Gullit wanted to book a European place before the final, despite slipping to seventh after losing three successive League games. A good result at St James's Park would put them back in the frame for a UEFA Cup spot. Newton said: 'This is another important game for us. We know we can't afford to just think about the Cup and have to get back to winning league games.' Gullit planned changes. 'We will see what happens from game to game but there are players coming back from injury, which is good. We know we need to be more consistent and we are working on it.'

Grodas wanted to commit the rest of his career to the club. Signed as cover, he forced himself into the limelight. 'As far as I'm aware, I am first choice at Chelsea now. Playing at Wembley in the FA Cup Final would be the high point of my career. I think only one other player from Norway has a winner's medal in the FA Cup, and ironically he is also a goalkeeper, namely Erik Thorstvedt. Hopefully, I can become the second. But I also want to become a regular at Chelsea for the future. It is a funny thing but in Norway when you reach thirty people think you are past it. That is part of the reason I came to England to play. People aren't so blinkered here. I hope to play at the top level for at least another six years, all with Chelsea if possible.'

Italian prodigy Gennaro Scarlato rejected a move to Chelsea. The Napoli midfielder, nineteen, walked out of his club to spend three days on trial. He returned to implore the Serie A club to take him back – and sign a contract worth just half of what he would have earned alongside Vialli, Di Matteo and Zola. 'Money isn't everything,' said Scarlato. 'I trained with Chelsea's youth squad, and Vialli was there as well. But I decided to return home – I felt bad about leaving Napoli without telling them. But the worst thing for me was the food. I wasn't eating well, and as a result my mind was filled with all sorts of unhappy thoughts. I would never have gone over had I foreseen that I would feel homesick.'

Gullit lined up his new international signings for next season to continue the transformation into championship contenders. First he won the £2.25m race for Nigerian whizz-kid, left wing-back Celestine Babayaro, beating off competition from Juventus, Inter Milan, Ajax, Deportivo La Coruña and Arsenal. The Babayaro deal was struck after Hutchinson held talks with Anderlecht. Babayaro, nineteen in August, stayed with Anderlecht for the rest of the season, arriving at the Bridge in the summer after signing a five-year contract at the Sheraton Hotel in Brussels in the presence of his lawyer and Hutchinson.

Known as Baba, he won an Olympic gold medal for Nigeria in Atlanta last summer and scored one of their goals in the final. He has been with Anderlecht from the age of fifteen and tracked by a pack of Europe's top clubs after impressive performances for the Belgian team in the Champions League and UEFA Cup. Gullit's worldwide reputation persuaded him to join Chelsea.

'I told Ruud I wanted to sign for Chelsea after only two conversations on the telephone,' Babayaro said. 'He told me, "Baba, you're a great player. Do you like Chelsea?" I said yes, and he says okay, he'll be glad to have me. I am very happy he wants me in his team and I am looking forward to a great season with Chelsea. I've watched all their top matches on TV and I have been impressed with Chelsea and their players. Ruud Gullit was always one of my heroes long before I spoke to him. Gianfranco Zola is an inspirational player and I am very excited about playing with him. It is my dream to play in England.'

He watched the FA Cup semifinal win over Wimbledon on television; he hoped to appear in the Belgian Cup final in June with Anderlecht in the semifinals. He joins Wimbledon's Efan Ekoku as the Premiership's second Nigerian international. 'I watched them defeat Wimbledon and I was very impressed. My assets, I think, are that I'm fast, good with my head and I can score.' He has been Belgium's 'African Player of the Year.'

Chelsea did not use an agent. Williams said, 'When we first heard about him six months ago fifteen agents were claiming he was their client and we found it difficult to make any headway. It was a confusing situation but in the end we cut through the lot of them and dealt straight with him and his lawyer.'

Hutchinson took advantage in a change in the rules. 'As recently as March Anderlecht were sticking out for £3.6m believing that, even when his contract expired in 1998, they would still collect compensation should he switch clubs because of his non-EC nationality. FIFA scuppered that by introducing, from April 1, a change in regulations allowing end-of-contract non-EC players playing for clubs in Europe to move within the EC without a transfer fee. Overnight Anderlecht's prize asset was squeezed. In just over twelve months Babayaro could move for nothing and, knowing how clubs, particularly Italians, enter into pre-contracts [rules allow these to be signed up to six months before a contract expires] Anderlecht decided to cash in after several failed attempts to get him to sign a new deal in Belgium. Eighteen months ago they were asking £4.5m for the exciting youngster.'

Uruguayan international Gustavo Poyet was tied up on a free transfer from Real Zaragoza. The twenty-nine-year-old was to join on June 30, when his contract ended in Spain, under the Bosman ruling. Poyet signed a three-year deal worth over £600,000 a season. He played in Zaragoza's Cup Winners Cup semifinal win over Chelsea in 1995, although he was suspended for the Stamford Bridge return. He helped them beat Arsenal 2–1 in the final. He scored eleven league goals from midfield this season, and managed another ten last year. Hutchinson said: 'Although he is Uruguayan, he has a Spanish passport and has dual nationality so doesn't need a work permit.' Poyet was named 'player of the tournament' in last year's Copa America, which Uruguay won. 'Zaragoza have been caught with their shorts down as far as the Bosman ruling is concerned because they have seven players out of contract this summer,' added Hutchinson. 'We knew Poyet from our tie in 1995, and he has got twenty international caps in the last three seasons. He's powerfully built, six feet one, twenty-nine, and scores goals from midfield.'

Zaragoza's captain and longest-serving foreign player scored sixty goals in 240 appearances for the Spanish club over seven seasons. 'Eighty per cent of his goals are from headers,' said Hutchinson. 'Players of his calibre don't usually become available on free transfers. Both the Madrid giants, Real and Atletico, showed interest, as did some Italian clubs. But it shows the pulling power of Chelsea and the Premiership that he has chosen to come to us. During recent weeks, injuries and suspensions have confirmed the need for us to add to the squad in readiness for next season.'

Hutchinson signed a new contract to keep him at the Bridge until 2002. Bates said: 'It is important to build off the field as well as on it. Colin is the best in the country. He is so highly regarded that several clubs wanted him to become the managing director of the Premier League following Rick Parry. Effectively, he is now going to stay with us until the end of his career.'

Unlucky Luca was given his chance with Hughes rested, only to injure himself in training and miss the afternoon flight. Gullit said: 'He twisted his ankle and the ligaments have blown up. I felt really sorry for him. He was to play against Newcastle and I had already told him that Mark Hughes knew that he was to be the odd man out.'

WEDNESDAY, APRIL 13
Newcastle United 3 Chelsea 1

With Vialli left behind, so too were the Chelsea defence. Gullit shook his head knowing his players had left their emotions and strength back at Highbury. It was hard for Gullit to be angry even though it was a shocking slump of four successive league defeats, a sorry sequence conceding ten goals, committing more errors against a Newcastle side that blasted their way into fourth spot.

Chelsea were hit by three blows. In the twelfth minute Darren Peacock won the ball bravely, lobbed it forward and then watched in delight as Leboeuf boobed with an attempted back-header. Shearer was on it in a flash to side-foot over Grodas as he came rushing from his line.

Chelsea put up mild resistance when Morris whiplashed a twenty-five-yard volley onto the bar, and Burley released a long-range missile which keeper Shaka Hislop pulled down from his top corner. Hughes then fed Zola who raced clear, only to see Hislop saving at his feet. Hughes blasted inches wide.

It was all a false dawn as Hislop launched a long clearance and Ferdinand got in above Leboeuf to flick on for Asprilla. The Colombian took two gazelle-like strides before touching the ball beyond Grodas with chilling accuracy. Minto made one desperate attempt to cut out the danger but only succeeded in injuring Grodas, who needed lengthy treatment. He hadn't fully recovered when Asprilla showed devastating skill to push the ball cheekily past Sinclair, reach it on the by-line and float over the perfect ball for Shearer to head in number three and his twenty-third Premier goal of the season; he needed another seven in the last five games to make it the fourth successive season on the thirty mark. Grodas was forced off with a hamstring problem before half-time giving Forrest his debut.

They put up a better fight in the second half with Zola whipping in a cross that Burley planted into the net in the sixty-second minute, bringing ironic cries from the Chelsea faithful of 'One nil in the second half'.

Gullit managed to smile as he analysed another Premiership setback. 'Maybe emotionally and physically they had given everything in the semifinal. Everybody was so tuned in for that game and it took so much out of them. So after the game I was not that disappointed, although I think we lost it on our own. I will forget this game and put it down to what happened on Sunday. I said to them afterwards what would have happened if we were really tuned in for it tonight. But I know everyone is tuned in for the final. But I want to win every game. That's what my job is all about. We had to come here and perform especially in the ambience of this St James's Park ground. But I didn't think we played a good game. If you make errors you can't catch them. It's not because they created, it's because we gave it to them. We made Shearer more popular than he already was. Yet in the second half we didn't play well, didn't make these errors and yet scored a goal. That sums up everything about the game. We gave it to Alan Shearer on a silver plate. Strikers like him will accept those gifts. We put Newcastle in the driving seat. You cannot coach players not to make individual errors.'

Shearer had won the players' Player of the Year, presented with his award by Ferguson at the Grosvenor House Hotel hours after Chelsea confirmed their place in the final. Shearer voted for Zola as his Player of the Year; it was Zola's turn to praise the England striker. 'Alan deserved to win the Player of the Year award. But if I was to judge his genius on a scale of one to ten, I would give him a nine. He played well against us and is a good striker. I would say, though, that Tino Asprilla created a lot more tension and problems for us. But I do like Shearer. He always seems capable of scoring whether he is using his feet or his head. I know him very well and his two goals against us were not a surprise for me. He is a very important player for Newcastle and England.'

FRIDAY, APRIL 18
Vialli's English had improved sufficiently for him to agree to express his true feelings about his rift with Gullit. The eighteen-month lease he'd taken on his dream home in Eaton Square confirmed his desire to stay, but his frustrations as being the 'supersub' were still evident. Seated alongside giant keeper Forrest and tiny Jody Morris, he hinted that if he still wasn't in the FA Cup Final team he would consider quitting the Bridge. 'I think my relationship with the players has been fantastic and my relationship with the fans is fantastic . . . With the manager there are some problems. But I want to forget them and think about the final and then after the final we shall have a chat, I think. And then I will decide what is better for me and what is better for Chelsea. I don't know what Chelsea think at this moment. I hope they are happy with me. If they're happy

with me I'd be happy to stay here. I can say I had some problems last week, but we have sorted them out and now I am positive in thinking about playing football, the final and the last matches in the Premier League.'

Vialli needed to produce something special in the few matches that remained or Zola or Hughes had to be injured for him to have any chance of starting at Wembley. 'To play would be fantastic. To be at Wembley would be fantastic as well. I have played football for sixteen years and I know sometimes something can go wrong, something is not like you would like it to be. I know you can go up and down, then suddenly something changes and you have to be ready. Now I'd like to play as soon as possible, but that is not up to me, that is up to the manager. I don't decide, the manager decides.'

He was worried his sharpness was suffering with lack of match practice. 'If you play regularly you can be fit very easily, but that's why it's important when you are sub and when sometimes the manager needs you you have to be ready and that means you have to train better than the other players. Your task when you come on would be more difficult. Yeah, I suppose I'm not tired!'

At his age Vialli was not content as a bit-part player. 'I'm not the kind of player who can only play for twenty minutes. I need to play for ninety minutes because I'm not like Jody. He's very light – I have a different style and I need to do running.' Vialli smiled spasmodically, laughing at his own jokes. Although no longer sulking, you could sense there was only a truce.

The Cup final distractions were a novelty for Gullit. 'It is important we end up the season well and for yourself it is important, week in and week out, to play good football, and I'm doing all my best to motivate my team. But it's very difficult because there's a circus around the Cup final. They're not talking so much about our game, but how they will organise their interviews, their song, and it's all new to me. It's difficult to concentrate with all this going on. I don't know if it's unprofessional because sometimes you can't avoid it. It's in the newspapers, people talk to you in the street. It's very difficult for the players because people remind them every day.'

Gullit would permit the circus to stay in town, but only until a week before the final. Then the players had to put their commercial pool to one side. Gullit said: 'It's not just about money. An amount of money will go to charity and it's not just about the players. It's for the young boys, the cooks, the people who work here, you give them something extra.'

It had been difficult enough before the semifinal, but now it was far worse. He added: 'Every time you're reminded of the fact there's an FA Cup and it's different for me, but people talk about it all the time so you can't blame anyone. I hope things change after the FA Cup. Next year they must do well in both the Cup and the championship, that's important. Maybe I ask too much of my players but I was used to it week in and week out. The first year in Italy we were focused on three trophies but the moment we won something it was easier for us. But I'll make sure a week before the final that these activities must be in the past. As far as I'm concerned, I'm already preparing for next season. It's part of the job.'

In a week when Dalglish and Robson ordered a halt to their players' drinking, Gullit allowed his stars to enjoy a pint – but warned them that their places were on the line. Gullit's philosophy was not to treat his 'children' like little naughty boys. Instead, he gave them the chance to prove that they were grown-ups. Gullit explained: 'I don't mind my players having a pint after a game. They know what my philosophy and attitude to this is. They know what it takes to be on this level. If they want to drink they know they risk throwing it away. I've given them their own responsibilities. I don't have to say to them what I want. They know. If they are in an environment with a party all the time, they will fall down. It will happen. I don't care what the players do outside of the training camp, but when they come here they have to do the job and to achieve that they have to live more seriously. I run it my own way. It's how the staff, how the chairman and the people around Chelsea cope with the situation. Everybody works with each other and learns from each other. It is wise to give people responsibilities as I feel they will think twice about doing something.'

The circus was in evidence as the youngsters mobbed the players after training, anxious for an autograph on shirt, ball or any scrap of paper, while the *Sun*'s female football reporter and photographer were busy snapping Zola as the newspaper's Player of the Year, voted by their readers. Eager young hands grabbed at little Zola as he posed with his trophy. Now he was favourite for the FWA's Footballer of the Year. 'In England there are many great players and it will be hard to decide who is best. I hope this award is the first of many trophies here; my next target is the FA Cup.' Zola was also voted Number One in *Goal*'s poll of the top 100 foreign stars in the English game.

One-to-one interviews with Gullit have to be prearranged through the accommodating Jon Smith at First Artist Corporation. Ruud refuses to accept fees for such interviews, but equally is choosy about doing them. Jon organises them on a sort of rota basis. I had saved my turn for their Cup final.

The press conferences over, Gullit strolled downstairs to continue his rehabilitation. An hour later, concerned that he might have forgotten our appointment, Williams reminded him. I found Ruud upstairs, looking at his watch – as if I had kept him waiting! After a warm greeting and even warmer smile we sat at the table overlooking the lush training fields and discussed a variety of subjects, concentrating on the FA Cup Final.

'Are you going to lead the team out at Wembley?' 'Lead the team out! What does that mean?' enquired Gullit. I explained that he would be at the head of his team as they come out of the Wembley tunnel. He smiled. 'I am learning something new about English football.' If it was expected of him he would do it. 'I don't want to do something different.'

He was coming to terms with the quaintness, peculiarities and tradition of the most prestigious cup final in the world. And it would be a unique occasion. Gullit made it so. The first foreign coach at Wembley. The first black coach in the Cup final. Gullit was making history that might never be repeated. 'When I heard that I didn't realise the importance. I really had to think about it, and it is quite an honour. I didn't really realise just how important the Cup final is here. I have been to many cup finals before, and each one has its own atmosphere.'

After two European Cup finals with AC Milan, this one was hardly going to faze him. 'I just let it come to me. I live by the day.' But the cold-eyed professional was lurking beneath the Mr Cool exterior. 'Yeah, I've been to several finals, but it's not the glamour that is important. My job will be to get everybody right – yourself right, the team right. Only then will we have a chance of winning it. And there is no point going there unless you are going to win. I don't want to be involved with other things, anything outside of the game itself. You must go to the final with the attitude to win, and I feel it already before the game.'

I informed Gullit that another part of the Cup final build-up is the intrusion of TV cameras on the team bus on its way to Wembley. 'I don't want that.' Well, I ventured to say, they usually pay an awful lot of money into the players' pool. 'It will be normal procedures as for every game,' said Gullit authoritatively. 'I had the feeling two or three weeks ago that everyone was asking me more about the final than about the Premier League. That showed me already how important it was. I come from a different country. I didn't know how to live with this period, how to come through this period. Now I know. I know how to do my job.'

Gullit is riveting company, serious one minute, laughing, smiling and joking the next. 'Are you going to wear a suit or a tracksuit when you lead the team out, Ruud?' He doesn't wear ties. 'Oh, yes, I do,' replied Ruud. 'I wear the club tie.' I suggested that he could always wear a suit with a tie to lead the team out, then nip around behind the bench and change into his tracksuit.

'Hmm.' Ruud likes to think things over.

I pressed him about his future.

'I see no reason to go away. I love it here. The people are great. In Italy they want to touch you . . .' he motioned to his chin and tugged at it! '. . . but the English are more reserved, just like the Dutch, but they are still happy about it.

'But I just want to thank everyone in England for their support. For myself I want to thank them for the wonderful reception they have given me when I first came to England. And, of course, the fans in general and Chelsea fans have been great. I want to stay, but I need a challenge in my life and we shall have to see.'

That challenge would be the chance of finishing at least second to win a place in the Champions League. In a frank exchange Gullit explained what motivates him. 'It is difficult for me to know what my future is because I am somebody who lives so much by the week. I will know what to do when the moment comes. I will think about it. I need a challenge in my life, that is the biggest thing. If I don't have that challenge in my life I would become lazy, sloppy. If I start something I want to do it one hundred per cent. That is why before I start anything I must think it over carefully. Next year is time enough to do that. At the moment I am very happy with what is happening. It is not so much about commitment, it is about seeing what happens next year. I never wanted the job. I was asked to take it on and I did. This year has been my first as a coach, and it was all new to me. Next year it will be different. Different because I will want to improve again.'

With a smile and nod, Gullit acknowledged that he wouldn't start a second season in charge if it hadn't worked out; it's worked out better than he anticipated both on and off the field.

His terms of reference with the board are one of the positive points. Managers resent interference from chairman and directors. Not Gullit. He welcomes it! Gullit only took the job on the pre-condition that he concentrated on playing, coaching and organising the team. The only management role he wanted was on the training pitch in total control of the team and in the choice of signings. Delegation was the key word – a pure continental-style approach to coaching and management. Gullit and Bates do not cross swords on any subject. Instead they pit their wits against each other with little jokes. Gullit said of his rapport with Bates: 'My relationship is very good. Interference? No! We have very good rules here at the club. I asked the club to get involved in transfers, money, which I didn't want to do. Everything is separated and everybody has their own island. That's why it works so well. Each person has carte blanche to express themselves.'

The one certainty about his future is that he has no intention of retiring as a player and will join his FA Cup finalists and new recruits for pre-season training. Once again 'enjoyment' was a key word when I asked him how long he intended to play on for. 'The most important thing is that I can enjoy it and that I can still do it. I cannot play again now because I had a bad injury, a broken ankle, but I will play next season, and I don't know how long I will go on for, I really don't know. It's really about attitude, not time. I want to give something when I play and I don't want to throw away the chance of playing if I can. I have worked very hard for it and I will play on while it is still fun.'

There are those who are convinced it is hard to combine playing and management. Gullit can manage the two – if anyone can. He was hailed as a great innovator, revolutionising the English game with his European thinking. A new philosophy for the game, a cult with new followers from the young players at the Bridge.

It was a surprise to listen to the Ruud Revolution according to Ruud. 'I don't know how the English see me. But I didn't come here to change something, or with the purpose to teach things. I came to England with the purpose of enjoying myself, for the football, for quality football. Suddenly, after one year as a player, I get this job as the coach. I have put into the game as a coach what I was used to as a player, with all my years of experience. Okay, so it has turned out that I have taught British players, or Romanian players, but I did not have that in mind when I arrived here. But if I have changed anything, it has been players' attitudes, and that is incredibly pleasing for me as the coach. The players are aware of what being a professional is all about.

'And, so far I have achieved nothing. I don't have that feeling that I have already done something very big.' That was the response to my assertion that to become the first foreign coach to make it to the Cup final was an extraordinary feat – notably in his first season in charge. So, I asked him what constitutes achievement in his eyes.

'To win the cup, of course. That would be an achievement, a big compliment for the players. But it would be only one moment. I have to think about next season – which players I want, things I want to change. Yeah, this year has been the easy part for me because everything was new. Next year it will be much different.'

Gullit always talked affectionately about 'the cup with the big ears'. You get the feeling that his ambitions have no limits. He will want to achieve as a coach what he managed as a player of enormous stature – the European Cup. That is why the Premiership is so important to him as a passport to that competition, particularly as second place also provides qualification. For that reason the cup in Italy, for example, is downgraded in importance and stature. Gullit explained: 'The "cup with the big ears" is what every manager would like, that is the dream. But I am not even thinking about it. At the moment it is not a possibility; maybe it will be later on. But why torture yourself by focusing on that when at this moment it is not realistic if Manchester United are winning the league all the time? Yeah, I want the cup with the big ears, but that would mean a team that is winning the championship all the time. And that means having a team of high quality.'

Gullit is in pursuit of that team of high quality for next season, and he would not object to Vialli being part of it. 'Yeah, I'd like him to stay.' But doesn't Vialli want to be wanted? Gullit agreed. 'I can understand that. I understand perfectly. But I treat Vialli as a professional and in doing that I have to separate my private relationship and must have a professional relationship instead.'

Will Vialli play in the final? Gullit's response was a challenge to Vialli to prove that he should be in the starting line-up. So far there was little to justify Vialli's claims, and plenty of evidence to support the manager. The majority of Chelsea fans sing Vialli's name, but didn't believe he should oust either Zola or Hughes. The big question was whether Gullit could accommodate all three. On whether Vialli will win a Cup final place he said: 'It all depends how everyone is doing. There is Zola and Mark Hughes who have played so well, and they are the facts.'

It might be even harder for Vialli once Gullit finalises his recruitment plans. 'Of course, as a coach you always need to improve the team. At the moment I have the players I need, and I'll let you know when we get the ones I want for next season.'

I asked Gullit what has been the most satisfying and most distressing aspects of management he has experienced. Dropping Vialli and Wise had been the most difficult. 'It has been a difficult situation with Vialli. And it hurts me in a way because of the personal relationship with my players. It is just the same also with Dennis. It hurts you personally but it has to be professionally separated. But it has given me great satisfaction when players come back from that, and when they understand what you mean by it. Dennis Wise immediately springs to mind, and now I feel he deserves a place in the national side. He definitely merits a place in the England team. He has become more consistent, and he is playing good football. I don't know why he isn't. I wish that he was in the team.'

Gullit was hurt when he was the victim of some savage and uncalled-for criticism because of his stance over Vialli. One vile attack from a former Dutch coach who had made a racist remark against Gullit was particularly wounding. 'Yeah, that sort of thing always hurts. But it was something I was always used to. I have played on a high level and knew how these things work. When you get closer to winning something, it is strange, the attacks are going to come. I had it in Holland and in Italy. Unfortunately it is a human thing. As we got close to the final I knew one day it would come. I didn't know from which angle or who would do it, but I knew it would happen. Really, I am not even worried about it. I am not even angry about it. It is part of the job.'

Overall, was he enjoying his new role as the Boss? 'Yeah! The most important thing is to enjoy it, and if you do the players notice that.'

Gullit's message to his Cup final team will be to enjoy the experience, play their football, but be tuned in, focused, concentrated, and above all else to produce their optimum and win. 'We have experienced players like Mark Hughes who are used to the Cup final, the same with Zola. Everyone has pleased me in their own way. No exceptions. Especially the young players like Jody and Paul Hughes.'

He doesn't contemplate defeat in the final, but knows it might happen. 'People made us favourites for some time. Wherever I have gone people have expected a lot. I am used to pressure. Ask any coach, ask Robson, it is not so nice when you lose a final. But at the beginning of the season no one really thought we would make it to the final. Now we are there we must go out to win. I remember one final, the European Championships, when we went to a concert the night before and still won. The reason? We had beaten the Germans in Germany and that was good enough for us.'

It's been a long season for Gullit in his dual role as player and coach, fighting injuries and pushing his team further forward in their development. What does he plan to do after the final?

'A n-i-c-e holiday.' Where are you off to? 'I am going a long way. I don't want to see any English, I don't want to see any Italian, I don't want to see any Dutch. I just want a quiet time.' Possibly a remote Portuguese villa.

Gullit believed Manchester United can win the 'cup with the big ears'. Gullit hoped Ferguson would emulate Sir Matt Busby because of the help the United boss gave him before his own great adventure into management at the start of the season. 'Manchester United's chances are very good. Yeah, there is no reason why they cannot beat Dortmund, even though they are a goal down. It's all down to self-belief and I sense that Manchester Untied possess it. If they want the trophy bad enough they will win it. That takes real confidence, and it is perhaps the most important ingredient – even more so than organisation.' Overcoming the Germans will be hard enough, but then champions Juventus are awaiting them in the final. Juve have already beaten the English champions twice in the Champions League. But Gullit said: 'If United play well in the final they could beat Juve. If you believe in yourself, you can achieve anything.' Gullit does not hide his admiration for the Manchester United manager. 'I admire Ferguson, the way he works. He was kind to me, spoke to me about the job of management, how things work. I appreciated it, he didn't have to do it.' The respect is mutual. Ferguson's big regret as United boss was not signing Gullit. 'Did he say that?' enquired Ruud. 'That was a nice compliment. I didn't know that, but I am very happy about it.' No chance of getting Gullit now!

SATURDAY, APRIL 19
Chelsea 2 Leicester City 1
Fifteen minutes before kick off Bates bounded into the press room to announce he had appointed a new manager because of the debate over a new contract for Gullit. He introduced the dreadlocked showjumper Oliver Skeete, a dead ringer for Ruud! Bates enjoyed his joke and said: 'Reaching the FA Cup Final is a platform for future growth. We intend to make our mark in Europe next season and go on to become a top club in Britain.'

Gullit's team had to either win the Cup or come out of their Premiership nose-dive. The end of their sequence of four successive defeats cheered up Bates, and indeed Gullit, who was looking to the future. 'Yes, I can spend more money. Ken Bates is backing me with his tremendous work off the field and together we can make Chelsea great. We have not discussed my future yet. I've got one year left of my existing contract and don't want to leave. I need a challenge in my life and I came here for a challenge. I'm certainly not here just for the money and I don't want people at Chelsea whose only aim is to chill out and enjoy London. I want committed players. My signings and I have proved that foreigners don't just come to England for the money. Today you saw the other side of Chelsea. We were very secure in defence.'

Zola stayed behind at the end to sign the autographs and personally shake the hands of the thirty-six excited seven-year-olds from form 2T of the Warren Park Primary School in Leigh Park Havant, who had made a record about him – a remake of the Kinks' sixties hit Lola, renamed Zola. 'When I received a cassette of the song I was surprised and amazed. To have a song written about you, especially by children, is one of the most satisfying things for any player. My grandfather always told me to listen to what children say.' He smiled. 'He said that's because they always tell the truth. Me too. Perhaps that is why they like me and I like them. That's why I say that what has happened to me in the five months since I came here is something I could only dream about.'

He paid for all the children and their two teachers to be his guests. Les Terry, teacher, composer and guitarist, strummed away as the children sang long and loud. Zola smiled and hummed along. 'We wrote the words, sent off a tape and were amazed when the club wrote back and said Gianfranco liked it,' said Terry. 'The kids weren't expecting anything. He must be swamped by things like this, but we're now here. We've had £500 worth of free tickets, we've all got pictures and autographs and are hoping to get a signed jersey. What a day. It's been brilliant.' Terry and Colin Harris, the Warren Park head, couldn't thank Zola enough. 'It's my pleasure and I hope I will see you again.'

Zola was about to experience his first FA Cup Final song with his team-mates. He was more nervous about his part in the song than playing at Wembley! 'I am very worried about the record, but at least it will be something we can remember for ever.'

The ever-modest Zola admitted that his move had gone better than he could ever have imagined after a small yet significant role as a substitute in a welcome win over the Coca-Cola Cup winners. 'It has been like a dream for me, and it would have been impossible to imagine the satisfaction that I have had since coming to Chelsea. I have been very pleased with the way it has gone so far and now I want to finish the season by winning the cup.'

He was quick to praise Hughes. 'He has had a fantastic season. He is a very important player, not just for myself but for the whole team. My game has been helped by his support, and he helps the team by holding the ball in attack. He keeps the ball at the right moments, giving team-mates time to recover. He is one of the best players that I have played with, very similar in style to Pierluigi Casiraghi. They do a similar job and bring stability to the team.' Zola added: 'We are a strange team, who can beat Manchester United and then lose to the bottom side. We have to concentrate more all the time. Ruud told us that it is not possible to play your best football all the time, and that sometimes you have to be solid and not give the opposition any chances. That is what Italy did against England. It is not just an Italian mentality. I saw Manchester United play like that at Liverpool. Chelsea have demonstrated that we can beat those sort of teams but we need to make some improvements if we are to be a top side. But we are not far from it. If you don't give chances it makes things hard for them.

'I was on the bench because Ruud said I needed a rest. I am okay but sometimes you need a break, we have so many games. I like to play all the time but I know it is not possible. It would be very bad if I got an injury now, especially because of the FA Cup.'

The Chelsea players lined up to applaud their Coca-Cola Cup-winning opponents onto the pitch before handing them each a bunch of flowers. Gullit said: 'It's done on the continent if a club has won something. Leicester knew about it because flowers are thought of as a cissy thing here. But flowers are nice; everyone likes them, especially women.'

The match itself was hardly the Chelsea Flower Show. Plenty of thorns, rather than roses. New boots, but the same Hughes, making the first goal and scoring the winner before limping off with fifteen minutes to go, off on the 6.45pm shuttle to Manchester, nursing the blisters that come from breaking in his smart new blue footwear. But again he showed why he is so important with his fourteenth goal of the season, Chelsea shaking off a persistent Leicester only when Hughes was reunited with Zola. By then it was clear why Gullit was right again about Vialli: his only meaningful contribution was to be involved in the first goal. At times both Hughes and Vialli hunted the same ball, and when Pontus Kaamark moved inside to pick him up Vialli found himself stifled by the specialist man marker, something he might have been used to in Italy. At the final whistle he was off and out of the Bridge in a chauffeur-driven limo, knowing he had blown another chance to force Gullit to think again.

Victory in the league at last, for after Minto had put the Blues ahead and Sinclair had put through his own goal, Leicester looked capable of sharing the points. Only the woodwork and a goal-line clearance prevented them as they came close in a feverish finish.

Later that night in a pre-recorded Alan Hansen documentary, *The Sack Race*, on BBC2, Gullit revealed the only occasion he really blew his top. The pressure was at its most intense for many reasons – the first match after Matthew Harding's death. 'Yes, I lost my temper; it was in the game against Tottenham Hotspur at home. I think we played very well and we were one-up, and in the last couple of minutes we made some terrible mistakes and I couldn't handle it. I was so frustrated about it. I went a little bit out of control in a moment and later on I got back again.' Gullit confessed that dropping his pals is the toughest task of being a manager. The change of role has meant a change in attitude. 'It's difficult. I must admit that was the worst part because I was with guys I normally play golf with, or go out with. Now I have to say to them, "Maybe you don't play," or you have to approach them in a different way and that is very hard. I had to make some decisions that were very difficult for me, yes, personal, but I had to do it as a coach.'

SUNDAY, APRIL 20

The Cup final squad joined pop star and Chelsea fan Suggs to record their Cup final song in a west London recording studio. Blue Is The Colour is a football classic of the seventies, now it was Blue Day under the name Team Chelsea. Suggs from Madness fronted the club's follow-up to 1994's vintage No One Can Stop Us Now – no one apart from Manchester United!

The 1997 version, written by Chelsea season-ticket holder Mike Connaris, became an emotional Cup final day anthem, with gems like:

> We've got some memories,
> Albeit from the seventies,
> When Ossie and Co restored our pride.
> Now we've got hope, and a team
> And suddenly it's not a dream.

Blue Day went into recording at the West Side Studios even before the players had agreed to do it; Suggs had performed the lead vocal days before, and the players went to the studios to join in the chorus and record the video. For the video the players came to the mike at random to sing in time to the music. When Luca strolled up for a solo he took a deep breath, hands clapping to the rhythm . . . and the tape ran out! Amidst the laughter David Lee shouted: 'Ruud's turned it off!' Hysterics followed, and it can be heard on the CD featuring a special karaoke mix.

Ruud wasn't there. He preferred to stay out of the limelight. Suggs said: 'I wouldn't hear a bad word said against him, but for some reason he wasn't that keen to join in with the record. He was probably more concerned with working on tactics for the big day.' Also missing was Hughes, who had flown home to Manchester for the weekend the day before, and Di Matteo, who flew home to Switzerland at the same time.

They all moved on to a photographic studio to shoot the cover for the CD. There was a piano there. Zola couldn't be persuaded to play, but Luca had a go.

Released twelve days before the final, Wise said: 'Blue Day really catches the team spirit. We had a great laugh recording it – but it's a good job we play football and don't sing for a living!'

Final rivals Boro teamed up with Bob Mortimer and pop legend Chris Rea to record a version of Let's Dance ... there was only going to be one Wembley sing-along winner.

MONDAY, APRIL 21

Chelsea faced a re-run of the semifinal at Selhurst Park, with Hughes doubtful. Williams said: 'Sparky did a bit of training today but may have to miss the Wimbledon game.' Youth team striker Joe Shearin, eighteen, was added to the squad. Wise and Clarke were still out with minor injuries. Johnsen was also sidelined with back trouble. Forrest continued to deputise for hamstring-injury victim Grodas, although Hitchcock was back in training. Leboeuf was available before a one-match ban came into effect.

Kinnear said, with more than a hint of envy, 'The only problem Ruud Gullit will have is whether to field his £30m team or his £20m team. But I have had to put up with that kind of thing from the opposition for six years and it isn't going to get easier.'

TUESDAY, APRIL 22

Wimbledon 0 Chelsea 1

Leboeuf was captain for the first time. Zola gave Wimbledon another footballing masterclass. There was also the obligatory Cup final injury scare.

Zola pulled up in pain in the final seconds, running for a loose ball, and was hastily replaced by young Sherrin. He immediately departed for treatment, clutching a hamstring, but Gullit was confident he would be fit for the final. Zola gingerly trudged off and Gullit said: 'He has a little muscle problem but it's not that bad. His thigh muscle has gone into spasm, we will not know the full extent of the damage for twenty-four hours. But I am not too worried about him for the Cup final because it is too early to say and, anyway, we have other players who can replace him. They do not have the same kind of skill but can certainly do a job for the team. He will go with the national team though I don't think he will be able to play, but I will allow him to travel with the squad. We didn't take any chance and he was having treatment as soon as he came off. While away he will be able to get treatment from the Italian doctor every day and that should help him.' The injury made him a big doubt for Italy in their World Cup qualifier against Poland in Naples, to take place on the same day England faced Georgia at Wembley.

Zola was determined to make the Wembley showpiece. 'I was running for the ball a minute from the end and felt a twinge. The muscle just went tight. I know exactly what these things are like so I didn't do anything silly. We'd already won the game and I thought the best thing was to get off the pitch as soon as I could. I'm not in any pain; it's just a matter of wait and see what the medical people tell me. I'm desperate to play for Italy because it's a very important game for us. But I will not be taking any chances. That's because the FA Cup Final is less than four weeks away and I definitely want to be ready for it. I'm travelling to Italy and will have treatment every day. Hopefully I will be fit for the Poland match, but I shall not take risks. I love Wembley and want to go there and score again.' Zola would have medical tests in Florence to determine the exact nature and severity of the problem.

There was no getting away from it. No Zola, no chance in the final. In terms of ability and invention, he was irreplaceable. Gullit admitted: 'He gives the team something extra.' Once again his performance underlined that fact. He'd scored in every round of the FA Cup except the fifth-round tie against Leicester. An admiring Kinnear said: 'Everybody would like a Zola in their side. I think he's been the pick of the foreign players this season. Zola can unlock sides when it's stalemate and win a game with one piece of skill. And when you think he's only been here since November he has settled in brilliantly.'

Chelsea made seven changes from the semifinal but were still too classy for Wimbledon. Sullivan made a string of fine saves, from Vialli and Nicholls in particular, to keep the score down.

The solitary goal came after a quarter of an hour. Zola's exquisite through pass sent Petrescu through alone on goal and he beat Sullivan. When Zola beautifully beat Perry out on the left and found Vialli with remarkable sleight of foot, Vialli's high shot was caught by Sullivan. Later, when Zola gave Petrescu another chance, Sullivan repelled the incursion, as he did when Nicholls forced him to turn the ball for a corner. And in the ninetieth minute Vialli, all alone and clearly desperate to score, was thwarted by the resilient keeper.

Wimbledon, without the backbone of their team and bringing Gayle on only late in the game, troubled Forrest just once. That was when, after thirty-one minutes, Jones got his head to Ardley's left-wing corner but Sinclair headed off the line.

Promising youngsters Hughes and Nicholls had lively games. Gullit said he was particularly pleased with the performances of Myers and Nicholls. But Zola was still the star of the show.

Gullit was displeased when, late in the second half, Forrest went down under a challenge by Euell, and when the ball was kicked out of play Jones took a normal throw-in. Gullit spoke darkly, if obliquely, of the 'bad example from Blackburn' the previous Saturday, when Arsenal had accused Sutton of flouting the unwritten rule of giving the ball back to the opposition when it has been put out after an injury. 'We saw another example of that and I hope it stops here and now. There is no need for it. Vinnie Jones just threw the ball back in when our goalkeeper was injured in a challenge with a Wimbledon player. There has been a code of honour among players, not only in England but everywhere the game is played. I hope this is not a new trend and I certainly don't want to see it spreading. If teams start getting away with things like that, then others will think they can too.'

Chelsea were gearing up for the final. Gullit said: 'I hope I have a selection problem for the final because that means everyone will be fit.' And their opponents were Boro – Juninho, Ravanelli and Emerson.

Juninho promised a devastating performance after the bitter disappointment of the Coca-Cola Cup battering from Leicester. Juninho, Man of the Match in the emphatic replay defeat of brave Chesterfield, wanted his boyhood heroes Pele and Zico to come to Wembley. Juninho knew how important it was for Boro to ensure European football at the Riverside if the club were to have any chance of keeping

Ravanelli and Emerson – and himself! 'I have already played twice at Wembley and now I am so happy to be going back there. It's a brilliant pitch and a fabulous atmosphere, which brings the best out of you. I can see why the English players think the FA Cup is the best competition in the world. Now it is important for us to bring a trophy back for the supporters.

'I came to England to win things and now that is starting to happen. We had a chance in the Coca-Cola Cup and it didn't happen, but now we have another chance. I think Chelsea will suit our style more than Leicester did. Like us, they always look to bring the ball down, pass and play. That can only be good for us, and for the crowd. I think I will get more space this time. But I have watched a lot of Italian football, and I know that Zola is an excellent player – different class. I think that the English supporters prefer Italian football to the South American game, but I have had a wonderful welcome in this country. Wherever I go people call my name and ask for my autograph. Not just Middlesbrough supporters, but all fans. I am very proud to be going back to Wembley, but what is even more important is that we stay in the Premier League.'

Robson said: 'People have had a go at my foreign lads but Juninho has been fantastic all season.' Their priority was survival and they faced an exhausting programme before the final. 'If we win the Cup and stay in the Premier League, it won't have been such a troubled season after all ... apart from all these grey hairs!'

FRIDAY, APRIL 25

Zola was declared fit to take on Poland – bad news for England, good news for Chelsea. 'As soon as I arrived in Italy and had all the tests with the Italian team medical staff, they all proved negative. I needed a couple of days of rest and now I'm ready to play.' The Italians called up Roberto Baggio from his long international exile as cover. 'It was nice to see Roberto back in the squad; it must have been hard for a great player like him to be left out all this time. For me it was great motivation to be playing when I knew somebody like him was waiting in the wings.'

SATURDAY, APRIL 26

Bates was accused of ripping off Chelsea fans by selling hospitality Cup final tickets and shares in the ground to qualify for a ticket. For £495 plus VAT fans received a £35 ticket for the final as part of a hospitality package which included lunch with celebrity speakers and travel to and from Wembley. The other deal offered fans the chance to buy two £35 tickets if they bought five £100 shares in the Chelsea Pitch Owners Association. The FA insisted that only they have the right to sell final tickets as part of hospitality packages.

FA spokesman Steve Double said: 'No club is allowed to sell corporate hospitality packages that include FA Cup Final tickets. The FA is the only organisation allowed to provide hospitality packages. The only way clubs should sell their FA Cup Final tickets is in the usual legitimate way through the box office.' Bates pointed out that the FA sell 4,000 of their own hospitality packages at £850 a time. Ironically Bates is on the FA match and grounds committee and had an input in deciding that the FA should sell up-market corporate hospitality packages. Bates believed the FA guilty of hypocrisy in suggesting Chelsea cannot sell hospitality packages while they are at liberty to do so because the money is channelled back into good causes such as 'grass-roots football'. Bates said: 'As far as I'm concerned, the FA speak with forked tongues. They say that this money from hospitality packages goes directly back into grass-roots football. Where is the specific grass-roots football fund? Is it separate from everything else? I don't think it is because I've never seen it. The FA trot out that their money goes to grass-roots football as a convenient excuse for everything.' He added: 'What we are doing is after consultation with the FA. Like the FA, we are ploughing profits from the hospitality package back into schemes such as Football in the Community and the club's youth policy. The most important issue is that the public have the right to know where all the FA Cup Final tickets go. As Cup finalists we received 25,000 tickets and so did Middlesbrough, so what has happened to the other 26,000 tickets?

'The FA packages at £850 are quickly snapped up by corporations that have nothing to do with football. But I supported the idea because there were companies selling these packages anyway and ripping off the FA. There is a need for this kind of service because you can't get a decent meal in VIP treatment at Wembley and there are people who don't want to go by tube and eat a hamburger. Our packages will give everyone a day out at Stamford Bridge, transport to Wembley and we've limited it to 500 – the number that can comfortably get into the Bridge. I consulted the chairman of the match and grounds committee, Jack Wiseman, and he made the point that provided the tickets are available to the people who don't want to buy hospitality packages and provided they are sold at face value it was okay by him. That has been confirmed in writing by the FA's solicitors. As for selling shares in the ground in conjunction with a Cup final ticket, I cleared that with Pat Smith of the FA and she said that if we allocated a certain number of tickets to a certain class of supporters, provided those tickets were sold at no more than face value, then it met with approval.'

Bates feared that with so many tickets not distributed by the Cup finalists, the perennial Cup final black market would be in operation. 'We have already discovered one travel agency trying to jump on the bandwagon purporting to sell hospitality packages in our name – and they've received a solicitor's letter from us.'

SUNDAY, APRIL 27

Vialli was in Barcelona playing for an all-star Europe team that lost 4–3 to the Rest of the World. 'It's a novelty for me to get a game,' he said. 'Chelsea give me so few chances to play. Now I'm looking ahead to the FA Cup Final, when some from among myself, Zola, Di Matteo, Festa and Ravanelli will become the first Italians to win a trophy in England. But it's no surprise to me – the reason English clubs have brought us in is to help them win things.'

Vialli was not contemplating going back home to Italy, but his future at the Bridge was still open to doubt. 'Back home I have had some successes. But I've achieved fairly little in London. There's no denying that I have fared worse than any of the other Italian players in the Premiership. I don't know where I'll be playing in England next season.' He dismissed talk of a move to Serie A side Atalanta. 'Those stories are lies – I have not spoken to anybody at the club. I have no desire to go back to play in Italy – my future lies elsewhere. I will be in England next season – but I don't yet know where. That doesn't necessarily mean I plan to leave Chelsea, but neither does it mean I will stay there. I still have so much to prove in England.'

In an interview with *4-4-2* magazine Vialli said he was hardly talking to Gullit any more. 'Sometimes I don't know what's happening between me and the manager. Gullit doesn't speak to the players much. I feel very frustrated but I'm trying my best to remain calm and then at the end of the season I'll decide what I must do. I signed for three years but I don't want to spend the next two years at Chelsea sitting on the bench. I am happy here, but only seventy-five per cent happy.

'I was very happy when Chelsea called me last summer because I wanted to learn English and go to England. I could have joined Rangers in Scotland but I love London and wanted to come here. Here I can live my own life, have my privacy, go shopping with a girlfriend or to the theatre or cinema and no one cares. That is fantastic. In Italy it was impossible to go out so I was always at home.

'The quality of football in Italy is higher. It's about mentality. That's why every time an English team plays an Italian team they lose. We are smarter. We know we have to win. When we play it's a war. We know we must win or afterwards our own fans will be waiting for us. That's why so many British players have failed in Italy. They just didn't have the right mentality. In Italy it's very tactical. We know everything about opponents – their corner and free-kick strategies, how fit they are, what they do when they're with their wives. When we play it's like a job. We're always under pressure. In England it's more relaxed because football is not so important and players try to enjoy themselves. That is very important when you're thirty-two. England is the right place to play when you want to enjoy yourself.'

MONDAY, APRIL 28
Zola, in the build-up to Italy's World Cup tie, hinted he favoured finishing his career in Italy, preferably with his former club Napoli! 'I will be at Chelsea next season – that is a hundred per cent certainty. But after that we will have to see. I am no longer a little kid – in fact I will be thirty-four by the turn of the century. I would like to finish my playing career in Italy, and I will do it for sure. I have made up my mind where I want to go, although I can't yet say where. I've got a plan and I know what I would like to do. I've already decided but I'm not going to say. It would bring me bad luck.' Napoli was believed to be his target. 'Napoli made me into the player I am today. I was a nobody when I joined them, but I had the chance to learn from Maradona. There was a real atmosphere about the place, and it was the most important stage of my career.' But moving to Chelsea has helped him recapture his best form. 'I am very glad I moved to England. It has helped me a great deal. I have improved as a player because nowadays I am more self-confident and I have more freedom to play my own type of game.'

Hutchinson responded: But he has three years left on his contract and has every intention of enjoying them to the full at Chelsea.' Zola later reiterated this news, adding that he'd like to play for his home town team Cagliari, in Sardinia.

TUESDAY, APRIL 29
The players' pool was in full swing, organised by soccer agent Paul Stretford. A number of agents vied for the lucrative pot, and a players' committee had the final choice. Stretford's task was to 'sell' the Cup final team for as much money as possible in the short space of time. Newspapers were one source of revenue. Stretford contacted the papers with players' interviews for sale. He had a three-tier price range. 'The big hitters' were on offer for between £7,000 and £12,000 each – Gullit, Wise, Leboeuf, Hughes and the three Italians. Category B was Petrescu, Clarke, Sinclair, Burley, Morris and Myers at £3,000 to £7,000. 'The supporting cast' were valued upwards of £1,000 – Rix, Forrest, Kharine, Grodas, Granville, Paul Hughes, Minto, Parker, Rocky and Lee.

Gullit was unaware of his involvement. After being told a few days after by his agent, Jon Smith, he opted out. Smith, who contacted Stretford to explain Gullit's policy, said: 'He felt the whole business of charging the media for interviews "silly". He has never done it and doesn't want to start now.' Zola was in talks about signing for Smith and he too would be taken out of the interview 'pot'. Once lucrative, the Players' Pool couldn't be sure of charging large sums for interviews with newspaper budgets so tight.

WEDNESDAY, APRIL 30

Di Matteo grabbed Italy's twenty-third-minute opener in the 3–0 defeat of Poland in Naples, his first international goal. Paolo Maldini notched up the second and Roberto Baggio scored a glorious third as Italy took control of the game that kept them top of World Cup qualifying Group Two. Italy were unbeaten on sixteen points, ahead of England on twelve with a game in hand. Baggio came on for Zola, who had struck the bar with a venomous shot in the first half and although put through was thwarted by the keeper. Zola limped off but his early exit was 'precautionary'. Zola was replaced after fifty-one minutes and was doubtful for Chelsea's final home game with Leeds.

MAY

The first foreign coach to lead out a Cup Final team.... Chelsea win their first mayor trophy in twenty-six years. Zola voted Footballer of the Year

THURSDAY, MAY 1

A third transfer coup – Tor Andre Flo, the twenty-three-year-old Brann Bergen striker, on a free transfer. The Norwegian, with eleven caps, nearly joined Everton in a pre-transfer deadline £2.6m deal after impressing against Liverpool in the European Cup Winners Cup. Royle's enthusiasm for the transfer was not shared by Goodison chairman Peter Johnson and led to them parting company. Chelsea were prepared to wait until November to secure Flo on a free as his contract expires on October 31.

The club claimed Chelsea broke the rules and threatened to complain to FIFA that the pre-contract was discussed outside the six-month rule. Hutchinson insisted he only jetted to Oslo to finalise the deal on May 1 to meet Flo and his lawyer and clinch the five-year contract, countering, 'I know what they are saying at Brann but we met on May 1, and completed the deal after four hours of talks. Erland Johnsen was returning to Norway and we were faxed by Rosenborg in December although he was not allowed to sign until January 1. But we have not reported Rosenborg.'

Hutchinson added: 'Flo is well known to us. We've watched him for over a year. He was put in the shop window for the English market with Brann's two Cup Winners Cup quarterfinal ties against Liverpool. Although we have a number of high-quality forwards, they are all more experienced players, so at twenty-three Flo represents a great capture with real potential.'

An enthusiastic Flo said: 'I am a big fan of English football and it has always been my ambition to play in the Premiership. I have had offers from England, Germany and Italy, but once I knew Chelsea wanted me my decision was made very easy. Playing with so many great players and being coached by Ruud Gullit can only make me a better player. It's a great move for me.' Gullit said: 'My new signings will add a dimension as we set about trying to win major honours. I have brought two players in on "frees" and Flo will be a very useful goal-scoring acquisition. But there should be more newcomers because Chelsea is now the club players want to join.'

Gullit was not satisfied just to become the fifth manager to reach the Cup final in Chelsea's history, planning ahead to next season with central defenders high on his list including West Ham's Slaven Bilic and Xavier Aguado of Real Zaragoza, with Johnsen going and Duberry and Lee recovering from long-term injuries as well as Marcel Desailly of AC Milan. But Gullit was also looking for English players, sending his specialist coach Niedzwiecki to run the rule over England international Flowers at Southampton. He had four goalkeepers in his first-team pool, but he would be prepared to offload two to finance a move for Flowers, who had already broken the British transfer record for keepers once when he joined Blackburn from Southampton for £2.4m. From abroad, Rossi showed no signs of leaving, Maldini was not allowed to leave Milan and so the favourite was Ed de Goey of Feyenoord.

But the row with Brann Bergen rumbled on as they threatened to register Flo for next season's European campaign if they didn't get a proper transfer fee. The Norwegian part-timers were furious their £2.3m-rated striker was heading for Stamford Bridge on a free transfer. If Brann carried out their threat to register Flo for Europe, he would be ineligible for the Blues until the quarterfinals – should Chelsea win the Cup.

Embarrassed Flo offered to pay Brann £200,000 out of his own pocket after delaying his departure until he became a free agent. But Brann president Lars Henrik Berge raged: 'We are very disappointed and a little bitter about what has happened. We had a gentleman's agreement with Flo that we would allow him to leave when we got a good offer for him. Suddenly we are losing the most valuable player in Norway and we are not getting anything for him. If I'd known this was going to happen I would have accepted Graeme Souness's offer when he first came in for Flo in October.'

Even Flo admitted: 'I don't feel too good about what has happened because I like Brann Bergen and owe them a lot. They have treated me very well and I would have liked them to have got some money for me.'

Chelsea offered £300,000 for Brann to release Flo immediately. Hutchinson said: 'When a player like Flo becomes available you've got to move in and take him, particularly when he's a free agent. We've signed him on a pre-contract and he officially joins us on November 1 on a free transfer. The only way that situation might change is if we sit down with Brann and work out a minimal deal for him to arrive earlier. A lot depends on how Brann are doing in the Norwegian championship.'

Gullit wanted to assemble a squad to rival Manchester United, prepared to field an entire side without a single British player. 'Every player here will have to get used to being on the bench. I know some will find that difficult. I found it strange when I was at Milan because I was used to playing all the time. But it's now impossible to play every game at a consistent level so I want twenty-two top players of equal ability who can cope with big demands all the time. I don't want us to be like Fiorentina, Paris St Germain or Schalke, who do well in the Cup competitions but are only midway in their leagues. We need to be more like Manchester United or Juventus. That's why we need more people of real quality.'

Gullit spent £14.3m on foreigners, with at least £4m to follow. 'I start fishing for players in January and make sure I'm in a good position to sign them as soon as they become available. We're in a very good position. A lot of players are being brought to me who are available and want to play at Chelsea. We are now being linked with the most important players in Europe and I'm very happy to be in this position. It's a compliment to us and the way we play.' Gullit told his players inconsistent league form will not be tolerated next season. 'I demand more of my team all the time. We have to do better than this year. We cannot kill off games and that has to change. We have already made good steps but there are still more to take.'

FRIDAY, MAY 2

Zola is named Footballer of the Year after just twenty-eight games in English football. Football writers cast their vote in favour of Zola despite playing only half a season in the Premiership. His spectacular goals, warm smile and willingness to take part in seemingly endless interviews, plus his match-winning ability that took Chelsea to the FA Cup Final, swayed the country's soccer writers. Zola only arrived from Parma in November and made a whirlwind impact, probably the most instantly successful foreign star ever. He was not only the first Italian to win the most prestigious individual award in the country, but the first Chelsea player in history. Not even Jimmy Greaves came close to winning the fifty-year-old trophy. Williams arranged for Zola to ring Dennis Signy at the FWA to comment. He said: 'Every footballer wants to win a prize like this and it is big honour for me. I feel very lucky. It is hard for me to explain with words what I am feeling. It is not easy to be voted Footballer of the Year because there are many good players in England.'

Zola polled twice as many votes as second-placed Juninho and Hughes put together. So, another success for the Blues – first and third in the awards. The top-placed Englishman was Beckham in fourth place. And Sir Stanley Matthews, winner of the original award in 1948, would be at the awards ceremony at the Royal Lancaster Hotel in two weeks' time to honour Zola.

Ironically, the votes were announced after Gullit demanded talks with soccer's authorities – and even Tony Blair's new government. 'Nobody is buying English players any more because nobody can afford them. I want to sign British players but every time I make an enquiry I'm quoted £8m and that's far too much when I can get players from abroad for nothing. It's very frustrating. All the talk, all the rumours of new signings and they are all foreigners. Englishmen aren't even being mentioned. Even Manchester United are now going abroad. We are reaching the situation where the Premiership is being flooded with foreigners who are not as good as the English players. But that is not the fault of the foreigners or the club owners. It's the fault of the system and we have to have a meeting to make English players cheaper.

'It's not a problem for me. I don't care if the British players are upset by all the foreigners and neither do the fans. As long as the team is winning I am happy. But home-grown players are suffering because you have to pay a fee for them and not for European signings. They are at a disadvantage and they must have the same rules for everyone. You have to adapt and become a part of Europe, even though many people in this country don't want to be. Maybe now you have a new government you can change the system and sort this problem out. There is no point in moaning about too many foreigners. You have to do something about it. The problem is that the transfer money is no longer circulating within the game. It's disappearing into someone's pocket.'

Zola wouldn't play again until the final after returning from Italy's World Cup win over Poland with a hamstring strain. He asked to be taken off after fifty-five minutes because of his nagging hamstring injury and underwent a scan. Gullit stressed that it was just a precaution and that the problem was not serious. Zola was given the all clear after the scan. 'It's good news. No damage, it's only a matter of muscle fatigue. A week's rest will do the job.'

Gullit had problems in defence, Leboeuf suspended and Clarke ruled out with a back injury. Burley was also doubtful with a knee injury but Grodas, Di Matteo, Wise and Hughes were all available again after being rested at Wimbledon. Hitchcock was back in the squad after playing in the reserves the previous night.

Gullit resumed training and physiotherapist Mike Banks said: 'Ruud had a crack in the fibula but it has healed very well. He is now busily strengthening up the muscles around his ankle, is running quite well and is not ruled out of the Cup final.' Gullit spent intensive sessions in a swimming pool, using hydrotherapy to get himself fit. He did not escape the Ade Mafe training treatment. 'I have to push him. I can't be too soft on him. He tries to shirk it sometimes, and he moans a bit, but he knows it's for his own benefit. He might be my boss but he's still a player and I tell him to get on with it.' But Ruud had no intention of pushing himself too hard, making the Cup final a target.

Bates stressed, in his match day programme notes, that Zola was not leaving halfway through his four-year contract. 'Zola is with us until the next century and can't be responsible for every Italian phrase taken out of context and/or misquoted.'

Zola cleared up any doubts. 'I hope I can stay here for a long time. I have a long contract and I hope to respect it. My family and my children have settled very well here. London is a fantastic city and I enjoy myself living here.'

SATURDAY, MAY 3

Chelsea 0 Leeds United 0

Gullit summed up the season in his final address to the fans in his programme notes: 'It has been a rollercoaster year. At least at home in most of the games we have done what we had to. I said already that Chelsea's ground has to be hell for the opposition, and it has been for the most part. That is thanks to you, the fans, as well as the players. We've played some very good football which I think you've appreciated. There've been very good vibes from both sides of us. It feels good. What is more, we had two games in a row against opposition that people have said we can't cope with. But against Leicester and Wimbledon we did and it was very useful. It gave me plenty to think about for next year and what is needed to beat such teams.

'We are now looking to end the season well. We owe this to ourselves. Then when we have finished against Everton we can start preparation for the FA Cup Final. Step by step.'

David Mellor's arrival in the Directors' Box was greeted with cries of 'He's on the dole, He's on the dole, Mellor's on the dole' by Leeds fans. Vialli sat alone in the dug-out, fag in hand, swigging from a bottle of beer. Long after a reluctant lap of honour with the rest of his team-mates, Vialli looked like a man taking one last glimpse at Stamford Bridge. The other members of the squad re-emerged from the tunnel and performed a patient tour, even troubling to applaud and wave to the deserted building site! Vialli, in T-shirt and flip-flops, performed a turn alone in the centre circle and jogged away. The farewell of a disillusioned man? Keeping his thoughts firmly to himself, he strolled across the pitch to be whisked quietly through the back door by his waiting chauffeur. Outside a main entrance still swarming with supporters, Sharpe, Rush, Palmer and Deane made an even more ostentatious exit in a huge white stretch limo.

Gullit refused to confirm that Vialli will leave but he was certain to be on the bench for the final. Given few chances by a mean Leeds defence to advance his claims, Vialli was convinced he should have been given a penalty when bundled over by Wetherall in the closing stages.

Johnsen, captain for the day in recognition of his last game at Stamford Bridge, was emotional as he said his goodbyes to the Chelsea ground staff. The Gullit revolution was only partially responsible for his decision to sign for Norwegian champions Rosenborg. 'I'm going when the club are on a real high but the way Chelsea are playing now does not really suit my game. The long-time professionals definitely get no advantage over the new arrivals and I feel that I should have had more first-team chances than I have this season. Chelsea have offered me a two-year contract but the time is right to go. If I'd stayed any longer it probably would have been too late to get a big club like Rosenborg.

'I am going to miss the players a lot and I must say thank you to the fans for the support they have given me. I was standing on the pitch at Highbury last month, beating Wimbledon with 25,000 Chelsea fans singing their hearts out, and I thought to myself, "What am I doing, going back to Norway?" It was such an emotional feeling being part of a big club like Chelsea with the best supporters in the country. Hopefully, I'll go with a Cup winners' medal in my pocket and I'm looking forward to coming back in a couple of years with Rosenborg for a Champions League game.'

Deprived of Zola, Chelsea were exposed by Graham's stifling approach as depressingly short of creative talent. Leeds' blanket defence smothered Chelsea so well that keeper Martyn, having shaken off tonsillitis, had only two saves to make. The best openings fell to Leeds but Lilley, surprisingly preferred to the unsettled Yeboah, missed two sitters.

Gullit admitted: 'I am not even thinking about the Cup final yet. No one will play on their reputation alone – they have to prove their fitness. Of course some people will be disappointed but I understand that. When I was at Milan I watched the European Cup Final against Marseille from the stands.'

MONDAY, MAY 5
Ravanelli pulled up as his hamstring went during Boro's gallant 3–3 draw at Old Trafford in their quest to beat the drop. Gullit was in the BBC studios with Des Lynam for the late-night *Match of the Day* programme. Asked by Des how he was coping with all the excitement of the final, Ruud made it clear he was still concentrating on the 'slight' chance of a UEFA Cup place with the last game at Everton. 'I am not participating in all the ... fuss.' He knew there would be some bitterly upset players when he named his Cup final team. 'It won't be a problem for me to leave people out. I think I have to pick up the best team, and the best players play. If you are fit and I think I can win the Cup with that team then I have to put them on the pitch. Of course I understand there will be some people disappointed. But I think if you win it everyone wins it, and if you lose it then everyone loses it. It's not true that only the eleven who play win it – it's good for everyone.' All his players were desperately battling to get involved on the big day. 'You can already see players that want to be part of it, players who were not fit, training like hell to be in that eleven. And that is good to see.'

He ruled himself out, even as a Wembley sub. 'No, I won't play. That would mean training all day and worrying about myself as well as the team – I'd be knackered! I think now I can concentrate myself more on the team and on the teambuilding.'

TUESDAY, MAY 6

Robson was hopeful Ravanelli would be fit. After a scan to establish the extent of the hamstring injury Robson, during a brief interview with *Channel Four Racing* at Chester, revealed the injury was not as serious as first feared. 'It's not snapped. It's not as bad as we first thought and hopefully we can get him fit for Wembley.' Ravanelli's prospects of playing looked remote when he left Old Trafford on crutches. But Robson's update appeared to improve the thirty-one-goal Italian's chances of recovering in time. Robson had already ruled Ravanelli out of Middlesbrough's two remaining Premiership matches at Blackburn and Leeds. Ravanelli said: 'I was quite scared at Manchester, but the news after the scan allows me to start hoping again. I feel I can make it for the final. I'm going to make sure and try my best to be there. There is no serious damage and I'm confident there is enough time.'

WEDNESDAY, MAY 7

The FA reprimanded Stretford for charging 'exorbitant' fees for interviews for the final. The FA stressed they did not hold the club responsible. Stretford hit back at adverse publicity for the way he was running the players' pool for the Cup final. 'The big stars are taking a cut but the money will also go to junior players, staff and a proportion to the Great Ormond Street Hospital. The players' pool doesn't make massive amounts of money for the big hitters. It enables us to share the cash out so that even people like the kit-men get a share.'

Middlesbrough issued a statement, making it plain that their players were not making such financial demands. Jon Smith of Wembley-based First Artist Management Corporation co-ordinated the media interest for Chelsea's Cup final opponents, and on his advice they threw out any plan to charge the media for interviews.

The FA were also upset when requests for information and interviews for the Wembley match programme were met by a fax from the agent. Wembley, who produce the match programme for the FA, wrote to Hutchinson asking for assistance. But the reply, by fax, came from Stretford's Pro-Active Sports Management. The fax said that the company would handle all media enquiries about 'Team Chelsea' and that they would get back with details in twenty-four hours. Wembley was still waiting. When a further specific request was made to talk to Hughes, it was claimed a 'contribution' would have to be made to Stretford's players' pool – but then Wembley again heard nothing more.

Wembley spokesman Martin Corrie said: 'I can't say we have been directly asked for cash by Chelsea, but their response means that we will have no interviews from them in the programme.'

Hutchinson said: 'I think someone's trying to stir it. If Wembley wanted to talk to the players why didn't they come to our regular Friday press conferences?' Stretford insisted: 'We have never intimated that Wembley would have to pay us.'

Gullit was not impressed by the rampant commercialism. Boot suppliers Mitre had a special pair of bright blue boots made for Hughes to lace up in the final. According to Mitre, Gullit told Hughes that the boots were a publicity gimmick and he didn't want him to wear them. Sparky had to make do with a pair of plain black Mitre boots instead. A spokesperson for Mitre said: 'We understand from Mark Hughes that Ruud Gullit does not want him to wear them at Wembley. It's a shame because they had been made specially for the occasion and I know he was delighted with the boots when they were sent to him.'

The players were furious over all the adverse publicity, branding them greedy for cashing in on their Cup final appearance. Clarke responded: 'We are all very upset about the negative publicity this issue has attracted. People have read that the big guns are charging a lot of money for interviews but that is not the idea. Our pool will be distributed among all the staff at Chelsea, from the ladies who clean the kit and run the canteen to the YTS boys. If we didn't have a pool the big-name players could take the money and run by going off and doing exclusives on their own. This way, everybody gets a share and the star names will probably end up with less money. The young players here on £200 per week are going to get a lot more out of it than the big earners relatively. We are also giving ten per cent of the proceeds to the Great Ormond Street Children's Hospital, a decision that was made before we got all this bad press.'

But Clarke admitted that the fuss generated by the issue could be just the spark Chelsea need to fire them up for Wembley. He added: 'Why do people have a pop at us? There seems to be an obsession with having a go at this club. Our attitude is, "Okay, if that is what you think about us, we'll show you." I think negative publicity brings the players a little bit closer together, especially if you have a good team spirit. We'll stick together and make sure we'll come through the other side smiling. It's like the situation before our semifinal with Wimbledon. We hadn't been playing particularly well before the semifinal and the media decided that because I'd raised my voice after our defeat at Coventry there was a crisis in the club. But these things happen in football and there would be something wrong if you didn't say anything after a defeat. Our performance in the semifinal was excellent and we proved that we can get ourselves up for the big games.'

FRIDAY, MAY 9

Zola missed the last league game to ensure his fitness, and in an ominous message to Boro he assessed his form. 'Since I came here I think I'm playing the best football of my life. I'm now more consistent every time I play so my game has got better in every match. All the things I've needed to play my football well have happened. I'm perfectly content on the pitch and off it with my family as well. It doesn't matter what job you do or what profession you're in, when you're relaxed, confident and happy you perform well – and that's certainly the case with me.'

Zola the Gola reckoned his match-winning effort in the vital World Cup qualifier against England went a big way towards helping him clinch that honour. 'I think that goal was very important for me. After that everybody knew me better. That goal was a very good step for me for getting this prize because all the country was watching that game, and it was a very, very important game. So if you win and you score you can get good popularity. But, yes, it was a big surprise for me to win it because it's a very important prize for a player. I'm playing in a top championship where there are some excellent players and I came here a couple of months after the season started. I thought it might be hard for me to settle in the beginning but everything has gone in the right way. And for that I have to thank my friends and Chelsea team-mates; they've helped me to be confident. I thought Shearer, Bergkamp or Juninho, or even Mark Hughes could have won it – they've all had great seasons.'

Gullit was not happy with the way his team had dipped in the league; he told them they should have already qualified for Europe. 'If you see the points that we've lost I think we could easily be in the top three. We lost stupid points and now you have to pay for it and that's a pity. In the last couple of games at least we haven't given any stupid goals away – that's changed already in our attitude. But of course that's too late and we have lost some good chances to already be in Europe – so that can cost you at the end of the season.' Beating Boro would get the Blues there, and Gullit added: 'For us it's an achievement to get into Europe – and if you can have it you have to fight for it. You need challenges in your life and if that's not a challenge then I don't know what is.'

He was ready for some hard selection choices for the final. 'I won't be sweating over it. I know I have decisions to make and I'll make them.' Everyone would be fit, that was for sure. 'They have good reason to be fit!'

Clarke summed up before the last league game: 'We're going flat out to win because we know we could get into Europe. And I think every player at the club is playing for his Cup final place. Not just those out on the park against Everton but in training this week there's been an added edge, and I think it'll be the same again next week.'

So close to the final, the feature writers, profile specialists and Sunday paper journalists swelled the media ranks at the training ground in force. They focused on Gullit's relationship with rebellious players, given that he had such a streak himself as a player. The Netherlands is a densely gifted footballing nation, where players feel compelled to speak their minds, and Gullit plagued a succession of Dutch managers. 'From the moment that people don't want to stay here,' said Gullit, 'then they are also not good for the group. If they are moaning all the time it's not good, then it's better for them to go. Yes, I was also stubborn.' Gullit impressively turned even that on its head. 'I recognise that in some of the players here. But I like stubborn players. At least they have an opinion. If they are right or wrong, this doesn't matter for me. At least they have some balls.'

Ruud has those in abundance. The tabloids have been circling, prying, probing into his privacy which he holds sacred. The broad shoulders showed no signs of slumping. 'I don't give a shit what they say about me. I'll live with that. I don't sleep worse, or whatever. It's part of my life. I accept it. It's part of being a celebrity.'

Uppermost in his thoughts was the match at Everton, but there was no escaping persistent questioning on the final. The traditionalists will wince at the Great Occasion becoming the most cosmopolitan final in the competition's 125-year history, and probably the most-watched ever across the world.

'Just a game,' said Mr Cool, then added: 'I first couldn't understand why it is so important and even now I can't because I am not born here.' But he had discovered its immense significance in the English scheme of things. 'I can feel it. I can sense it. I have seen it. It's a happening and now I want to feel what it is.'

Zola v. Juninho, the battle of the little men, was seen as the most intriguing aspect. Gullit said he would not depute a man to shadow Juninho – 'though it depends where he plays' – even if Leicester City's Pontus Kaamark showed in the Coca-Cola Cup Final that it might be a sound strategy.

Boro stood on the verge of relegation, and their final game at Leeds would determine their mood before Wembley. 'If they could do the championship again they would never be in a position to be relegated,' said Gullit. He added that he had 'seen what I have seen' when it comes to devising a game plan to beat them. Gullit's only clue: 'You need to have patience but still play fast. Patience doesn't mean playing slow because it is easy for the opposition. Keep the speed in there and you will find the openings. It has been a year of development for us, but you cannot do everything in a year and we have to learn to play for results. Against the big teams we have done well. Only if you also beat the smaller teams do you win the championship. Look at Manchester United. Twice recently they have been two goals down and still managed to get a draw. We know what must be done to reach that level. But it is a discussion for the dressing room.'

Gullit has obviously been concentrating on his coaching while he's been out of the side injured. 'It can be an advantage, but I think it's easier to be only a player or only a manager. Both things at the same time is very difficult. So the injuries I've had have this year helped me to concentrate myself more on being a manager. It's been my first year as a manager and I've enjoyed it very much. And if I can carry on enjoying it like this, yes, I'd like to continue being a manager. The most important thing with my life is that I have always been looking for challenges. This is again a new challenge. It keeps you fit, keeps you awake and you learn something.'

After their Coca-Cola Cup Final defeat, it would be hard on Robson's side should they end the season with nothing but relegation to show for their brave attempt to join the Premiership's elite.

SUNDAY, MAY 11
Everton 1 Chelsea 2

With Zola given another day off to rest his ankle, Vialli was offered the chance to stake his Wembley claim; it was depressingly snatched off him after only twenty minutes. Grodas was sent off. Ferguson, looking suspiciously offside, raced onto Watson's long clearance. The big striker, three yards outside the penalty area, lifted the ball past the onrushing Grodas, but in trying to go after it was pulled down by the keeper. Referee Peter Jones brandished a red card after speaking to his assistant. Gullit had no option but to bring off someone for substitute keeper Hitchcock. It just had to be Vialli! He sprinted straight past Gullit, standing on the touchline reorganising his formation, without a sideways glance, and without breaking stride headed straight back to the dressing room. Once again the body language said it all: maybe he wouldn't be back for another Premiership game!

Gullit said: 'I have no complaints; the linesman raised his flag although I felt their player was in an offside position. What did annoy me was that we had five players booked when maybe it should have been only three.'

Chelsea took control from the start and Vialli demanded a full-length save from Southall after only four minutes. But twenty minutes was hardly enough time in his last game in the league to stake a Cup final place.

It was no surprise when Chelsea took the lead in the fourteenth minute. Hughes dispossessed Ball and hared off down the right wing, before releasing a low cross into Everton's goalmouth. Di Matteo missed it and the ball went to Wise on the far side of the penalty area in a position which invited a centre. From an acute angle he chipped the ball over Southall and into the far corner.

Instead of being inspired at the prospect of playing against ten men, Everton did not react as positively as Chelsea. Their defence was opened up again in the thirty-sixth minute. Wise won a tussle with Thomsen and floated the ball to Petrescu on the right wing. His centre fell between Watson and Dunne, and Di Matteo stepped in to head past the stranded Southall. Ferguson, Hottiger and Barmby each missed a chance before Barmby was left with a tap in after Watson's header was pushed out following a corner kick. Everton ended the game applying more pressure but Watson said: 'That performance just about sums up a terrible season. We never got going even against ten men.'

Gullit said: 'That was an excellent performance because despite having only ten men we created a lot of chances. We played a lot of good football. While the Cup final is only six days away the players also had the chance of qualifying for Europe and I was pleased with their commitment. Aston Villa won, which means we have not qualified for the UEFA Cup. But really we threw it away in the past couple of weeks.' Impressed Everton caretaker manager Dave Watson tipped Chelsea to win the FA Cup.

Hughes limped off on the hour after stretching for a ball but Gullit insisted it was a precaution to protect an ankle injury the player had had for two weeks. 'Mark is okay. We took him off as a precaution, that is all. He felt his ankle a little bit. It is something that has been troubling him recently.' But who is going to report injured before the final? No one. Gullit added: 'It is strange that maybe two weeks ago we had only half a squad and now everyone is fit. That's no coincidence – it's the healing powers of Wembley. I know my Wembley line-up, but it's like a rough diamond – you try to polish it, polish it and we still have a week to go to work on a few more details.' The players had been working on a passing programme designed to make the best use of the Wembley pitch, and he felt it showed in this game. 'We've been training for the last few weeks on certain exercises and you could see it coming out.'

There were tears, heartbreak and recriminations as Boro were relegated. Juninho, Emerson and Ravanelli were expected to quit. Robson's side slumped into the First Division despite a thirty-one-goal haul from Ravanelli. Formerly at Inter Milan, Gianluca Festa, veteran of three Serie A relegation battles with home town club Cagliari, accused Boro of lacking the bottle to avoid the drop. 'It has been an utter waste of a season. I know full well what sort of fighting spirit is needed to stay up – and Middlesbrough don't have what it takes. Relegation is a tragedy both for myself and also for the club.'

A back injury had forced Ravanelli to sit out the 1–1 draw at Leeds that condemned Boro to the Nationwide League. 'I don't have the words to describe how I feel. This is absolutely terrible.' Will he play in the final? 'I hope to be able to make it, but I have only got a fifty per cent chance.'

Robson blamed the Premier League. 'We deserved to stay up because we won more points on the football field than Coventry City, Sunderland and Nottingham Forest. The Premier League took away three points my players won fairly and squarely. I still don't understand how they can do that.' Middlesbrough had three points deducted when they pulled out of a match at Blackburn Rovers in December. Chairman Steve Gibson hinted that the club could take the matter to the High Court. A decision was to be made after the Cup final. But, in reality, Boro had little chance of resorting to the law.

Chelsea's odds to win the FA Cup were reduced by Ladbrokes to 1–2 from 4–7 following Middlesbrough's relegation; Boro were rated 6–4, out from 11–8.

MONDAY, MAY 12

Four days of open training sessions to the media.

Clarke welcomed Gullit's continental revolution; the current squad was the strongest they have ever had. The latest imports were likely to squeeze British players Burley and Minto out of contract in the summer. 'We've got three new foreign signings but it would be good to see a couple of British players signed to keep the balance right. You need players who are experienced in the Premiership and know what it's all about. I think the foreign boys would be the first to admit that some of the games have been a bit of a culture shock to them.' But he accepted that the winds of change rejuvenated both Chelsea and the game in this country.

'I've been here since the bad old days, when we stuttered along from season to season with no real purpose. Glenn Hoddle arrived three years ago and changed all that. We got to the FA Cup Final in his first year, which was a good achievement with the players we had. Things have improved every year since then and we now have better quality players and the best squad I have known. The good thing this year is that a few kids such as Jody Morris and Mark Nicholls have come through from the youth team.'

But it hadn't damaged every British player's chances. Sinclair is one home-grown product who decided to stay and fight for his place, and his reward has been a regular place in the side. Sinclair opened talks about a new long-term contract in the summer. 'I was concerned about my situation at the start of the season because I was coming back from injury, and people were playing well. Ruud explained to me that it was a squad game and you have to be patient. If you get a game and do well you earn the right to stay in the team. Some people didn't fancy it and they've gone, but I stuck with it because I like playing for Chelsea and now I'm talking about a new contract, even though I've got two years to run. It's security for me and for the club. Ruud wants to win things and you need a big squad with good players on long contracts.'

Clarke's first sighting of Gullit was fourteen years ago. Clarke and Gullit were nineteen-year-old opponents in a UEFA Cup tie between St Mirren and Feyenoord. 'Even then he was massive. And he had dreadlocks so it was hard to miss him. But what was really clear was the immense range of talents he had. The best illustration of that is that he played on the right wing for the first hour – then dropped back to sweeper. That's versatile for a teenager. We lost the first leg 1–0. I marked him in the second leg out there and, although we lost 2–0, I think I acquitted myself well against him. He does remember the game – he says because it was so cold and, also, because he got racial abuse from the crowd. He told me the St Mirren chairman apologised to him afterwards.'

Clarke is astonished by the steely self-belief beneath Gullit's laid-back swagger. He believed Gullit was transforming a club once riddled with self-doubt. That was never clearer than at half-time in the fourth-round tie against Liverpool, the most crucial turning point of the route to Wembley. 'In the past, we'd have just attempted a damage limitation exercise in the second half. We'd have accepted the result already. Gullit came in and said: "That wasn't very good," and that was it, the first half dismissed. Then it was bang, bang, change the tactics, get the goal early on and you'll be back in this. That's exactly what we did. We scored early, the place came alight and we ended up winning 4–2.'

TUESDAY, MAY 13

Team Chelsea line-up was Leboeuf, Hughes, Burley and Minto.

Burley and Minto rejected new contract offers. Burley said: 'They offered me a four-year contract just after Christmas but we couldn't agree terms and I rejected it. They haven't been back with a new offer and there's no more talks planned. What I've been offered looks to me like a take-it-or-leave-it job. I can't say I'm particularly happy with it but perhaps this is not the right time to be talking about it. I don't want to leave Chelsea, but the terms have got to be right. I'm not happy with what's been offered. This has got nothing to do with any new players arriving here. I'm not worried about the competition for first-team places next season. But I'm not going to be rushed into any decision and right now I'm not sure if I'll be staying. I'm not on a transfer list and still have a year of my current contract to run. So we'll just have to see what happens after the Cup final.'

Minto looked likely to be in his final game for the club. 'I turned down a three-year contract in February and a four-year deal in March and I've not spoken to them since then. Personal terms are the problem. I'd like to have some more negotiations after the final because I'm out of contract in the summer. It's no secret I'm looking for a better deal, but I don't want to leave Chelsea and I'm going to wait on any further negotiations until after the Cup final.'

They were both reluctant to destabilise the team effort so close to the biggest game for the club in years, yet they had made a contribution and were determined not to sell themselves short and get left behind in the wage scale.

Leboeuf pledged his future to Chelsea following Marseille's interest in trying to lure him back to France. 'I will definitely be at Chelsea next year. There is no doubt about that. I have three more years here and I am very happy. Why would I want to leave? Even if I did change I would go to another club in England or a different country. I am not going back to France.'

Hughes signed a vastly improved two-year contract worth £2.5m, elevating him to the Vialli wage league. 'It has all been sorted out. I've spoken to my wife about the situation and though being in London is not ideal this is a great opportunity for me professionally.' Hughes flies down from his Cheshire home twice a week to stay in a flat near the Heathrow training ground provided by the club. He had been aware that newly promoted Bolton were ready to offer him one last lucrative move. He had been convinced since the Liverpool tie that Chelsea's name was on the Cup. 'Every year there's always one team whose name appears to be on the Cup. This year we have been labelled with that tag. But we still have to go out and win it.'

Hughes, a Chelsea fan since childhood, had great sympathy for Vialli's plight. 'I actually feel sorry for Luca. He is a world-class player and I know that if I don't produce my best he is waiting there to take my place. That's what has inspired me to play so well. Luca has actually been unlucky. He suffered some injuries early on so when Gianfranco Zola arrived it was me who partnered him. It could easily have been the other way around. Luca is a lovely guy. A really nice bloke. Dennis Wise wears his "We love you Luca" T-shirt not for effect but because he means it. Luca is great. He understands the situation and there has never been a problem between us. We talk all the time about football, about golf – he even asks me for help with his English.'

Hughes could see some similarities in the development of Chelsea and his former club. 'I remember at United there were times when the fans just felt we would never win the championship again. But look how that's changed. And at Chelsea the fans used to just hope we would do something. Now they expect us to do well. I think Ruudi has really settled into the job now. I actually believe he enjoys it as much as when he was playing. Ruudi likes challenges and likes trying to overcome any problems set in front of him. He has certainly made a success of his first year and the way he is gearing up for next year he will take the club even further. He has this laid-back character but don't be fooled. He does lose his temper and is not slow to tell you when he's not happy. There are different ways of doing it, obviously. Alex Ferguson at United was in the teacup-throwing department but Ruudi's not like that. But he does say what he feels in no uncertain terms and that he expects better – usually in just a couple of sentences.

'If he sees something in a match or training that he is not happy about he will let you know that he will not accept it. For instance, at the beginning of the season he said he was going to change a few things. He said there was going to be a squad of players that he was going to pick from and if you wanted to be a part of Chelsea you were okay. But if you didn't want to stay and be a part you would have to go and he stuck to that. Some players have had to leave.'

He paid tribute to Gullit for giving him a new lease of life. 'At Manchester United I would chase full-backs and tackle midfield players all the time. It looked good at the time but I was expending too much energy in other areas and couldn't get into the box when I was needed. As soon as Ruud took over he said he wanted his strikers to stay fresh and get on the end of things, and I have felt such a big difference. I feel so much sharper in front of goal these days. But it's taken me fifteen years to realise I've been playing the wrong way.' Hughes, chasing a fourth winners' medal, added: 'There are certain players who rise to the big occasion, grace the whole thing, love every minute, every ball they kick. I hope I have now become one of those players. I was only twenty-one when I played in my first final and I didn't particularly enjoy it, apart from the fact that we won. I was the new boy in the side and had no one to enjoy it with. I was very much on the periphery. There was no one in the side I could hug and say we'd done it together. I enjoyed it so much more when I developed some proper friendships at United. And now I have my new friends at Chelsea and I will enjoy this one as well.'

Bates hosted a select media lunch at Drakes after providing the senior soccer writers from the daily papers with a tour of the new development. On the menu were the futures of Vialli, Gullit and the club. He gave Gullit the go-ahead to keep Vialli, even if he remained as a £1m-a-year supersub. 'He has a three-year contract and he is very happy here to be driven by his chauffeur and to have the odd fag when he doesn't think anybody's watching. London is his kind of town as well, but I wouldn't expect any player to be happy if he's not in the team. That's the same for a seventeen-year-old or a thirty-seven-year-old or for the highest paid player. But equally I expect loyalty and I expect dissatisfaction from anyone not in the team. If you are not satisfied under those circumstances performances would drop, you would give up striving. If Gullit wants him here and he doesn't want to stay I would just point out that he has another two years of his contract and that's the end of the story.

Bates sympathised with Vialli when he was substituted after just twenty minutes of the last Premiership game. 'Luca was one of the first out of the dressing room and on the coach. I saw him, and we just hugged. I said, "You're not having any sort of luck at the moment; you're even being substituted for a goalkeeper!"' Bates insisted that Vialli shouldn't be upset. 'Why should he be in the team if we keep on winning?' Bates stressed Vialli was not being picked on and was a vital part of the new regime.

'Two great things happened this season concerning team selection after which nobody could take exception. The first thing is that the manager dropped Dennis Wise, and the reason was valid – he was playing crap! But more importantly the message came across that it didn't matter whether you were the team captain – if you were not good enough you would be left out. Then the manager himself was injured. Craig Burley came in the side and when the manager was fit he left Burley in the team because he was playing well and deserved to be picked. The message again was that "I'm the manager; I can walk back in, but I won't." So, whether you are the team manager or the team captain, nobody was guaranteed a place. There were no differences within the club, and in my view that makes a very happy club.' Bates felt Vialli was happy socially – all he craved was a place in the side.

Bates planned to present Gullit with a lucrative new two-year extension to his contract after the Cup final, keeping him at the Bridge until the year 2000. Bates was confident that Gullit would sign the deal. 'It's a question of what would he do elsewhere that he couldn't do at Chelsea? He's so rich that, let's face it, he doesn't have to go anywhere for the money. It is up to him. His contract comes to an end next season, but we will be offering him a new one. He doesn't want to talk about it before the final and after the Final he will f*** off on holiday and we will talk about it when he comes back from holiday. But don't forget that last year he signed an extension in the summer and I can't see him going anywhere else. First of all, who can afford him? Where would he want to live other than here? He's very happy in London with his lady, Estelle.'

Gullit's phenomenal success in his first season as a coach intensified speculation that he will end up at AC Milan one day. Bates disagreed. 'He wouldn't want the president interfering and that's what they do over there. He would not last in that league. Milan! Is that a better move? You haven't seen the San Siro stadium lately. I know where I'd prefer to be. Their pitch is dreadful at the moment. We have just authorised £165,000 on our pitch to improve the quality of the grass and the surface. It will be more like a bowling green. The season after next we will have a 44,000 capacity and then we'll be able to take on Man United in terms of finance as, don't forget, we charge more on gates. The transformation is under way.'

Bates wanted Gullit as the focal point of Chelsea's long-term plan to challenge Manchester United for supremacy. Season ticket sales were at a record level for a third year in a row. A proud Bates said: 'We've sold 10,117 season tickets already and forty-five per cent of them are new season ticket holders. We expect to sell between 12,000 and 15,000 season tickets this summer. As we stand, we've taken £7m in advance sales. I remember a time we didn't take £7m all year through all forces.'

He added: 'We never doubted Ruud would be the man to take over when Glenn Hoddle left. We had been talking to him for a year and got to know the guy and he is something different. He was an influence behind the scenes – even under Hoddle. Most player-managers fail because, instead of working ten hours a week they are now working sixty – they can't cope. A football club today is not like it was twenty years ago; it's a big business. So we decided to let him concentrate on his playing and coaching. We organised others to look after the administration and deal with the press and players' contracts. That arrangement started with Hoddle – getting him in was the first stage. He made a great number of changes at all levels and he brought in Mark Hughes and Gullit. He made some mistakes, bought some bad players, but that was the platform. When he went to the England job, Ruud took it on. They have different styles. Glenn was into reflexology, alternative medicine, a dietician. Gullit is into fitness. He brought in Ade Mafe and a different style of coaching. He bombed out the dietician, reflexologist and masseur. Gullit said to me: "The players rebelled against the dietician, telling them what they should eat. If I say 'you must eat this' they won't eat at the training ground, will go elsewhere and get it. You have to get them to realise the only person who can really look after them is themselves. If they don't realise that, they won't be in the team." Some make the transition from player to manager easily, others find it a problem. John Hollins found it hard. As a player, he was one of the ones that took the mick out of the manager behind his back. Now his team-mates were doing it to him. Ruud has not had a problem like that.'

WEDNESDAY, MAY 14

Team Chelsea switched to the Bridge press room, with Vialli leading in Zola, Newton and Morris. The background was a sponsors list: BBC Sport, Yves St Laurent, Cerruti, Coors, Umbro and the Great Ormond Street Hospital. Vialli wore a 'Make the tear disappear' T-shirt, and the boys were decked out in YST.

Zola gave the best possible Wembley news. He had had a full week's rest but was now gradually stepping up his training. 'I rest for one week. I'm improving my condition. I started training three days ago. I don't have a problem. Day by day I am improving.' He didn't accept it would be a huge setback if Chelsea were not in Europe. 'We would like to play in Europe to give a good impression of Chelsea. A place in Europe is important for all the team, not just me. I shall try to do my best for all reasons. But it doesn't matter for me. If we don't succeed it doesn't matter – we will do good next year. Everything at Chelsea is in front of me.'

Most important for Zola was to win the Cup. He sensed the importance of the occasion. 'Yeah, the feeling for this game is special, absolutely special. You can feel the atmosphere around you everywhere you go, in the newspapers, all the people talk about it. I hope Chelsea play a special game for all our supporters.'

As he worried about his acceptance speech for the Footballer of the Year award the next day, he explained how playing in the Premiership had made him a better player. 'Playing here has increased my skill. I have become more complete than when I played for Parma.' He did not accept that English defences were weaker than in Italy. 'It is a different situation. In England there is a different mentality. In Italy they think defensively, in England it's the opposite and that's a point for me. I've played good seasons against good defenders. What is important is that you have to be confident and have to be right – I am confident and I am right.' He expects that he will be closely watched at Wembley. 'They are going to try to stop me playing, it's normal. I have to think about it and to find the way to put myself in confidence in the game. This season has given me great satisfaction. I never thought I could play like that. I have to thank all my team-mates who have helped me give of my best. I have to thank Chelsea and all our supporters, they have been fantastic for me. I hope to deserve all their satisfaction. I hope to give them all my best in the next games.'

Vialli resigned himself to a place on the Wembley bench; but he wasn't going to see out the remaining two years of his contract on the sidelines. 'I don't expect to be part of the starting eleven against Middlesbrough but I am used to that now. It won't be the first time for me on the bench so my disappointment was a long time ago. Now I understand the situation and accept it. This is the first time in my career that I have not been the first choice and it has been very difficult for me. I will sit down and talk with the manager and the chairman some time after the final and try to sort the problems out. But I have only two years of my career left and I don't want to spend them on the bench. I want to play as much football as possible. I get so upset when I don't play that my stomach hurts me so much with the tension inside.'

He was smiling, but only on the outside. Inside he was hurt. 'I have learned to become a good actor. I have discovered that I must always be in control of my emotions and to be patient when I am not playing. I must always be nice with my girlfriend when I go home! I have to smile even if inside I feel very disappointed. I have to be a great actor.

'Ruud is the manager and I am a player. That is our relationship. We are both professionals trying to do our best for the team. But it is a difficult situation for me because the manager only needs me if the team is playing badly or they are not winning. Do I hope to come on or not? Perhaps for the last five minutes after Gianfranco has scored a hat-trick!

'The final is like a movie. Gullit will be our director, Zola the superstar main character and the other players will be the support actors. But you need all those people to make a movie. Even Gianfranco can't play on his own. And if I am not playing it is important I still help everyone as much as I can. I hope I get at least five minutes at Wembley but the most important thing is to see Dennis Wise lift the Cup. The Cup final is just not the same in Italy. In England it's more important than the Premier League. I am very proud just to be part of such a fantastic occasion.'

Vialli responded to Bates. 'I'm happy to hear nice things from the chairman about me but I have to consider all that has happened this season. I have played for Cremonese, for Sampdoria and for Juventus, and this is the first time in my career that I have not been the first choice. And that has been very difficult. It is important to consider everything. I love living in London, my relationship with my team-mates is fantastic and I have a great feeling for the supporters. I will have talks with the manager and the chairman about the matter. But not until after the final. Now it is important for the team to be relaxed. I do not want to cause any trouble. Let's think of the final for now and sort things out at the end of the season.'

Vialli wasn't the only Italian on the move after the final. His former Juventus strike partner Ravanelli was also set for a Wembley farewell, with Vialli admitting: 'I think it could be his last game in England. I spoke to Fabrizio last week. He was going back to Italy for treatment on his injury and was very worried because he would miss Middlesbrough's last two games. Now he is hoping to play in the final, although I don't think he will decide until five minutes before the game. It will be better for Chelsea if he is not playing because he is a very good player who can score goals, work hard and cause problems. But he is my friend and I hope he does play.'

THURSDAY, MAY 15

More than 120 journalists from all over the world crammed into the upstairs canteen area for a mega-audience with the players and Gullit, an FA-organised event for all sections of the media with every single member of the Chelsea squad and the manager available for interview.

Di Matteo's family flew over from Italy to see him at Wembley, but younger sister Concetta is practically blind and relies on a special commentator to talk her through the Cup final action. The twenty-four-year-old Concetta suffers from the rare eye disease retinitis pigmentosa; she can only see shadows and the condition is irreversible. Before the final league game she was wandering around the busy forecourt at the Harlington training ground, white stick in hand. FA Cup success would justify Roberto's decision to leave the family home to make his name in England. He might not generate the same headlines as fellow Chelsea imports, but his contribution was never underestimated by Gullit.

'We have always been very close,' said Concetta, five years older than Roberto, who would be twenty-eight in two weeks. 'I was naturally worried when he came to England to join Chelsea. It was a big step but he is very happy here and has never expressed any thoughts of leaving although one day we expect he will come home. I cannot see Roberto play, of course, but my father tells me what is happening on the field and how he is doing. I can sense the atmosphere for myself and it is wonderful joy for me to go to football matches.' She had made three previous visits to her brother, staying with her father and an uncle at Roberto's flat.

Roberto was determined to hand her a Cup winners' medal as a reward for the bravery and constant cheerfulness she has shown over the years. 'The way Concetta has handled her problems has been an inspiration to me. Hopefully, my success will now help her. My family give me my power for the game. And it has been very difficult for me because it is the first time in my life I have ever been on my own. In Italy I always lived with my family. Now when I go home there is no one waiting there for me. And that is not so nice. Normally I live on my own and it is not so nice to come back to an empty house but now I go home and they are there. It makes it very nice and comfortable for me and I can get more confidence in what I do when they are around.

'Concetta and my parents come over as often as they can. They have been to our training ground many times and now they will be with me at Wembley, and that makes me very happy. For my first two months at Chelsea it was even worse because I was living in a hotel. Even now that I have bought a flat in Kensington it still hasn't been easy. But I have learned to live on my own. Now I know how to cook for myself but I still have a cleaner to help me around the apartment. In England I can go wherever I like without being mobbed. I don't like to go out on my own too much but when my friends come over from Italy there are some very good shops and nightclubs where we can go without any problems.'

His girlfriend refused to join him in London and his settling-in process was hardly helped when his flat was flooded by a burst pipe while he was back in Italy on international duty. Now he was relishing his new life at Chelsea. 'I am a better player now than I was at Lazio. In Italy I was a purely defensive player. Ruud Gullit has given me much greater freedom to go forward and score goals. I was already a technically good player when I came to England. But I can protect myself better in the tackles and on the high balls. Every time I play for Italy all the players now ask me about the Premiership. They see how much we are enjoying it here and they all want to come over as well.'

Leboeuf knew the word went round the Premier League that he couldn't handle the physical side of English football after being roughed up by Wimbledon. He came through that test and he was ready for another in the final. 'I hope he [Ravanelli] will play because I remember playing against him last summer in my first game for Chelsea and we won. In defence we did well that day; that's why I'm not afraid about him or Beck or anyone. It doesn't matter for me who plays. Of course I respect them as players. I am certainly not scared of them. It is only a game of football.

'The first game against Wimbledon was just down to circumstances. I was watching the ball and didn't see the man. I had the same in France a couple of seasons ago when I fractured my jaw but that came after eight seasons with no problems. I saw a lot of newspapers talking about my football and everyone seemed to think I could be intimidated if the man comes at me very strong. I was happy to prove against Wimbledon the next time that that was just a legend.

'Before our semifinal against Wimbledon last month everyone was saying I would be intimidated because I am not a hard player. A lot of people believed I couldn't cope with the strong powerful strikes after that first Wimbledon game. But I think I proved in that semifinal that I can play a physical game when I have to. It wasn't a big problem. We were concentrated all the game and won easily. We proved we are a strong team, and now we have to do the same in the final. Now I am very happy because I have shown what I am really.'

Gullit made it clear if Vialli wanted to go no one would stand in his way. Equally he could stay if he wanted to. 'I don't want players who are not enjoying themselves hanging around the place with long faces. Everyone is welcome to stay. I don't want any player to leave my squad. But if they want to leave that's different. It happened earlier this season with John Spencer and Gavin Peacock. I wanted them to stay, but I couldn't make them. Okay, they were still under contract and I suppose I could have told them they must honour it. But what is the point in that? I had conversations with them and they just said they didn't want to stay under these circumstances, so it's over. It sent a message because a whole lot of players then came to me and said, "I want to be part of Chelsea, I don't want to go," so I accepted that. Strangely, players I had meetings with played more. I don't want to have players who don't want to stay here. If you don't want to stay here you're not enjoying yourself. You come with a long face every day and it has no meaning for me to pick you.'

Vialli was again quizzed about his future. Once again he responded with good humour and diplomacy. 'I'm proud of my behaviour this year. It's been a very difficult year for me. When you live in a difficult football situation, you have to learn always to be positive with team-mates. You have to show you are a good professional even if you don't play. It has not been easy for me but I think Chelsea is happy with me. I don't like to stop doing something without finishing my job. I signed a contract for three years and I would like to stay here for all my contract. I can't say now if it's possible or not. I don't want to think about that now. I will talk to the chairman and club later. Now I am only thinking of the final and our chance to go into Europe. Afterwards everyone has got time to sort out his own problems.'

Vialli and Wise made an unlikely duo, but for some bizarre reason they were close. Wise had his own peculiar theory for building team spirit, dragging Vialli down to Venables's bar in Kensington (now sold). 'It was a few weeks into the new season and we'd all been to Steve Clarke's testimonial dinner. I decided on the spur of the moment to take Luca out for a few beers and we ended up in Scribes on karaoke night. Luca just loved it. He was standing there, bottle of beer in his hand, and couldn't believe we were allowed to carry on like that. I spent all night trying to get him up on stage to sing a song, but he was having none of it. But he still had a great time. When all these big stars started turning up at the club the rest of us were all wondering what was going to happen. These guys had been treated like gods in Italy and some people thought they'd look down their noses at the rest of us. But those nights out showed me that these stars are just like the rest of us. They do the same things, enjoy the same laughs. It was so important that Luca came out for that drink. That's the time we became a real team. It was obvious then there would be no "them and us" situation in the camp. You always think these guys are completely different. But when you get to know them you realise they're just like the rest of us – nice and down to earth. The only difference is that they have been blessed with this incredible talent on the football field.'

Wise dealt with the foreign culture shock. 'I've had no problems because I speak a foreign language as well – fluent cockney. But the quality the foreign guys have brought to the club is amazing. They turn bad moves into good ones and you have to get better yourself just by being on the same pitch as them. I don't captain guys like Zola, Di Matteo, Luca and Frank Leboeuf; I just let them get on with it. And with the team we now have, we're capable of achieving a lot of success in the next few years. We need to get over the obstacle of the first trophy and then we'll really take off.'

Gullit was not worried by the burden of being favourites. 'We have been favourites since we beat Liverpool in the fourth round and we have lived with that. Being favourites is okay and there is no pressure because I am confident in what my players can do. When I played my first final with Milan against Steaua Bucharest we were also favourites and we just did the job. They have made us favourites for a whole lot of games; they thought maybe that would put some pressure on us. But I don't see it, especially when we played against Wimbledon. There was a lot of pressure built up for that game. But if you're confident about yourself you know what your strengths are, then you don't have to worry about anything. I'm very confident because I know what my players can do and the experience they have. But I don't think we are favourites by much. We are only confident about our possibilities and strengths but we have a lot of respect for Boro. I don't approach them as a relegated team. I approach them as a top team. I don't think they deserved to go down. With the quality I've seen and the way they play it is strange for me that they were relegated.'

Gullit, previously a staunch advocate of fielding three central defenders and two wing-backs, now looked certain to stick to the 4–4–2 system which overwhelmed Wimbledon in the semifinal. 'I just needed to do it, especially when we played against Wimbledon. That distracted them because they never thought I could do it. Afterwards I saw they really enjoyed playing that way, and then when we played against Everton with ten men we could still produce good football. That would be difficult with three at the back. This is more solid. The good thing is I can change whenever I like.' His refusal to discuss tactics in any detail suggested he had something up his sleeve. He was not too bothered by Boro's plans, even to the extent of dismissing talk of Ravanelli's injury. 'I will prepare myself for the strongest team they have.'

Grodas would be a key player. The eccentric Norwegian said: 'I'm a normal person most of the day, but the minute I pull on my goalkeeper's shirt I'm a changed man. I become more aggressive, shouting and screaming. You have to be mad to do this job because you put yourself into situations where you're going to get kicked. I've been a goalie since I was five years old and it's the best feeling in the world when you pull off a great save. It's even better than scoring a goal, and I should know because I once beat the Swedish national goalie with a clearance from my eighteen-yard box.' He often charged into the opposition's penalty area for corners during his Lillestroem days and he said he'd go up again at Wembley if he got the nod from Gullit. 'The gap between hero and clown is so small for every keeper.

'I've made plenty of mistakes in the past but I've learned how to handle them. If you can't do that as a keeper, you've got no chance. I used to be a very superstitious person. Between 1989 and 1994 I always wore the same pair of shoes. Then I'd always have the same shirt on under my kit and I'd listen to the same music in my car on the way to the game. But I just got to the stage where I said, "That's enough,

I'm out of this." I couldn't be worrying about all those things any more. I just realised that it really didn't matter what shoes I wore; it wasn't going to have the slightest bearing on what happened in the match.'

Grodas owned up to 'a couple of goals that were down to me' but insisted: 'I don't think there are many goalkeepers in England who have not made mistakes this season.' Like David James? 'I see him as one of the top two or three goalkeepers in this country. I'm sure he will be back next year. If you make a mistake you just have to forget it. It's all part of the position. I'm thirty-two now, I've played a lot of important matches and I'm sure I can handle this one.'

Zola was presented with the Footballer of the Year award at a glittering night at the Royal Lancaster at the Soccer Writers' dinner, an occasion made all the more special for him by the presence of his father, Ignazio. He had come to England for the first time in his life from his Sardinian home to watch his son play in the Cup final and Zola insisted that he accompanied him to the Royal Lancaster. 'He deserves the satisfaction of being there with me. It's my first award and I will be very proud to have him beside me tonight.' He was presented with the fiftieth anniversary award by the first recipient, Sir Stanley Matthews, for the season 1947/48.

With Ruud sitting close to him, a nervous Zola made a lengthy speech. The guest comedian remarked later: 'I understood him better than I do Gascoigne!' Zola thanked those who had voted for him but humbly said: 'I think the jury must have been a bit drunk.' He captured the hearts of the audience by stumbling through his acceptance speech in broken English. Zola said: 'I must thank my team-mates, my coach and the Chelsea supporters who helped me settle down very quickly. It's very great to receive an honour like this. Every player would like to receive it. And looking at the past winners it's very easy to imagine what I feel. I have a little emotion.'

Ignazio, the sixty-six-year-old former truck driver and bar owner, said: 'I am so proud of my boy. I only read about his award in the papers. Franco is so modest that he didn't want to tell me about it. That is the way he has always been, ever since the best player in Sardinia told him at the age of seven he was going to be a great footballer. Everyone back in our home town of Oliena will be watching the game on pay TV in the local bar but I will be at Wembley and I am very happy to be here.' Zola smiled. 'My father is not serious when he says I am modest. He wants to hide my real personality. If I told you what I am really like I would end up in prison! But I am very proud my father can be with me. He deserves to be beside me because he has supported me all the way. I will be very proud at Wembley Stadium.'

On the way to the Royal Lancaster I bumped into David Rocastle on the Central Line. He was out of the final through suspension, which would have been a major shock-horror story a few years ago. In reality, he wouldn't have been involved even if he wasn't banned. Once one of England's brightest stars, he was just a back number at Chelsea and desperate for a move to revive his reputation which nose-dived into near anonymity after his flop £2m move from Highbury to Leeds in 1992. 'I had a foot injury all last season but I'm well over that now and just don't know why it has all gone wrong for me.' The only 'serious football' he has played in two years was on loan to First Division Norwich at the back end of the season. And he was sent off there after a bust-up in a reserve match, bringing him a suspension which started on Monday. 'The ban doesn't actually mean a thing as I know I'll never be given an opportunity here.'

He was back at Chelsea because hard-up Norwich could not offer anything like his Stamford Bridge pay cheque to sign him permanently. 'Ruud Gullit told me last

June I wouldn't be in the side this season. I was staggered. I thought it was an amazing thing to say when I hadn't even been given a chance to show what I could do, and I just don't know why he took that attitude. When Glenn Hoddle signed me I was hopeful it would set me up again in London. I had a nightmare at Leeds, where I hardly got into Howard Wilkinson's side, and he eventually swapped me for David White from Manchester City where I thought I did okay. Chelsea have even bigger ambitions now under Ruud Gullit, but I'm obviously not part of them. I've a year to go on my contract and then I'll be on a free transfer, but I'd move anywhere now just to get a game. The trouble is, the club don't seem to want to move me on, even though it seems certain they have no further use for me.

'It has occurred to me other clubs may be suspicious of me. They may be thinking, "Why has he just faded out of the picture?" But you can ask anyone here – I haven't missed a day's training this season and feel really sharp. People like Gianfranco Zola come up to me and ask why I'm not playing. He doesn't understand it either. But even when we had four players suspended and a few others out injured for the Arsenal game a few weeks ago I knew I wouldn't be considered. As far as I know, I've done nothing to upset anyone. It seems obvious I have to go. I was thirty the other week but I'd even be prepared to have a trial somewhere to prove myself again.'

Parker was another ex-England hero on his way out after two months. 'It was a nice surprise to jump back into the Premiership again but, to be fair, Chelsea never promised me anything more than the rest of the season. But I was hopeful I could make an impression and get a longer contract. It hasn't worked out, though.' Parker was once considered one of Europe's top defenders but was jeered mercilessly by a section of Chelsea fans for mistakes he made against Arsenal in his only start for the first team last month. 'It looks as if I must find another club now, but I know I can still do a good job for someone.'

FRIDAY, MAY 16

Gullit broke the bad news to Parker and Clement that they did not make the seventeen travelling to Wembley, with third-choice keeper Nick Colgan only going along 'for the ride'.

Juninho prepared to bid adieu to this country at Wembley with Spanish giants Atletico Madrid, money no object, the destination of the twenty-four-year-old. The Brazilian pinned his hopes on saying his final farewells to the Boro faithful by giving them one last sight of him in full flow in what he believed would be an open game. 'Chelsea have some great players but I'm happy that we're playing them. It will be a great game to watch because Chelsea like to play football. They play beautiful football, and when we play teams who play like that we tend to play well ourselves.' Gullit does not believe in man-marking and that thought brightened Juninho, recalling the two Coca-Cola Final matches against Leicester when Pontus Kaamark did not leave his side. 'I hope not!' laughed the man from São Paulo. 'You have to let the players play. Chelsea have players like Zola, Di Matteo and Hughes and you have to let them show their football. If they are all man-marked it would be an ugly game.'

Juninho wanted to impress the man who used 'the beautiful game' as part of the title of his autobiography – Pele. His most famous predecessor in that Brazilian number ten shirt was at Wembley to watch him, as he was two years ago when Juninho first made his impact on the British game in the 3–1 Umbro Cup win over England. 'I have good memories of that game,' said Juninho, whose glittering talents, summed up by the most exquisite of free kicks, illuminated the foulest of days. 'That was my best moment for Brazil, a great game for me and Brazil.'

This is the first FA Cup Final in Middlesbrough's 121-year history. In fact, they had never been beyond the quarterfinals before. The last time they reached the last eight was in 1978. Chelsea, by contrast, were playing in their fifth final, although, like Boro, they have never won at Wembley; they lifted the Cup in 1970 after a 2–1 replay win over Leeds at Old Trafford.

Juninho and Emerson became the first Brazilians to play in an FA Cup Final, while Petrescu become the first Romanian to do so. Whatever happened, there would be Italian Cup winners for the first time. Boro were hoping not to join an elite group of three other clubs, Manchester City (1926), Leicester (1969) and Brighton (1983). All reached Wembley in the season they were relegated from the top flight. All lost.

Hughes was aiming to become the first player this century to play in four FA Cup Final winning teams. Hughes, who played for Manchester United in 1985, 1990, 1994 and 1995, would join Joe Hulme, Johnny Giles, Pat Rice, Frank Stapleton and Ray Clemence as a five-time Wembley Cup finalist.

Five hundred and seventy-four clubs, twelve rounds, thirty-seven weeks and 572 matches decide which two clubs will be at Wembley. Gates have been topside of two million. Not one of the Cup's all-time top eight – Manchester United, Tottenham, Aston Villa, Arsenal, Blackburn, Newcastle, Everton and Liverpool (52 wins between them) – went beyond the fourth round. The last final which didn't involve at least one of them was twenty-two years ago.

Middlesbrough would break new ground, a place in the European Cup Winners Cup and relegation from the Premiership in the same season. But Chelsea, who had averaged more than three goals a round and overcome the likes of Liverpool, Leicester and Wimbledon, were clear favourites.

A worldwide television audience of 400 million in more than fifty countries awaited the final . . .

SATURDAY, MAY 17
Chelsea 2 Middlesbrough 0
Ruud strolled into an ecstatic Wembley winners dressing room carrying the FA Cup minus its top and plinth. The skipper had just finished a TV interview. 'Look at the Yeti!' Wise shouted across the room. A broad smile creased Gullit's features. The twenty-seven-year wait was over.

For those fans who were there, it will be memories to savour for the rest of their lives. They were there for the greatest carnival I can ever recall for a Wembley Cup final. There was a real family atmosphere as Gullit insisted his players made the fans part of their celebrations. His 'lovely boys' had won the Cup; not even the cockney captain's irreverence would spoil it. It was party time, and Ruud can party with the best. The job had been done; it was time to unwind and enjoy.

But that scene encapsulated Gullit's management technique. Still one of the boys, he didn't take offence at the dressing-room banter, he revelled in it; yet he still remained aloof and would pick a team for the right result. It was fascinating how he coped with seemingly incompatible roles. The outcome fully vindicated his stance over Vialli.

Vialli gave a dressing-room interview to Clubcall providing every indication that he wants to stay to win the championship with Chelsea. He issued an emotional 'thank you' to the fans and talked enthusiastically about winning more trophies for the club. 'I wish that this is not the last one. I hope we can win something bigger next season; it is difficult because the FA Cup is very special. But there's Europe, the Premier League, the Champions League – you never know. We have a great future and I will try to win everything we can for us, the chairman, for Colin and of course the supporters.' He paid homage to the fans. 'I could hear them shouting; I was very happy because the feeling was fantastic. So I'd like to thank you. I think we won the Cup also because they were fantastic all the season.'

Vialli contrasted the occasion with his tears from his last appearance at Wembley in a final. 'You know, I have been here with Sampdoria and at the end of the match I was crying because we lost the Champions League [against Barcelona] and I wanted to leave winning something. Today the atmosphere is completely different. I am very happy to be part of the final; it was great.'

Even in his cameo Cup final role there was just a sniff of a chance; he knew it wouldn't go his way. 'I think this has not been a lucky year for me so when I received the ball I always knew something would happen. It doesn't matter because the result mattered. We win.'

The spiritual presence of Matthew Harding was felt by Gullit and the fans. His widow, Ruth, dressed in emerald green, kissed Suzannah as the Cup was finally won. Ruth was one of the official party of twenty-nine FA guests, the list provided by the club. Ruth also joined the all-night party at London's Waldorf Hotel. She said: 'The final would have been the best day in Matthew's life, and it was the best day of mine. I felt he was upstairs looking down on the occasion.'

Girlfriend Vicky was not on the official guest list, but she was also at the final. She decorated the outside of her leafy London home with a Chelsea flag and balloons before leaving to watch Matthew's team at Wembley. She heard them pay him a moving and emotional tribute as the Chelsea faithful chanted, 'Matthew Harding's blue and white army'. She said: 'They are the ones we mustn't forget – the fans who queued up to get tickets for the match, who queued up to be there. Matthew was a fan, but he was a great believer in other people.'

The team coach departed their hideaway hotel, the West Lodge Park near Barnet, at 12.30, and was parked outside the dressing rooms at 1.08. A relaxed, shirtsleeved Ruud sat in the front with Rix as his players stepped off the bus and were soon on the pitch. Vialli stood there taking in the scene with a white handkerchief in his pocket instead of the buttonholes of his team-mates and manager. Wearing a baseball cap, he blew bubbles with his gum. The Boro bus arrived a little later, and the players headed straight for the pitch where Vialli and Ravanelli greeted each other warmly. The cropped silver-haired Ravanelli grabbed his little Italian team-mate Zola in a head lock.

Ninety minutes before the kick off Gullit wrote out the names of his team on the blackboard. Vialli was on the bench. Vialli wished his team-mates the luck to win the Cup. 'I am not selfish person. I am looking forward to shaking the hands of members of the royal family.'

Sinclair was interviewed on the pitch and made a significant comment. Three years ago he was a Wembley loser, he said. 'They told me to enjoy the day. But they forgot to tell me that to enjoy it you have to win.' The concentration, determination and will to win was written over all the Chelsea players' faces.

Boro fans booed throughout the presentations, aggrieved at the Premier League's docking of three points. Sir Cliff Richard led the communal singing with Abide With Me. The atmosphere was electric. Now they knew for the first time what an English FA Cup Final was all about.

In the 1997 FA Cup Final Gullit taught Chelsea how to win a trophy, their first in just over a quarter of a century, and he planned to make it into a winning habit. Chelsea's life vice-president, Dickie Attenborough, stood in the royal box as long as any of the Chelsea faithful taking part in the longest-ever celebrations after the quickest Wembley Cup final goal on record.

In the Foreigners' Final there was a distinct division between Robson's collection of authentic world-class stars and the way Gullit integrated his overseas captures into a successful team strategy.

Gullit broke the mould to become the first foreign coach to win a trophy in English football. But he wasn't satisfied. This was not the end of the saga to bring silverware to the Bridge for the great underachievers with twenty-six barren years, but just the beginning. Gullit said: 'As a coach you must improve and I'd like my players to improve, and what is important is they now know the feeling of winning and we want to keep it going now that we have broken the chain. They had never tasted winning something. Now they have there is something to build on. I just did what I had to do. I knew that winning this Cup meant a lot to the club. It is also a boost, qualifying for Europe, because of the way we play and also our players are now famous around the world. This team didn't know its limits. If anything, I have taught them how to be winners and my next aim is win even more.'

Can Chelsea be champions? Gullit said: 'I certainly want to do better, and how good we can be depends on next season. We have made mistakes, all of us, but it's still been a very good season. We have played very well against the big teams and played some good football, but you don't win the championship or finish in second place to qualify for the Champions League unless you beat also the small teams.'

His first experience of the FA Cup Final moved him. 'There was a lot of noise, a great day out and I'm a little bit more proud as a coach than maybe I have been as a player, because I had a hand in the tactics and throughout the year shaped this team into how you see our football. I need challenges. I have taken this challenge and I have succeeded, and I have to thank the players and the whole environment at the club for that. I'm really proud of this day. I feel I've grown up as a person. It's a great day, a great year ... and it went very fast.'

The chant of 'Ruudi, Ruudi,' went up when Gullit first appeared on the pitch, after a BBC TV interview, to join in the start of the celebrations. He raised his arm in appreciation. He had become the club's most popular boss in just one remarkable season.

Gullit stood back, admiring each of his players as they climbed the famous Wembley steps to receive the FA Cup and their medals, having already individually acclaimed them with personal hugs and kisses, even a cuddle for Vialli. But as Wise lifted the Cup and each player in turn was handed the famous trophy, Gullit had to be reminded by FA official Adrian Titcombe that he had to collect his medal! Gullit sprinted across the pitch, past the bench, almost knocking over a cameraman, and up the steps.

What did he plan to do with it? 'My other medals are in a box. I didn't have time to unpack them, but after a while they will all have their places.' Gullit doesn't have a trophy cabinet nor does he have pictures of his successes adorning the walls. 'No pictures to do with football because my home is another environment, and I'm not that vain.' Clearly Gullit would eventually unpack; there was no sign of him moving on. 'I'm happy to stay at Chelsea. I'm not thinking about leaving the club. I've no intention of leaving Chelsea.' If there was any lingering doubt about his future, that statement of intent surely dispelled it.

Gullit not only extended his players' after-match stay on the Wembley pitch for an unprecedented sing-song, he also summoned his chairman to join in. Bates almost slid down the steps. When he got onto the pitch Ruud signalled as if to say, 'There you are.' Gullit explained: 'He deserved it also because all the time he's under pressure, but he wants the best for Chelsea and people don't realise it. He was very proud of us.' Gullit not only ensured that his players stayed on the pitch for a second lap of honour to share their experience with the fans, but also took his entire backroom staff for a picture, acknowledging their vital contribution. It had a real continental flavour as they all held hands in the centre circle, and ran into the goal mouth before diving, with Wise eager to catch up and diving while holding the cup in his hands.

Gullit said: 'It was a disciplined performance in very hot and humid conditions – everybody did exactly what they were supposed to. We didn't need anybody to do things on their own because it was a big occasion. And I am delighted that it went the way we asked. The defence was perfect; they didn't have a shot. I am very proud and I am very proud of the team. They deserve all credit. People have said to me that it is hard to understand what the FA Cup means here and what it has meant to Chelsea to go so long without winning anything. I think it will begin to sink in in a few days. This is as big for me as when I won my first European Cup with AC Milan. I'm happy for the chairman, Ken Bates, and also for the memory of Matthew Harding, who's been with us spiritually all year.'

In truth, the celebrations were better than the game!

When Di Matteo struck that marvellous dipping thirty-yarder after just 42.4 seconds, Chelsea seemed certain to fulfil their destiny. Wise won possession, and his pass bypassed Zola to give Di Matteo plenty of space in a centre circle vacated by the opposition. Robson's midfield was on the missing list. Emerson was left in Di Matteo's slipstream, and with the defence backing off, Pearsons preoccupied with Hughes, the Italian's wickedly dipping shot whipped over Roberts. That goal gave Di Matteo the confidence to strike up a Man of the Match performance. After nine minutes his precision pass could easily have given Minto a goal, but his scrambled shot was half stopped as it went through the keeper's legs and didn't have enough pace to cross the line.

Boro suffered a massive set-back after twenty minutes, when Juninho's glorious pass gave Ravanelli first sight of goal. But the first time he had to break into a full stride his hamstring gave way a split second after Sinclair made a telling tackle. Without their thirty-one-goal striker, Boro looked tame in attack, with Beck replacing him. Juninho looked their only hope, although just before the interval Festa headed into the corner from Stamp's cross but was caught marginally offside. Just before that, after Leboeuf was tripped, Zola had made his first telling contribution with a thirty-yard free kick tipped round the post.

In the seventieth minute a tantalising Zola dribble past three defenders was finally ended with a ferocious shot the keeper pushed out. Grodas made his one vital save nine minutes later when Juninho took a quick free kick after he was fouled by Clarke, to put substitute Vickers through, but the Norwegian smartly smothered the shot.

Finally, the irrepressible Zola helped create Chelsea's second goal eight minutes from the end. Newton began the move and Petrescu's delicate chip to the far post seemed beyond Zola, but his delightful back flick was finished off from close range by Newton.

The chant for Vialli went out and after eighty-eight minutes and thirty-three seconds he came on for Zola, who departed a hero and paid homage to Vialli as he came on. It was a touching moment. Vialli's cameo appearance might have only been a matter of minutes, but it proved beyond doubt that those who peddled the tales of jealousy and envy failed to understand Gullit. No such feelings exist. Only the good of the team was the motive behind Gullit's decision to leave Vialli on the bench in favour of the Zola–Hughes attacking partnership.

Gullit would create for himself even more team selection problems next season by building up his squad to the levels to challenge on the domestic and European fronts; he'll enjoy pitting his managerial wits in even more challenging circumstances. 'I've been consistent. For me that was priority number one as well as being honest with everyone, giving everyone the same chances. If you give them that feeling everyone will work with you and want to go with the team. At the start some players were moaning, but some of them played on Saturday. This is life. Some didn't want to stay. Some wanted to stay. They wanted to be part of it and now they are Cup winners.'

He declined to discuss Vialli, but his fellow Italians planned to spend the next two weeks on tour trying to convince Vialli to stay. Vialli hinted that he would be willing to consider a move to another Premiership club when he said: 'This is my first winners' medal in England but I hope it won't be my last. I will put this medal alongside the one I won with Juventus in the European Champions Cup last year. It means just as much to me, even though I only had a couple of minutes.'

Vialli had been given the loudest cheer of the day when he'd made his appearance. 'The reception I was given was fantastic. My relationship with the supporters and my life in London will be the two biggest factors when I come to decide what I will do next season. But now is not the time to talk about my future. Now is the time to enjoy our Cup success. And soon I will sit down and decide what is best for my career.'

Mark Hughes had become an FA Cup legend. As he collected his fourth winners' medal he raised four fingers in front of the cameras. 'It's been a good day all round. The early goal settled us down and in the first half we knocked the ball around and caused them a few problems. They looked a bit more solid in the second half, but we also looked like we could cause them more problems. It was great for Di Matteo to score and also great there was a goal for Eddie Newton. He's one of our unsung heroes. It's been a rollercoaster of a season for Boro and it's been very trying for them. But they'll be back.' Asked if this win would help him settle his new contract, he told a reporter, 'No. I signed a new contract yesterday!'

Without surviving film footage and action replay evidence, no one can ever be certain, but the early goal in the 1895 FA Cup Final was probably the fastest goal ever scored. Repeated examination of video evidence showed that Di Matteo's shot crossed the goalline 42.4 seconds after kick off, the fastest Cup final goal since Jackie Milburn scored for Newcastle after forty-five seconds when they beat Manchester City 3–1 in 1955, and only the third time a goal had been scored in the first minute of a Wembley FA Cup Final. The only other occasion was when James Roscamp scored for Blackburn after fifty seconds when they beat Huddersfield 3–1 in 1928.

The quickest Cup final goal in the competition's 126-year history was scored 102 years ago in 1895 when Aston Villa took the lead within forty seconds of the kick off against West Bromwich Albion at the old Crystal Palace. It was the only goal of the match. Although there is no precise timing of the goal, all the surviving evidence places it as being scored between thirty and forty seconds after the kick off. The only matter that will never properly be resolved is which player actually scored it as it has been credited to both Villa inside-forward Bob Chatt and centre-forward John Devey in equal measure through the years.

Di Matteo's goal was also the second fastest ever scored at Wembley in a first-class match. The fastest, after thirty-eight seconds, came when England beat Yugoslavia 2–1 in a friendly on December 13, 1989. The scorer was Bryan Robson.

Roberto didn't even know he'd made history; he was unaware he'd won a place in the record books until more than an hour after the final whistle. As he groomed himself in front of the dressing-room mirror, he laughed, 'Yes, my hair is okay. Was it the fastest goal ever? Surely not. I didn't know that I'm in the record books. But it's not too bad, is it? When I scored it did my head in. I didn't know where I was for two minutes afterwards. I was surprised that they let me run so far. Maybe they didn't expect me to shoot. But I just shot and I was lucky because it dipped. I've been very lucky. I think my sister Concetta will have heard the crowd when I scored and she will have been celebrating. My father was giving her a running commentary.'

So, why no Roman pose? 'It was so quick, I was so excited, I couldn't calm down. It was an unbelievable feeling, so great an emotion, the first time I had anything like this.' As for the Cup final atmosphere, 'It was better than I ever think about the Cup final.' Di Matteo finished the season playing more games than anyone else, starting forty-three and scoring eight goals, a season's best. 'This one was my best goal.'

Goalkeeper Ben Roberts said: 'Di Matteo dipped for fun. We knew he was a class player and that we would have to close him down. He ran something like fifty yards then hit a screamer. You get a feeling for these sort of things and I thought it was going over the bar. But when it went in, and so early on, I just thought, "What else can go wrong this season?"'

Newton scored to crown an emotional return to the big time. He conceded a penalty in the defeat by Manchester United in 1994 and missed much of the past two seasons with a broken leg followed by a serious knee injury. 'It was the worst day of my life when I conceded that penalty. This is the best day of my life. I'm from Hammersmith so it's great for a local boy to get on the score sheet – although I supported QPR as a kid. I had a bet with Frank Sinclair about who would score the most goals each season. I have missed a lot of games, but I've equalled him by scoring one goal in the last game of the season.'

The celebrations continued into the small hours at the Waldorf Hotel. Gullit's speech praised his entire back room staff. Bates gave an insight into that private dinner. 'It was wonderful. He picked out every single person individually down to the groundsman, the kitman and "our girls at the training ground who cook for us". We had Pele as our guest and Jimmy Tarbuck as our host who made a special presentation to Erland Johnsen who is now leaving us. The game was repeated on TV screens without the sound and the BBC had produced a special eight-minute edited highlight of the final. Di Matteo scored ten times – and that was before he went to bed!'

Ruud stunned the audience when he coolly announced that Estelle was pregnant. He would be a dad for the fifth time.

Bates had tried to give Gullit his lucky leprechaun, Rory, when his manager came up to collect his Cup final medal. Gullit opted not to parade the cuddly toy around Wembley. Bates explained: 'He told me it was style that won us the Cup, not luck. He also said "Well, Chairman, are you happy now?" I couldn't help but laugh. Steve Clarke said: "It's been too bloody long." And Dennis Wise told me: "I did it for you, Batesy."'

Williams slept with the cup. 'It wasn't all that comfortable because it has a lot of different parts and edges to it, plus a plinth!'

SUNDAY, MAY 18

Ruth mingled with Blues supporters who turned out to cheer their heroes as they left the Waldorf in the morning, heading for the civic reception without her. She signed autographs and chatted with friends. 'It was a shame there weren't more families allowed to be there. There were a lot of FA men in grey suits who didn't follow one team or the other, but were just there because the FA had given them tickets.' Vicky took the teenage son of Matthew's pal, Raymond Deane, to bury his dad's ashes. Ray, forty-three, was alongside Matthew when the helicopter crashed. Vicky said: 'There are helicopters flying by every five seconds and whatever you do you can't forget.' Asked how he would be feeling about the result, she added: 'Wherever he is, he's smiling and crying.'

Between 60,000 and 100,000 fans paid a blue and white tribute to the players and Gullit aboard the open-top bus. Outside the Fulham and Hammersmith Town Hall the bus pulled up and Gullit told the fans: 'We're happy to make your dream come true. We love you all.' A stream of blue lined the streets, the sun shone and *their* song rang out time and again just as it had at Wembley. It was a Blue Day again.

In scenes not seen for twenty-seven years, fans jammed every corner of the streets in west London, sitting on each other's shoulders, perching up in lampposts and even climbing up on rooftops, to catch a glimpse of their heroes. The heat was muggy, the crowd overbearing and the hangovers still evident, but nothing could stop the massive cheers that went up as fans saw Wise lift the coveted silver trophy above his head yet again.

The streets echoed with the sounds of favourite terrace chants as the double-decker slowly made its way from the Waldorf Hotel to the Town Hall on Fulham Broadway, yards from the Stamford Bridge stadium. Street tannoys blasted out the club's two FA cup anthems, Blue is the Colour and Blue Day, as tears rolled down the cheeks of fans starved of FA Cup glory for nearly three decades. Fans wore wigs with Gullit's trademark dreadlocks, with some even dying their hair blue for the occasion. One woman, wearing a sparkling blue Gullit wig, told how she banged on the side of the bus and shouted for Vialli. He handed her the life-size cardboard cut-out of Wise that had been on the front of the bus, and autographed it. Somehow she sneaked past the 'tight' security and was in the civic reception along with half a dozen other fans in their element as they searched for autographs and had pictures taken with the Cup.

Hutchinson said: 'The supporters have been absolutely magnificent. I don't think I've witnessed the crowd stay on so long after a game. It was just one big happy family together, celebrating something that they waited for a long time and which they deserve. It's only a pity that Matthew could not be with us, but I am sure he is here in spirit.'

The crowd erupted into a chorus of 'There's only one Di Matteo'. He said: 'This is very special. We have got to enjoy the moment. But we have got to get on with the momentum we have achieved this season.' Asked if he thought the European Cup Winners Cup would also form part of the Stamford Bridge silverware next season he smiled and said: 'I think so.' Zola's smile was endless. 'It's beautiful, fantastic.' Andrea Zola took pictures like any Italian tourist and the other wives were just as astonished.

Twenty-seven years after Dave Sexton's side paraded the FA Cup along the King's Road, most of Gullit's foreign legion have probably never heard of former Shed idols like Osgood, Hudson and Chopper Harris. For long-suffering Clarke, the exploits of those seventies swingers were a constant reminder of their own shortcomings. He said: 'Before the kick off I said to Wisey, "Let's make sure after this game they're all talking about the team from the 1990s and not the 1970s." It's so nice to finally put an end to all that stuff. It was great for the guys who did so well for the club in 1970 but it had gone on far too long. It had become like a huge weight on our shoulders but we've finally laid this ghost once and for all. Now, with the quality we now have in the side, it's important we go on to bigger and better things. We don't want to wait another twenty-seven years for our next trophy.

'This club has come a hell of a long way in the last few years, and I'm better qualified to comment than anyone. I was here when we were just playing at being a big club. Now it truly is that, and the FA Cup is another step on the road to becoming a really successful operation. We've had a good season and played a lot of good football but there was a danger we'd end with up nothing after throwing away automatic qualification for Europe. So Wembley was a really big game for us because with the players we've got we should be in Europe every season.'

Hughes added: 'It would be nice to be mentioned in the same breath as Osgood and Bonetti by future Chelsea fans.'

Wise said: 'Long live the nineties. You lot are going to see the best of us for the rest of the century. I joined Chelsea from Wimbledon because they're a bigger club and I wanted to win trophies. But I've had to wait seven years to achieve that and this is the best feeling I've ever had in football. Picking up the trophy as captain made it even more special than beating Liverpool with the Dons. We've missed out too many times in the past. We'd been to a final and a couple more semifinals and kept messing it up.

'But there was no way we were going to muck it up this time. Steve Clarke told me before the game there was no way we were going to lose. Sometimes you just get that feeling when you know you're going to win. And this was one of those occasions. Now we've all agreed that we've got to take things on from here. We needed to get over this hurdle of landing our first trophy and now that obstacle is out of the way. The last time we were in the Cup Winners Cup we got to the semis. Without the quality we've already got, plus the new players Ruud has signed, a few people might be worried about us next time. We've been an okay side capable of putting a decent cup run together for the past few seasons. But we're not an okay side any more. We're a real quality team.'

Leboeuf wanted to retain the team spirit forged by this Cup run. 'We need the new players but must not destroy the atmosphere we have already. Winning the FA Cup is fantastic but it is in Europe where we really need to make our mark. We will have to be strong for the Premier League championship as well as the Cup Winners

Cup. But we have the ambition and we want to win everything.'

Ruud dispensed with his tracksuit and sat in the banqueting hall alongside Estelle and Ted Troost, relaxed, wearing a white polo shirt. He smiled politely for everyone who asked for an autograph or an interview.

Wise dedicated the Wembley success to Bates. 'I've always admired Batesy and loved him as a person because of what he's done for this club. He puts his money where his mouth is and is always prepared to have a go. There would be no Chelsea without him. He kept it going and this win is his greatest dream come true. I'm happier for him than anyone else and that's why I invited him down from the royal box to show off the Cup. He's waited such a long time for this and put so much into the club that he deserves the applause more than anyone.'

Bates had been the first of the official party to arrive at the Town Hall opposite Fulham Broadway Station and he had taken it upon himself to assist the DJ with the communal singing. He told me, 'This has been the greatest party in the history of English football. This is the carnival cup, the happiest cup. Euro '96 was the summer of love for the English game but this has been electric. I can't believe that I've just seen the biggest street party since the Notting Hill Carnival. I thought I'd seen it with the greatest party on the pitch at Wembley. We've seen so much knocking over the years and this is the best answer to it all. We want to be in Europe every year. We had already signed three more internationals before we even played in the FA Cup Final. Winning the FA Cup has added at least £2.5m to the club.'

The reception was scheduled for just an hour, to finish at 2pm to allow time for Gullit, Hutchinson and the players to travel to the airport for an evening departure for a tour, after which Ruud planned to 'disappear' for a well-earned break in Portugal with Estelle before returning to Holland.

The tour was another money-spinner. Bates said: 'It shows how the image of Chelsea has grown. We're one of the top draws in Europe. Soon we'll be the most successful.' The FA Cup winners signed up with Channel 5 for exclusive live coverage of their European Cup Winners Cup campaign. Bookmakers William Hill quoted Chelsea at 5–1 to win the trophy.

Channel 5 will show live coverage of the cup winners' Thursday home matches in the European Cup Winners Cup. The deal also included exclusive rights to the south-east Asia tour to Hong Kong, Thailand and Brunei. Hutchinson said: 'Signing Chelsea is a scoop for Channel 5 and, for our part, we're very happy to team up with them. They are keen to feature football, have some good ideas and showed some sharp shooting by signing an option before the Cup final! Channel 5 are linking up with Chelsea at a time when interest in the Blues is sky-high. Let's hope we prove a winning partnership.' Channel 5's commitment to showing every home match in the competition was a major attraction.

'We experienced major problems in 1994/95, with broadcasters unable or unwilling to schedule football live on Thursdays. This was frustrating for us and our supporters. Channel 5 has given us a guarantee of scheduling every home game in the European Cup Winners Cup live. This gives continuity and allows those Chelsea fans unable to attend matches to follow our progress.' Channel 5 chief executive David Elstein said: 'Chelsea are one of the most cosmopolitan teams in the UK. This agreement shows 5's commitment to bringing the best of European football action free of charge to our viewers, and is absolutely in line with our ambition to show great events on 5.'

The south-east Asia tour kicked off in Hong Kong against South China FC. 'If they thought it was hot and humid at Wembley they're in for a shock,' said match organiser Julian Kam as Hong Kong sweltered at 30° and 78% humidity. The game was the first major match at the new Siu Sai Wan stadium, managed by Wembley International, but could be Vialli's last game in a Chelsea shirt. Kam added: 'They don't even have time to celebrate in London. We've organised some champagne so they can carry on here.'

In Gullit's absence the club was launching a Dutch-style concept to find a Beckham for Chelsea. He wanted to break Manchester United's monopoly on nurturing the best of English talent like Beckham, the Neville brothers, Butt and Scholes. Gullit went back to his roots in Holland where the kids are enticed to a professional club with the chance of being coached by the stars. Clubs rely on the traditional methods of scouting, going out to trial games where most of the best kids are already known.

The 'Search for a Star' programme started a week after the final when Stamford Bridge was open to 150 young hopefuls at £15 a time. Gullit planned to be present personally on a further session later in the year. Bates said: 'With Chelsea's commitment to youth development, this is a special opportunity for young Chelsea supporters to show off their soccer skills on the hallowed Stamford Bridge pitch. Who knows, there could be a future Chelsea star amongst them!' Chelsea's events director Mike Beaufoy, said: 'Ruud Gullit spoke to chairman Ken Bates about a system operated in Holland whereby clubs encourage young footballers to show off their skills during open days at the stadium under the supervision of the club scouts and coaches. The objective is to spot hidden talent in order to sign them up for a school of excellence and ultimate stardom.'

Bates departed early from the mayhem and, despite being a Chelsea pensioner, never broke his stride as he walked along the King's Road. 'Why are you walking?' enquired one fan. Bates responded, 'I'm saving money to afford Gullit's wages.' He strode purposefully more than a mile along the King's Road, shaking hands with all the fans. During his presidential-style walkabout he was generally treated like a hero. 'The same fans, no doubt, who were chanting "Bates Out" a year ago,' he laughed. Bates never refused an autograph and he posed for endless photographs with fans from all ages from babies to pensioners. Cars hooted him, fans waved at him, shook his hand and congratulated him. Not all of them, though. Some abused him because the team bus had missed out the King's Road.

It took him twenty minutes to finally arrive at Leonardo's restaurant where two flags were out in triumph. He was applauded when he entered, and one fan sent over a bottle of champagne. People came off the streets to thank him, but there were the few who continued to attack him. Something like 10,000 fans were stranded in the King's Road while the open-topped red bus took the triumphant team and the FA Cup along the Fulham Road. They bitterly complained that the King's Road was the traditional haunt of the now-trendy-again football club. Bates pointed out that the route had been devised in conjunction with the police and had been well published in the programme and on Club Call. He didn't know that one Sunday paper had published the King's Road as the route!

After a lunch that lasted until 5.30, Bates was up in the restaurant in a woman's white floppy hat dancing with Suzannah. The impromptu dance spilled out into the King's Road where diners joined in. It was all good-natured until Ken disappeared down the road still mobbed by well-wishers, only to be attacked by a yobbo who poured a pint of beer over his head. Bates recalled: 'I had never seen the man in my life. He appeared out of nowhere and threw a pint of beer over me. Mind you, it was very hot so it only served to refresh me. I must admit by then I'd had a few, but I think I ought to get into the *Guinness Book of Records* ... I was so annoyed that I gave chase. I was like a gun out of a bullet as this guy ran off. Just imagine it, I'm sixty-five and he was about twenty-eight, but after giving him a four-yard start I caught him in twenty – admittedly he was about eighteen stone. I swung him around about to land one on him when five Chelsea supporters grabbed me from behind and stopped me. They said, "You don't need this; just carry on shaking hands and having a good time." They grabbed the bloke and the last I saw of him he had a well-placed boot up the backside.'

Generally, the vast majority of fans were marvellously well behaved, but the police had their work cut out. From Saturday night a helicopter was buzzing overhead down the Fulham Road with so many fans out to celebrate. A policeman said: 'Well, many have had too much to drink for two days solid and they probably don't know what they are doing.'

In the general hysteria it was hard to put this success in context. Osgood tried. 'I actually wrote: "May 17: Chelsea – Cup Final" in my diary months ago. That's how confident I was. I reckon the second half against Liverpool when we came back from 2–0 down was the best forty-five minutes seen at the Bridge since our great days. We contested five major finals in eight years, and I'd like to think these lads can do even better than that. Though, to be honest, I think we're still two or three players short of having a championship-winning squad.'

The seventies team went on to land the Cup Winners Cup, but were underachievers in the league. Osgood said: 'We were all so young, twenty-three or twenty-four, that it was hard to take in the fact we'd just beaten Real Madrid, the greatest name in world football. That's why I'm really pleased there are so many talented youngsters at the Bridge today. This team, like ours, will have the chance to grow together. Ruud Gullit can feel well pleased. An FA Cup victory and sixth in the league in his first season in charge isn't a bad start.'

Gullit had laid the groundwork even before the final, clinching three deals before Wembley and two more after the final. In came an impressive array of new foreign talent, all internationals – goalkeeper Ed de Goey, Uruguayan Gustavo Poyet, French central defender Bernard Lambourde, Nigerian left-wing back Ceslestine Babayaro and Norwegian centre forward Tor Andre Flo. Gullit brought the foreign contingent to thirteen. The summer was a time for reflection on the glory of the FA Cup and renewed expectations for Europe and in the Premiership. The quest for the Champions League was under way.

The fans remembered at Wembley and again outside the Town Hall: 'There's only one Matthew Harding.' Minister of Sport Tony Banks, sporting his favourite blue and white scarf at the reception, dedicated the FA Cup celebration to his memory. 'Matthew would be crying his heart out now but because he's one of the Chelsea family he'll never be forgotten. That is all for him.'

The team had delivered that precious piece of silverware that was worth more than his personal fortune to him.

RIP Matthew Harding.